"With the publication of *God's Acts for Israel, Gentiles, and Christians*, Joshua Jipp puts on full display what we have come to expect of him: exemplary skills as a reader of Scripture and masterful attention to both historical and theological concerns. Jipp's well-established reputation as a trusted voice for grappling with the message of Acts is only advanced with this collection of essays that, together, illuminate Luke's portrait of God's faithfulness. Students, pastors, and scholars alike will benefit from reading this compelling contribution to our understanding of the Acts of the Apostles."

—JOEL B. GREEN
Fuller Theological Seminary

"Since the publication of his 2013 monograph *Divine Visitations*, Joshua Jipp has emerged as one of the leading interpreters of the Lukan writings. *God's Acts for Israel, Gentiles, and Christians* conveniently combines unpublished and previously published (and occasionally expanded) essays into one collection. The result is a veritable feast that explores theological themes of Luke and Acts in both their ancient and contemporary contexts. Highly recommended for students and scholars alike!"

—MIKEAL C. PARSONS
Baylor University

"Jipp's collection of essays is a rich tapestry of learning, insight, and interest across a variety of issues within, and arising from, the book of Acts. Anyone seeking a deeper appreciation of that book would do well to study this one with care."

—CONSTANTINE CAMPBELL
Australian University College of Divinity

"Joshua Jipp has distinguished himself as a trusted expert on the book of Acts. In this academically rigorous and wide-ranging set of studies, the connecting theological thread is Jipp's view of Acts as a narrative of the living God revealed in Jesus Christ and the Spirit-gifted church. In Jipp's telling, Luke invites readers to discern and respond to divine activity—activity that is evident in Acts and also in readers' everyday lives. Jipp has offered a weighty book on a weighty topic. Highly recommended."

—NIJAY K. GUPTA
Northern Seminary

"Joshua Jipp offers a collection of cutting-edge studies on Israel, Gentiles, and Christians in Luke-Acts that will benefit a wide audience. It is full of learned insights and new perspectives on contested topics. Jipp's volume is necessary reading for anyone interested in Luke-Acts scholarship and in how Luke's story of Jesus and the early church can speak to our own world today."

—Michael F. Bird
Ridley College

"Joshua Jipp has placed students, pastors and scholars in his debt by this excellent collection of essays on Luke-Acts. Jipp's consistent theme of God being active for the salvation of people in and through the work of Jesus and the power of the Spirit is lucidly expressed, engaging, and persuasive. Readers will find him a sure-footed guide to Luke and Acts, and a strong encourager and help in living out the message of those books today."

—Steve Walton
Trinity College, Bristol

"The industrious Joshua Jipp is at it again, producing yet another volume with original, judicious insights that exhibit his fine command of scholarship and the primary sources. Most refreshing are the Jewish facets of the theology of Acts, which Jipp is able to explicate with great effectiveness and which attest to a pivotal moment in the field of Luke and Acts studies. I have learned much from Jipp's scholarship and highly recommend this book."

—Isaac W. Oliver
Bradley University

God's Acts for Israel, Gentiles, and Christians

A Theology of the Acts of the Apostles

Joshua W. Jipp

William B. Eerdmans Publishing Company
Grand Rapids, Michigan

Wm. B. Eerdmans Publishing Co.
2006 44th Street SE, Grand Rapids, MI 49508
www.eerdmans.com

© 2025 Joshua W. Jipp
All rights reserved
Published 2025
Printed in the United States of America

31 30 29 28 27 26 25   1 2 3 4 5 6 7

ISBN 978-0-8028-8378-0

Library of Congress Cataloging-in-Publication Data

Names: Jipp, Joshua W. author
Title: God's Acts for Israel, gentiles, and Christians : a theology of the Acts of the
   Apostles / Joshua W. Jipp.
Description: Grand Rapids, Michigan : William B. Eerdmans Publishing Com-
   pany, [2025] | Includes bibliographical references and index. | Summary:
   "A collection of essays focusing on theological themes within the biblical
   book of Acts"—Provided by publisher.
Identifiers: LCCN 2024038417 | ISBN 9780802883780 hardcover |
   ISBN 9781467467575 epub
Subjects: LCSH: Theology
Classification: LCC BS2625.52 .J56 2025 | DDC 226.6/06—dc23/eng/20250529
   LC record available at https://lccn.loc.gov/2024038417

To Luke Timothy Johnson

Contents

Preface ix

List of Abbreviations xi

Part One: God's Acts for Israel

1. The Paul of Acts 3
   Proclaimer of the Hope of Israel or Teacher of Apostasy from Moses?

2. Paul as Prophet of God's Resurrected Messiah 23
   Prophecy and Messianism in the Lukan Depiction of Paul

3. Luke's Scriptural Suffering Messiah 43
   A Search for Precedent, a Search for Identity

4. Abraham in the Synoptic Gospels and the Acts of the Apostles 65

5. "For David Did Not Ascend into Heaven . . ." (Acts 2:34a) 84
   *Reprogramming Royal Psalms to Proclaim
   the Enthroned-in-Heaven King*

Part Two: God's Acts for Gentiles

6. Does Paul Translate the Gospel in Acts 17:22–31? 103
   A Critical Engagement with C. Kavin Rowe's One True Life

CONTENTS

7. "Hospitable Barbarians"   123
   Luke's Ethnic Reasoning in Acts 28:1–10

8. Paul's Areopagus Speech of Acts 17:16–34
   as *Both* Critique *and* Propaganda   144

9. Why Did Gentiles Convert to Christianity?   169
   Storytelling and the Rise of Christianity

Part Three: God's Acts for Christians

10. The Beginnings of a Theology of Luke-Acts   187
    Divine Activity and Human Response

11. The Migrant Messiah and the Boundary-Crossing Messianic
    Community in Luke-Acts   209

12. Jesus, the Church, and Mental Illness   225

13. Philanthropy, Hospitality, and Friendship   240

14. The Economics of Jesus in the Context of the Roman Empire
    and Israel's "Sacred Economy"   248

Acknowledgments   279
Bibliography   281
Index of Authors   305
Index of Subjects   310
Index of Scripture   312
Index of Other Ancient Sources   325

Preface

The following set of essays stems from the conviction that the Acts of the Apostles is best understood as a text that narrates the implications of the God of Israel's divine actions for ancient Jews and gentiles, and also for Christians who continue to read the text as scriptural communication. I trust it will be clear to the reader that I am not offering a comprehensive theological description of Acts. I do hope, however, that these essays will help careful readers understand "what makes the Acts of the Apostles tick." These fourteen essays set forth some of the primary aspects of the theology of Acts, including

- the earliest Christians' messianic interpretation of Israel's Scriptures;
- the foundational role that Jesus's resurrection from the dead plays in the earliest Christians' understanding of salvation, history, and the Holy Spirit;
- how Acts invites its readers to discern divine activity in history;
- how the Christian movement claimed continuity with its Jewish heritage despite accusations that their leaders, especially Paul, were apostates from Moses's teachings;
- how the earliest Christians engaged Greco-Roman religion, philosophy, and culture;
- the centrality of the practices of hospitality, friendship, sharing possessions, and healing;
- how the Christian movement grew and expanded by telling stories that made claims to be a superior cult, community, and philosophy; and
- how Acts might be used for contemporary Christians' understanding of how to respond to mental illness, questions of race and ethnicity, and immigration.

PREFACE

All but two of the chapters have been published elsewhere. I offer my heartfelt thanks to the original publishers for the permission to include these essays in this collection. Thank you also to Trevor Thompson, Laurel Draper, and everyone at Eerdmans for the encouragement and opportunity to create this book. Many thanks also to Lydia Bindon, my remarkable graduate assistant at Trinity Evangelical Divinity School, for her ongoing help with the project.

I have had many fine teachers, but I would like to dedicate this book to my doctoral supervisor, teacher, and friend, Luke Timothy Johnson. I count it as one of the greatest gifts from God to have had him as a teacher and mentor. I do not have the space here to share all of the ways he continues to influence me. I remember his frequent encouragements to me and others to, yes, work hard at our craft and our studies, but also pay attention to the world that we live in, not only to develop a curiosity for ancient texts but also to live deeply and meaningfully now. The joining together of text and life, history and existence is one that I seek to emulate, and I trust that some of those impulses are on display in these essays.

Abbreviations

1 Apol.	Justin, *Apologia i*
1 En.	1 Enoch
1QpHab	Pesher Habakkuk
2 Apol.	Justin, *Aoplogia ii*
4QFlor	Florilegium
4QRPa	Reworked Pentateuch
AB	Anchor Bible
ABD	*Anchor Bible Dictionary*
ADA	Auflage dieser Neuauslegung
Aen.	Virgil, *Aeneid*
Ag. Ap.	Josephus, *Against Apion*
ALBO	Analecta Lovaniensia Biblica et Orientalia
Alex.	Lucian, *Alexander the False Prophet*
Alex. Fort.	Plutarch, *De Alexandri magni fortuna aut virtute*
AnBib	Analecta Biblica
ANRW	*Aufstieg und Niedergang der römischen Welt*
Ant. Rom.	Dionysius of Halicarnassus, *Antiquitates romanae*
Apol.	Xenophon, *Apologia Socratis*
Apol.	Plato, *Apologia*
ASNU	Acta Seminarii Neotestamentici Upsaliensis
Att.	Cicero, *Epistulae ad Atticum*
AYBC	Anchor Yale Bible Commentary
AYBRL	Anchor Yale Bible Reference Library
Bacch.	Euripides, *Bacchae*
BBR	*Bulletin for Biblical Research*
BCE	Before Common Era
BDAG	F. W. Danker, Walter Bauer, William F. Arndt, and F. Wilburt Gingrich, *Greek-English Lexicon of the New Testament and Other Early Christian Literature*. 3rd ed. Chicago: University of Chicago Press, 2000 (Danker-Bauer-Arndt-Gingrich)

ABBREVIATIONS

Ben.	Seneca, De beneficiis
BETL	Bibliotheca Ephemeridum Theologicarum Lovaniensium
Bib	Biblica
BibInt	Biblical Interpretation
BibInt	Biblical Interpretation Series
BZNW	Beihefte zur Zeitschrift für die Neutestamentliche Wissenschaft
C. Ap.	Contra Apionem
CBOT	Coniectanea Biblica: Old Testament
CBQ	Catholic Biblical Quarterly
CE	Common Era
CEB	Common English Bible
CNT	Commentaire du Nouveau Testament
Conf.	Philo, De confusione linguarum
CP	Classical Philology
Curios.	Plutarch, De curiositate
Cyr.	Xenophon, Cyropaedia
Demetr.	Plutarch, Demetrius
Diatr.	Epictetus, Diatribai (Dissertationes)
DJG	Joel B. Green, Jeannine K. Brown, and Nicholas Perrin, eds. Dictionary of Jesus and the Gospels. Downers Grove, IL: InterVarsity Press, 2013.
DOTP	T. Desmond Alexander and David W. Baker, eds. Dictionary of the Old Testament: Pentateuch. Downers Grove, IL: InterVarsity Press, 2003.
Ep.	Seneca, Epistulae morales
Eth. nic.	Aristotle, Ethica nicomahea (Nicomachean Ethics)
Euthyphr.	Plato, Euthyphro
FAT	Forschungen zum Alten Testament
Flac.	Cicero, Pro Flacco
FRLANT	Forschungen zur Religion und Literatur des Alten und Neuen Testaments
Her. mal.	Plutarch, De Herodoti malignitate (On the Malice of Herodotus)
Hist.	Herodotus, Histories; Thucydides, History of the Peloponnesian War
Hom. Act.	Chrysostom, The Homilies on the Acts of the Apostles
HTKNT	Herders Theologischer Kommentar zum Alten Testament
HTR	Harvard Theological Review
HTS	Harvard Theological Studies
ICC	International Critical Commentary
Int.	Interpretation: A Journal of Bible and Theology
ISBL	Indiana Studies in Biblical Literature
JAC	Jahrbuch für Antike und Christentum
JBL	Journal of Biblical Literature
Joseph	Philo, On the Life of Joseph
JRE	Journal of Religious Ethics
JSNT	Journal for the Study of the New Testament
JSNTSup	Journal for the Study of the New Testament Supplement Series
JSOT	Journal for the Study of the Old Testament
JSOTSup	Journal for the Study of the Old Testament Supplement Series
JSPSup	Journal for the Study of the Pseudepigrapha Supplement Series

Abbreviations

JSS	*Journal of Semitic Studies*
JTI	*Journal of Theological Interpretation*
JTS	*Journal of Theological Studies*
J. W.	Josephus, *Jewish War*
KEK	Kritisch-exegetischer Kommentar über das Neue Testament (Meyer-Kommentar)
LCL	Loeb Classical Library
LD	Lectio Divina
Leg.	Cicero, *De legibus*
Legat.	Philo, *Legatio ad Gaium*
Lives	Diogenes Laertius, *Lives of Eminent Philosophers*
LNTS	The Library of New Testament Studies
LSTS	The Library of Second Temple Studies
LXX	Septuagint
Mem.	Xenophon, *Memorabilia*
Metam.	Apuleius, *Metamorphoses*; Ovid, *Metamorphoses*
Mos. 1, 2	Philo, *On the Life of Moses 1, 2*
Mut.	Philo, *De mutatione nominum*
Nat. d.	Cicero, *De natura deorum*
NE	Aristotle, *Nicomachean Ethics*
NICNT	New International Commentary on the New Testament
NIGTC	New International Greek Testament Commentary
NovT	*Novum Testamentum*
NovTSup	Supplements to Novum Testamentum
NPNF	*Nicene and Post-Nicene Fathers*
NRSV	New Revised Standard Version
NSBT	New Studies in Biblical Theology
NT	New Testament
NTS	*New Testament Studies*
NTSI	New Testament and the Scriptures of Israel
OBT	Overtures to Biblical Theology
Od.	Homer, *Odyssea* (*Odyssey*)
Off.	Cicero, *De officiis*
Opif.	Philo, *De opificio mundi*
Or.	Demosthenes, *Orations*; Dio Chrysostom, *Orations*; Julian, *Orations*
OT	Old Testament
Phaed.	Plato, *Phaedo*
Phaen.	Aratus, *Phaenomena*
Pol.	Aristotle, *Politica* (*Politics*)
Prob.	Philo, *Quod omnis probus liber sit*
PRSt	*Perspectives in Religious Studies*
Ps. Aristotle	Pseudo-Aristotle
Pss. Sol.	*Psalms of Solomon*
Quaest. conv.	Plutarch, *Quaestionum convivialum libri IX*
R&T	*Religion and Theology*
RB	Revue Biblique

xiii

ABBREVIATIONS

Rep.	Cicero, *De republica*
RSR	*Recherches de Science Religieuse*
SBLDS	Society of Biblical Literature Dissertation Series
SBLMS	Society of Biblical Literature Monograph Series
SBLSP	*Society of Biblical Literature Seminar Papers*
SBLSymS	Society of Biblical Literature Symposium Series
SBS	Stuttgarter Bibelstudien
SBT	Studies in Biblical Theology
SJT	*Scottish Journal of Theology*
SNTSMS	Society for New Testament Studies Monograph Series
SP	Sacra Pagina
SPCK	Society for Promoting Christian Knowledge
Spec.	Philo, *De specialibus legibus*
SR	*Studies in Religion/Sciences Religieuses*
SSEJC	Studies in Scripture in Early Judaism and Christianity
Stoic. abs.	Plutarch, *Stoicos absurdiora poetis dicere*
SUNT	Studien zur Umwelt des Neuen Testaments
Superst.	Plutarch, *De superstitione*
SVF	*Stoicorum Veterum Fragmenta*
SZNW	Studien zum Neuen Testament
TDNT	Theological Dictionary of the New Testament
TynB	*Tyndale Bulletin*
TZ	*Theologische Zeitschrift*
Verr.	Cicero, *In Verrem*
Virt.	Philo, *De virtutibus*
WMANT	Wissenschaftliche Monographien zum Alten und Neuen Testament
WUNT	Wissenschaftliche Untersuchungen zum Neuen Testament
Xen.	Aristotle, *De Xenophane*
ZAW	*Zeitschrift für die alttestamentliche Wissenschaft*
ZNW	*Zeitschrift für die neutestamentliche Wissenschaft*
ZTK	*Zeitschrift für Theologie und Kirche*

Part One

God's Acts for Israel

1

The Paul of Acts

Proclaimer of the Hope of Israel or Teacher of Apostasy from Moses?

Some contemporary scholars of early Christianity have thought of Paul as a former Jew, as an apostate from his religious faith, and as a "self-hating Jew who rejected Torah and caricatured Judaism."[1] The narrative of Acts testifies that some of Paul's fellow first-century Jews were sympathetic with this assessment. Upon Paul's arrival in Jerusalem, James and the elders inform Paul of some nasty rumors circulating about Paul and his teaching: "You see, brother, how many thousands of believers there are among the Jews, and they are all zealous for the law. They have been told about you that you teach all the Jews living among the gentiles to forsake Moses, and that you tell them not to circumcise their children nor to observe the ancestral customs" (Acts 21:20–21). James has not underplayed the seriousness of these rumors about Paul's character, for when Paul is nearing the completion of his Nazarite vow in the Jerusalem temple, some fellow Jews from Asia begin to shout: "Fellow Israelites, help! This is the man who is teaching everyone everywhere against our people,

---

All translations are my own in the following essays unless otherwise noted.

1. See the quote and broader discussion by Patrick Gray, *Paul as a Problem in History and Culture: The Apostle and His Critics through the Centuries* (Grand Rapids: Baker Academic, 2016), 118. See also Paul's controversial and mixed reception among contemporary Jews as helpfully described by Daniel R. Langton, *The Apostle Paul in the Jewish Imagination: A Study in Modern Jewish-Christian Relations* (Cambridge: Cambridge University Press, 2010). Nevertheless, Langton also recounts numerous Jewish theologians, musicians, novelists, artists, and psychologists who engaged Paul as one who wrestled with the meaning of Jewish identity and who brought the God of Israel to the gentiles. See also John G. Gager, *Who Made Early Christianity? The Jewish Lives of the Apostle Paul* (New York: Columbia University Press, 2015), 37–52.

PART ONE: GOD'S ACTS FOR ISRAEL

our law, and this place; more than that, he has actually brought Greeks into the temple and has defiled this holy place" (21:27–28). Paul is accused of being a Jew who is faithless to God, who is a dangerous rebel against the teachings of Moses. And this is exemplified in his lack of loyalty to some of the major pillars of Israel's heritage, namely, God's election of Israel ("against our people"), Torah, and Temple.[2] Are the rumors true? Is Paul faithless to the God of Israel? Do his teachings undermine God's election of Israel, Torah, and Temple?[3]

In what follows, I will argue that the answer to these questions from Luke's perspective is an emphatic NO! Paul is, in every way, faithful to his Jewish ancestral customs. His teaching that God has raised Israel's Messiah from the dead is the singular hope of Israel.[4] Embracing this Messiah constitutes faithfulness to the God of Israel and Israel's ancestral customs. This messianic conviction results in a re-evaluation (not rejection) of Israel's primary identity markers that will only be embraced if one grants Paul's claim that the hope of Israel is identified with Jesus of Nazareth as the resurrected and enthroned messianic ruler of Israel and the nations. If one does not grant Paul's claim that Jesus is the resurrected Messiah of Israel, then the rumors lodged against Paul are right and his teachings should be rejected as an absurd, dangerous, and inappropriate understanding of what constitutes faithfulness to the God of Israel.[5]

---

2. I find it interesting that these charges correlate closely with Seth Schwartz's argument regarding how, within first-century Palestine, "the three pillars of ancient Judaism—the one God, the one Torah, and the one Temple—cohere in a neat, ideological system." See Seth Schwartz, *Imperialism and Jewish Society: 200 B.C.E. to 640 C.E.* (Princeton: Princeton University Press, 2001), 49. See the entirety of his chapter 2.

3. A brief methodological caveat: Throughout this essay I am talking about the "Lukan Paul." Regardless of how one navigates the relationship between the Paul of Acts and the Paul of the epistles, the Lukan Paul's agency stems from Luke's composing hand. The similarities of the charges lodged against Stephen (6:11–14) and Paul (21:27–28), along with the abundance of Luke's parallels in characterization of his protagonists, further demonstrates this point.

4. Though our evaluations of Luke and Judaism differ, I agree here strongly with Shelly Matthews who emphasizes that it is "disingenuous" for scholars "to celebrate [Luke's] universalism without attending to its hegemonizing force." See Shelly Matthews, *Perfect Martyr: The Stoning of Stephen and the Construction of Christian Identity* (Oxford: Oxford University Press, 2010), 32.

5. I think the same argument can be made for Stephen in Acts 6:8–8:1 where similar rumors and charges are lodged against him (see 6:11–14). Again, see Matthews, *Perfect Martyr*, 33. For both the Lukan Stephen and the Lukan Paul, "faithfulness to the God of Israel" is singularly defined by confessing Jesus as the Christ.

Paul, the Faithful, Torah-Observant Jew

One can give a simple and correct response to the rumors brought against Paul, namely, there is simply nothing to them according to Luke's narrative. And many recent commentators, rightly recognizing Luke's concern to portray Paul as a faithful Jew, simply note that, at least for Luke, the charges are false. If ancient notions of ethnicity center upon shared ancestral customs, family, paideia, land, language, and the gods and their cults, then Luke's Paul can be seen as making a powerful and repetitive argument regarding the importance of his Jewish ethnic identity.[6] For example, in his first defense speech in Acts 22, Paul speaks Hebrew (22:2), proclaims "I am a Jewish man" (22:3a), claims his education took place under Gamaliel in Jerusalem (22:3b), and testifies that he has been extremely zealous for his people's ancestral customs (22:3c; cf. 26:4–5). Lukan scholars such as Jacob Jervell, Robert Brawley, and David Moessner, among others, have reacted against interpretations of Luke's narrative that posit the origins of the Christian church within and as a result of the rejection of the Jewish people.[7] Israel's election is still in place, Torah observance for Jews is still non-negotiable, and the Jewish Scriptures remain revelatory. Ironically, their star witness for Luke's positive view of Judaism is the apostle Paul.

In his defense speeches in Acts 22–28, Paul emphasizes that he is faithful to his Jewish heritage in every way.[8] He is a Pharisaic Jew who is zealous for the God of Israel and is Torah observant (21:20–26; 22:1–3; 23:1, 5; 26:4–5).

---

6. On ancient constructions of ethnicity and their relationship to the gods, see Paula Fredriksen, "How Jewish Is God? Divine Ethnicity in Paul's Theology," *JBL* 137 (2018): 193–212.

7. Jacob Jervell, *Luke and the People of God: A New Look at Luke-Acts* (Minneapolis: Augsburg, 1972); Robert L. Brawley, *Luke-Acts and the Jews: Conflict, Apology, and Conciliation*, SBLMS 33 (Atlanta: Scholars Press, 1987); David P. Moessner et al., eds., *Paul and the Heritage of Israel: Paul's Claim upon Israel's Legacy in Luke and Acts in the Light of the Pauline Letters*, vol. 2 of *Luke the Interpreter of Israel*, LNTS 452 (London: T&T Clark, 2012). See also Simon David Butticaz, *L'identité de l'église dans les Actes des apôtres: De la restauration d'Israël à la conquête universelle*, BZNW 174 (Berlin: de Gruyter, 2011); David L. Tiede, *Prophecy and History in Luke-Acts* (Philadelphia: Fortress, 1980). On the divergent evaluations of Luke's assessment of Judaism among scholars from the eighteenth to the twentieth centuries, see Joseph B. Tyson, *Luke, Judaism, and the Scholars: Critical Approaches to Luke-Acts* (Columbia: University of South Carolina Press, 1999).

8. See further the helpful essay by Reidar Hvalvik, "Paul as a Jewish Believer—according to the Book of Acts," in *Jewish Believers in Jesus: The Early Centuries*, ed. Oskar Skarsaune and Reidar Hvalvik (Grand Rapids: Baker Academic, 2017), 121–51.

PART ONE: GOD'S ACTS FOR ISRAEL

Paul believes everything that is written in the Law and the Prophets (24:14–15; 26:22–23). Paul stands on trial because of his loyalty to the promise made by "God to our ancestors, the promise our twelve tribes hope to attain" (26:6–7; 28:20).[9] He circumcises Timothy (16:1–5),[10] celebrates Jewish festivals such as Pentecost (20:16) and Yom Kippur (27:9), and participates in the rituals of the Jerusalem temple (21:23–27; 22:17; 24:11–14).[11] There are no instances of Paul doing anything that would suggest intentional breaking of the laws of Torah such as working or traveling on the Sabbath or eating non-kosher foods. Isaac Oliver has even made the bold claim that Luke's deep knowledge of Torah observance and halakha demonstrates the likelihood that the author of Luke-Acts was both born and raised as a Torah-observant Jew.[12] Oliver argues that there is nothing within Luke-Acts that would justify speaking of the abrogation of the Pentateuchal food laws.[13] In fact, Paul's opponents such as the high priest who commands Paul to be struck (23:3) and the Jews who conspire to murder Paul before his trial (23:12–22; 25:3) are set forth as the ones who violate the law.[14] "The effect," as noted by David Miller, "is to present Paul and other Jewish Christ-believers as faithful to the terms of the covenant—as those who listen to Moses and Jesus, and who thereby inherit the promises to Abraham."[15]

Luke's Paul assumes that Jews within the Jesus movement will and must continue to read and observe the Torah. Matthew Thiessen has shown that the eighth-day circumcision of John, Jesus, and Isaac indicate that Luke "consistently stresses its rightful timing [and] does not denigrate circumcision."[16] Luke insists upon the necessity of Jewish believers circumcising their children,

---

9. See here especially Jervell, *Luke and the People of God*, 153–83.

10. On this episode, see Shaye J. D. Cohen, *The Beginnings of Jewishness: Boundaries, Varieties, Uncertainties* (Berkeley: University of California Press, 1999), 263–307.

11. Seen also Isaac W. Oliver, "The 'Historical Paul' and the Paul of Acts," in *Paul the Jew: Rereading the Apostle as a Figure of Second Temple Judaism*, ed. Gabriele Boccaccini and Carlos A. Segovia (Minneapolis: Fortress, 2016), 51–80, here 56.

12. Isaac W. Oliver, *Torah Praxis after 70 CE: Reading Matthew and Luke-Acts as Jewish Texts*, WUNT 2/355 (Tübingen: Mohr Siebeck, 2013), 447–48.

13. For this paragraph, see Oliver, *Torah Praxis after 70 CE*, 320–98.

14. So Jervell, *Luke and the People of God*, 169.

15. David M. Miller, "Reading Law as Prophecy: Torah Ethics in Acts," in *Torah Ethics and Early Christianity Identity*, ed. Susan J. Wendel and David M. Miller (Grand Rapids: Eerdmans, 2016), 75–91, here 82–83.

16. Matthew Thiessen, *Contesting Conversion: Genealogy, Circumcision, and Identity in Ancient Judaism and Christianity* (Oxford: Oxford University Press, 2011), 122.

and the rejection of the same need for gentile believers. Thus, "Jews continue to be Jews. Gentiles continue to be Gentiles. The ethnic ties linking Abraham and his descendants remain intact and significant for Luke."[17] Thus, the claim that Paul teaches Jews who live among the gentiles to refrain from circumcising their children and walking in the customs of Moses is held up as patently false (21:21–26). And he declares as a summary statement to his fellow Jews in Rome: "I have done nothing against our people or the customs of our ancestors" (οὐδὲν ἐναντίον ποιήσας τῷ λαῷ ἢ τοῖς ἔθεσιν τοῖς πατρῴοις, 28:17).[18] He visits Jerusalem in order to give alms (24:17–24; cf. 9:36; 10:2, 31). Paul consistently carries out his missionary work among Jews within the synagogues (e.g., 9:19–29; 13:4, 42–43; 14:1; 16:12–13; 17:1–11; 18:4, 19; 19:8)—so much so that Jacob Jervell refers to Paul as "the teacher of Israel."[19] Thus, Luke's portrait of the Torah-observant Paul indicates, as Isaac Oliver has stated, Luke's "concern for the preservation of Jewish identity within the Jesus movement through the perpetuation of Torah observance, and hardly teaches his audience to play the Jew merely for the sake of proselytizing."[20] We can conclude, then, that the Lukan Paul's defense speeches demonstrate that Paul "is not against his people (13:26; 28:19), against the law (13:27; 22:12; 23:3; 24:14; 26:22; 28:23), or even . . . against the temple (21:26; 22:17)."[21]

Paul, Teacher of Apostasy from Moses

Luke's narrative makes it clear, however, that not everyone sees Paul as a faithful, Torah-observant Jew. James recounts the rumor that there are countless thousands of Jewish believers in Jesus who are zealous for the law and have been told that Paul teaches Diaspora Jews to forsake Moses, their ancestral customs, and the practice of circumcision (21:20–21). The language of "apostasy [ἀποστασίαν] from Moses" indicates Paul is viewed by many as one who

17. Thiessen, *Contesting Conversion*, 139–40.
18. It is worth noting that Acts presents Jewish believers in Jesus as "the sect of the Nazarenes" (24:5b; cf. 24:14; 28:22), not unlike the sect of the Sadducees (5:17) and the Pharisees (15:5; 26:5).
19. Jacob Jervell, *The Theology of the Acts of the Apostles* (Cambridge: Cambridge University Press, 1996), 82–94.
20. Oliver, *Torah Praxis after 70 CE*, 186.
21. Craig S. Keener, *Acts: An Exegetical Commentary*, vol. 3, *15:1–23:35* (Grand Rapids: Baker Academic, 2014), 3146–47.

PART ONE: GOD'S ACTS FOR ISRAEL

has directly rebelled against or defected from the God of Israel (see LXX Josh 22:22; 2 Chr 29:19; Jer 2:19).[22] James's recounting of the rumors against Paul echoes the crisis recounted in 1 Maccabees where, from the perspective of the author, the pagan king's officers were compelling Jews to apostatize from Moses and their ancestral customs (see οἱ καταναγκάζοντες τὴν ἀποστασίαν, 1 Macc 2:15; cf. 1 Macc 1:41–43, 51–52). The abandonment of their ancestral customs, whether enforced or chosen voluntarily, gives rise to Mattathias's (and his family's) full-throated articulation of their zeal for the law and commitment to never abandon the law and their ancestral ways (1 Macc 2:19–28, 49–70). And there are plenty of other examples from Josephus (*J. W.* 7.47–53), Philo (*Joseph* 254; *Mos.* 1.31), and Maccabean literature (4 Macc. 4:26) that mention negative examples of Jews who have abandoned their ancestral customs and mention them as warnings to other Jews to remain loyal to their heritage.[23] Thus, James's recounting of the rumors about Paul indicate that many Jews believe him to be a dangerous threat to other Jews and one who seeks to turn them from their faithfulness and loyalty to the God of Israel. This accusation continues in Paul's trial scenes where non-Jewish governors and rulers declare that Paul is on trial due to disputes about Jewish laws and customs (18:13–15; 23:29).

And Luke does not minimize the controversial nature of Paul and his message in the Jewish synagogues. After Paul's encounter with the risen Messiah, he proclaims that Jesus "is the Son of God" and spends his time "proving that Jesus is the Messiah" to the Jews in the synagogues in Damascus (9:19, 22). The result is that "the Jews plotted to kill him" (9:23). After his sermon in Pisidian Antioch many of the Jews "followed Paul and Barnabas" and listened to their message about "the grace of God" (13:43). On the other hand, when Paul and Barnabas show up on the next Sabbath and find the "whole town assembled to hear the word of the Lord," a group of Jews are filled with jealousy and attack Paul and his message (13:44–45). Paul famously responds, "It was necessary that the word of God should be spoken first to you. Since you reject it and judge yourselves to be unworthy of eternal life, we are now turning to the gentiles" (13:46–47; cf. Rom 1:16–17). This inspires some Jews to further stir up trouble for Paul and Barnabas, such that they shake "the dust off from their feet" as a sign of judgment against them (13:49–51). This is the first of three scenes where Jewish rejection of Paul's message results in Paul uttering a word

---

22. Keener, *Acts*, 3:3128.
23. See also Keener, *Acts*, 3:3128; see further Stephen G. Wilson, *Leaving the Fold: Apostates and Defectors in Antiquity* (Minneapolis: Fortress, 2004), 23–65.

of judgment against those who reject the message that Jesus is the Messiah (also in Corinth in 18:5–6 and Rome in 28:23–28). But in addition to Pisidian Antioch, Corinth, and Rome, Paul's message also creates controversy and inspires hostility and rejection by some Jews in the cities of Iconium (14:2–5), Lystra (14:19), Thessalonica (17:5–9), and Berea (17:13). Commenting on Paul's missionary work in the Diaspora synagogues, Loveday Alexander rightly notes that "The overall effect of the whole narrative section from ch. 13 to ch. 19 is to leave the damaging impression that Paul's mission causes trouble wherever it goes (17.6): prudent magistrates might well conclude that any well-regulated city would be better off without it."[24]

A few matters should be noted regarding Luke's recounting of these scenes. First, Paul never stops going to the Jewish synagogue with his message. Surprisingly, immediately after his words of judgment in Pisidian Antioch and Corinth, Paul still continues to proclaim his message in the Jewish synagogue (so in Iconium in 14:2–5; and Ephesus in 19:8). Second, Luke frequently recounts a mixed Jewish reception to Paul's message; in other words, Paul does not receive blanket hostility and rejection from his fellow Jews (e.g., 13:43; 17:4; 18:8). Third, after Paul receives opposition and rejection from his fellow Jews in the synagogue, Luke portrays Paul's message as being received and taking root in gentile households rather than in the synagogue (16:11–15; 17:1–9; 18:1–8; cf. Luke 10:1–13). Luke constructs a consistent pattern of the hospitable gentile household precisely to draw attention to gentile receptivity.[25] Interpretations of Luke's depiction of the Jewish people and the synagogue often have a difficult time maintaining the tension and complexity of the narrative. What we have seen is that Paul's proclamation of the gospel has resulted in some limited positive reception from his Jewish audience. Not all Jews who hear Paul's proclamation of the Messiah are resistant to his message. But we have also seen that there is constant opposition to Paul and his message. So much so, in fact, that almost every city has a group of Jews who, often together with the civic authorities, violently seek to drive Paul out of their cities.

Luke's characterization of Paul, then, does not shy away from recounting his person, activity, and message as controversial and unsettling to many of his fellow Jews. Luke's depiction of Paul portrays Paul as one who is faithful and loyal

---

24. Loveday Alexander, *Acts in Its Ancient Literary Context* (London: T&T Clark, 2005), 199.

25. See further David Lertis Matson, *Household Conversion Narratives in Acts: Pattern and Interpretation*, JSNTSup 123 (Sheffield: Sheffield Academic, 1996); Joshua W. Jipp, *Divine Visitations and Hospitality to Strangers in Luke-Acts: An Interpretation of the Malta Episode in Acts 28:1–10*, NovTSup 153 (Leiden: Brill, 2013), 240–47.

to the God of Israel, the law of Moses, and the Jewish people. And it portrays Paul as one who is deeply controversial to many other Jews' understanding of what constitutes faithfulness to God, Moses, and the Jewish people. So much so, in fact, that Paul is viewed as an apostate from his ancestral heritage.

Paul, Messianic Interpreter of Israel's Scriptures and Ancestral Traditions

There is, in my view, an internal tension within Luke's characterization of Paul that does not fit neatly into easy answers to the question, Was Paul faithful to his Jewish heritage or not? This tension is what accounts for the radically different scholarly configurations of Luke's portrait of Judaism, ranging from those who see the Jewish people as excluded from their own covenant, unable to rightly understand their own Scriptures, and as violently contributing to the split between the synagogue and the church to those who see the deepest relationship of continuity between Israel and the Jesus-movement, who lament the break between the church and the synagogue, and who see Luke as holding out hope for all of Israel.[26] I want to suggest, then, that understanding the Lukan Paul's relationship to his Jewish ancestral heritage is best approached by taking into account both Luke's depiction of Paul as Torah-observant and faithful to his ancestral customs in every way and as one whose reputation is that he is a teacher of apostasy from Moses whose person and message is viewed as a destabilizing threat to the Jewish ancestral way of life.[27]

---

26. My sentiment is stated clearly by Daniel Marguerat, *The First Christian Historian: Writing the "Acts of the Apostles,"* trans. Ken McKinney, Gregory J. Laughery, and Richard Bauckham, SNTSMS 121 (Cambridge: Cambridge University Press, 2002). The first view is associated with scholars such as Jack T. Sanders, *The Jews in Luke-Acts* (London: SCM, 1987); J. C. O'Neill, *The Theology of Acts in Its Historical Setting* (London: SCM, 1961), 71–93; Lawrence M. Wills, "The Depiction of the Jews in Acts," *JBL* 110 (1991): 631–54; Ernst Haenchen, *The Acts of the Apostles: A Commentary* (Philadelphia: Westminster, 1971).

27. I should note here that speaking about Paul's (or Jesus's) relationship to the laws of Moses is complex given that determining *what* was the written Torah, what counted as proper Torah observance, and what traditions were used to guide Torah observance were deeply contested. See especially, Philip S. Alexander, "Jewish Law in the Time of Jesus: A Clarification of the Problem," in *Law and Religion: Essays on the Place of the Law in Israel and Early Christianity*, ed. Barnabas Lindars (Cambridge: Clark, 1988), 44–58. With respect to the historical Jesus, see here John P. Meier, "The Historical Jesus and the Historical Law: Some Problems within the Problem," *CBQ* 65 (2003): 52–79.

The Paul of Acts

I propose, then, that we explore how the Lukan Paul construes the meaning and significance of Israel's Scriptures and ancestral traditions (i.e., "Judaism"). I don't want to get sidetracked here into the impossible task of trying to give a definition of "Judaism," but I do want to argue that the Lukan Paul should be viewed as a participant in the construction and definition of his own ancestral heritage and way of life.[28] And here the Lukan Paul is emphatic and nothing but clear in his unrelenting association between the hope and history of Israel as centering upon God's resurrection and heavenly enthronement of Israel's Davidic Messiah. It is no surprise that the Lukan Paul agrees with the broader narrative of Luke-Acts. Luke's narrative begins with the angel Gabriel's promise to Mary that her son will be called "great and the son of the Most High" and will be given "the throne of David his father and he will reign over the house of Jacob forever and his kingdom will have no end" (Luke 1:32–33; cf. Pss 2:7; 89:27–38; 132:11–12).[29] Peter's Pentecost speech in Acts 2 interprets Jesus's divine sonship as finding its climax in God's resurrection of Jesus from the dead whereby Jesus is enthroned as Messiah and Lord (esp. 2:30–36; cf. Ps 110:1).

Let me set forth two primary pieces of evidence from the Lukan Paul to justify this claim. The first is found in Paul's sermon in Pisidian Antioch, and the second at his trial before Felix in Caesarea.

Paul's Synagogue Sermon in Pisidian Antioch (Acts 13:13–41)

First, Luke provides a representative sermon for how Paul proclaims the gospel to the children of Israel in the synagogue in Pisidian Antioch (Acts 13:13–41).[30]

---

28. On the complexities involved in using the word "Jew" and its relationship to contemporary notions of race, ethnicity, and religion, see Cynthia M. Baker, *Jew*, Key Words in Jewish Studies (New Brunswick: Rutgers University Press, 2017), esp. 16–46. I have benefited here from Michael L. Satlow, *Creating Judaism: History, Tradition, Practice* (New York: Columbia University Press, 2006), 1–14, who argues for "a definition of Judaism that can better account both for its immense diversity and its unifying features" and thereby centers upon "large overlaps of shared characteristics" (6–7). These three shared characteristics are: (1) locating oneself within the history of God's election of Israel (i.e., a narrative and historical claim); (2) textual tradition; and (3) religious practices and customs.

29. See here the helpful essay by Jens Schröter, "Salvation for the Gentiles and Israel: On the Relationship between Christology and People of God in Luke," in *From Jesus to the New Testament: Early Christian Theology and the Origin of the New Testament Canon*, trans. Wayne Coppins, Baylor-Mohr Siebeck Studies in Early Christianity (Waco, TX: Baylor University Press, 2013), 227–46, here 230–31.

30. See here Joshua W. Jipp, *Reading Acts* (Eugene, OR: Cascade, 2018), 106–9.

Both the synagogue leader's request that Paul speak "to the people" (πρὸς τὸν λαόν, 13:15) as well as Paul's reference to his audience as "Israelites" (13:16) and "brothers" (13:26, 38) make the point that Israel, the people of God, is embodied in Paul's contemporary audience.

Paul's sermon presents a mini-history of God's people, whereby Paul emphasizes God as beneficently electing and caring for his people Israel. Paul's summary of Israel's history should be seen as his intentional attempt to frame and interpret the meaning and significance of Israel's history, not unlike Stephen's retelling of the history of Israel in Acts 7, Ezra's history centering upon Israel's exile as a consequence of covenant unfaithfulness (Neh 9:6–36), or the Animal Apocalypse's lengthier summary of Israel's history culminating in the remnant of faithful sheep (1 En 90:6–12).[31] In other words, Paul's summary of Israel's history is preparing the reader and audience to accept Paul's definition of the meaning of Israel's history.[32] Paul's election theology is explicit in his first sentence: "The God of this people [τοῦ λαοῦ τούτου] Israel chose our fathers and exalted the people [τὸν λαόν]" (13:17). Throughout the sermon, God is the subject who cares for his people Israel: he compassionately leads his own people out of Egypt (13:17), provides for them in the wilderness (13:18), gives them land for an inheritance (13:19), and grants them judges and prophets (13:20). Second, without so much as even a singular mention of Torah, Sinai, or Temple, Paul orients God's climactic actions for Israel in relation to King David (13:21–22). God has "raised up David" as the king who will do that which God desires (13:22b). As God elected Israel to be his people, so God elected David as the monarch of his people. The pinnacle of the argument comes in v. 23 where Paul roots his message about Jesus in Israel's traditions about David: "From this person's seed, according to the promise, God has brought to Israel the Savior Jesus." This language of "promise" and "seed" alludes to the promises made to David in 2 Samuel 7:12–14 where God declares that one of

---

31. On the role of these summaries of Israel's history within a variety of Jewish texts, including Acts 7 and 13, see Joachim Jeska, *Die Geschichte Israels in der Sicht des Lukas: Apg 7,2b-53 und 13,17-25 im Kontext antik-jüdischer Summarien der Geschichte Israels*, FRLANT 195 (Göttingen: Vandenhoek & Ruprecht, 2001); Robert Hall, *Revealed Histories: Techniques for Ancient Jewish and Christian Historiography*, JSPSup 6 (Sheffield: Sheffield Academic, 1991).

32. As Satlow, *Creating Judaism*, 4 notes, "Essentialist and normative definitions [of Judaism] are useful for communal self-definition.... One Jewish group that wants to define itself against both non-Jews and other, competing Jewish groups will naturally try to cast itself as more 'authentic.' It will draw upon history to create a definition of Judaism to which it is the true heir and other claimants are not. Judaism's essence... becomes identical with that of the particular claimant."

David's "seed" will have his kingdom established forever (7:12; cf. 2 Sam 22:51; 1 Chr 17:4–14; Ps 89:20–38).

The most striking component of the speech's first stage is that it situates Jesus within Israel's election-history, not only as the promised heir of David's throne, but as the long-awaited Savior of Israel (13:23b). "Savior" is a distinctively Lukan title for Jesus, and it comports well with Luke's overall concern to narrate how the message of Israel's Davidic king will be good news for the gentiles.[33] Thus, Paul's thesis is given in verse 26: "Men, brothers, sons of the family of Abraham, and those among you who fear God, the word of this salvation has been sent forth to us." While Luke concentrates upon the promises made to David, it is God's election of the people Israel, through the promises made to Abraham for descendants, which sets the wider context for God's salvation-history.

The climax of Paul's sermon is the simple statement in 13:30: "But God raised him from the dead." But what does this resurrection of the Messiah mean? Paul, like Peter in Acts 2:22–36, interprets God's resurrection of Jesus from the dead as God's fulfillment of the promises he made to David. So Paul explains (13:32–37):

> We also are proclaiming to you the good news of the promise made to the fathers, that God has fulfilled this for us, their children, by raising up Jesus. Just as even in the second Psalm it has been written, 'You are my son. Today I have begotten you.' And because he raised him from the dead, no longer to return to corruption, so he has spoken, 'I will give to you the holy and faithful things of David.' And therefore, in another place he says, 'You will not give your holy one to see corruption.' For David, who served the will of God in his own generation, fell asleep and he was added to his fathers and he saw corruption. But the one whom God has raised, he has not seen corruption.

We have already seen Paul in 13:23 refer to how God brought forth Jesus, as a descendant of David, to bring salvation to Israel in fulfillment of the promise. Here too Paul invokes Israel's Scriptures that spoke of the Davidic king's enthronement as a means of interpreting Jesus's resurrection as his own heavenly enthronement (Ps 2:7; Isa 55:3; Ps 16:10). Thus, the fulfillment of the promise for the children comes about through "the raising up of Jesus" (13:32). This "raising up of Jesus" is what "has been written in the second Psalm" (13:33b),

---

33. E.g., Luke 2:30–32; 3:4–6; Acts 13:46–48 ("eternal life"); 28:28.

PART ONE: GOD'S ACTS FOR ISRAEL

namely, God's enthronement of his Davidic Son to a position of rule in Zion. The most difficult part of Paul's speech is found in his citations of Isaiah 55:3 and Psalm 16:10 in 13:34–35. The primary point here is that God's resurrection of Jesus from the dead is the act that unleashes the salvific blessings for Israel. Justification and forgiveness of sins is now available for those who submit to God's messianic king, whereas those who fail to trust in him are warned of judgment (13:38–41).

Paul's Trial for the Hope of Israel, i.e., the Messiah's Resurrection from the Dead

When Paul is given the opportunity to speak in his defense speeches, he essentially has three basic claims. We have noted the first one already: Paul has nothing against his people; he is a faithful Torah-observant Jew; and he believes everything written in the Law and the Prophets—his loyalty to his Jewish ancestral customs cannot be questioned.

Paul's second claim is that the real reason he is on trial and in chains is due to his proclamation of the hope of Israel. And this hope of Israel is defined by Paul as God's resurrection of Messiah Jesus from the dead. God has visited his people by resurrecting the Messiah and has offered repentance and salvation in his name. And this is all in fulfillment of Jewish Scriptures. Thus, it is not simply "resurrection" that Paul proclaims, it is God's resurrection of the Messiah—Jesus of Nazareth.[34] Paul states, then, to Felix that he "believes everything laid down according to the Law or written in the Prophets" (24:14). But in the next breath Paul defines the content of the Law and the Prophets as centering upon a future resurrection from the dead for both the just and the unjust (24:15). Paul declares to Herod Agrippa II that he is "saying nothing beyond what the Prophets and Moses said would take place" (26:22b).[35] And Paul is absolutely convinced that the content of their writings is "that the messiah would suffer, and would be the first to be resurrected from the dead, and would proclaim the message of light to both the people and the gentiles" (εἰ παθητὸς

---

34. See here Alexandru Neagoe, *The Trial of the Gospel: An Apologetic Reading of Luke's Trial Narratives*, SNTSMS 116 (Cambridge: Cambridge University Press, 2002), 195–218; Robert F. O'Toole, *Acts 26: The Christological Climax of Paul's Defense (Ac 22:1–26:32)*, AB 78 (Rome: Pontifical Biblical Institute, 1978).

35. Alexander, *Acts in Its Ancient Literary Context*, 205, argues that Herod Agrippa II functions as something of a "symbolic spokesman for Diaspora Judaism" within the narrative setting of Paul's speech and that Agrippa "has the best claim to be identified as the ideal (and doubtless idealized) target audience for the apologetic in Acts."

ὁ χριστός, εἰ πρῶτος ἐξ ἀναστάσεως νεκρῶν φῶς μέλλει καταγγέλλειν τῷ τε λαῷ καὶ τοῖς ἔθνεσιν, 26:23). This is why Paul believes he is on trial "on account of my hope in the promise made by God to our ancestors, a promise that our twelve tribes hope to attain. . . . Why is it thought incredible by you that God raises the dead?" (26:6–8). And again, in Luke's summary of Paul's speech to the Jews in Rome, Paul declares "I am bound in chains because of the hope of Israel (28:20b).[36] Predictably, Paul's explanation of this hope centers upon the kingdom of God and Jesus as the climax of the Law and the Prophets (28:23). In other words, Paul's Jewish ancestral traditions center upon and demand a positive response to God's resurrection of the Messiah; and this event, for Paul, has taken place. When Paul says that he is simply proclaiming that the fulfillment of Moses and the prophets has taken place in the Messiah's suffering and resurrection, he is claiming that God has now begun to fulfill and complete the promises he made to his people in their Scriptures.

In Paul's third claim he is emphatic that God's resurrection of the Messiah from the dead is the prior event that gives rise to his mission to the gentiles. The Lukan Paul sees God's welcoming of the nations into his people as something that was also foretold in the Law and the Prophets. Once God acted to restore Israel, the way was open for Paul to take God's light and salvation to the gentiles (Acts 13:47 quoting Isa 49:6; cf. Luke 2:30–32).[37] And Paul declares that his gentile mission is rooted in his obedience to the risen Messiah who appeared to him and called him to take the message of salvation to the gentiles (22:21; 26:18–19).

Assessing the Lukan Paul's Faithfulness to His Jewish Ancestral Heritage

In light of what I've argued about the Lukan Paul, let me conclude with a few theses.

---

36. The phrase "the hope of Israel" functions within Paul's defense speeches as a pithy summary of the content of Paul's proclamation about Jesus. See Klaus Haacker, "Das Bekenntnis des Paulus zur Hoffnung Israels nach der Apostelgeschichte des Lukas," *NTS* 31 (1985): 437–51.

37. For the Lukan Paul (and the other Jesus-believing characters in Acts), the gentile mission is also rooted in Israel's Scriptures (e.g., Isa 49:6 in Acts 13:47; Amos 9:11–13 in Acts 15:16–17). This is a point frequently emphasized by Jervell. E.g., Jervell, *Luke and the People of God*, 44–64.

PART ONE: GOD'S ACTS FOR ISRAEL

(1) *I want to affirm emphatically one more time that Luke's view of Paul is that he is a faithful, Torah-observant Jew, faithful to his ancestral heritage in every way.* He does not teach anything against his people, against Moses, or against the temple. He believes everything written in the Law and the Prophets. His entire life and mission are devoted to what he calls "the hope of Israel." As Paula Fredriksen has noted in her work on Paul's letters, even the language of "messiah" and "resurrection from the dead" are words and ideas that are specific to Judaism.[38] Fortunately, it seems to me that the days of seeing Acts as marginalizing and denigrating Judaism as a religion of the past which has now been superseded by the universal gospel of Paul and Christianity are over. Instead, in the words of a recent re-evaluation of the Lukan Paul, the book of Acts should be seen as a "promoter rather than archiver of Israel's history and heritage in the Messiah Jesus."[39]

(2) *But, secondly, I suggest that Luke's preservation of the rumors of apostasy lodged against Paul by fellow Jews and his recounting the depictions of Paul's message provoking violent conflict should be taken seriously.* Taken seriously in that they remind us that no matter how faithfully Jewish Luke wants us to see Paul, many, if not most, Jews viewed Paul and his message as a destabilizing, problematic threat to their own understanding of what constituted faithfulness to God. Let me state this another way: Luke's Paul does not simply add "belief in Jesus of Nazareth as Israel's Messiah raised from the dead and enthroned to the right hand of God" as a piece of information to his beliefs and convictions; rather, Paul's association of the hope of Israel with the Messiah's resurrection results in a reconfiguration and re-evaluation of the very meaning of his Jewish ancestral heritage and what counts as faithfulness and loyalty to the God of Israel. If one does not accept Paul's equation of the hope of Israel with the Messiah's resurrection, then Paul is an idiosyncratic Jew at minimum and perhaps even a dangerous, destabilizing teacher of Israel at worst.[40] Thus, I'm sympathetic to the perception by some of Paul's fellow Jews that his message could be construed as having negative implications for the people of Israel, the law of Moses, and the sanctity of the temple (21:27–28). I won't expand on these with the detail they deserve, but Paul's message might be reasonably rejected because it was perceived as:

38. Fredriksen, "How Jewish Is God?," 211–12.
39. See the heading in the conclusion by Moessner et al., eds., *Paul and the Heritage of Israel*, 321.
40. John M. G. Barclay, *Jews in the Mediterranean Diaspora: From Alexander to Trajan (323 BCE–117 CE)* (Berkeley: University of California Press, 1996), 381–95, refers to him as an "anomalous Diaspora Jew."

(a) *Against the people.* We are not always given as much information as we would like for why non-believing Jews in the Diaspora so violently react against Paul's message of the risen Messiah. Often enough, however, Paul's claim to turn to the gentiles with his message provokes conflict or intensifies the conflict (e.g., 13:47–52; 22:21–22). Paul's "Christology" of a once crucified and now resurrected-enthroned-in-heaven Davidic Messiah has as its corollary a new definition of who the people of God are and what constitutes faithfulness to the God of Israel.[41] Faithfulness to the God of Israel is based now primarily on whether one is loyal to this enthroned Messiah; gentiles are now included within God's people and receive the promised Abrahamic blessings simply based on giving the same appropriate response to the Messiah (cf. Acts 3:22–26); and the legitimate leaders of Israel are, no surprise, not those who are connected to the Jerusalem Temple but the Messiah's apostles, prophets, and teachers (see Luke 22:24–30 and the turf war battles in Acts 1–5). Those Jews who are not sympathetic to Paul's proclamation that Jesus is Israel's Messiah receive harsh words of prophetic judgment as Paul plays the role of the prophet Isaiah while his fellow Jews who reject his message take on the guise of those ancient Israelites who rejected the prophet (Acts 28:25–27; Isa 6:9–10). Thus, based not only on Paul's teaching but also the broader narrative of Acts, I can sympathize with the accusation lodged against Paul that his teaching has dangerous or at least very surprising implications for one's definition of the people of God—a definition that is absurd if one does not grant Paul's prior christological claims.[42]

A second way in which Paul's teaching may be construed as "against the people" can be seen in its potential consequences for the social life of the Diaspora synagogues. Paul is accused by those in the Diaspora synagogue of tampering with their customs and laws for how they worship (17:5–8; 18:5–6, 12–13). And here it seems likely that Paul's practice of calling gentile "godfearers" (who were sympathetic to the God of Israel and their laws) to reject their native pagan gods, to cease from sacrifices and participation in their pagan temples, and to give their exclusive allegiance to the God of Israel and Messiah Jesus could have serious negative repercussions for these diaspora synagogues.[43] In other words, those gentiles who rejected their ancestral gods

---

41. See Marguerat, *First Christian Historian*, 146–47.
42. On this connection between "Christology" and "ecclesiology" in Luke's broader narrative, see Schröter, "Salvation for the Gentiles and Israel," 236–37.
43. On the presence of gentiles within the Jewish synagogue and who were sympathetic, in some form, to the God of Israel, see Gager, *Who Made Early Christianity?*, 53–85; Cohen, *Beginnings of Jewishness*, 140–74.

and customs obviously risked giving offense to their families and friends, and this could then result in deeper hostility, suspicion, and anger directed against these Jewish synagogues (see esp. Acts 16:20–23). As Paula Fredriksen has stated clearly, "Such a destabilizing and inflammatory message [i.e., to turn away from their native cults and gods to the God of Israel], radiating from the synagogue, could make the Jewish urban community itself the target of local anxieties and resentments. Alienating the gods put the city at risk; alienating the pagan majority put the diaspora synagogue at risk—especially when the behavior occasioning that risk, an exclusive commitment to the god of Israel, was so universally and uniquely associated with Jews themselves."[44] The well-being of the Jewish Diaspora synagogues was dependent upon, says Martin Goodman, "Jews not interfering in the civic life, not least the religious civic life."[45] Thus, once again, the rumor that Paul and his message shows little concern for the Jewish people seems, from one perspective, to have strong substance to the claim.[46]

(b) *Against the law of Moses*. Clearly not all Jews, even Jewish believers in Jesus as the Messiah of Israel, agreed with Paul (and the broader argument of Acts) that gentiles should be welcomed into God's people Israel apart from circumcision. The "believing Pharisees" in Acts 15:1–5, for example, view gentile salvation and inclusion in God's people apart from circumcision as overriding "the custom of Moses" (15:1 and 5). Despite Luke's portrait of unified agreement and harmony in response to this dispute, it is likely that Luke's preservation of disagreement over how gentiles can be saved continued on the part of Jewish believers in Jesus. Paul's insistence that Jews and gentiles are saved, have their sins forgiven by faith in the Messiah, and receive God's Spirit apart from the law is easily capable of being interpreted as failing to honor the law of Moses (further, 11:15–18; 13:38–39; 15:7–11).[47]

---

44. Paula Fredriksen, *Paul: The Pagans' Apostle* (New Haven: Yale University Press, 2017), 92.

45. Martin Goodman, "The Persecution of Paul by Diaspora Jews," in *The Beginnings of Christianity: A Collection of Articles*, ed. Jack Pastor and Menachem Mor (Jerusalem: Yad BenZvi Press, 2005), 379–87, here 385.

46. The social situation of 1 Peter seems relevant here, as the author addresses gentiles who are receiving hostility and persecution as a result of having rejected their "foolish lifestyle inherited from your ancestors" (1 Pet 1:18).

47. Giving hermeneutical priority to these texts, particularly Acts 13:38–39, has resulted in some scholars arguing that Luke has repudiated the Jewish law and sees it as a custom of a bygone period of early Christian history. E.g., Stephen G. Wilson, *Luke and the Law*, SNTSMS (Cambridge: Cambridge University Press, 1983), 103–17.

The Paul of Acts

Paul's declaration that the law of Moses could not provide justification from Israel's sins (13:39), not to mention Stephen's accusation that God's people did not obey the law (7:53) and Peter's reference to the law as a yoke that "neither our ancestors nor we have had the ability to bear" (15:10), should not be minimized or ignored when evaluating Paul's relationship to the Torah.[48] In addition, while I by no means intend to take away from my earlier argument regarding Luke's depiction of Paul following and obeying various laws of Moses, the Lukan Paul is portrayed as much less interested in reading the law of Moses as laws and commandments as he does in reading the law of Moses as prophetic utterances about the Messiah and his resurrection (again, 24:14–15; 26:22–23; 28:20, 23).[49] In other words, for the Lukan Paul, Moses functions as a prophetic anticipation of, and is thereby subordinated in terms of importance to, Messiah Jesus.[50] Paul's understanding of Moses as an anticipatory prophet-like-Jesus is, of course, something also insisted upon by Peter (3:18–26) and Stephen (7:14–53)—though with violent repercussions from those who reject their claim (4:1–4; 7:54–8:3).[51] Stated simply, if one does not agree with Luke's risen Jesus who declares that Moses and the Prophets all speak and testify about the risen Jesus, then the accusation against Paul's understanding of the law of Moses should also be rejected (Luke 24:25–27, 44–49).[52]

(c) *Against the temple.* By Luke's reckoning, Paul does nothing that can be

---

48. So Daniel Marguerat, "Paul and the Torah in the Acts of the Apostles," in *Torah in the New Testament: Papers Delivered at the Manchester-Lausanne Seminar of June 2008*, LNTS 401, ed. Peter Oakes and Michael Tait (London: T&T Clark, 2009), 98–117.

49. Again, this does not mean Paul is "anti-Jewish" or making a break with the law of Moses. See, for example, Jonathan Klawans, *Josephus and the Theologies of Ancient Judaism* (Oxford: Oxford University Press, 2012), 137–79, who has shown how the sects mentioned by Josephus had variegated hermeneutical approaches to interpreting and observing the Torah.

50. Miller, "Reading Law as Prophecy," 91, states my sentiments well: "The law in Luke's writings plays a supporting role behind his overwhelming interest in Jesus. While Luke does not think they conflict, it is the example of Jesus, much more than the demands of Torah, that serves as the primary paradigm for the main characters in Acts, and hence for Luke's Gentile readers."

51. On the depiction of Jesus as a prophet-like-Moses, I have learned much from Paul S. Minear, *To Heal and to Reveal: The Prophetic Vocation According to Luke* (New York: Seabury, 1976); David P. Moessner, *Luke the Historian of Israel's Legacy, Theologian of Israel's "Christ": A New Reading of the "Gospel Acts" of Luke*, BZNW 182 (Berlin: de Gruyter 2016), 205–37; Jocelyn McWhirter, *Rejected Prophets: Jesus and His Witnesses in Luke-Acts* (Minneapolis: Fortress, 2013).

52. See here Matthews, *Perfect Martyr*, 34.

construed as directly against the Temple in Jerusalem, and as we saw earlier Paul's piety is often expressed through his worshipping in the Jerusalem Temple (e.g., Acts 22:17; 24:11–17). But if the temple is viewed as sacred due to its functions as God's chosen dwelling place amongst his people and as the central institution that mediates God's forgiveness for the sins of his people, then once again Paul's teaching may be viewed as giving too little respect and attention to the Jerusalem temple. All of God's salvific blessings for Israel and the gentiles, including the forgiveness of sins, are mediated to God's people through Messiah Jesus (13:34–39; 26:18). Furthermore, access to God's presence is consistently connected to the resurrected and heavenly enthroned Messiah. Sacred space is not localized for Paul, or for the broader narrative of Acts, to one geographical locale, but is rather connected to wherever the heavenly Messiah chooses to make himself known. As a result, God's revelatory presence is often mediated through heavenly Christophanies, dreams and visions, and outpourings of the Holy Spirit (e.g., 2:1–13; 4:23–31; 8:14–17; 10:1–11:18; 16:6–10; 22:1–21; 26:15–18).[53] Is Paul against the temple? From Luke's standpoint, absolutely not; but understandably from another viewpoint, the Lukan Paul's teaching is not deeply interested in the Jerusalem temple and it may not be by accident that his one speech in the Jewish synagogue presents the history of Israel without even a single mention of the temple.[54]

(3) *Reckoning with Luke's dual characterization of Paul both as someone who was faithful to his Jewish ancestral heritage, never envisioning himself as abandoning his commitment to God's election of Israel, and as one who was perceived as a dangerous and destabilizing threat to the Jewish people and the practice of their ancestral customs is necessary for a balanced evaluation of the legacy of the Paul of Acts.* On the one hand, not unlike the Paul of the epistles, Paul did not reject the Torah for Israel. Paul did not deny Israel's election. Paul did not replace Judaism with Christianity. The Paul of Acts does not criticize his fellow Jews for failed observance of the Torah, for legalism, for hypocritical judgment

---

53. For the way in which the enthroned-in-heaven Messiah creates sacred space and impacts the narrative of Acts, see Matthew Sleeman, *Geography and the Ascension Narrative in Acts*, SNTSMS 146 (Cambridge: Cambridge University Press, 2009).

54. Within Acts 1–7 the Jerusalem temple often provides the setting for opposition against those proclaiming Jesus's resurrection from the dead (e.g., Acts 4:1–6; 5:17–21). See here especially Geir Otto Holmås, "'My House Shall Be a House of Prayer': Regarding the Temple as a Place of Prayer in Acts within the Context of Luke's Apologetical Objective," *JSNT* 27 (2005): 393–416.

of others, or for national pride. In short, Paul is not a critic of, let alone one who rejects or abandons, his Jewish ancestral heritage (cf. Rom 3:1–2; 7:7, 12; 9:4; 11:1). The Lukan Paul, thus, stands as a witness against supersessionist forms of Christian theology that have dispensed with the ongoing significance of God's election of Israel, which view Christianity or the church as replacing Judaism, and which denigrate Judaism as particularistic and now superseded by the universal gospel of Paul.[55]

On the other hand, one cannot ignore the historical consequences of Paul's emphatic definition of Israel's history (Acts 13:13–41) and Israel's hope (Acts 22–28) as centering upon the crucified Jesus of Nazareth, resurrected from the dead, enthroned at God's right hand, and responsible for pouring out God's Spirit on Jewish and gentile believers in Jesus. Thus, Paul's foundational commitment to Jesus as the risen Messiah results in a totalizing and hegemonic appropriation of Israel's ancestral heritage, customs, and Scriptures.[56] God's election of Israel finds its significance, for the Lukan Paul, in Messiah Jesus; those who violently oppose Paul or reject his message of the resurrected Messiah find themselves excluded from their own covenantal blessings (13:46; 18:6; 28:25–28). Those who speak of Luke's positive view of Jews and Judaism cannot (or should not) ignore the fact that Luke is positive regarding Jews who believe in Jesus as the Messiah of Israel. Those Jews who do not believe Jesus is the Messiah are spoken of by Luke as "jealous" (5:17; 13:45; 17:5), as instigating mob violence (e.g., 7:54–60; 14:1–7, 19; 17:5–9), and blind to the meaning and significance of their own institutions and Scriptures (e.g., Luke 19:41–44; 28:25–28). While this does not mean that the Lukan Paul's teaching was anti-Jewish, that he denied or rejected God's election of Israel, or that he replaced "Judaism" with "Christianity," his refashioning of the significance of Israel's history and

---

55. See, however, the attempt by many now to reckon with Christian theology's supersessionist past and to chart a better way forward. E.g., Willie James Jennings, *The Christian Imagination: Theology and the Origins of Race* (New Haven: Yale University Press, 2010); Robert W. Jenson, "Toward a Christian Theology of Israel," *Pro Ecclesia* 9 (2000): 43–56; R. Kendall Soulen, *The God of Israel and Christian Theology* (Minneapolis: Fortress, 1996); Soulen, *Distinguishing the Voices*, vol. 1 of *The Divine Name(s) and the Holy Trinity* (Louisville: Westminster John Knox, 2011).

56. Again, while I think Luke-Acts is involved in an earlier intramural debate or argument in terms of what constitutes faithfulness to the God of Israel, and while I think the similarities between Acts and the second-century Christian *Adversus Judaeos* tradition are overplayed, Matthews rightly emphasizes this point and pushes against those who emphasize Luke's positive view of Judaism. See Matthews, *Perfect Martyr*, 35–36.

hope did lay the ground for later Christian discourse. And this discourse was rarely able to simultaneously maintain Paul's commitment to Israel's election and the significance of Jewish ethnic identity and a commitment to the resurrected Messiah as the mediator of God's saving blessings for gentiles and Jews alike.[57]

---

57. For example, Justin Martyr's interpretation of Israel's Scriptures, many of which are the same Scriptures interpreted in Luke-Acts, consistently sees the prophetic oracles of Israel as global statements of judgment *against the entire Jewish people* and sees Christians as the "true Israel" who inherit all of God's promises made to Israel. See here Susan Wendel, *Scriptural Interpretation and Community Self-Definition in Luke-Acts and the Writings of Justin Martyr*, NovTSup 139 (Leiden: Brill, 2011). On the rhetoric of Christian discourse which subsumed Israel within an economy of salvation and spoke of its replacement by Christianity, see Soulen, *God of Israel and Christian Theology*.

2

PAUL AS PROPHET OF GOD'S RESURRECTED MESSIAH

Prophecy and Messianism in the Lukan Depiction of Paul

In chapter 1 I probed the accusation made against the "Lukan Paul," and reported by the "Lukan James," that there are "thousands of believers . . . among the Jews," all of whom are "zealous for the law," who have heard that Paul teaches "all the Jews living among the gentiles to forsake Moses" (Acts 21:20–21).[1] Seven days later, Jews from Asia grasp hold of Paul and claim that Paul is the man "who is teaching everyone everywhere against our people, our law, and this place [i.e., the temple]" (21:28). Neither James the character nor Luke's narrative as a whole, of course, agrees with the assessment that Paul rejects Moses. And thus begins the lengthy section of defense speeches in Acts 22–28 where Paul consistently answers the charges that he opposes his own people and ancestral customs (e.g., 24:10–13; 25:10–11; 28:17).[2] One of the obvious rhetorical functions of Paul's speeches is to persuade his listeners that Paul is a faithful Jew and that the charges brought against him are false. More than half of Paul's words, in fact, are taken up by these apologetic speeches highlighting the fact that, at the time of the writing of Acts, Paul was both well-known, controversial, and (for Luke) in need of a strong apologetic.[3]

---

1. The present chapter expands upon some of the claims made in Joshua W. Jipp, "The Paul of Acts: Proclaimer of the Hope of Israel or Teacher of Apostasy from Moses," *NovT* 62 (2020): 60–78.

2. On Acts 27:1–28:10 as offering a reminder of Paul's missionary activity among the gentiles see Joshua W. Jipp, *Divine Visitations and Hospitality to Strangers in Luke-Acts: An Interpretation of the Malta Episode in Acts 28:1–10*, NovTSup 153 (Leiden: Brill, 2013), 219–87.

3. Jacob Jervell, *The Theology of the Acts of the Apostles* (Cambridge: Cambridge University Press, 1996), 86.

PART ONE: GOD'S ACTS FOR ISRAEL

Paul's repetitive arguments conform nicely to definitions of ancient notions of ethnicity, namely, shared ancestral customs, family, *paideia*, land, language, and the gods and their cults.[4] In the Hebrew (or Aramaic) language (Acts 22:2), Paul claims that he is a "Jewish man" (22:3), educated at the feet of Gamaliel in Jerusalem (22:3b), and is zealous for his people's ancestral customs (22:3c; also 26:4–5). Paul emphasizes that he is a Pharisee according to Torah observance (23:5–6; 24:14–16). His visit to Jerusalem was not in order to profane the temple but, rather, in to give alms "for my *ethnos*" (εἰς τὸ ἔθνος μου, 24:17b). From the Lukan Paul's standpoint, Israel is God's elected people; Torah observance for Jews is good; and the Law and the Prophets reveal the will of God. But if the charges brought against Paul are nonsense, then why does Luke so frequently portray Paul as encountering intense opposition among the Jewish people in every city and synagogue he frequents? Paul is chased from city to city precisely by those fellow Jews to whom he proclaims his message (e.g., 13:42–52; 14:4–7).

Making sense of the plausibility of the charges of apostasy brought against Paul requires, I suggest, an understanding of the two central "christological" threads of Acts and their implications for Luke's depiction of the people of God, namely, the messianic and prophetic aspects of Lukan Christology. Jens Schröter has rightly argued, in my view, that "the conception of the people of God developed by Luke must be viewed in close connection with the Christology of his work."[5] I will argue first (and more briefly given I've written on this elsewhere) that the Lukan Paul's primary claim is that Jesus of Nazareth is the resurrected and enthroned Messiah who has, through his life, death, and especially his resurrection, inaugurated Israel's restoration and deliverance. But Jesus is also understood by Luke as Israel's greatest prophet who warns God's people to repent in light of God's visitation of his people. Paul's ministry is best understood as an extension of Jesus's prophetic ministry as he, Luke's star witness, testifies that God has sent the Messiah and raised him from the dead thereby offering salvation to both Israel and the gentiles. The Lukan Paul believes that the divine plan for Israel's restoration consists in God's resurrection of the Messiah (as the foretaste of the final resurrection from the dead). Paul does not give up on Israel as God's elect people, though he—like

---

4. See here, for example, Paula F. Fredriksen, "How Jewish Is God? Divine Ethnicity in Paul's Theology," *JBL* 137 (2018): 193–212.

5. Jens Schröter, "Salvation for the Gentiles and Israel: On the Relationship between Christology and People of God in Luke," in *From Jesus to the New Testament: Early Christian Theology and the Origin of the New Testament Canon*, trans. Wayne Coppins, Baylor-Mohr Siebeck Studies in Early Christianity (Waco, TX: Baylor University Press, 2013), 227–46, here 242.

Paul as Prophet of God's Resurrected Messiah

Jesus—prophetically warns the Jewish people of the consequences of failing to recognize the fulfillment of God's covenantal purposes brought to fruition in the resurrected Messiah. I unpack how the messianic and prophetic strands of Lukan Christology are necessary for understanding the Lukan Paul in three steps. First, Luke depicts Jesus as the Davidic Messiah who will save Israel and establish an everlasting kingdom over Israel. But Jesus also prophetically warns Israel to embrace this divine visit. Second, while Israel's leaders reject and crucify the agent of the divine visitation, the Lukan Paul argues that this act conforms to the foreknowledge of God and is, ironically, the means by which God fulfills his promises to restore the Davidic monarchy, namely, by means of resurrecting and enthroning in heaven the Davidic Messiah. Third, and finally, the Lukan Paul is God's prophet who proclaims repentance to Israel and the nations. Paul is a rejected prophet in the mold of Jesus.

JESUS THE ESCHATOLOGICAL PROPHET AND DAVIDIC MESSIAH IN THE GOSPEL OF LUKE

To set some critical context for understanding Paul's Jewishness in Acts, a look at Luke's infancy narrative will be helpful as it sets forth both the centrality of Luke's presentation of Jesus as Israel's Davidic Messiah *and* his birth into a prophetic people. Both themes are critical for understanding the Lukan Paul as, I will argue, the Gospel of Luke anticipates and the book of Acts narrates how Jesus of Nazareth is the agent who fulfills God's promises to reconstitute the Davidic monarchy and establish an everlasting kingdom over his people. But even as Luke emphasizes Jesus's primary role as Israel's Messiah, he shows how Jesus is born into a family and a people of prophets.[6] Luke's infancy narrative (Luke 1:5–2:52) is peppered with pious Torah-observant Jews who are waiting for "the consolation of Israel" (2:25) and "the redemption of Jerusalem" (2:38). They are filled with the Holy Spirit and give prophetic utterances that interpret God's work of salvation for Israel within history (see, for example, 1:15–17; 1:41–56; 1:67; 2:28b–32; 2:36–38). Their prophetic role, evidenced especially in John the Baptist, is also seen in their task to prepare Israel for God's new work by calling the people to repentance (1:16–17, 76). More specifically, these prophetic characters engage in all kinds of liturgical expressions of praise, confession, and prayers expressing the conviction that Jesus is the one who

---

6. Helpful here is Luke Timothy Johnson, *Prophetic Jesus, Prophetic Church: The Challenge of Luke-Acts to Contemporary Christians* (Grand Rapids: Eerdmans, 2011), 54–56.

will inherit the promises made to David *and* the one who will reign *forever* as Israel's messianic king (see Luke 1:31–35).[7]

Jesus's role as Davidic Messiah is indicated through the following literary features of the infancy narrative:

- Gabriel's claim to Mary that her child will be called "Son of the Most High" and that God will give him "David's throne" so that "he will reign over the house of Jacob forever and his kingdom shall never end" (Luke 1:32–33).
- The parallels between Luke's infancy narrative and 1 Samuel 1–2, which centers upon stories of barren women and their royal hymns (see esp. 1 Sam 2:1–10; Luke 1:46–55).[8]
- Luke's note that Jesus has Davidic lineage given that Mary is engaged to Joseph—a man who is "from the house of David" (1:27). Jesus is, furthermore, born in Bethlehem "the city of David" (2:4, 11; cf. Mic 5:2).
- The use of scriptural messianic titles such as the "horn of salvation in the house of David" (1:69–70); "the dayspring from on high" (1:78–79); and the "Savior who is the Messiah, the Lord" (2:11).

The infancy narrative is emphatic that the target of God's salvation through Messiah Jesus is Israel. Jesus is the agent who will fulfill the covenantal promises made to Israel's patriarchs (1:54–55, 73–74), the embodiment of God's visitation for the redemption of his people (1:68, 78), and the one who inaugurates "the consolation of Jerusalem" (2:38; cf. 2:25). God's provision of Israel's restoration is the impetus for the extension of salvation to the nations. Simeon expresses Luke's convictions that this salvation for the nations cannot bypass Israel: "My eyes have seen your salvation that you have prepared before the presence of all peoples, that is, a light for revelation to the nations and glory for your people Israel" (2:30–32). Israel and the nations are *distinguished* even as both are recipients of God's salvation. Throughout Luke-Acts, in line with many of Israel's prophets (e.g., Isa 42:6; 49:6; 60:1–11), salvation for the gentiles requires *first* the restoration and redemption of Israel.[9]

Isaac Oliver helpfully summarizes how Luke 1–2 make the point that Jesus, as the Davidic Messiah, is the agent of Israel's restoration: "The soteriological

---

7. See, further, Mark L. Strauss, *The Davidic Messiah in Luke-Acts: The Promise and Its Fulfillment in Lukan Christology*, JSNTSup 100 (Sheffield: Sheffield Academic, 1995).

8. In more detail, see Sarah Harris, *The Davidic Shepherd King in the Lukan Narrative*, LNTS 558 (London: T&T Clark, 2016), 41–43.

9. Isaac W. Oliver, *Luke's Jewish Eschatology: The National Restoration of Israel in Luke-Acts* (Cambridge: Cambridge University Press, 2021), 36–37.

Paul as Prophet of God's Resurrected Messiah

terminology in Luke 1–2, be it in the declarations of Mary, Zechariah, Simeon, or Anna, could not be more Jewish in texture.... Nothing in Luke's infancy narrative suggests that this salvation for Israel should be denied, internalized, spiritualized, or transferred to another realm. Restoration is to be experienced by Israel on this earth."[10] Oliver's point cannot be stated too strongly: God is acting to help "his servant Israel" (1:54); Jesus the Messiah will reign "forever over the house of Jacob" (1:33); the salvation of God results in "glory to your people Israel" (2:32).

And yet the Lukan infancy narrative tempers one's hopes through its character's frequent prophetic warnings. The task of John the Baptist, for example, is that of announcing repentance and thereby making a people ready to respond to God's visitation of his people (1:16–17; 1:76–79; also 3:4–6; 7:27). John is called a "prophet of the Most High" (1:76) whose task is "to turn many of the sons of Israel to the Lord their God" (1:16). His prophetic goal is to make the people ready and prepared to "see the salvation of God" (3:6). A second, and more ominous, prophetic warning is found on the lips of Simeon who, immediately after his prophetic declaration of Jesus as the agent of salvation for Israel and the nations, declares to Mary, "Behold this one is appointed for the falling and rising of many in Israel and for a sign that will be opposed—and even your soul will be pierced by a sword—for the revelation of the thoughts of many" (2:34b–35). Simeon testifies to what Jervell refers to as the Lukan notion of "the divided people of God," namely, how Jesus and his followers will provoke a division within Israel.[11] While it is possible that the "falling" and "rising" refer to a temporal sequence of Israel's experiencing judgment and then salvation, I think it more likely foreshadows the mixed response of Israel to the proclamation of Jesus's messiahship.[12] Throughout Luke-Acts, Jesus's messiahship is the "sign that will be opposed" even to the very end of the Acts of the Apostles where Paul describes how fellow Jews "oppose" him and his message (28:19, 22). Simeon's prophecy anticipates how most of Israel will reject Jesus as Israel's messianic deliverer and, yet, the oracle looks forward equally to a "rising" of Israel, that is, a day when the people will be restored.[13]

Jesus himself plays the role of Israel's eschatological prophet who warns the people of God of the consequences that follow should they reject him as the

---

10. Oliver, *Luke's Jewish Eschatology*, 39.

11. See Jacob C. Jervell, *Luke and the People of God: A New Look at Luke-Acts* (Minneapolis: Augsburg, 1972), 41–74.

12. For the former interpretation, see Mark S. Kinzer, *Jerusalem Crucified, Jerusalem Risen: The Resurrected Messiah, the Jewish People, and the Land of Promise* (Eugene, OR: Cascade, 2018), 33–34.

13. Oliver, *Luke's Jewish Eschatology*, 39.

messianic agent of God's visitation. For example, in Luke 11:37–54, Jesus speaks prophetic words of "woe" against the Pharisees and accuses them of continuing their ancestors' practice of rejecting the prophets: "Woe to you! For you build the tombs of the prophets whom your ancestors killed. So you are witnesses and approve of the deeds of your ancestors; for they killed them, and you build their tombs" (11:47–48 NRSV). Note that Jesus declares that *this generation* (ἀπὸ τῆς γενεᾶς ταύτης, 11:50, 51) will be held responsible for "the blood" of all the rejected and killed prophets, a comment that indicates Jesus sees himself as "*the* consummating point of all the prophets' tragic sending."[14] Jesus is the final eschatological prophet calling the people of Israel to repent and recognize the time of salvation so that they might escape divine judgment.

Similarly, in Luke 13:31–35 Jesus warns some Pharisees to welcome their divine visitation as he makes his way to Jerusalem (see 9:51–56).[15] His words are portentous, however, for Jesus knows that prophets are not welcome in Jerusalem and that the people will not embrace him (13:33–34). Like Israel's prophets who warned the people of the consequences for the temple if they failed to repent (e.g., Ezek 9–11; Jer 7:8–15; 12:7; 22:5), so Jesus pronounces a conditional warning of judgment against the temple and its leaders should they reject him: "Behold your house is left to you" (13:35a).[16] Jesus's final statement, "You will not see me until you say, 'blessed is the one who comes in the name of the Lord'" (13:35b; Ps 118:26), is a warning to respond to the divine visitor with the welcome of blessing. Given the Lukan use of sight as recognition, the reader understands that those who proclaim the blessing on Jesus see him as the agent of God's visitation. Jesus's warning is fulfilled in 19:28–40 as Jesus enters Jerusalem as Israel's messianic lord (19:31, 33; cf. 2:11). Some in the crowd rejoice and praise God, using the language of Psalm 118:26: "Blessed is the one who comes, the King, in the name of the Lord" (Luke 19:38). The language of kingship and lordship draws the reader back to the messianic destiny and vocation marked out for Jesus in Luke's infancy narrative, particularly the promises that Jesus would have an everlasting kingdom as the Davidic Messiah. The people's cry draws upon Jesus's promise in 13:35 and thereby marks them as those who see Jesus's entrance into Jerusalem as the messianic Lord's coming to his city. But, of course, it is notable that within the scene there are no priests, scribes, or temple leaders; the Pharisees, in fact, demand that the Mes-

14. David P. Moessner, "Paul in Acts: Preacher of Eschatological Repentance to Israel," in *Luke the Historian of Israel's Legacy, Theologian of Israel's "Christ": A New Reading of the "Gospel Acts" of Luke*, BZNW 182 (Berlin: de Gruyter, 2016), 292–301, here 294.

15. I have written on this in more detail in *Divine Visitations*, 231–33.

16. See Klaus Baltzer, "The Meaning of the Temple in the Lukan Writings," *HTR* 58 (1965): 263–77.

Paul as Prophet of God's Resurrected Messiah

siah silence his followers (19:39).[17] And this leads to Jesus's climactic prophetic warning of judgment as he weeps that the people have rejected his offer of peace (19:41–44). The destruction of Jerusalem will be, Jesus declares using the language of Jeremiah (see Jer 6:15 LXX), "because you have not recognized the time of your visitation" (Luke 19:44b). Jesus's words of judgement, however, do not indicate the rejection of Israel as God's people. Again, Oliver: "Luke mixes Jesus's condemnation of Jerusalem with an emotional quality that expresses a strong attachment to the city, an affection that Israelite prophets frequently show even when they relay oracles of judgment against their own people."[18]

Allow me to make two summary comments. First, Luke depicts Jesus as the final Davidic Messiah *and* the eschatological prophet. Second, both the messianic and prophetic aspects of Lukan Christology are significant for understanding Jesus's relationship to Israel. Given that Jesus is God's promised Davidic Messiah whose vocation is to establish an eternal kingdom over Israel, the time of Israel's restoration has arrived. Jesus's prophetic role consists in calling Israel to repent by recognizing God's eschatological visit and warning of the dire consequences of rejecting God's salvation.

Paul's Proclamation of the Resurrected Messiah in the Acts of the Apostles

Luke reports two of Jesus's disciples giving voice to their belief that the crucifixion of Jesus has shattered their hopes for Israel's salvation and restoration. Their response to the resurrected-and-disguised Jesus on the Emmaus Road is as follows:

> The things about Jesus of Nazareth, who was a prophet powerful in word and deed before God and all the people, and how our chief priests and rulers handed him over to the sentence of death and crucified him. But we had hoped that he was the one about to redeem Israel [ὁ μέλλων λυτροῦσθαι τὸν Ἰσραήλ]. And even more it is now three days since these things happened. (Luke 24:19–21)

The words of the two disciples foreshadow what is perhaps the major theme of Acts as well as what animates the activity of the Lukan Paul, namely, how

---

17. See Brent Kinman, "Parousia, Jesus' 'A-Triumphal' Entry, and the Fate of Jerusalem (Luke 19:28–44)," *JBL* 118 (1999): 279–94.

18. Oliver, *Luke's Jewish Eschatology*, 79.

the resurrection of Jesus the Messiah constitutes the hope for Israel's salvation. That is, the two disciples voice their fear that Jesus's death marks the end of the hopes for Israel that were declared by so many pious prophetic Jews in the Lukan infancy narrative, whereas in fact Israel's hope of salvation is wed to the resurrection of the Messiah who is "the first to rise from the dead" (Acts 26:23). While Israel's leaders are accountable for their sin of rejecting and crucifying Jesus, their acting in ignorance is the means whereby God's plan to resurrect the Messiah and set him at God's right hand initiates restoration for Israel and salvation for the nations. Their putting Jesus to death is, in fact, the means by which God, according to the Lukan Peter, "has fulfilled all the things which he foretold through the mouth of all the prophets, namely, that his Messiah should suffer" (3:18). Therefore, now is the time for Israel to repent and turn to God, which will unleash God's promised covenantal blessings from the resurrected and enthroned-in-heaven Messiah (3:20–21).

Luke portrays Paul, then, as Torah-observant, devoted to Jerusalem, and loyal to the people of Israel. But the Lukan emphasis is clearly upon arguing the controversial claim that Paul's faithfulness to his ancestral customs and heritage consists in his proclamation that Jesus is the resurrected Davidic Messiah, the one who fulfills the hopes of Israel. Paul's proclamation reaffirms the expectations and hopes for Israel's redemption narrated in the infancy narrative, albeit in a new era of salvation history. As I have recently made this argument in more detail elsewhere, I will be briefer here and offer three lines of evidence which indicate how the Lukan Paul associates Israel's restoration and salvation with the resurrection of the Messiah.[19]

Paul's Formulaic Proclamation of Jesus as the Resurrected Messiah

After his transformative encounter with the risen Jesus, Paul proclaims that Jesus is risen from the dead. It is notable that the location for Paul's proclamation are the Jewish synagogues in Damascus (9:19–25) and Jerusalem (9:26–30). The honorifics Paul uses to proclaim the significance of Jesus are one's the reader is familiar with from the Lukan infancy narrative, namely, Jesus is "the Son of God" (οὗτός ἐστιν ὁ υἱὸς τοῦ θεοῦ, 9:20; e.g., Luke 1:31–35) and "the Messiah" (οὗτός ἐστιν ὁ χριστός, 9:22; Luke 2:11, 26). These summary statements preview the content of the Lukan Paul's proclamation in his later missionary journeys. So, in Thessalonica, we are told that it was Paul's regular habit to attend the synagogue meetings, just as it was Jesus's custom (κατὰ δὲ

---

19. Jipp, "Paul of Acts," 68–72.

Paul as Prophet of God's Resurrected Messiah

τὸ εἰωθὸς τῷ Παύλῳ, Acts 17:2a; κατὰ τὸ εἰωθὸς αὐτῷ, Luke 4:16b), and to expound from the Jewish Scriptures that "it was necessary for the Messiah [τὸν χριστὸν] to suffer and to be raised from the dead, and saying 'This is the Messiah Jesus [οὗτός ἐστιν ὁ χριστὸς ὁ Ἰησοῦς] whom I am proclaiming to you'" (Acts 17:2b–3; cf. 17:31–32). Likewise, Luke narrates that Paul's regular habit in Corinth was to try to persuade "both Jews and Greeks" that "Jesus is the Messiah" (εἶναι τὸν χριστὸν Ἰησοῦν, 18:5).

Paul's Davidic-Messianic Interpretation of Israel's History and Scriptures

In his narration of Paul's time in Pisidian Antioch, Luke offers his readers one representative scene that contains Paul's proclamation to "the sons of Israel" (9:15) in the synagogue (Acts 13:13–41). Paul's sermon is given during the weekly "reading of the Law and the Prophets" (13:15). The note that Paul is speaking "to the people" (13:15), referring to his audience as "Israelite men and those who fear God" (13:16) and "brethren" (13:26, 38), makes the point that Paul is addressing the elect people of God. Paul engages in the common literary practice of retelling the history of Israel, here beginning with God's election of Israel and redemption out of Egypt up until the time of King David. Paul's summary of Israel's history should be seen as his intentional attempt to frame and interpret the significance of Israel's history, not unlike Stephen's retelling in Acts 7, Ezra's history centering upon Israel's exile and covenant unfaithfulness (Neh 9:6–36), or the Animal Apocalypse's summary of Israel's history culminating in the remnant of faithful sheep (1 En. 90:6–12).[20] In other words, Paul's summary of Israel's history is preparing the reader to accept Paul's very particular and controversial interpretation of the meaning of Israel's history. I will make three points.

First, Paul's sermon is oriented toward God's reconstitution of the Davidic monarchy. Paul's interpretation of Israel's history focuses on *God's* consistent activity and working within his people Israel but moves quickly to its high point, namely, God's "promise" to raise up a "descendant" from David's house who would reign forever over Israel. Israel requested a king, and so God gave them Saul, whose disobedience resulted in God having him "removed" (13:21–22a), but God "raised up David as a king for them" since he was

---

20. On the role of retellings of the history of Israel in a variety of Jewish texts, see Robert Hall, *Revealed Histories: Techniques for Ancient Jewish and Christian Historiography*, JSPSup 6 (Sheffield: Sheffield Academic, 1991).

PART ONE: GOD'S ACTS FOR ISRAEL

"a man according to my heart who will do the entirety of my will" (13:22b).[21] It is "from the seed of [David]" (ἀπὸ τοῦ σπέρματος κατ᾽ ἐπαγγελίαν) that God, "according to his promise," has sent Jesus as Israel's "Savior" (13:23). The language of "promise" and "seed" clearly draw upon the oath that God made to David in 2 Samuel 7:12—"I will raise up your offspring after you who will come from your loins and I will establish his kingdom" (so also 2 Sam 22:51; 1 Chr 17:4-14; Ps 89:20-38).

Second, God has fulfilled this promise to rescue Israel through a descendant of David by raising Jesus from the dead (13:30). Paul interprets the Psalter's (Ps 16:10 [15:10 LXX]) claim that God's holy one will not "see decay" (ἰδεῖν διαφθοράν, 13:35b) to refer not to David who "saw corruption" (εἶδεν διαφθοράν, 13:36) but to his descendant Jesus "whom God has raised, he has not seen corruption" (ὃν δὲ ὁ θεὸς ἤγειρεν, οὐκ εἶδεν διαφθοράν, 13:37). God's resurrection of Jesus from the dead is the means whereby God establishes his plan to give one of David's descendants an everlasting reign over the people of God (13:34b). God's promise is brought to fruition through his "raising up Jesus" (13:33), which is what was promised in Psalm 2:7—"You are my son. Today I have begotten you" (13:33b). Given that the entire discussion of 13:33-37 focuses upon a scriptural demonstration of Jesus's resurrection as his enthronement as the messianic king, this "raising up" makes best sense not as a reference to God's act to bring Jesus into the world but, rather, as referring to God's resurrection of the Messiah as his enthronement and installation of God's king (see also Ps 2:1-2 in Acts 4:25-27). Thus, Psalm 2, originally a declaration of God's election of the Davidic dynasty, is now fulfilled in the messianic Son of God's resurrection and enthronement.[22]

Third, Paul's messianic interpretation of Israel's history and claim that God has raised the Messiah from the dead means that covenantal blessings of salvation are available for those who embrace Jesus. Note, for example, Paul's claim that God "has brought to Israel a Savior—Jesus" (ἤγαγεν τῷ Ἰσραὴλ σωτῆρα Ἰησοῦν, 13:23) and that his sermon is a "message of salvation" (ὁ λόγος τῆς σωτηρίας, 13:26) for the children of Israel. Paul claims that God's resurrection of the Messiah results in the unleashing of God's promise from Isaiah 55:3—"I will give to you the holy and faithful things of David" (δώσω ὑμῖν τὰ ὅσια Δαυὶδ τὰ πιστά, 13:34b). Oliver comments on the phrase, "Whatever its precise meaning, it seems to concern an ensemble of blessings . . . sworn to David, the fulfillment

---

21. See Oliver, *Luke's Jewish Eschatology*, 64.
22. So Luke Timothy Johnson, *Septuagintal Midrash in the Speeches of Acts*, The Père Marquette Lecture in Theology 2002 (Milwaukee: Marquette University Press, 2002), 61.

of which Paul proclaims in Acts to the people of Israel."[23] In other words, God's climactic act to reconstitute the Davidic kingdom results in justification and forgiveness of sins for Israel while grave warnings of judgment are spoken for those who would refuse to submit to the resurrected messianic king (13:40–41).

Paul's Identification of the Hope of Israel

Paul's defense speeches in Acts 22–28 revolve around two broad themes. First, Paul is in every way a faithful and Torah-observant Jew who is loyal to his people and his ancestral customs. He speaks Hebrew and was educated in Jerusalem (22:1–3), he believes everything written in the Law and the Prophets (24:14–15; 26:27), and he does nothing against his own people (28:17–19). But, second, Paul is emphatic that he is on trial for "the hope of Israel," which he identifies as God's resurrection of Messiah Jesus (see 24:14–15; 26:6–8; 26:19–23; 28:17–20).[24] Paul does not proclaim "resurrection" or "the Messiah" as a replacement of, or in contrast to his Jewish heritage but, rather, as the true content of the Scriptures of Israel. God's resurrection of the Messiah is the sign, the foreshadowing of the final eschatological resurrection of the dead—which Paul refers to as something "the twelve tribes" hope to obtain (26:7) and "the hope of Israel" (28:20). The Messiah is "*the first* among the resurrection of the dead" (Acts 26:23a). Again, Oliver: "In Luke's estimation, to uphold the resurrection of the messiah is to sustain the hope in the resurrection of the dead, which remains indissolubly linked with Israel's eschatological destiny."[25]

PAUL AS THE MESSIAH'S PROPHETIC WITNESS TO ISRAEL AND THE NATIONS

Given the Lukan Paul's emphatic association between Israel's restoration and the Messiah's resurrection, Luke's primary characterization of Paul is that he is God's eschatological prophet sent to both Israel and the nations in order to proclaim the necessity of repentance. Luke draws upon a variety of prophetic motifs and intertexts from both the Scriptures of Israel *and* his Gospel in order

---

23. Oliver, *Luke's Jewish Eschatology*, 65.
24. See Klaus Haacker, "Das Bekenntnis des Paulus zur Hoffnung Israels nach der Apostelgeschichte des Lukas," *NTS* 31 (1985): 437–51.
25. Oliver, *Luke's Jewish Eschatology*, 128; see also Kinzer, *Jerusalem Crucified, Jerusalem Risen*, 133–34.

PART ONE: GOD'S ACTS FOR ISRAEL

to explain why Paul's Jewish audience so often rejects him. In what follows, I argue that the importance of Luke's prophetic characterization of Paul enables one to better understand how he can simultaneously be depicted as one who is loyal to the God of Israel and yet considered a pest or even an apostate by many of his Jewish contemporaries.

Paul the Commissioned Prophet

Luke provides three accounts of the risen Christ's initial appearance to Paul (Acts 9, 22, and 26), and scholars are right to prefer the language of call/commission (rather than conversion) to describe the event whereby Paul becomes a prophetic witness for the risen Christ.[26] First, Paul experiences not just a theophany but, rather, a Christophany (9:1–9). Note here the blinding light "from heaven" (ἐκ τοῦ οὐρανοῦ, 9:3b), heaven now being the location of the risen Christ (e.g., 1:9–11; 2:30–36; 3:19–21),[27] the voice that declares "I am Jesus whom you are persecuting" (9:5), and the repeated title "Lord"—a Lukan designation for the resurrected Jesus (9:1, 5, 10, 11, 13). Luke speaks of Paul as one elected for a task. Thus, Paul is Christ's "chosen instrument" (σκεῦος ἐκλογῆς, 9:15); the "God of our ancestors has chosen you" (προεχειρίσατό σε, 22:14); and Christ has "appointed you" (προχειρίσασθαί σε, 26:16). Many have recognized that Paul's call conforms to the pattern of God's commissioning of Israel's prophets—most notably that of Isaiah and Jeremiah (e.g., Isa 6:1–13; Jer 1:1–19).[28] For example, the risen Christ declares to Paul, "I will rescue you from the people and from the gentiles to whom I am sending you" (Acts 26:17). To Jeremiah, God declares, "You will go to all to whom I send you.... I am with you to deliver you, says the Lord" (Jer 1:7, 8). Or compare Acts 26:17–18, where the risen Christ commissions Paul "to open their eyes and to turn them from darkness to the light," with the Isaianic servant who is appointed as "a light to the gentiles, in order to open the eyes of the blind ... who sit in darkness" (Isa 42:6–7).[29]

---

26. For example, Paul S. Minear, *To Heal and to Reveal: The Prophetic Vocation According to Luke* (New York: Seabury, 1976). Also, see Benjamin Hubbard, "The Role of Commissioning Accounts in Acts," in *Perspectives on Luke-Acts*, ed. Charles H. Talbert (Edinburgh: T&T Clark, 1978), 187–98.

27. See here Matthew Sleeman, *Geography and the Ascension Narrative in Acts*, SNTSMS 146 (Cambridge: Cambridge University Press, 2009).

28. See here, for example, Jocelyn McWhirter, *Rejected Prophets: Jesus and His Witnesses in Luke-Acts* (Minneapolis: Fortress, 2013), 117; also, Craig S. Keener, *Acts: An Exegetical Commentary*, vol. 2, *3:1– 14:28* (Grand Rapids: Baker, 2013), 1609.

29. On these parallels, see Dale C. Allison Jr., *The Resurrection of Jesus: Apologetics, Polemics, History* (New York: T&T Clark, 2021), 85–86.

Paul as Prophet of God's Resurrected Messiah

Second, the risen Christ commissions Paul with the prophetic task "to take my name before nations and kings and the children of Israel" (9:15b). The purpose of Paul's Christophany is consistently seen to be that of enabling Paul to engage in testimony to the risen Christ (Acts 22:14–16; 26:15–16). This conforms to the risen Christ's initial commission of the disciples as "my witnesses [μου μάρτυρες] in Jerusalem, in Judea and Samaria, and until the end of the earth [ἕως ἐσχάτου τῆς γῆς]" (1:8b). Note here that Christ's commission is in response to their question as to whether *now* is the time when "you will restore to the kingdom to Israel" (ἀποκαθιστάνεις τὴν βασιλείαν τῷ Ἰσραήλ, 1:6b). Space precludes providing the necessary details, but suffice it to say that the disciples' question raises the same expectant hopes as did the characters in the Lukan infancy narrative *and* that Acts also makes the closest of links between the hope of Israel *and* the resurrection of Israel's Messiah. If Luke only has the disciples *ask* the question in order to portray them as foolish, then Luke's emphasis here on the kingdom of God, the Spirit, the distinctly Israelite geographic language in 1:8, and the emphasis on Jesus as the enthroned Davidic Messiah are inexplicable.[30] Here I simply note that the language of "my witnesses" and "the ends of the earth" derive from Isaiah 40–66, where the people of God will function as prophetic witnesses to God's accomplishment of salvation and restoration of Israel (Isa 43:10–12; 44:8).[31] Furthermore, the language of "the end of the earth" also alludes to Isaiah 40–66, where the phrase evokes how the servant accomplishes salvation for the gentiles. So, Isaiah 49:5–6:

> And now the LORD says,
>   who formed me in the womb to be his servant,
> to bring Jacob back to him,
>   and that Israel might be gathered to him, . . .
> he says,
> "It is too light a thing that you should be my servant
>   to raise up the tribes of Jacob
>   and to restore the survivors of Israel;
> I will give you as a light to the nations,
>   that my salvation may reach to the end of the earth." (NRSV)

---

30. I have argued this in more detail in Joshua W. Jipp, *Reading Acts* (Eugene, OR: Cascade, 2018), 34–38.

31. See David W. Pao, *Acts and the Isaianic New Exodus*, WUNT 2/130 (Tübingen: Mohr Siebeck, 2000), 88–93.

Paul himself quotes this portion of Isaiah in his response to some Jews in Pisidian Antioch who reject his proclamation of the word of God.[32] He has, as Isaiah foretold, spoken God's word *first* to the Jews and now he is taking it "to the gentiles" (13:46). Paul plays the role of the Isaianic servant when he claims the Scriptures spoke about him: "I have appointed you as a light for the nations so that you may bring salvation to the end of the earth" (13:47). The characters of Acts, then, including Paul, play the role of the Isaianic servant in bearing witness to Israel's restoration and salvation—an event which results in salvation going to the gentiles.[33]

Third, Paul is equipped for his prophetic task through divine intervention and Christophanies. For example, Christ sends him the disciple Ananias who grants Paul hospitality, the Holy Spirit, and baptism (9:17–19; also 22:16). The risen Christ continues to make epiphanic appearances to Paul whereby he encourages him and strengthens him for his prophetic task. For example, Paul's so-called first missionary journey (Acts 13:1–14:28) begins when the Holy Spirit speaks to the "prophets and teachers" (13:1) in Antioch: "Set apart [ἀφορίσατε] for me both Barnabas and Saul for the work to which I have called them [εἰς τὸ ἔργον ὃ προσκέκλημαι αὐτούς]" (Acts 13:2).[34] After experiencing hostility in Corinth, the Lord appears to Paul in a vision and says, "Do not fear, but speak and do not be silent, for I am with you and no one will lay a hand on you to harm you. For I have many people in this city" (Acts 18:9–10). The promise "fear not" resonates with numerous oracles in the Scriptures of Israel, not least the mission of the servant in Isaiah (Isa 41:10; 43:1–5; see Acts 13:47). But most important here for the Lukan Paul's mission is the commission of Jeremiah who not only proclaims God's word to Israel but is also "a prophet to the nations" (Jer 1:5b; also 1:10). So, in one account of Paul's commissioning, Christ declares, "I am sending you to [the nations]" (Acts 26:17a). God's promise to Paul is similar to his promise to Jeremiah: "Do not be afraid of them, for I am with you to deliver you, says the Lord" (Jer 1:8 NRSV). Christ continues to appear to Paul either to encourage him or to move him in new directions. Thus, during Paul's imprisonment in Jerusalem, Luke declares, "That night the Lord stood by [Paul] and said, 'Be courageous! For just as you have testified about me [διεμαρτύρω τὰ περὶ ἐμοῦ] in Jerusalem so you must testify [μαρτυρῆσαι] about me in

---

32. The explicit quotation of Isaiah 49:6 (LXX) in Acts 13:47 supports the claim that this portion of Isaiah also lies behind Acts 1:8 (and Luke 24:47). So Pao, *Acts and the Isaianic New Exodus*, 96–97.

33. See here Holly Beers, *The Followers of Jesus as the "Servant": Luke's Model from Isaiah for the Disciples in Luke-Acts*, LNTS 535 (New York: T&T Clark, 2015), 130–33.

34. See also Acts 16:7–10.

Rome" (23:11). While onboard the ship bound for Rome, the imprisoned Paul receives visits from "God's angel" (27:23) to encourage Paul that he will indeed make it safely to Rome as will everyone on the boat (27:24–26).

Paul the Rejected Prophet

The portrayal of Paul as the preacher of eschatological salvation and repentance to Israel comes to a tragic climax (for Luke) when he is rejected by his fellow Jews in Rome. I'll focus my comments here, then, primarily on Acts 28:17–31 where we see four themes which establish Paul as Israel's prophet.[35]

First, in Acts 28:17–20 Paul's trials parallel Jesus's trials.[36] Both are faithful to the Jewish law (Luke 23:14–16; 24:26–27); neither have acted against the Jewish people (Luke 23:14–15); both have been delivered into the hands of the Romans (Luke 24:7, 20); neither deserve death (Luke 23:15, 22); and both are declared innocent (Luke 23:4, 15, 22). Paul's prophetic suffering witness, then, recapitulates and follows the same pattern as that of Jesus. The parallels between Paul and Jesus, however, are ominous as they suggest that Paul's fate will mirror that of Jesus as his fellow Jews will again reject the agent of the divine visit.

Second, Paul's chains are a sign of his loyalty to "the hope of Israel" (Acts 28:20b). He has been called to take "the name" of the Lord not only to the gentiles but also to "the sons of Israel" (9:15b). His regular practice of seeking out the local Jews when he arrives in a new city confirms this.[37] Despite opposition and persecution, Paul never ceases from proclaiming to the Jewish people that this hope of Israel has been fulfilled through the resurrection of the Messiah Jesus (23:6; 24:15; 26:6–7). Throughout the trial scenes Paul declares that he stands trial as a result of his commitment to the promised hope of Israel for which the twelve tribes have been longing (26:6–7a). Paul spends night and day trying to persuade the Roman Jews by "giving witness" to the kingdom of God based on interpretations "from the law of Moses and the prophets" (28:23b). Paul, then, is no Jewish apostate. He is a faithful, loyal, and persistent prophet to Israel as he proclaims the fulfillment of God's promises and warns of the consequences of rejecting them. His chains, representative of the Jewish people's rejection of his message, confirm his status as God's rejected prophet to Israel.[38]

---

35. In more detail, see my argument in Jipp, *Divine Visitations*, 272–81.
36. Walter Radl, *Paulus und Jesus im lukanischen Doppelwerk: Untersuchungen zu Parallelmotiven im Lukasevangelium und in der Apostelgeschichte* (Bern: Lang, 1975), 252–67.
37. See here Acts 13:5, 14; 14:1; 16:13; 17:1; 18:2–4; and 19:8.
38. Paul's chains in his imprisonment are referred to in Acts 22:29; 23:26–35; 24:27; 26:29, and 31.

Third, Paul's quotation of Isaiah 6:9-10 marks him out as continuing the Isaianic prophetic ministry. Commentators note correctly that Luke has been saving this text for the final scene in Acts 28, but fewer comment upon Luke's decision to include the command given to the prophet, "Go to this people and say..." (πορεύθητι πρὸς τὸν λαὸν τοῦτον καὶ εἰπόν, Acts 28:26).[39] The effect of Luke's inclusion of Isaiah 6:9a is that it allows the reader to identify Paul as the prophet who fulfills the command given to Isaiah. The language of the sending of the prophet reminds the reader of Paul's call to the gentiles, which, as we have seen, is also cast in the form of a prophetic call narrative (Acts 9:15-16; 18:9-10; 22:10-21; 26:15-18).[40] The evocation of Paul's prophetic call and his identification with God's mandate to Isaiah evoke Luke's larger literary pattern of the rejected prophet, preparing the reader for Paul's final encounter with the Jews.[41] The scene functions as Paul's third and final encounter with Jewish resistance to his message, resistance which has taken place in Asia at Pisidian Antioch (13:14, 42-47), in Greece at Corinth (18:1-6), and now in Italy at Rome (28:16, 23-28).[42] The three scenes follow the pattern: (a) proclamation to the Jews, (b) Jewish rejection of the proclamation of the message of salvation, (c) a statement by Paul that he will turn to the gentiles, and (d) gentile acceptance of Paul's message.

Paul acts the role of the prophet in Pisidian Antioch as the proclaimer of the word of God. So, Paul proclaims "a word of exhortation" (λόγος παρακλήσεως, 13:15) and "this word of salvation" (ὁ λόγος τῆς σωτηρίας ταύτης, 13:26) by means of interpreting "the Law and the Prophets" (13:15). He criticizes those leaders of Israel who put Jesus to death for their "ignorance of the words of the prophets [τὰς φωνὰς τῶν προφητῶν] which are read every sabbath" (13:27). Paul warns them lest they too act the part of those who hear the words of the prophets but reject their warnings. Furthermore, when some Jews hear "the word of the Lord" (τὸν λόγον τοῦ κυρίου, 13:44) and then reject "the word of God" (τὸν λόγον τοῦ θεοῦ, 13:46), Paul and Barnabas perform a prophetic sign: "They shook off the dust from their feet against them" (13:51; cf. Luke 10:11).

---

39. See, however, Daniel Marguerat, *The First Christian Historian: Writing the "Acts of the Apostles,"* trans. Ken McKinney, Gregory J. Laughery, and Richard Bauckham, SNTSMS 121 (Cambridge: Cambridge University Press, 2002), 225.

40. David P. Moessner, *Lord of the Banquet: The Literary and Theological Significance of the Lukan Travel Narrative* (Minneapolis: Fortress, 1989), 298-99.

41. See Luke Timothy Johnson, *The Literary Function of Possessions in Luke-Acts*, SBLDS 39 (Missoula, MT: Scholars Press, 1977); Marguerat, *First Christian Historian*, 139-40.

42. So also David P. Moessner, "Paul in Acts: Preacher of Eschatological Repentance to Israel," *NTS* 34 (1988): 96-104, here 101-3.

Paul as Prophet of God's Resurrected Messiah

This leads to Paul's claim that he will turn to the gentiles who "give glory to the word of the Lord" (ἐδόξαζον τὸν λόγον τοῦ κυρίου, 13:48). Luke's concluding statement regarding Paul's prophetic ministry here is, "So the word of the Lord [ὁ λόγος τοῦ κυρίου] spread throughout the region" (13:49). Paul is, then, clearly an agent of the divine word. Similarly, in Corinth, Paul's proclamation of the word of God is rejected by the Jews resulting in Paul, again, "shaking out his garments" (18:6; cf. Luke 10:11) as a testimony against them for their rejection of the word, and he claims that now he will go to the gentiles (18:6b).

While the response is notably less hostile, Luke also interprets the Roman Jews' response to Paul and his message as one of rejection. After Paul's christological witness to the Jews, Luke tells the readers that "some were persuaded by his words while others did not believe" (οἱ μὲν ἐπείθοντο τοῖς λεγομένοις, οἱ δὲ ἠπίστουν, 28:24). Luke's narration of a mixed response is stereotypical (cf. Acts 2:12–13; 13:42–45; 17:32–34; 18:4), and there is no reason to deny that Luke presents some Jews as convinced by Paul's message. Yet given the heightened intensity of the scene it is apparent that Luke intends that the reader view Paul's preaching as an anticlimactic failure. Luke's emphasis is found in the tragedy that Paul's preaching about Jesus produces "disunity" in the Jewish people (ἀσύμφωνοι δὲ ὄντες πρὸς ἀλλήλους, 28:25). Luke's portraits of the unity of the early Christian community and their ability to overcome conflict (e.g., Acts 2:42–47; 4:32–35; 8:1–25; 10:1–11:18) stands in contrast to the division of the Jewish people in Acts 28:24–25.[43] Further, the disunity of the Roman Jews stands in contrast to the unity of the witness of Paul, the prophet Isaiah, and the Holy Spirit who all agree in their "one word" of judgment: "Paul spoke *one word*, 'Rightly did the Holy Spirit speak through the prophet Isaiah to your fathers'" (εἰπόντος τοῦ Παύλου ῥῆμα ἕν, ὅτι καλῶς τὸ πνεῦμα τὸ ἅγιον ἐλάλησεν διὰ Ἡσαΐου τοῦ προφήτου πρὸς τοὺς πατέρας ὑμῶν, 28:25b). As a result of their rejection, Paul takes on the role of the prophet Isaiah while the people take on the guise of the ancient Israelites who rejected the prophets. Paul identifies the Roman Jews with the people of Isaiah's time by referring to the latter as "your fathers" (28:25b; cf. Luke 6:23; 11:48; 13:33–34; Acts 7:51–53).[44]

Fourth, Paul speaks a prophetic word of judgment to the unbelieving portion of Israel. Paul quotes Isaiah 6:9–10 in full as a message of judgment against

---

43. So David W. Pao, "Disagreement among the Jews in Acts 28," in *Early Christian Voices: In Texts, Traditions, and Symbols; Essays in Honor of François Bovon*, ed. David H. Warren, Ann Graham Brock, and David W. Pao, BibInt 66 (Leiden: Brill, 2003), 109–18.

44. See also Marguerat, *First Christian Historian*, 225; Susan Wendel, *Scriptural Interpretation and Community Self-Definition in Luke-Acts and the Writings of Justin Martyr*, NovTSup 139 (Leiden: Brill, 2011), 193–95.

them. They have had ample opportunity to "hear" (ἀκοῇ ἀκούσετε) and "see" (βλέποντες βλέψετε), but their sensory perceptions are dull and hardened (28:26b). Luke heightens the intensity of the scene and the literary finality of Paul's mission to the Jews by moving the Isaiah 6 quotation from Jesus's parable of the sower (Mark 4:12; Matt 13:14-15) and saving the bulk of it for this final scene. In Luke 8:10 Jesus explains that to those who do not receive the mystery of the kingdom, the parables work such that "while seeing they may not see and while hearing they may not understand" (Luke 8:10b). But the full quotation is not yet used against them in judgment. The first rejection of the divine visitation through Jesus is explained briefly with the short quote from Isaiah, but the final rejection of the *second visitation* through the prophetic emissaries receives a note of rebuke with a full citation of Isaiah 6:9-10 and occurring as it does at the end of the narrative.[45]

The inability of the Roman Jews to "see" God's salvation is ironic and tragic given that one of the fundamental components of Jesus's ministry was to give sight to the blind.[46] In his inaugural and programmatic sermon in Nazareth, Jesus quotes Isaiah 61:1 and declares that the Spirit of the Lord "has sent me ... to open the eyes for the blind" (Luke 4:18). Given that the healing of blindness is one of the main components of Jesus's mission, one finds that vision and the healing of blindness function as metaphors for salvation and the recognition of God's salvation throughout Luke-Acts (see Luke 7:21-23; 10:23-24; 18:35-43; Acts 9:1-19; 26:18).[47] The connection between vision and God's salvation is stated clearly by Simeon who, upon encountering the child Jesus gave praise to God and declared, "My eyes have seen your salvation" (Luke 2:30). This salvation is said to be not only for Israel but also "a light of revelation for the gentiles" (Luke 2:32a; cf. Acts 13:47). But already in Jesus's promise to heal the blind there is an ominous note of rejection sounded by the Nazareth synagogue (Luke 4:24-28), foreshadowing that Jesus's promised healing will not be embraced by everyone. Further, in Luke 3:4-6 John the Baptist quotes another Isaianic text at length, this time Isaiah 40:3-5, which ends with the promise that "all flesh *will see* the salvation of God" (Luke 3:6).[48] Here too salvation is something that is seen by all peoples, but again it is something which will not be met with full acceptance (Luke 3:7-9). Luke's literary project

---

45. So also Luke Timothy Johnson, *The Acts of the Apostles*, SP 5 (Collegeville, MN: Liturgical Press, 1992), 476; Pao, *Acts and the Isaianic New Exodus*, 105.

46. Cf. Robert C. Tannehill, "Israel in Luke-Acts: A Tragic Story," *JBL* 104 (1985): 69-85.

47. See Dennis Hamm, "Sight to the Blind: Vision as Metaphor in Luke," *Bib* 67 (1986): 457-77.

48. On this cluster of Isaianic texts, see Pao, *Acts and the Isaianic New Exodus*, 105-9.

Paul as Prophet of God's Resurrected Messiah

is, then, bracketed by Isaianic references to sight and blindness. Between this Isaianic inclusio centering on sight, light, and salvation (Luke 3:4–6; 4:18–19 and Acts 28:25–28), Luke also narrates Paul's mission through an Isaianic lens whereby Paul's task is to illumine the gentiles with God's salvific light: "For so has the Lord commanded us: 'I have appointed you as a light to the gentiles [εἰς φῶς ἐθνῶν] so that you may bring salvation to the end of the earth'" (Acts 13:47; Isa 49:6). Before Herod Agrippa II, Paul summarizes his prophetic ministry as an encounter with the exalted Lord who commissions Paul "to open their [i.e., Jews and gentiles] eyes" (ἀνοῖξαι ὀφθαλμοὺς αὐτῶν) and to bring them "to the light" (εἰς φῶς, 26:18; cf. 26:23). Thus, the Gospel begins with the promise of the vision of God's salvation for "all flesh" and "gentiles" (Luke 3:6//Isa 40:5; cf. Luke 2:30–32) and with Jesus's mission to give sight to the blind (Luke 4:18//Isa 61:1), a prophetic mission which is continued in Acts by the apostolic witnesses who are commissioned by the exalted Lord to bring light to the gentiles (Acts 13:47 and 26:18//Isa 49:6) but concludes with a judgment against the Jews who have "seen" but not "perceived" and have closed their eyes to God's salvific healing (τοὺς ὀφθαλμοὺς αὐτῶν ἐκάμμυσαν, 28:27b). Isaac Oliver strikes the right balance between judgment and hope for Israel: "Luke accordingly cites Isa 6:9–10 to account for the *present* condition of the Jewish people rather than to deny Israel's *future* restoration. At the end of Acts, Luke reaches an impasse."[49]

The Lukan Paul's "Jewishness" in Acts

In this chapter, I have argued that the Lukan Paul's relationship to his Jewish heritage is best understood by way of Luke's two major christological categories: messianism and prophecy. Paul's messianic convictions result in a strong appropriation of Israel's ancestral heritage. Lukan messianic Christology has direct implications for understanding his view of the people of God. On the one hand, there is no doubt that Luke wants his audience to embrace the view that Paul is Torah-observant, faithful to his ancestral customs, and loyal to his own people. Nevertheless, he does not shy away from tackling what must have been a significant perception of Paul as an apostate from Moses and as one who provokes his fellow Jewish contemporaries. It is not just that Paul equates the hope of Israel with the resurrection from the dead that is disruptive; rather, it is Paul's argument that the hope of Israel has surprisingly taken place, at least

---

49. Oliver, *Luke's Jewish Eschatology*, 135.

PART ONE: GOD'S ACTS FOR ISRAEL

as a foretaste, through Jesus of Nazareth, the crucified, resurrected, and now enthroned-in-heaven Messiah that provokes controversy. God's resurrection of the Messiah has inaugurated Israel's restoration, but full restoration, the final resurrection of the dead, requires repentance and an embrace of the messianic king. It seems easy to imagine listening to Paul's sermon, for example, in Pisidian Antioch and agreeing with Paul's Davidic-messianic interpretation of Israel's Scriptures and history *or* advancing arguments that would contest his interpretation and offer a different alternative. The starting point, however, would depend upon whether one grants Paul's claim that God has indeed raised Jesus form the dead and enthroned him to a heavenly position.

Luke portrays Paul as a prophet of the risen Messiah in order to explain his task of calling both Israel and the nations to repentance as well as to establish a precedent that legitimates his (and Jesus's) rejection by most of his Jewish contemporaries. Luke employs a variety of prophetic motifs and prophetic scriptural intertexts that work to establish Paul's task as consisting in testimony to the risen Messiah and to explain why his mission was consistently rejected by his fellow Jewish contemporaries. Acceptance of Luke's pro-Jewish depiction of the Lukan Paul should not be at the expense of or minimization of the fact that Luke is positive regarding Jews who believe in Jesus as Israel's Messiah. Those Jews who do not believe Jesus is the Messiah are characterized as those who reject and kill the prophets, that is, they are "jealous" (5:17; 13:45; 17:5), instigate mob violence (e.g., 7:54–60; 14:1–7, 19; 17:5–9), and are blind to the meaning and significance of their own institutions and Scriptures (e.g., Luke 19:41–44; Acts 24:25–27). This puts one in the place of simultaneously affirming that the Lukan Paul does not in any way reject God's election of Israel *and also* affirming that the significance of God's election of Israel is found in Jesus the Messiah. This results in a situation where those who oppose Paul and reject his message of the Messiah find themselves excluded from their own covenantal blessings (13:46; 18:6; 28:25–28).

3

Luke's Scriptural Suffering Messiah

A Search for Precedent, a Search for Identity

Jesus's post-resurrection appearance in Luke 24 has proved to be a hermeneutical conundrum for NT interpreters. Luke 24:44–46 illustrates the problem.

> Then he [Jesus] said to them, "These are my words that I spoke to you while I was still with you—that everything written about me in the law of Moses, the prophets, and the psalms must be fulfilled." Then he opened their minds to understand the scriptures, and he said to them, "*Thus it is written that the Messiah is to suffer and to rise from the dead on the third day.*"[1]

The problem is obvious—where do Israel's Scriptures speak of a suffering messiah? Attempts to identify where "it is written" have been unconvincing. Likewise, scholarly efforts to find the concept of a suffering messiah in the Second Temple Jewish literature have proved fruitless. As Lloyd Gaston notes, "Nowhere is it even intimated that the Messiah should suffer, neither in the Bible as written nor in the Bible as read in first century Judaism."[2] Joel B. Green represents many when he refers to the concept of a scriptural suffering messiah as an "oxymoron" and a "hermeneutical innovation."[3] Many scholars have labeled Luke's "scriptural suffering messiah" a Lukan invention. In an attempt to explain the difficulty, Mark L. Strauss has argued that Luke's suffering

---

1. Note also Luke 24:26: οὐχὶ ταῦτα ἔδει παθεῖν τὸν χριστὸν καὶ εἰσελθεῖν εἰς τὴν δόξαν αὐτοῦ (Was it not necessary for the Messiah to suffer these things and then enter into his glory?).
2. Lloyd Gaston, *No Stone on Another: Studies in the Significance of the Fall of Jerusalem in the Synoptic Gospels*, NovTSup 23 (Leiden: Brill, 1970), 292.
3. Joel B. Green, *The Gospel of Luke*, NICNT (Grand Rapids: Eerdmans, 1997), 848–49.

messiah must be a fusion of the concept of the Davidic king and the Isaianic suffering servant.[4] Interpreters have usually been content to draw on the figure of Isaiah 53 or to note that pre-Christian Judaism had no concept of a suffering Christ figure; they therefore remark that Luke's scriptural suffering messiah is an early Christian invention or oxymoron.[5] In this article, however, I will argue that Luke's "suffering messiah" is not an oxymoron and that his narrative gives readers all the clues necessary to identify the Scriptures to which Luke's Jesus is referring.

It is my contention that many scholars have not adequately accounted for the enormous role the book of Psalms plays in Luke's narrative, specifically with respect to the suffering anointed one.[6] Although many have rightly noted Luke's reliance on the psalms in his interpretation of Jesus's resurrection and exaltation (primarily Pss 16; 110; and 132), fewer have noted the important role the psalms play in Luke's narrative in answering the question, Where is it written that the messiah must suffer? Luke's use of psalms in his passion narrative is undoubtedly indebted to earlier tradition, but it is Luke who most clearly interprets Jesus's death against the psalms.[7] Among NT authors, only Luke

---

4. Mark L. Strauss, *The Davidic Messiah in Luke-Acts: The Promise and Its Fulfillment in Lukan Christology*, JSNTSup 110 (Sheffield: Sheffield Academic, 1995), 256–57, 266–67.

5. I. Howard Marshall, *The Gospel of Luke: A Commentary on the Greek Text*, NIGTC (Grand Rapids: Eerdmans, 1978), 896–97; Joseph A. Fitzmyer, *The Gospel according to Luke X–XXIV: A New Translation with Introduction and Commentary*, AB 28A (Garden City, NY: Doubleday, 1985), 1565–66, 1581.

6. My thoughts on this matter have been influenced by the helpful article of Peter Doble, "Luke 24.26, 44—Songs of God's Servant: David and His Psalms in Luke-Acts," *JSNT* 28 (2006): 267–83. Additionally, although he has not made this specific proposal regarding Luke's use of the psalms, I should note my indebtedness to conversations with Richard B. Hays on the NT's use of the psalms. See, among other articles, his essay "Reading Scripture in Light of the Resurrection," in *The Art of Reading Scripture*, ed. Ellen F. Davis and Richard B. Hays (Grand Rapids: Eerdmans, 2003), 216–38.

7. Although tradition undoubtedly played a role in Luke's appropriation of the psalms, my method is primarily literary and not redactional in that I am attempting to answer internally how and why Luke says that the Scriptures declare that the messiah must suffer. I do, however, note instances in which Luke has enhanced or added to Mark's prior use of the psalms. For Luke's debt to tradition in his passion narrative, see Raymond E. Brown, *The Death of the Messiah: From Gethsemane to the Grave; A Commentary on the Passion Narratives in the Four Gospels*, AYBRL (New York: Doubleday, 1994); Donald Juel, *Messianic Exegesis: Christological Interpretation of the Old Testament in Early Christianity* (Philadelphia: Fortress, 1988), 89–117; and Frank J. Matera, *Passion Narratives and Gospel Theologies: Interpreting the Synoptics through Their Passion Stories*, Theological Inquiries (New York: Paulist, 1986).

refers explicitly by name to ψαλμοῖς (Psalms) as a distinct group of Israel's Scriptures, once, as previously mentioned, from Jesus's own lips speaking with respect to his suffering and resurrection (Luke 24:45).[8] It is in the psalms that one consistently finds the sufferings of King David, the anointed one, and the assurance of his vindication. Although Jesus's Davidic messiahship is arguably important for all the gospel writers, it is Luke who manifests an intense interest in David and the psalms.[9] Furthermore, while the book of Isaiah itself clearly figures prominently in Luke's Gospel, the figure of Isaiah 53 plays only a minor role in Luke's narrative (see Luke 22:37; Acts 8:26–40).[10] Luke's description of Jesus is an amalgamation of scriptural traditions, but he does nothing explicitly to develop Isaiah 53 as a background for interpreting Jesus's death.[11] I suggest that Isaiah 53 has proved to be more of a red herring than a solution for how Luke conceives of the scriptural suffering messiah.[12] It is David, not the Isaianic servant, upon whom Luke consistently draws in order to describe Jesus's persecution, death, resurrection, and exaltation.

In this chapter, I argue that Luke's scriptural suffering messiah is primarily indebted to the psalms and their depiction of King David's sufferings.[13] Luke found in the Davidic psalms something of a portrait of the messiah's career, and thus a precedent for the messiah's sufferings and subsequent exaltation. Luke not only has embedded multiple allusions to the psalms in the passion narrative but also has consistently referred to the persecutors and enemies of the messiah, especially in Acts, with language drawn from the psalms' portrayal of David's persecutors. Engaging in a broad study of Luke's use of the psalms to describe the sufferings of Jesus and the early messianic community

---

8. In addition to Luke 24:45, see Luke 20:42; Acts 1:20; 13:33.

9. This is true despite the fact, as François Bovon notes (*Luke: The Theologian*, 2nd rev. ed. [Waco, TX: Baylor University Press, 2006], 103–6) that no one has analyzed the figure of David in Luke's writings. This lacuna has been remedied by Yuzuru Miura, *David in Luke-Acts: His Portrayal in the Light of Early Judaism*, WUNT 2/232 (Tübingen: Mohr Siebeck, 2007).

10. For the programmatic role of Isaiah in Luke's ecclesiological program, see David W. Pao, *Acts and the Isaianic New Exodus*, WUNT 2/130 (Tübingen: Mohr Siebeck, 2000).

11. As noted by David L. Tiede, *Prophecy and History in Luke-Acts* (Philadelphia: Fortress, 1980), 101.

12. The influence of Isaiah 53 on the NT has been contested famously by Morna D. Hooker, *Jesus and the Servant: The Influence of the Servant Concept of Deutero-Isaiah in the New Testament* (London: Nisbet, 1959).

13. Of course, many of these quotations and allusions may have in fact been mediated through Mark's Gospel. Although my methodological approach is primarily literary, I suggest that Luke has in many instances enhanced these allusions and quotations in his redaction of Mark.

PART ONE: GOD'S ACTS FOR ISRAEL

will contribute to a fuller understanding of Luke's distinctive use of the OT in establishing the scriptural necessity of the messiah's suffering.

DAVID AND THE PSALMS

Before examining Luke's use of the psalms, it will be helpful to make a couple of short methodological comments with respect to the relationship between David and the Psalter concerning the following: (1) eschatology and messianism, and (2) David as the royal righteous sufferer.

The extent to which eschatology and messianism are present in the Psalter is evident not only in the way it was appropriated by the early Christians but also by the fact that the editor(s) of the Psalter retained its royal shape long after the demise of the Davidic monarchy.[14] What happens, for example, when Psalm 2 or Psalm 132 is read in a context where the monarchy has failed and is now but a distant memory? The obvious answer is that the psalms are reinterpreted and invested with an eschatological meaning.[15] The picture of Yahweh ruling the nations through the Davidic prince, or that of Yahweh's reclamation of Zion for the Davidic monarchy from the postexilic period onward, could have produced only eschatological expectations.[16] The failed monarchy thus gives rise to a royal messianic reinterpretation of the psalms that looks forward to the fulfillment of the Davidic promises.[17]

One may ask if there are any specific examples of pre-Christian messianic appropriation of the psalms. Psalms of Solomon 17 and 18 use Psalm 2 in their description of a coming Davidic Messiah. Moreover, one could describe Psalm of Solomon 17:21-32 as a midrash on Psalm 2. For example, the coming Davidic figure is depicted as bringing forth punishment ἐν ῥάβδῳ σιδηρᾷ (by an iron rod;

---

14. On this, see Gerald H. Wilson, *The Editing of the Hebrew Psalter*, SBLDS 76 (Chico, CA: Scholars Press, 1985); G. Wilson, "The Use of Royal Psalms at the 'Seams' of the Hebrew Psalter," *JSOT* 11/35 (1986): 85-94.

15. David C. Mitchell (*The Message of the Psalter: An Eschatological Programme in the Book of Psalms*, JSOTSup 252 [Sheffield: Sheffield Academic, 1997]) has argued that the similarities between the psalms and Zechariah 9–14 demonstrate the eschatological reworking of the psalms.

16. Richard B. Hays, "Christ Prays the Psalms: Paul's Use of an Early Christian Exegetical Convention," in *The Future of Christology: Essays in Honor of Leander E. Keck*, ed. Wayne A. Meeks and Abraham J. Malherbe (Minneapolis: Fortress, 1993), 122-36, here 130.

17. On this, see Georg P. Braulik, "Psalter and Messiah: Towards a Christological Understanding of the Psalms in the Old Testament and the Church Fathers," in *Psalms and Liturgy*, ed. Dirk J. Human and Cas J. A. Vos, JSOTSup 410 (London: T&T Clark, 2004), 15-40, here 26-27.

Ps Sol 17:24), an exact replication of Psalm 2:9. The vocabulary of Psalm 2:9 of σκεῦος κεραμέως συντρίψεις αὐτούς (you will crush them into pieces as a potter's vessel) is echoed in Psalm of Solomon 17:23b–24a with ὡς σκεύη κεραμέως . . . συντρῖψαι. The use of Psalm 2 by Psalms of Solomon, therefore, provides further evidence of the eschatological and messianic nature of Psalm 2.[18]

Perhaps most important, however, is the psalms' frequent depiction of a Davidic figure under intense duress and persecuted by his enemies. While suffering and hostility at the hands of one's enemies are potentially common to all humanity, it is King David who is portrayed as the righteous, royal sufferer par excellence (Pss 7:4; 69:4; 109:3).[19] His enemies surround him to mock and afflict him (e.g., Pss 22; 69; 89). David's plight frequently brings him to the point of despair, wondering if God has abandoned and forsaken him, giving him over to death and Hades (Pss 22:14–18; 38:5–8; 69:16–20). Yet despite his sufferings and persecution, David maintains his fidelity and hope in God. In the Davidic psalms one finds the paradoxical combination of kingship and righteous suffering. The point is not so much that David is the paradigmatic example of a "righteous sufferer" as he is the "righteous suffering *king*."[20] This anomaly, namely, that David, God's anointed one, undergoes persecution and suffering, has great importance for Luke's conception of Jesus, the suffering Anointed One.

The Psalms and the Death of the Messiah (Luke 23:33–46)

It is striking that, with the abundant references to Davidic traditions and the promise of a Messiah in Luke's infancy narrative (e.g., 1:27, 32, 69; 2:4, 11),

---

18. Joachim Schaper, *Eschatology in the Greek Psalter*, WUNT 2/76 (Tübingen: Mohr Siebeck, 1995), 74–76. See also Schaper, "Die Septuaginta-Psalter als Dokument jüdischer Eschatologie," in *Die Septuaginta zwischen Judentum und Christentum*, ed. Martin Hengel and Anna Maria Schwemer, WUNT 2/72 (Tübingen: Mohr Siebeck, 1994), 38–61.

19. I am not, however, presupposing or commenting on a fixed, generic concept of "the righteous sufferer" or "righteous one" from the psalms or first-century Judaism against which Luke interpreted the sufferings and death of Jesus as one finds, for example, in Lothar Ruppert, *Jesus als der leidende Gerechte? Der Weg Jesu um Lichte eines alt- und zwischentestamentlichen Motivs*, SBS 59 (Stuttgart: Katholisches Bibelwerk, 1972). On this motif, see also Karl Theodor Kleinknecht, *Der leidende Gerechtfertigte: Die alttestamentlich-jüdische Tradition vom "leidenden Gerechten" und ihre Rezeption bei Paulus*, WUNT 13 (Tübingen: Mohr Siebeck, 1988).

20. In other words, though the psalms' characterization of David as a "righteous" sufferer is extremely significant, it is his royalty and kingship that are crucial for Luke's appropriation of the Davidic psalms.

David is largely absent from the end of Luke's infancy narrative to 18:38, where his presence again is strongly felt.[21] The parable of the pounds (19:11–27), the triumphal entry and temple scene (19:28–44), and Psalm 110's riddle (20:41–44) are rife with royal elements. The overall absence of Davidic references from the bulk of Luke's narrative and their subsequent reappearance in 18:38 through the rest of the Gospel may indicate prima facie that Jesus's Davidic messiahship is bound together with the events of the passion week. Luke's plethora of psalm quotations and allusions in the brief account of Jesus's death is of great importance for understanding the necessity of the Messiah's death.

The Gospel's Crucifixion of a King

It is commonly recognized that the Gospels depict Jesus's crucifixion as an ironic royal enthronement. The crucifiers engaged in intentional irony as they "exalted" the "insubordinate transgressors by displaying a deliberately horrible mirror of their self-elevation."[22] Luke's account of Jesus's death reverses this irony by depicting the sufferings and death of Jesus as the gateway to the Messiah's royal coronation—the resurrection (Acts 2:32–36). Jesus's enemies repeatedly confess what the reader already knows, namely, that Jesus's kingship is connected with his suffering and death.[23] Thus, one finds the following on the lips of Jesus's opponents: (1) "Let him save himself if he is the Messiah, the chosen one of God" (σωσάτω ἑαυτόν, εἰ οὗτός ἐστιν ὁ χριστὸς τοῦ θεοῦ ὁ ἐκλεκτός, 23:35b); (2) "Save yourself if you are the King of the Jews" (εἰ σὺ εἶ ὁ βασιλεὺς τῶν Ἰουδαίων, σῶσον σεαυτόν, 23:37); and (3) "Are you not the Messiah? Save yourself and us" (οὐχὶ σὺ εἶ ὁ χριστός; σῶσον σεαυτὸν καὶ ἡμᾶς, 23:39b). The epitaph on the placard likewise reads, "This one is the King of the Jews" (ὁ βασιλεὺς τῶν Ἰουδαίων οὗτος, 23:38b). The mockery hurled at Jesus by three groups (the Jewish rulers, the Roman soldiers, and the criminal) finds its home in the scoffing and reviling words of the enemies of the psalms' anointed. It is the Psalter that most clearly depicts the righteous king as one who becomes an object of scorn by the arrogant. For Luke, Jesus's messiahship

---

21. Perhaps scholarship's general tendency, at least since Hans Conzelmann's work (*The Theology of St. Luke* [Philadelphia: Fortress, 1982]) to disregard Luke 1–2 as an integral part of Luke's narrative has, in part, prevented scholars from seeing the significance of the Davidic Messiah for Luke's passion narrative.
22. Joel Marcus, "Crucifixion as Parodic Exaltation," *JBL* 125 (2006): 73–87, here 78.
23. Green, *Gospel of Luke*, 818–19.

is not only compatible with his suffering and crucifixion, but is, in light of the psalms, actually at the heart of his kingship.[24]

The Psalms' Use as Lukan Intertexts in the Passion Narrative

It is striking that within the span of thirteen verses (Luke 23:34-46) Luke peppers his passion narrative not only with an abundance of royal imagery but also with frequent quotations of and allusions to explicit Davidic psalms.[25] The psalms function as Luke's premier intertext whereby the voice of David is transposed onto the suffering messiah. In what follows I will show how Psalms 22, 69, 31, and 38 function as intertexts for Luke's passion narrative.

Luke begins his description of Jesus's death by alluding to Psalm 22:18 (LXX 21:19) as a picture of Jesus's persecutors' mockery: διαμεριζόμενοι δὲ τὰ ἱμάτια αὐτοῦ ἔβαλον κλήρους (and distributing his garments, they cast lots [Luke 23:34b]).[26] Although a minor change, Luke enhances the echo of Psalm 22:18 by using the transitive verb ἔβαλον, whereas Mark uses the participle βάλλοντες (Mark 15:24).[27] Luke then draws further attention to the psalm by describing the mocking speech of Jesus's persecutors in language taken from Psalm 22. Luke uses the rare word ἐξεμυκτήριζον (to ridicule), drawn from Psalm 22:7 (LXX 21:8), to describe the rulers' mockery of Jesus (Luke 23:35). Whereas the parallel passage in Mark 15:31 has ἐμπαίζοντες (to mock), Luke's use of ἐξεμυκτήριζον suggests that he is enhancing Mark's allusion to Psalm 22. These "rulers," in their persecution of God's Anointed, play the role of Zion's enemies, as exemplified in Psalm 2:1-2. The soldiers' mockery of Jesus's royalty also evokes Psalm 89:19-20 (LXX 88:20-21), where the Anointed One is referred to as ἐκλεκτὸν ἐκ τοῦ λαοῦ μου (my chosen one from the people) as well as Δαυιδ τὸν δοῦλόν μου . . . ἔχρισα αὐτόν (David my servant . . . I have anointed him). The use of this title for the Messiah is unique to Luke (23:35) and Psalm 89

---

24. John T. Carroll, "Luke's Crucifixion Scene," in *Reimaging the Death of the Lukan Jesus*, ed. Dennis D. Sylva, Athenäums Monografien, Theologie 73 (Frankfurt am Main: Anton Hain, 1990), 108-24, here 114-15.

25. For Mark's use of the psalms, see Joel Marcus, *The Way of the Lord: Christological Exegesis of the Old Testament in the Gospel of Mark* (Louisville: Westminster John Knox, 1992).

26. Many good manuscripts have κλῆρον instead of κλήρους (e.g., 𝔓[75], ℵ, B, C, and D).

27. It is possible that Luke may have known Hebrew, but, unlike in Matthew's Gospel, there is little reason to assume that a Hebrew text type has influenced his use of OT citations. For a detailed discussion, one may refer to Bovon, *Luke: The Theologian*, 92-95, 106-17. Quotations are taken from Alfred Rahlfs and Robert Hanhart, eds., *Septuaginta* (Stuttgart: Deutsche Bibelgesellschaft, 1935).

PART ONE: GOD'S ACTS FOR ISRAEL

(LXX 88:4, 20). Likewise, although lacking strong linguistic echoes, the soldiers' abuse is quite similar to that of the mockers from Psalm 22.

Luke 23:35b:

ἄλλους ἔσωσεν, σωσάτω ἑαυτόν, εἰ οὗτός ἐστιν ὁ χριστὸς τοῦ θεοῦ ὁ ἐκλεκτός.

He saved others, let him save himself, if this one is the chosen one, the Messiah of God.

Ps 22:8 (LXX 21:9):

ἤλπισεν ἐπὶ κύριον ῥυσάσθω αὐτόν σωσάτω
αὐτόν ὅτι θέλει αὐτόν.

He hoped in the Lord, let that one rescue him,
let that one save him, because he desires him.

In Psalm 22 it is the sufferer's confidence in God to save, as well as the sufferer's relationship with God that is derided (vv. 9–10). Luke, however, draws attention to the apparent incongruity between Jesus's shameful death on the cross and his messianic identity. The Jewish rulers, the Roman soldiers, and even the criminal take up the words of David's enemies from Psalm 22:8, mocking Jesus's claim to royalty. The irony is thick as Luke draws on the voice of David in Psalm 22 in order to show that suffering and royalty not only are not in contradiction but actually constitute the very foundation of the psalms' vision of the Anointed One. In other words, the sufferings of Jesus identify him as exactly who his mockers believed him not to be.

In case readers have not yet perceived Luke's allusions to the psalms, Luke, like Mark and Matthew, further evokes the sufferings of David by echoing Psalm 69:21 (LXX 68:22): "The soldiers were mocking him, coming to him and offering him sour wine" (Luke 23:36).[28] Instead of offering a beverage fit for a king, the soldiers make sport of Jesus's kingship by offering him bad wine (ὄξος).[29] In Jesus's sufferings, just as in David's, friends and comforters look on

---

28. Although Luke 23:36 and Psalm 69:21 share only the word ὄξος, an allusion to Psalm 69 is still likely in light of Luke's consistent portrayal of Jesus as the psalms' royal sufferer. See Scott Cunningham, *"Through Many Tribulations": The Theology of Persecution in Luke-Acts*, JSNTSup 142 (Sheffield: Sheffield Academic, 1997), 161.

29. Brown, *Death of the Messiah*, 997.

Luke's Scriptural Suffering Messiah

at a distance while mockers and persecutors surround him. It is worth noting that the portrait of Psalm 69 is, like that of Psalm 22, one of a royal figure who suffers unjustly but continues to commit himself to God.

With his last breath, Jesus speaks the very words of David, this time nearly a direct quotation from Psalm 31:5 (LXX 30:6): εἰς χεῖράς σου παραθήσομαι [Luke 23:46: παρατίθεμαι] τὸ πνεῦμά μου (Into your hands I place my spirit). Luke has here intensified the echo of the Davidic psalms by inserting Psalm 31:5, a text that is unique to Luke's Gospel. When David's words are placed on Jesus's lips, the reader is led to identify Jesus's crucifixion with the psalm's depiction of the suffering righteous king.[30] We have seen how the opponents of Jesus, in taking up the language of Psalm 22, deride Jesus not only as a messianic pretender but also for his confidence in God. The psalm on which Jesus draws before his last breath is paradigmatically a psalm of hope in God despite suffering and mockery from the wicked. It is no accident that Jesus responds to the enemies' taunts of Psalm 22:8/Luke 23:35 ("He hoped in the Lord, let him deliver him") with a quintessential royal psalm of the righteous king's hope in God.[31] The sufferings of the righteous king are vivid and disturbing. He is the scorn of his adversaries, like a corpse, plotted against by many (vv. 10–14), and yet the king declares, "But I trust in you, O Lord; / I say, 'You are my God'" (Ps 31:14; LXX 30:15). Jesus thereby takes on the role of the psalm's speaker as one in whom royalty, suffering, and hope in God are embodied. Immediately after Jesus's last breath, Luke informs the readers that Jesus's companions were far from him at his death. Luke 23:49a states, Εἱστήκεισαν δὲ πάντες οἱ γνωστοὶ αὐτῷ ἀπὸ μακρόθεν καὶ γυναῖκες αἱ συνακολουθοῦσαι αὐτῷ (and all the companions stood at a distance from him and the women who had followed him). The resonance with Psalm 38:11 (LXX 37:12) is strong: καὶ οἱ ἔγγιστά μου ἀπὸ μακρόθεν ἔστησαν (and my companions stood at a distance). Note that where Mark refers only to Jesus's female followers (15:40a), Luke again has heightened the allusion to Psalm 38:11 by including Jesus's male followers with the female companions. Even in this small detail Luke has not lost the opportunity to remind readers of the psalms' depiction of the righteous king abandoned by his companions.

When the reader reaches the statement of the Roman officer—"truly this man was righteous" (ὄντως ὁ ἄνθρωπος οὗτος δίκαιος ἦν, Luke 23:47b)—it

---

30. See the excellent discussion of this text in J. Samuel Subramanian, *The Synoptic Gospels and the Psalms as Prophecy*, LNTS 351 (New York: T&T Clark, 2007), 85–89.

31. See Peter Doble, "The Psalms in Luke-Acts," in *The Psalms in the New Testament*, ed. Steve Moyise and Maarten J. J. Menken, NTSI (New York: T&T Clark, 2004), 83–119, here 115.

PART ONE: GOD'S ACTS FOR ISRAEL

becomes an inescapable inference to conclude that Luke is climactically portraying Jesus as the psalms' righteous, royal sufferer. Given the fact that Luke has just quoted Psalm 31, the psalm that portrays the sufferer as δίκαιος (31:18; LXX 30:19), it becomes increasingly likely that the centurion is unwittingly identifying Jesus as the righteous, royal sufferer of the psalms.[32] The sufferings of the righteous king in Psalm 31 match well the sufferings of Jesus: both figures are verbally mocked and persecuted, friends stand at a distance, and each one's murder is premeditated by his enemies.[33] Luke emphasizes throughout both volumes that Jesus is righteous and without fault (see Luke 23:4, 14–15, 41, 47; Acts 3:14; 7:52; 22:14). Luke's decision to delete Mark's ὁ ἄνθρωπος υἱὸς θεοῦ (the Son of God, Mark 15:39b) and replace it with δίκαιος dramatically suggests that the Davidic psalms are Luke's intertext.[34] It is the Psalter, after all, that begins with an *inclusio* whereby the "righteous" are blessed in opposition to the wicked scoffers who persecute God's Anointed.

Psalm 1:5–6

> For this reason, the wicked will not rise up in the judgment
>   nor sinners in the council of the righteous [ὁδὸν δικαίων],
>   because the Lord knows the way of the righteous [δικαίων]
>   and the way of the wicked will perish

Psalm 2:12 [Eng. 2:11]

> Lay hold of instruction lest the Lord become angry
>   and destroy you from the way of the righteous [ἐξ ὁδοῦ δικαίας]
>   when his wrath is kindled quickly.
> Blessed are all those who put their trust in him.

Scholars have long noted that Psalms 1–2 function as a preface to the Psal-

---

32. On Luke's intentional use of irony in this scene, see James M. Dawsey, *The Lukan Voice: Confusion and Irony in the Gospel of Luke* (Macon, GA: Mercer University Press, 1986), 7–8; see also Peter Doble, *The Paradox of Salvation: Luke's Theology of the Cross*, SNTSMS 87 (Cambridge: Cambridge University Press, 1996), 137–38.

33. See also Subramanian, *Synoptic Gospels*, 87–88.

34. Note Luke's penchant for the adjective δίκαιος: Luke 1:6, 17; 5:32; 12:57; 14:14; 15:7; 18:9; 20:20; 23:47, 50; Acts 3:14; 4:19; 7:52; 10:22; 22:14; 24:15.

ter, thereby introducing a hermeneutic to the whole work.[35] As Psalm 1 indicates, one of the major motifs of the Psalter is the opposition between the righteous and the wicked. The word δίκαιος itself appears over fifty times throughout the Psalter. Psalm 2 attaches an eschatological and, most important, a royal messianic interpretation to the righteous–wicked contrast. This combination is found in Psalm 31, which presents the royal sufferer declaring himself as the "righteous one" (τοῦ δικαίου [LXX 30:19]). Thus, in Luke 23:46, Jesus, the Anointed One, speaks the words of David, the Anointed One, from Ps 31:5 (LXX 30:6), entrusting himself in hope to his Father, and one verse later (v. 47) the royal centurion testifies from the language of the Psalter that this Jesus is the royal righteous sufferer.

Isaiah's Servant or David's Suffering Messiah?

Reading the statement of the Roman officer in 23:47, one would find it odd that scholars argue for a reference to the Isaianic servant when Luke has so heavily interwoven the crucifixion account with royal imagery and texts from the psalms. This is, however, exactly what one frequently encounters in the scholarly literature on Luke's passion narrative or his concept of soteriology. Vincent Taylor comments that Luke's passion narrative "depicts Jesus as the Servant of the Lord without using the name."[36] Green, who has made the most detailed case for interpreting Jesus's death against the Isaianic background, argues similarly, "Luke's Christology focuses especially on the Isaianic Servant of Yahweh. Indeed, we might be so bold as to say that the Servant-theme makes up something of the substructure of Luke's two-part narrative."[37] The Isaianic servant stands out, for Green, as the primary category against which to view Jesus's sufferings for two reasons: (1) the presence of Isaianic material in Luke's passion account, and (2) the use of δίκαιος in tandem with Isaianic servant language in Acts 3. The presence of the servant terminology to which Green refers is the connection between Acts 3:13, ἐδόξασεν τὸν παῖδα αὐτοῦ (he has glorified his servant), and Isaiah 52:13, ὁ παῖς μου καὶ ὑψωθήσεται καὶ δοξασθήσεται σφόδρα (Even my servant will be greatly lifted up and glori-

---

35. Mitchell, *Message of the Psalter*, 73–74.
36. Vincent Taylor, *The Passion Narrative of St. Luke: A Critical and Historical Investigation*, ed. Owen E. Evans, SNTSMS 19 (Cambridge: Cambridge University Press, 1972), 138.
37. Joel B. Green, "The Death of Jesus, God's Servant," in *Reimaging the Death of the Lukan Jesus*, ed. Dennis D. Sylva, Athenäums Monografien, Theologie 73 (Frankfurt am Main: Hain, 1990), 1–28, here 19.

PART ONE: GOD'S ACTS FOR ISRAEL

fied).[38] For Green, Luke conflates the category of messiah with servant "so as to articulate the suffering role of the Messiah."[39] To this Green adds the appellation ὁ ἐκλεκτός in Luke 23:35, which, he maintains, recalls Isaiah 42:1.[40]

Is Green right in asserting that Luke is interpreting Jesus's death in light of the Isaianic servant? The high frequency of quotations and echoes from the Davidic psalms and the absence of any quotations from Isaiah in Luke 23–24 raise questions about the plausibility of this thesis.[41] Crucial for Green's argument is the occurrence of the title τὸν παῖδα αὐτοῦ (Acts 3:13; 4:25), yet surely it is significant that the psalms' Davidic sufferer also is referred to as God's "servant" (παῖς in LXX 68:18; δοῦλος in LXX 18:12; 77:70; 88:4; 108:28; 131:10). "Servant" is, in fact, a proper designation for the royal figure portrayed in the psalms.[42] Furthermore, Acts 4:27 explicitly maintains a connection between Jesus as "servant" (παῖδα) and the anointed (ὃν ἔχρισας) Davidic figure of the psalms (note the preceding use of Psalm 2 in 4:25–26).[43] The same connection between David and "servant" is seen in Luke's infancy narrative as well (ἐν οἴκῳ Δαυὶδ παιδὸς αὐτοῦ [1:69]). In fact, in light of the high frequency of psalm intertexts in Luke's passion account, I suggest that Psalm 89 provides a much more plausible context for understanding both the Roman officer's statement (Luke 23:47) and the so-called Isaianic servant material in Acts 3:13–14. Psalm 89:4 (Heb.; LXX 88:4; Eng. 89:3) states:

Διεθέμην διαθήκην τοῖς ἐκλεκτοῖς μου,
ὤμοσα Δαυιδ τῷ δούλῳ μου

I have established a covenant with my elect ones.
I have sworn to David my servant.

Similarly, in Ps 89:20–21 (Heb.; LXX 88:20–21; Eng. 89:19–20) one finds the common elements of exaltation (ὕψωσα), the chosen one (ἐκλεκτόν), and my anointed servant David (Δαυιδ τὸν δοῦλόν μου ... ἔχρισα αὐτόν).[44]

---

38. Green, "Death of Jesus," 20–21.
39. Green, *Gospel of Luke*, 827; see also Strauss, *Davidic Messiah*, 331–32; Darrell L. Bock, *Proclamation from Prophecy and Pattern: Lucan Old Testament Christology*, JSNTSup 12 (Sheffield: JSOT Press, 1987), 207.
40. Green, "Death of Jesus," 21.
41. Luke does quote Isaiah 53 in 22:37.
42. John H. Eaton, *Kingship and the Psalms*, SBT 2/32 (London: SCM, 1976), 149–50.
43. Luke uses παῖς in reference to Israel (Luke 1:54), David (Luke 1:69; Acts 4:25, 27), and the boy Jesus (Luke 2:43).
44. Green ("Death of Jesus," 21–22) claims that in Luke 22:39–46 no fewer than five fea-

Luke's Scriptural Suffering Messiah

Why, it must be asked, should one read Luke's references to παῖς as unambiguous references to Isaiah 53? The most explicit reference to the Isaianic servant comes in Acts 8, where the Ethiopian eunuch is converted by Philip. It is telling that there are no explicit mentions of Jesus as παῖς or ἐκλεκτός in this account. Therefore, there appears to be little reason to employ the Isaianic servant in Luke's portrait of the death of Jesus. The distinctly "Isaianic servant" terminology for which Green argues is actually used for David by the psalmist.[45] Does one find the same use of the psalms in Luke's second volume?

The Psalms and the Messiah's Enemies (Acts 1–4)

Luke's second volume adds support to the thesis that Luke interpreted the necessity of Jesus's sufferings and death in relation to the psalms' portrait of a kingly sufferer. Although Luke uses the psalms also as evidence predicting the messiah's resurrection and exaltation, here I discuss those texts in which the apostles are presented as interpreting the necessity of the messiah's death *as well as their own sufferings* against the backdrop of the Davidic psalms.[46]

Judas (Acts 1:15-26)

Two quotations from the psalms appear in Peter's first speech (Acts 1:15-26; Ps 69:25 [LXX 68:26]; Ps 109:8 [LXX 108:8]), which centers on Judas's defection from the apostolate and his replacement.[47] At this point in the narrative what is most striking is Luke's portrait of Peter as an interpreter of Israel's Scriptures.[48] Peter's speech begins with these words (1:16a):

---

tures of the account point toward Jesus as the Isaianic servant. Each of Green's five features is quite general, completely lacking in linguistic parallels to Isaiah; they can just as easily be applied to the psalms' suffering king.

45. Doble, "Luke 24.26, 44," 275.

46. Luke Timothy Johnson (*Septuagintal Midrash in the Speeches of Acts*, The Père Marquette Lecture in Theology 2002 [Milwaukee: Marquette University Press, 2002], 11–12) notes that one of Luke's distinctive uses of Scripture is that he extends its use beyond the Christ event to include the messianic community.

47. For the structure of Peter's first apostolic speech, see Marion L. Soards, *The Speeches in Acts: Their Content, Context, and Concerns* (Louisville: Westminster John Knox, 1994), 26–31.

48. Scholars have confirmed that the apostolic speeches are Lukan creations. See, e.g., Ulrich Wilckens, *Die Missionsreden der Apostelgeschichte: Form und traditionsgeschichtliche Untersuchung*, WMANT 5 (Neukirchen-Vluyn: Neukirchener Verlag, 1961).

55

PART ONE: GOD'S ACTS FOR ISRAEL

ἄνδρες ἀδελφοί, ἔδει πληρωθῆναι τὴν γραφὴν ἣν προεῖπεν τὸ πνεῦμα τὸ ἅγιον διὰ στόματος Δαυὶδ περὶ Ἰούδα

Brothers, it was necessary for the Scripture to be fulfilled that the Holy Spirit spoke beforehand through the mouth of David concerning Judas.

Two points call for comment. First, Peter's words ἔδει πληρωθῆναι τὴν γραφὴν (it was necessary for the Scripture to be fulfilled) function to make a link with the ending of Luke's first narrative, as they strongly recall Jesus's final words, which provide the hermeneutical key for interpreting his death—δεῖ πληρωθῆναι πάντα τὰ γεγραμμένα (Luke 24:44; see also 24:26-27).[49] A paradigm shift has taken place with respect to Peter's hermeneutics of scriptural interpretation. Thus, the hermeneutical program instituted by Jesus on the Emmaus road is taken up by Peter in his messianic sermons.[50] Even before the outpouring of the Spirit and Peter's multiple missionary speeches, the apostle provides the necessary interpretation of Jesus's death through Israel's Scriptures. Whereas prior to Jesus's resurrection it was Jesus himself or the narrator who clued the reader in to the necessity of his death, now it is Peter, formerly unable to understand the necessity of the Messiah's death (see Luke 18:34), who provides the link between Jesus's death and the divine necessity according to Israel's Scriptures.[51]

Second, that Peter connects the fulfillment of Scripture to that which was spoken specifically by "the Holy Spirit through *the mouth of David*" (διὰ στόματος Δαυὶδ) explicitly links his interpretation of Judas's act in the arrest and subsequent death of Jesus to the Davidic psalms. I have observed that Luke's specific mention of the psalms as a distinct category of Israel's scriptural canon is unique among NT writers, occurring four times (Luke 20:42; Acts 1:16; 2:25; 4:25), as is

---

49. See Robert C. Tannehill, *The Narrative Unity of Luke-Acts: A Literary Interpretation*, vol. 2, *The Acts of the Apostles* (Minneapolis: Fortress, 1990), 20.

50. This is argued nowhere as strongly as in the work of Jacques Dupont, "Les discours de Pierre dans les Actes et le Chapitre XXIV de l'évangile de Luc," in *L'Évangile de Luc: Problèmes littéraires et théologiques; Mémorial Lucien Cerfaux*, ed. F. Neirynck, BETL 32 (Gembloux: Duculot, 1973), 329-74; and Dupont, *L'utilisation Apologétique de l'Ancien Testament dans les discourse des Actes*, ALBO 40 (Paris: Publications Universitaires, 1953). Many of Dupont's most important essays have been reprinted in his *Études sur les Actes des apôtres*, LD 45 (Paris: Cerf, 1967).

51. On Luke's use of δεῖ and its link between Israel's Scriptures and the death of Jesus, see Luke 22:37; 24:26, 44; Acts 1:16, 21; 3:21; 17:3. See also Charles H. Cosgrove, "The Divine Δεῖ in Luke-Acts: Investigations into the Lukan Understanding of God's Providence," *NovT* 26 (1984): 168-90; John T. Squires, *The Plan of God in Luke-Acts*, SNTSMS 76 (Cambridge: Cambridge University Press, 1993).

Jesus's reference to the role of the psalms in predicting his death (Luke 24:44). Furthermore, although Peter will use two specific Davidic psalms as foreshadowing Judas's treachery, here at the beginning of the speech he simply maintains that Judas's deed was generally spoken of beforehand by the psalms. One is thereby given a hint as to how the early Christians read the psalms, namely, as royal texts that foreshadow the life and experiences of David's royal son.[52]

Understanding Luke's portrayal of Peter's role as the primitive church's exegete of Israel's Scriptures, specifically the psalms, is a prelude to Peter's interpretation of the act of Judas in Jesus's arrest and death. Judas's act of betrayal and subsequent death become public knowledge to the people of Jerusalem (1:18b–19).[53] Both Judas's betrayal and his destruction were already predicted of David's enemies in the psalms. Peter's claim that Judas's act was in some way "a necessity" (1:16), without providing reason or motive for his act of betrayal, again points to the psalms' depiction of the suffering righteous king. Luke melds together Psalm 69:25 (LXX 68:26) and 109:8 (LXX 108:8) to describe Judas's fate as an enemy of the suffering king.[54] Acts 1:20 reads,

> For it has been written in the book of the Psalms [βίβλῳ ψαλμῶν], "Let his dwelling place become uninhabited and let no one dwell in it" [Ps 69:25] and, "let another take his office" [Ps 109:8].

I have already discussed the significance of Psalm 69 in Luke's portrait of Jesus's death. It bears repeating, however, that the Davidic psalm portrays a suffering righteous king, God's own servant (69:17), unjustly persecuted by his own enemies (vv. 1–4, 19–29) and crying out to God for vindication (vv. 1–2, 30–36). Likewise, Psalm 109 describes the persecution of the righteous king whereby he prays for curses against his enemies. The psalm ends with David's words of praise to God as the one who vindicates the "servant" (δοῦλος [LXX 108:28]), stands at the "right hand" (v. 31) of those unjustly persecuted, and gives retribution to the wicked (vv. 28–31). It may be significant that Luke uses Psalm 109 to describe the imprecation upon David's enemies, which, of course, moves into

---

52. David's name occurs frequently in the apostolic speeches (Acts 1:16; 2:25, 29, 34; 4:25; 7:45; 13:22, 34, 36; 15:16).

53. On Luke's presentation of Judas, see Arie W. Zwiep, *Judas and the Choice of Matthias: A Study on Context and Concern of Acts 1:15–26*, WUNT 187 (Tübingen: Mohr Siebeck, 2004).

54. For a short but incisive discussion of Luke's connection of these two psalms, see L. Johnson, *Septuagintal Midrash*, 14–15. More generally, see Jacob Jervell, *Luke and the People of God: A New Look at Luke-Acts* (Minneapolis: Augsburg, 1972), 75–112; Pao, *Acts and the Isaianic New Exodus*, 123–27.

Psalm 110, where God vindicates and exalts the righteous Davidic figure to his "right hand" (ἐκ δεξιῶν μου [LXX 109:1]) from his enemies (vv. 1-2, 5-6). The significance of the portrait of an exalted Davidic figure in Psalm 110 for Luke's understanding of Jesus's resurrection is enormous (Luke 20:41-44; Acts 2:22-36; 5:31).[55] I suggest that Luke was naturally prompted, as he read Psalm 110 and its picture of an exalted and *vindicated* figure, to read also the previous psalm, with its prayer for vindication from the wicked and its affirmation of trust in God as the one who stands at the "right hand" of his righteous servant (109:27, 31), as predicting both Judas's persecution of Jesus and his ultimate demise.

Commentators frequently pass over Acts 1:20 and the quotation of Psalms 69 and 110 without realizing their larger hermeneutical implications.[56] Although Peter's second apostolic speech in Acts 2 unambiguously proclaims Christ's resurrection as the fulfillment of the Davidic psalms, it is his first speech that demonstrates the scriptural necessity of Christ's suffering.

The Rulers of Israel, Herod, and Pilate (Acts 4:1-31)

Luke's use of the psalms reaches its pinnacle in Acts 2:22-36 and 13:13-41, where Peter and Paul respectively portray the resurrection and exaltation of the Messiah against the backdrop of Psalms 2, 16, 132, and especially 110.[57] While a study of these psalms would confirm my thesis that Luke reads the psalms as a portrait of the life and experiences of Jesus the Messiah, it is my intention to demonstrate

---

55. Literature on the use of Psalm 110 in Luke's writings and early Christianity is copious. See, e.g., David M. Hay, *Glory at the Right Hand: Psalm 110 in Early Christianity*, SBLMS 18 (Nashville: Abingdon, 1973); Jacques Dupont, "'Assis à la droite de Dieu': L'interprétation du Ps. 110, 1 dans le Nouveau Testament," in *Resurrexit: Actes du Symposium International sur la Résurrection de Jésus (Rome 1970)*, ed. Edouard Dhanis (Vatican City: Libreria Editrice Vaticana, 1974), 94-148; David P. Moessner, "Two Lords 'at the Right Hand'? The Psalms and an Intertextual Reading of Peter's Pentecost Speech (Acts 2:14-36)," in *Literary Studies in Luke-Acts: Essays in Honor of Joseph B. Tyson*, ed. Richard P. Thompson and Thomas E. Phillips (Macon, GA: Mercer University Press, 1998), 215-32; Doble, "Psalms in Luke-Acts," 90-97.

56. For example, in his important study *Judas: Betrayer or Friend of Jesus* (Minneapolis: Fortress, 1996), William Klassen does not comment on the role or usage of the psalms in Judas's death. The same is true of Daniel Marguerat, *Les Actes des Apôtres (1-12)*, CNT (Geneva: Labor et Fides, 2007), 60-63. A major exception, however, is again Jacques Dupont, "La Destinée de Judas Prophétisée par David (Actes 1,16-20)," CBQ 23 (1961): 41-51, here 50-51.

57. For Acts 2, see, Robert F. O'Toole, "Acts 2:30 and the Davidic Covenant of Pentecost," JBL 102 (1983): 245-58; C. Kavin Rowe, *Early Narrative Christology: The Lord in the Gospel of Luke*, BZNW 139 (Berlin: de Gruyter, 2006), 189-96. With respect to Acts 13, note Robert F. O'Toole, "Christ's Resurrection in Acts 13,13-52," Bib 60 (1979): 361-72.

my thesis by an examination of Luke's use of the psalms with respect to Jesus's sufferings and death. Numerous issues and questions are raised in Acts 4, but of greatest importance are the uses of Psalm 118 (Acts 4:11), Psalm 146 (Acts 4:24b), and Psalm 2 (Acts 4:25b–26) within the broader narrative.

A significant change takes place with respect to Luke's use of the psalms in Acts 4. Whereas previously the Davidic psalms were applied to the sufferings, death, and exaltation of Jesus, now the psalms are employed also with respect to the experiences of the early Christians. The large number of similarities between Peter's and John's encounter with Israel's leaders in Acts 4 and Jesus's interaction with the leaders in Luke 20:1–19 suggests that these passages be read in light of each other.[58] Both scenes are dominated by the hostile presence of Israel's leaders (Luke 20:1, 19; Acts 4:1, 5–6, 8), and a significant act in the Jerusalem temple has captured the admiration of the people (Luke 19:45–48 [Jesus's action in the temple]; Acts 3:1–4:4 [the apostles healing and teaching in the temple]. In both instances, the leaders of Israel ask "by what authority" and "by what power" Jesus and the apostles are doing these acts (Luke 20:2; Acts 4:7).

The hostile questioning by Israel's leaders provokes Jesus's parable of the wicked tenants, in which Jesus foretells the role that Israel's leaders will have in his death, to which the disciples reply, "May it never be!" (Luke 20:16b). Having failed to enlighten the disciples regarding his impending death, Jesus asks them the meaning of what has been written in Psalm 118:22 (Luke 20:17b). It is at this point that Jesus in Luke (and the apostles in Acts) respond with an explicit reference to Psalm 118:22 (LXX 117:22). In both the Gospel and Acts the psalm text is quoted against the rulers and authorities of Israel, indicting them for their role in the death of Jesus.

Acts 4:11, quoting Psalm 118:22, states,

> οὗτός ἐστιν ὁ λίθος, ὁ ἐξουθενηθεὶς ὑφ' ὑμῶν τῶν οἰκοδόμων,
> ὁ γενόμενος εἰς κεφαλὴν γωνίας.

> This is the stone that was despised by your builders;
> this has become the head stone.

This aphorism functions in Luke's narrative as a memorable synecdoche, whereby the one verse encapsulates the whole psalm. The narrative of the psalm moves from distress, rejection, and suffering (Ps 118:5–9) to salvation

---

58. Tannehill, *Narrative Unity of Luke-Acts*, 2:69–70.

PART ONE: GOD'S ACTS FOR ISRAEL

and exaltation (vv. 15-29).[59] Despite the persecutions and distress caused by the psalmist's enemies, the psalmist sings of confidence in the Lord against the unrighteous rulers. In light of the frequent references to Israel's "rulers" in Acts 4 (τοὺς ἄρχοντας [4:5, 8; see also 4:1-2, 6]), the psalm's emphasis on trusting in God rather than humans is significant. Note Psalm 118:8-9 (LXX 117:8-9):

> It is better to trust in the Lord
>   than to trust in humanity [ἐπ' ἄνθρωπον].
> It is better to hope in the Lord
>   than to hope in rulers [ἐπ' ἄρχοντας].

To those, like the psalmist, who put their confidence in God and not humanity, God will bring forth the divine "right hand" for "salvation" (vv. 14-17). J. Ross Wagner has noted the significant influence of Psalm 118 on Luke's two-volume narrative. He points out that it is here, however, in Acts 4:11 that Luke explicitly connects Psalm 118 with the death and resurrection of Jesus.[60] What Jesus had declared cryptically in Luke 20:17 is herein proclaimed by the apostles with clarity and boldness. As in Acts 1, Peter proves himself a capable interpreter of Israel's Scriptures as he employs Jesus's lesson from Luke 24:26, 44-47.

At the core of Acts 4 (and Psalm 118) is the motif of reversal. As interpreted by the early Christians, Psalm 118:22 not only portrays the death of the Messiah but also looks forward to his resurrection. In a similar manner, it encourages the apostles to place their confidence in God as opposed to the "rulers" (118:8-9).[61] Salvation is offered not through the rulers of Israel but rather through the rejected and vindicated Messiah (Ps 118:14-15 / Acts 4:11-12). It is not unlikely that the psalmist's confident hope in God for salvation strongly influenced Peter's bold and exclusive offer of salvation in Acts 4:12.

Psalm 118:14-15 (LXX 117:14-15) reads,

---

59. On the structure and historical background of Psalm 118, see James A. Sanders, "A Hermeneutic Fabric: Psalm 118 in Luke's Entrance Narrative," in *Luke and Scripture: The Function of Sacred Tradition in Luke-Acts*, ed. Craig A. Evans and James A. Sanders (Minneapolis: Fortress, 1993), 140-53, here 143-48.

60. J. Ross Wagner, "Psalm 118 in Luke-Acts: Tracing a Narrative Thread," in *Early Christian Interpretation of the Scriptures of Israel: Investigations and Proposals*, ed. Craig A. Evans and James A. Sanders, JSNTSup 148, SSEJC 5 (Sheffield: Sheffield Academic, 1997), 154-78.

61. Wagner, "Psalm 118 in Luke-Acts," 173-74.

The Lord is my strength and my praise
and he has become salvation for me [ἐγένετό μοι εἰς σωτηρίαν],
the voice of rejoicing and salvation [σωτηρίας] is in the tents of the righteous.
The right hand of the Lord has done powerfully.

Acts 4:12 reads,

And there is salvation [ἡ σωτηρία] in no one else, for there is no other name under heaven that has been given to human beings by which it is necessary for us to be saved [ἐν ᾧ δεῖ σωθῆναι ἡμᾶς].

The Jewish rulers' persecution of the early Christians not only was hinted at in Psalm 118 but can also be discerned in the use of Psalms 2 and 146 in the community's prayer. Upon Peter's and John's release from the custody of Israel's leaders, the community lifts up their voice to God and prays. In Acts 4:24b they declare,

δέσποτα, σὺ ὁ ποιήσας τὸν οὐρανὸν καὶ τὴν γῆν καὶ τὴν θάλασσαν καὶ πάντα τὰ ἐν αὐτοῖς . . .

Lord, you who made the heaven and the earth and the sea and all the things that are in them . . .

Although these words are a standard introductory prayer formula, there are good reasons for seeing this prayer as an echo of Psalm 146:5b–6a (LXX 145:5b–6a):

ἡ ἐλπὶς αὐτοῦ ἐπὶ κύριον τὸν θεὸν αὐτοῦ
τὸν ποιήσαντα τὸν οὐρανὸν καὶ τὴν γῆν
τὴν θάλασσαν καὶ πάντα τὰ ἐν αὐτοῖς

His hope is in the Lord his God,
the one who made the heaven, the earth,
the sea and all the things that are in them.

There are two reasons for positing Acts 4:24b as an echo of Psalm 146. The most simple and obvious reason is that the Christians' prayer linguistically matches Psalm 146 more closely than any other OT text. The most convincing

PART ONE: GOD'S ACTS FOR ISRAEL

reason, however, is found in the psalm's metaleptic connection with Psalm 118 and Acts 4.[62] Note Psalm 146:3 (LXX 145:3):

μὴ πεποίθατε ἐπ' ἄρχοντας
καὶ ἐφ' υἱοὺς ἀνθρώπων οἷς οὐκ ἔστιν σωτηρία

Do not trust in rulers,
even in the sons of humans in whom there is no salvation.

The echoes of Psalm 118 and Acts 4 are strong: do not put your "trust" for "salvation" in mortal "rulers" who persecute and reject the righteous.[63] Psalms 118 and 146 are metaleptically melded together, with their common concern to reject confidence in human rulers and to create the prefiguration not only of the rejection and vindication of the Messiah but also the experience of the early Christians.

Luke's use of Psalms 118 (Acts 4:11) and 146 (Acts 4:24b) leads seamlessly into the quotation of Psalm 2:1-2 in Acts 4:25b-26. One may say that next to Psalm 110, it is Psalm 2 that exerts the most influence on the early Christians in their conception of the messiah, his relationship to God, and the opposition and persecution that Christians must endure at the hands of Israel's leaders. One finds echoes of and allusions to Psalm 2 in Luke's narrative already in the angel Gabriel's proclamation of the birth of the Messiah (1:31-35), Jesus's baptism (3:22), and his transfiguration (9:35). Psalm 2 can be divided into three parts.[64]

1. Vv. 1-3: The kings, peoples, and rulers of the earth conspire against the reign of God and of God's "anointed."
2. Vv. 4-9: God laughs at the futility of the enemies, responding by installing God's son as king.
3. Vv. 10-12: The kings and the rulers are invited to cease their opposition and submit to God and God's anointed son.

---

62. By metalepsis I refer to Luke's allusive references to the OT, which recalls the larger context of the psalms. On this, see Richard B. Hays, *Echoes of Scripture in the Letters of Paul* (New Haven: Yale University Press, 1989). With respect to Luke-Acts, however, note Robert L. Brawley, *Text to Text Pours Forth Speech: Voices of Scripture in Luke-Acts*, ISBL (Bloomington: Indiana University Press, 1995).

63. Doble ("Psalms in Luke-Acts," 100-101), with characteristic insight, is the only scholar I have found who notes the intertextual connections between Psalm 145 and Acts 4.

64. See W. J. C. Weren, "Psalm 2 in Luke-Acts: An Intertextual Study," in *Intertextuality in Biblical Writings: Essays in Honour of Bas van Iersel*, ed. Sipke Draisma (Kampen: Kok, 1989), 192-96.

Despite the absence of linguistic connections, the psalm shows striking similarities to 2 Samuel 7:12–14, where God promises David to establish a father-son relationship with David's progeny, which will result in an eternal dynasty. In Peter's prayer, Luke reproduces the first two verses of Psalm 2. Acts 4:25–26 states:

> ὁ τοῦ πατρὸς ἡμῶν διὰ πνεύματος ἁγίου στόματος Δαυὶδ παιδός σου εἰπών·
> ἱνατί ἐφρύαξαν ἔθνη
> καὶ λαοὶ ἐμελέτησαν κενά;
> παρέστησαν οἱ βασιλεῖς τῆς γῆς
> καὶ οἱ ἄρχοντες συνήχθησαν ἐπὶ τὸ αὐτὸ
> κατὰ τοῦ κυρίου καὶ κατὰ τοῦ χριστοῦ αὐτοῦ.

> Our father, through the Holy Spirit, through the mouth of David your servant said:
> Why do the nations rage
> and the peoples plot in vain?
> The kings of the earth take their stand
> and the rulers are gathered together for the same purpose
> against the Lord and against his Christ.

Lest readers make any mistake, Luke provides a clear interpretation of Psalm 2 through the mouth of Peter in what follows. Luke has unambiguously linked David with Psalm 2 in two ways: (1) both David and Jesus are referred to as God's παιδός (4:25, 27, 30);[65] and (2) in Luke's interpretation of Psalm 2, Jesus is referred to as the one "whom you [God] anointed" (ὃν ἔχρισας [4:27]). This "whom you anointed" most naturally refers to the coronation of the Davidic king in Ps 2:6–7. In other words, Jesus is given the same messianic position as that of David in the psalm, the one described as God's "Christ" (2:2).[66] As Peter Doble states, "Here, in this prayer, Jesus' history is retold as *fulfilled*

---

65. I have argued that the language of παῖς is connected with David both in the psalms and in Luke's narrative. There is no textual reason to argue that Luke is melding Isaianic material with the psalms' Davidic sufferer in Acts 4:25–31, as is done in J. J. Kilgallen, "Your Servant Jesus Whom You Anointed (Acts 4,27)," *RB* 105 (1998): 185–201. See also Jacques E. Ménard, "*Pais Theou* as a Messianic Title in the Book of Acts," *CBQ* 19 (1957): 83–92.

66. For the NT's use of Psalm 2 in connection with the Davidic Messiah, see Jacques Dupont, "'Filius meus es tu'. L'interpretation de Ps 2,7 dans le Nouveau Testament," *RSR* 35 (1948): 522–43.

scripture."[67] Israel's rulers, Herod, Pilate, and even the people of Israel play the role of the enemies of God and God's Christ in Psalm 2 (see Luke 23:12).[68] In 4:29-30 Peter and John take on the role of the Anointed One of Psalm 2 as they, the messianic community, also suffer at the hands of these leaders.

The Psalms and the Suffering Christ

In this chapter I have argued that Luke's portrait of a suffering messiah need not be characterized as an oxymoron. Although it is largely recognized that Luke uses the psalms as evidence predicting the resurrection and exaltation of Jesus, I have attempted to show that Luke reads the psalms also as the autobiographical speech of the suffering Davidic Messiah, now climactically embodied by Jesus himself. I have identified reasonably clear quotations and allusions to Psalms 2, 22, 31, 38, 69, 109, 118, and 146—all used by Luke as foreshadowing the suffering and death of the Messiah and/or the persecution of the early Christians.

Too often the psalms' depiction of a suffering king has been ignored or subordinated to the Isaianic servant by interpreters of Luke.[69] Perhaps Luke's portrait of a scriptural suffering Messiah has seemed too paradoxical to associate with anything royal or Davidic. Yet it is no accident that quotations and allusions to Israel's prayer book abound in Luke's passion narrative as well as in the apostolic speeches of Acts. I suggest that Luke (and many of his predecessors and contemporaries) found in the psalms exactly that combination of royalty and righteous suffering that had been embodied in the crucified Jesus of Nazareth.

---

67. Doble, "Psalms in Luke-Acts," 103.
68. L. Johnson (*Septuagintal Midrash*, 32-34) convincingly demonstrates the methodological parallels between Luke's interpretation of Psalm 2 and such Qumran pesharim as 1QpHab and 4QpPa.
69. C. H. Dodd (*According to the Scriptures: The Sub-Structure of New Testament Theology* [London: Collins, 1952], 106), for example, suggests that the Davidic Messiah held little, if any, significance for the early Christians in their development of Christology.

CHAPTER 4

Abraham in the Synoptic Gospels and
the Acts of the Apostles

Within the canonical Gospels and the Acts of the Apostles, the biblical patriarch Abraham plays a significant, if not primary, role in determining the identity of the people of God, establishing continuity between God's covenantal dealings with Israel *and* Jesus of Nazareth and his followers, establishing a connection between the Abrahamic promise for seed and God's promise to David to raise up seed for him, and in setting forth a paradigm for the ethical behavior demanded by the God of Israel. In what follows, I will examine the role of Abraham within the canonical Gospels and the book of Acts. While I will attend on occasion to important traditions that may have influenced these writings, my primary interest and emphasis is on the literary nature of the compositions and the role that Abraham plays within their broader narrative worlds.

The Gospel of Matthew

Matthew begins his Gospel by describing Jesus Christ with two titles—he is "Son of David" and "son of Abraham" (Matt 1:1). While Matthew's primary interest is in portraying Jesus as Israel's Davidic Messiah (e.g., 2:5–6; 21:9–15),[1]

---

1. The centrality of Jesus as Davidic Messiah for Matthew is argued for in a variety of important works. See, for example, Nicholas G. Piotrowski, *Matthew's New David at the End of Exile: A Socio-Rhetorical Study of Scriptural Quotations*, NovTSup 170 (Leiden: Brill, 2016); Anthony LeDonne, *The Historiographical Jesus: Memory, Typology, and the Son of David* (Waco, TX: Baylor University Press, 2009).

his royal-messianic identity only makes sense in light of the way in which Israel's Davidic traditions presuppose and expand upon the Abrahamic traditions (cf. Gal. 3:16). The seed of David is, then, the heir of the promises made to Abraham. This can be seen immediately in the way Matthew structures his genealogy as neatly moving from three periods of fourteen generations, moving from Abraham (1:2–6a), to David (1:6b–11), to the Babylonian exile (1:12–16), and culminating with the birth of Jesus the Messiah (1:16–17). We will have to attend to Matthew's narrative to discern the precise meaning and significance of Jesus's identity as "son of Abraham," but already it would seem justifiable to claim that Matthew is presenting Jesus Christ as the goal of God's election of Israel. Matthew's reference to Jesus as the "son of Abraham" draws, then, the identity of Jesus together with God's election and origins of Israel as his people. Anders Runesson rightly notes that one cannot "understand Matthew's story and focus on Israel without also acknowledging the notion of Israel's election as implied."[2] Matthew's genealogy thereby demands that his Gospel be interpreted in such a way that there is deep continuity between Matthew's story and God's election of Israel.[3]

Matthew is adamant that Abrahamic descent does not provide a safeguard against divine judgment. John the Baptist, forerunner of Jesus's proclamation of repentance for the forgiveness of sins (3:2; 4:17), preaches that Abrahamic descent and election does not translate into salvation. John's call for repentance is situated within the warning directed toward "the Pharisees and Sadducees" (3:7) that only "fruit worthy of repentance" rather than confidence that one has "Abraham as our father" (3:8–9) will enable one to escape "the coming wrath" (3:7). God has the power, in fact, to create "children for Abraham" (τέκνα τῷ Ἀβραάμ) out of the stones and rocks at the Jordan River (3:9). As Jon Levenson has noted, the election of Abraham and genealogical descent from his family is quite simply irrelevant as it pertains to salvation and the avoidance of God's wrath.[4] Nothing that the Baptist states here is necessarily in conflict with the assertion of God's election of Abraham and his family in Matthew 1:1–17, nor *should* his statement be seen as implying God's rejection of his election of Israel. John's warning, however, does preview Matthew's ongoing polemic against Israel's religious leaders who, Matthew warns, must not

---

2. Anders Runesson, *Divine Wrath and Salvation in Matthew: The Narrative World of the First Gospel* (Minneapolis: Fortress, 2016), 182.

3. Richard B. Hays, *Echoes of Scripture in the Gospels* (Waco, TX: Baylor University Press, 2016), 110.

4. Jon D. Levenson, *Abraham Between Torah and Gospel*, The Père Marquette Lecture in Theology 2011 (Milwaukee: Marquette University Press, 2011), 34.

presume that their descent from Abraham provides them with an excuse to refuse John's and Jesus's proclamation of the kingdom of heaven and the need for repentance. This is the beginning of Matthew's narration of the conflict with the Pharisees and Sadducees and the pronouncement of judgment for their refusal to repent.[5] John's message previews Jesus's parable of the owner of the vineyard (Matt 21:33–45), an owner who in response to the tenants' failure to procure fruit "takes away the kingdom of God [from Israel's authorities] and gives it to a people [ἔθνει] producing its fruit" (21:43). That this is directed against Israel's authorities (rather than the people of Israel) is made explicit in 21:45 where the chief priests and Pharisees understand that Jesus directs the parable against them.[6] John's demand that only the fruits of repentance will enable one to avoid God's wrath is consistent with the narrative's broader portrayal of entrance into the kingdom of God as contingent upon repentance, obedience, and doing what Jesus teaches (e.g., Matt 7:13–23; 16:27).

Finally, Jesus declares that sharing in the eschatological banquet with Abraham and the patriarchs is contingent upon a faithful response to his person and teaching. In Jesus's encounter with the Roman centurion (8:5–13), Jesus responds to the man's understanding of and submission to Jesus's authority with the pronouncement, "Truly I tell you, I have not found anyone in Israel with so great a faith" (8:10). Jesus portrays this non-Jewish man as an exemplar of "the many" when he declares that "many will come from the east and west and will recline with Abraham, Isaac, and Jacob in the kingdom of heaven, but the sons of the kingdom will be cast out into the outer darkness where there is weeping and the gnashing of teeth" (8:11–12). God's election of Abraham and the patriarchs and his affirmation of the divinely created origins of Israel are upheld, and yet Jesus's pronouncement again engages in a surprising definition of who will experience the hospitality of the kingdom and who will be excluded. In Hays' words, "In the Matthean narrative context, this can only mean that the centurion exemplifies 'many' *non-Israelites* who will ultimately be included in salvation and the great final eschatological feast."[7] Again, it would be too simplistic and wrongheaded to interpret this as a contrast between gentiles who are welcomed and Jews who are excluded. Jesus's exaltation of the cen-

---

5. On this theme and the way in which the warning is directed *primarily* to the authorities of Israel (rather than the people as a whole), see Matthias Konradt, *Israel, Church, and the Gentiles in the Gospel of Matthew*, trans. Kathleen Ess, Baylor-Mohr Siebeck Studies in Early Christianity (Waco, TX: Baylor University Press, 2014), 167–264.

6. For a further defense of interpreting this parable in a non-supersessionist manner, see Konradt, *Israel, Church, and the Gentiles*, 173–93.

7. Hays, *Echoes of Scripture in the Gospels*, 181.

PART ONE: GOD'S ACTS FOR ISRAEL

turion's faith is spoken to those Jews "who are following" him (8:10), namely "the large crowds" (8:1; cf. 4:25) listening to his proclamation of the Sermon on the Mount. The commendation of the centurion's faith thereby functions as an exhortation to the crowds who are listening to his teaching (7:28–29). Entrance into the eschatological banquet with Abraham is mediated through one's response to Jesus, and therefore a faithless or hostile response will result in a situation where even "the sons of the kingdom" are excluded (8:12).

While many have seen here a reference to Israel's exclusion, it may make better sense to understand the warning to "the sons of the kingdom" as referring to those who have heard and responded to Jesus's teaching but are in need of further exhortations to follow. This makes good sense of the fact that the parallel phrase "sons of the kingdom" in Matthew 13:38 refers to "the good seed" in Jesus's parable of the wheat and the tares (13:36–43) as well as the literary context of 8:5–13, which seems much more concerned with exhortations and warnings to followers of Jesus to continue to listen and respond to his teaching (cf. 7:21–29).[8] However, Jesus's note that "many will come from east and west" (8:11) almost certainly previews the fulfillment of the Abrahamic promises that the nations will be blessed through the seed of Abraham (Gen. 12:1–4; 15:1–6; 17:1–5). Just as Isaiah 25:6–8 envisioned a banquet for "all the peoples" and "all the nations," (Isa 25:7), so Matthew 8:5–13 portrays participating in the eschatological banquet as for both Jews and gentiles who respond positively to Jesus.

Thus, Matthew's initial statement that Jesus is "the son of Abraham" (1:1) would seem to have universalistic connotations, and this possibility may be further strengthened by the fact that, as is often noted, Matthew's genealogy includes four non-Jewish women in Jesus's family lineage (Tamar, Ruth, Rahab, and Bathsheba).[9] As the climax of God's dealings with his people Israel, the Messiah thereby opens up salvation to the nations; for this reason, one finds within Matthew a variety of texts speaking of the extension of salvation to Jews *and gentiles* as fulfilling scriptural texts that signal God's faithfulness to his promise to Abraham that *through him* he would bless the nations (e.g., Matt 2:1–12 and Isa 60:1–6; 4:15–16 and Isa 9:1–2; 12:15–21 and Isa 42:6–7; 28:16–20 and Dan 7:13–14).[10]

---

8. More typical, however, are interpretations that follow Siker's conclusion that "Jews who do not demonstrate faith will be cut off from the kingdom, while the Gentiles who do exhibit faith will find themselves included in the kingdom and will sit at table with Abraham." See Jeffrey S. Siker, *Disinheriting the Jews: Abraham in Early Christian Controversy* (Louisville: Westminster John Knox, 1991), 84.

9. See, for example, Ulrich Luz, *Matthew 1–7: A Commentary*, trans. Wilhelm C. Linss (Minneapolis: Augsburg Fortress, 1985), 107–11; Jason B. Hood, *The Messiah, His Brothers, and the Nations: Matthew 1.1–17*, LNTS 441 (New York: T&T Clark, 2011).

10. Whether Matthew envisions the nations as saved *qua* the nations *or* as proselytes

Abraham in the Synoptic Gospels and the Acts of the Apostles

THE GOSPEL OF MARK

Abraham is only mentioned by name in one place in the Gospel of Mark as part of his response in 12:18-27 (cf. Matt 22:23-33; Luke 20:27-38) to some Sadducees who challenge Jesus by asking him about a woman married (consecutively) to seven different men: "Whose wife will she be in the resurrection? For the seven men had her as a wife" (12:23).[11] Their question is intended, it would seem, to trip up Jesus by mocking the belief in the resurrection from the dead. Jesus rebukes them, however, for failing to understand both "the Scriptures and the power of God" (12:24b). Jesus argues that their own Scriptures testify to the doctrine of the resurrection for the dead, and he appeals to Exodus 3:6: "I am the God of Abraham, Isaac, and Jacob. He is the God of the living, not the dead. You are greatly deceived" (12:26b-27; cf. Acts 3:13; 7:32). Joel Marcus notes that this is "hardly the sense that the formula 'the God of Abraham, of Isaac, and of Jacob' had in the original . . . [and that it] means that just as he delivered those patriarchs from their distress, so will he now liberate and succor their enslaved descendants."[12] And yet if God is the God of life who continues to demonstrate his power and covenant faithfulness to his people, then it is not too far removed to suggest that the recipients of his faithfulness "will ultimately be crowned by their liberation from the power of death itself."[13] Jesus's response is congruent with Luke's parable, which will depict Abraham and those in his bosom as participants in some form of blessed postmortem existence (Luke 16:22-23).

THE GOSPEL OF LUKE

In the Gospel of Luke and the Acts of the Apostles, the author draws upon Abraham in order to establish "a connection and continuity between the history of Abraham and the events of which he himself is writing."[14] Abraham is the father of Israel, the recipient of God's promises, the father of the repentant,

---

cannot be entered into here. See, for example, Runesson, *Divine Wrath and Salvation in Matthew*, 364-73.
    11. Their question presumes the practice of levirate marriage (e.g., Gen 38:8).
    12. Joel Marcus, *Mark 8-16*, AYBC 27A (New Haven: Yale University Press, 2009), 835.
    13. Marcus, *Mark 8-16*, 835. See further the argument of Jon D. Levenson, *Resurrection and the Restoration of Israel: The Ultimate Victory of the God of Life* (New Haven: Yale University Press, 2006).
    14. Nils A. Dahl, "The Story of Abraham in Luke-Acts," in *Studies in Luke-Acts*, ed. Leander E. Keck and J. Louis Martyn (Mifflintown, PA: Sigler, 1966), 139-58, here 140.

the outcasts, and marginalized within Israel, and the one through whom God will bless all the families of the earth.

Unlike Matthew, however, who draws a more obvious or explicit connection through his fulfillment citations, Luke accomplishes a similar end through subtle hints that his story is a continuation of God's covenantal promises made beginning with Abraham. The miraculous conceptions of John and Jesus resonate powerfully with the stories of the barren women in Israel's Scriptures, not least that of Sarah (Gen 12–21) and Hannah (1 Sam 1–2). Joel Green has set forth an impressive list of the parallels between the God's powerful mercy to the barren Sarah and God's opening of the wombs of Elizabeth and Mary in Luke 1–2.[15] To give just a few examples: Sarai and Elizabeth are barren (Gen 11:30; Luke 1:7); promises are made that share the common language of greatness, blessing, and seed (Gen 12:2–7; 13:14–17; Luke 1:15, 32, 55, 73); the recipients of the promise are advanced in age (Gen 17:1; Gen 18:11–13; Luke 1:7, 18); both are recipients of divine/angelic visitations (Gen 17:22; Luke 1:11, 38). Many more parallels could be adduced, but enough have been invoked to indicate Luke's intention to portray to the reader that God's merciful kindness to Abraham has not been forgotten, and that in the event Luke is narrating in his Gospel (and the second volume as well) God is continuing the story and promises he had initiated with Abraham in Genesis. Both the speeches of Mary and Zechariah interpret God's act to open the wombs of Mary and Elizabeth in relationship to the promises made to Abraham. Thus, Mary: "[God] has helped his servant Israel, to remember mercy [μνησθῆναι ἐλέους], just as he spoke to our ancestors, to Abraham and to his seed forever" (Luke 1:54–55). Similarly, Zechariah declares that God has "shown mercy [ἔλεος] with our fathers and remembered [μνησθῆναι] his holy covenant, the oath which he swore to Abraham our father" (Luke 1:72–73). For Luke, then, Abraham functions as the initial and primary recipient of God's promises, and thus God's opening of the wombs of Elizabeth and Mary functions as the concrete display of God's merciful remembrance of these promises.[16] Despite lacking the literary adornment of Matthew, Luke's genealogy does not surprise the reader when it lists Abraham and the patriarchs as the ancestors of Jesus (3:34).

Yet, even within Luke's infancy narrative, the reader is alerted to the expectation that God's merciful remembrance of his promises to Abraham will not take place without conflict or division. Thus, Simeon prophesies to Mary that

---

15. Joel B. Green, "The Problem of a Beginning: Israel's Scriptures in Luke 1–2," *BBR* 4 (1994): 61–86, here 68–71.

16. Dahl, "Story of Abraham in Luke-Acts," 142.

her son has been "appointed for the fall and rising of many in Israel and a sign to be spoken against and that even a sword will pierce your soul" (2:34b–35a). Mary's hymn has interpreted God's actions to be good news for the poor, hungry, and humiliated and judgment for the proud, powerful, and rich (1:51–53). John the Baptist's primary task is to lead Israel to turn back to God so that there will be a "people made ready, prepared for the Lord" (1:17, 76; 3:1–6). Not unlike what we have seen in Matthew's Gospel, the Baptist functions as a sign that God's election of Abraham does not translate into salvation *apart* from a believing response to John and Jesus.[17] Thus, just as in Matthew's Gospel, John warns them that their paternity of Abraham is irrelevant apart from producing fruit that is worthy of repentance (3:8a). Unrepentant, non-fruit bearing trees will be "cut off and cast into the fire" (3:9). John describes this repentant, fruit-bearing response in embodied and tangible terms of sharing one's possessions and refusing to engage in exploitation of the vulnerable (3:10–14).[18]

Luke's remaining explicit references to Abraham serve to highlight the surprising recipients of God's merciful kindness and the response of right behavior or the fruits of repentance. Thus, in Jesus's healing of the woman "bent over," who is "unable to stand up straight," and is plagued by an unclean spirit for fourteen years (13:11, 16), Jesus heals her and publicly declares her to be "a daughter of Abraham" (13:16a).[19] Luke describes her as coming to the synagogue on the Sabbath (13:10) and responding "giving glory to God" in response for her healing. She is one of Israel's poor but pious worshippers of the God of Israel described by Mary in Luke 1:51–53. Her identity as a daughter of Abraham reveals that she and others like her, those considered to be excluded from or on the margins of the society of Israel, are in fact the target of Jesus's mercy (e.g., Luke 4:18–29).[20] Jesus's healing releases her from the bondage of Satan and vindicates her as Abraham's daughter (13:16) and functions as a surprising literary fulfillment of Zechariah's hymn that links God's remembrance of his covenant to Abraham with the promise of deliver-

---

17. Siker, *Disinheriting the Jews*, 108: "Luke rules out completely the notion that mere physical descent from Abraham gives one a special claim on God's mercy. Only repentance and ethical behavior that demonstrates this repentance counts before God."

18. Dahl, "Story of Abraham in Luke-Acts," 140, may overstate the point when he denies that Luke portrays Abraham as a model or prototype for behavior.

19. On Jesus's overturning the prevalent and negative stereotyping based upon bodily attributes and appearance, see Mikeal C. Parsons, *Body and Character in Luke and Acts: The Subversion of Physiognomy in Early Christianity* (Grand Rapids: Baker, 2006).

20. See further, Joel B. Green, "Jesus and a Daughter of Abraham (Luke 13:10–17): Test Case for a Lucan Perspective on Jesus' Miracles," *CBQ* 51 (1989): 643–54, esp. 651–53.

ance from God's enemies.[21] A similar designation of Zacchaeus, the rich but short-in-stature tax collector (19:1–3), occurs in Luke 19:9 when Jesus declares him to be "a son of Abraham." As Zacchaeus engages in his quest to *see Jesus* (19:3a), Jesus makes eye contact with the tax collector in the tree (19:5) and demands that Zacchaeus receive Jesus hospitably in his own home: "Hurry up and come down, for I must receive welcome in your home today" (19:5).[22] The shared hospitality between Jesus and Zacchaeus creates the context whereby Zacchaeus is able to engage in repentant practices of sharing possessions and making restitution for his former exploitative practices.[23] As a result of the shared hospitality and Zacchaeus's repentance, Jesus grants salvation to the former outcast and refers to him as a son of Abraham (19:9, 10). Just as Abraham was remembered as hosting the divine strangers in his dwelling and thereby received the promise of Isaac as a gift in return, so Zacchaeus welcomes the traveling Lord in his home and receives salvation. His sharing of his possessions for the poor demonstrates that he is one who will do the deeds of the hospitable Abraham (cf. Gen. 18:4).[24]

There are two further significant texts from Luke's Gospel that portray Abraham as granting or alternatively excluding individuals from eschatological fellowship/hospitality. We have already examined the parallel pericope of Luke 13:23–30 in our discussion of Matthew's Gospel (Matt 8:5–13). In response to someone's question whether only a few will be saved (13:23), Jesus declares that some will seek entrance to the eschatological banquet and will demand, "Open up for us" (13:25) and even declare to him, "we ate and drank together with you" (13:26). But Jesus will respond, "I never knew you, depart from me all of you workers of injustice" (13:27; cf. LXX Ps 6:9). Jesus warns that they will experience torment "when you see Abraham, Isaac, Jacob, and all the prophets in the kingdom of God, and you are cast outside and they will come from east and west and from north and south and will recline in the kingdom of God" (13:29). The parable contributes to Luke's reversal motif, for Jesus concludes the

---

21. This point is made clearly by Siker, *Disinheriting the Jews*, 111–12.

22. I have discussed the relationship of Luke 19:1–10 to the broader theme of hospitality in Luke-Acts in my *Divine Visitations and Hospitality to Strangers in Luke-Acts: An Interpretation of the Malta Episode in Acts 28:1–10*, NovTSup 153 (Leiden: Brill, 2013), 228–29.

23. I remain convinced of the traditional interpretation of this episode as a story of salvation. See, for example, the important parallels with Luke 5:27–32. For further defense, see Dennis Hamm, "Luke 19:8 Once Again: Does Zacchaeus Defend or Resolve?," *JBL* 107 (1988): 431–37.

24. Some of these parallels are set forth by Andrew E. Arterbury, "Zacchaeus: 'A Son of Abraham'?" in *Biblical Interpretation in Early Christian Gospels*, vol. 3, *The Gospel of Luke*, ed. Thomas R. Hatina, LNTS 376 (London: T&T Clark, 2010), 18–31, here 26–27.

parable with the words, "Behold, the last will be first and the first will be last" (13:30; cf. 14:11). This warning of impending eschatological inhospitality within the context of Luke's reversal motif is directed precisely against those who, within Luke's narrative, grumble and complain about Jesus extending salvation and welcome to those "sinners" and outcasts on the margins of society. They are warned not to presume their election will act as a safeguard for them, all the while continuing to act as "workers of injustice" (13:27; cf. 3:8). Just as John had stated, Jesus declares that they will be cut down like trees and cast into the fire if they remain unrepentant (13:6–9). More precisely, Jesus's parabolic warning is directed to those Pharisees who, in the very next chapter, eat and drink with Jesus but as a means of testing him (14:1; cf. 7:36–39; 11:37–44) and who refuse to receive the invitation to the master's "great feast" (14:16–24). Their grumbling at Jesus's extension of hospitality and table fellowship with tax collectors and sinners (15:1–2) shows them to be like the elder brother in the parable of the prodigal son (15:1–32) who refuses to join in with the joyous celebration of the father who has received back his son (15:28–29). Thus, Luke portrays eschatological salvation through the imagery of food, hospitality, and fellowship with Abraham and the patriarchs.[25]

A similar image of feasting or reclining with Abraham can be found in Jesus's parable of the rich man and Lazarus in 16:19–31. The parable functions as a critique of the greed of the wealthy who fail to show hospitality and perform acts of mercy to the poor.[26] The rich man "clothed in purple and fine linen joyously feasts in luxury every day" (16:19b) while Lazarus suffers "having been tossed outside his [i.e., the rich man's] gate" (16:20). At the very least, the rich man was obligated to show hospitality to the stranger "lying at his gate"—an obligation that is obvious to those familiar with Torah (e.g., Deut 14:28–29; 15:1–8). Poor Lazarus, covered in sores, longs "to be filled with some food falling from the table of the rich man" (16:21; cf. 15:16), but even table scraps are denied him. When the two men die, Lazarus is accompanied "by the angels" (16:22; cf. 15:10) into "Abraham's bosom," while the rich man descends to Hades (16:22b–23) where "he sees Abraham at a distance and Lazarus in his bosom" (16:23b). Contributing to the ironic reversal throughout the parable is the likelihood that "Abraham's bosom" (16:22–23) functions as the heavenly

---

25. There are a variety of Jewish and early Christian texts that speak of eschatological salvation in relationship to Abraham and the patriarchs. See, for example, Peter-Ben Smit, *Fellowship and Food in the Kingdom: Eschatological Meals and Scenes of Utopian Abundance in the New Testament*, WUNT 2/234 (Tübingen: Mohr Siebeck, 2008), 151–52.

26. I have written in more detail about this episode in my *Saved by Faith and Hospitality* (Grand Rapids: Eerdmans, 2017).

and eschatological counterpart to the earthly banqueting of the rich man. The reason for the rich man's punishment is obvious; his punishment is not the result of his wealth but is his luxurious consumption and refusal to share with the poor stranger at his gate. Not unlike Jesus's warning to "workers of injustice" in 13:27, so here the man's unjust use of possessions and lack of deeds of mercy result in his being barred from fellowship with Abraham in paradise.

Jesus's use of "Abraham" as character and "Abraham's bosom" as image of the messianic feast is not accidental given Abraham's reputation as a paragon of hospitality. Had the rich man been a son of Abraham he would have bestowed hospitality upon the stranger at his gate. It is fitting, then, that the inhospitable rich man is denied access to the feast with the hospitable Abraham, for the rich man is not of the same lineage or heritage (cf. Luke 3:8; 13:26–29). Those who do not extend hospitality to those to whom the Messiah bestows welcome will not share in the Messiah's feast.[27] Further, in response to the rich man's request to send Lazarus back to warn his household, Abraham twice tells him, "They have Moses and the Prophets, let them listen to them" (16:29; cf. 16:31). According to Jesus, the rich man is a Torah-breaker and Prophet-rejecter, for these Scriptures teach hospitality to the poor, love of neighbor, and the extension of one's possessions to those in need (cf. 11:37–54).[28]

The Acts of the Apostles

In the Acts of the Apostles, Abraham is invoked in the speeches of Peter (3:13, 25), Stephen (7:2–8, 16–17, 32), and Paul (13:26) primarily to demonstrate continuity between God's election of Israel *and* the life, death, and resurrection of Jesus of Nazareth. After the healing of the lame man at the temple (3:1–10), Peter engages in a lengthy speech that has the primary purpose of arguing that this healing has taken place as an example of the restoration blessings proceeding from the resurrected and enthroned Jesus of Nazareth (3:11–26). Robert Brawley rightly notes that the "healing of the lame man at the Temple gate is a concrete case of God's bestowal of Abrahamic blessings."[29] The man functions as an instance of how God's Abrahamic blessings reach all peoples.

---

27. On the conceptual blending and background of the image of "Abraham's bosom," see Alexey Somov and Vitaly Voinov, "'Abraham's Bosom' (Luke 16:22–23) as a Key Metaphor in the Overall Composition of the Parable of the Rich Man and Lazarus," *CBQ* 79 (2017): 615–33.

28. E.g., Isaiah 61:1 and 58:6 in Luke 4:18–19; Leviticus 19:16–18, 33–34 in Luke 10:26–29; Deuteronomy 15:7–11 in Acts 4:32–35.

29. Robert L. Brawley, "Abrahamic Covenant Traditions and the Characterization of

Abraham in the Synoptic Gospels and the Acts of the Apostles

The theme of continuity between God's election of Israel and his resurrection of Jesus is set forth clearly in 3:13: "The God of Abraham, Isaac, Jacob, the God of our fathers, has glorified his servant Jesus" (ἐδόξασεν τὸν παῖδα αὐτοῦ Ἰησοῦν). The rhetorical force of this statement is brought forth in Peter's depiction of Jesus as one that Israel's leaders handed over to Pilate to be crucified but "God raised him from the dead" (3:15b). God has ironically used their ignorance and rejection of the Messiah as a means of fulfilling his scriptural promises (3:17–18). But God has resurrected Jesus from the dead, and thus Peter exhorts the people to repent so that they might experience "times of refreshment from the face of the Lord" (3:19–20). The God of Abraham who has resurrected Jesus from the dead enables the glorified Messiah to send forth times of refreshment (3:21). Therefore, Peter exhorts them to turn to God and to pay attention to what God has done. They are "the sons of the prophets and of the covenant which God established with your fathers saying to Abraham, 'In your seed [ἐν τῷ σπέρματί] all the peoples of the earth will be blessed'" (3:25). Peter quotes the Abrahamic promise from Genesis (here Gen 12:3; 22:18) that Abraham would be the means whereby God would bless all the peoples of the earth.[30] But here the emphasis is upon Peter's call to Israel to embrace their Messiah, for "to you first, God has raised up his servant and has sent him *in order to bless you* [εὐλογοῦντα ὑμᾶς] in order that each one of you might turn away from your evil deeds" (3:26). Luke creates a connection here between God's promise to bless all the families of the earth "in his seed" (3:25b) *and* Jesus who blesses Israel (3:26).[31] God's fulfillment of his promises to Abraham are universal in scope and will reach to all the nations, but Peter is emphatic that the order is first Israel *and then* the nations (cf. Luke 2:30–32).

In Paul's sermon in Pisidian Antioch (Acts 13:16–41), he too seeks to establish continuity between God's election of Israel (13:16–23) and God's resurrection of Jesus the Davidic Messiah (13:23–37). Though Abraham is not invoked directly, Paul's beginning statement that "the God of this people Israel has chosen our father and the people" is a simple affirmation of God's election of

---

God in Luke-Acts," in *The Unity of Luke-Acts*, ed. J. Verheyden, BETL 142 (Leuven: Leuven University Press, 1999), 109–32, here 125.

30. On the inclusion of the gentiles through the fulfillment of the Abrahamic promises, see Jacob Jervell, *Luke and the People of God: A New Look at Luke-Acts* (Minneapolis: Augsburg, 1972), 58–61.

31. A good case can be made for understanding "seed" in Acts 3:26 as referring to both Israel and the Messiah from the line of David. See further the helpful comments by Susan Wendel, *Scriptural Interpretation and Community Self-Definition in Luke-Acts and the Writings of Justin Martyr*, NovTSup 139 (Leiden: Brill, 2011), 223–24.

PART ONE: GOD'S ACTS FOR ISRAEL

Abraham and Israel as his covenant people. Paul's selective retelling of Israel's history is quite clearly geared toward David as the historical retelling of Israel's history drives toward God's fulfillment of promises made to David in 2 Samuel 7:12–14: "God has, from [David's] seed, and according to his promise, brought forth for Israel the Savior Jesus" (13:23). Just as in Peter's speech, so here Paul situates the basic christological kerygma within Israel's history and then exhorts his contemporary audience, "Men, brothers, children of the people of Abraham, and those among you who fear God, this word of salvation has been sent to us" (13:26). Just as Peter exhorts his audience as "the sons of the covenant" to pay attention to what the God of Abraham and the patriarchs (3:13) has done in raising Jesus for their benefit (3:25–26), so Paul now exhorts the synagogue in audience to recognize that the meaning of Israel's history and the election of Abraham are now discerned only in God's act of raising Jesus from the dead (13:30–37). Both Peter's and Paul's speeches are more directly concerned with God's promises to David, but Nils Dahl is right that Luke understands that "all messianic prophecies reiterate and unfold the one promise to the fathers, first given to Abraham."[32]

Stephen engages in some sustained reflection upon the patriarch Abraham in his lengthy defense speech (7:2–53). Stephen's emphasis upon Abraham centers upon his relation to the land and minimizes the covenant of circumcision.[33] Unsurprisingly, Stephen begins his speech with God's calling and election of Abraham in Mesopotamia (7:2). Thus, Stephen's argument, like Peter's in Acts 3 and Paul's in Acts 13, situates God's actions in Jesus of Nazareth (albeit here in an analogous or typological rather than kerygmatic form) within the context of God's election of Abraham and the people of Israel. This is all rather typical to form for Luke-Acts, but Stephen surprisingly emphasizes Abraham as an immigrant and sojourner who encounters God outside of the land of Israel.[34] Thus, "the God of glory appeared to our father Abraham while he was in Mesopotamia" (7:2); God called him to leave his land and his family to a new place (7:3); Abraham dwelt in Haran (7:4); God brought him into Canaan but gave him none of the land as his own possession (7:5).[35] David

---

32. Dahl, "Story of Abraham in Luke-Acts," 148. On the relationship between God's promises to Abraham and David, see Brawley, "Abrahamic Covenant Traditions," 111–15.

33. See further Joachim Jeska, *Die Geschicte Israels in der Sicht des Lukas: Apg 7,2b-53 und 13,17–25 im Kontext antik-jüdischer Summarien der Geschichte Israels*, FRLANT 195 (Göttingen: Vandenhoeck and Ruprecht, 2001), 155–61.

34. See throughout Craig S. Keener, *Acts: An Exegetical Commentary*, vol. 2, *3:1–14:28* (Grand Rapids: Baker Academic, 2013), 1351–1362.

35. Siker, *Disinheriting the Jews*, 121: "Luke highlights in particular the relationship be-

Abraham in the Synoptic Gospels and the Acts of the Apostles

Moessner rightly notes that "movement to the 'land' is the dynamic pivot of the plot" in Stephen's speech.[36] Later, Stephen makes the surprising comment that Jacob and his sons were buried "in the tomb that Abraham purchased for some silver from the sons of Hamor in Shechem" (7:15–16). This is in tension with the LXX which indicates that Jacob was buried in Hebron (LXX Gen 49:29–32). However we explain the incongruity, Stephen's note that Jacob and his sons were buried outside Judea fits the portrait of Abraham who encountered God outside the land of Israel and who spent his life as a sojourner without a homeland. This fits with one important theme of Stephen's speech, namely, the common theme that Israel's patriarchs and heroes encountered the God of Israel outside the land of Israel and beyond the Jerusalem temple.[37]

Worthy of note is Stephen's quotation of Genesis 15:13–14 in Acts 7:6–7 to the effect that God had foretold that Abraham's offspring would be sojourners in a strange land, would be enslaved for four hundred years, and after these things would then "worship me in this place" (7:7b). Luke here has actually conflated Genesis 15:13–14 and Exodus 3:12. Whereas the former indicates that after God's judgment upon Egypt, "they shall come out with great possessions" (Gen 15:14), the latter text notes that "you will serve God upon this mountain" (Exod 3:12). As numerous commentators have noted, the effect of this change or conflation is to center the promise to Abraham upon worshipping God in the land. And this aspect of Stephen's speech makes an important connection with Zechariah's hymn in Luke 1:68–79, which links God's covenantal mercies to Abraham with the promise of deliverance from one's enemies (1:72–75).[38] One of the effects of Stephen's linkage of the land with worship, then, is to declare that those who commit idolatry and do not worship the God of Abraham cut themselves off from the Abrahamic promises and blessings (cf. 3:22–26).[39]

---

tween Abraham and the land, but he does so in such a way that he actually undercuts the significance of the promise of the land per se."

36. David P. Moessner, "'The Christ Must Suffer': New Light on the Jesus—Peter, Stephen, Paul Parallels in Luke-Acts," in *Luke the Historian of Israel's Legacy, Theologian of Israel's "Christ": A New Reading of the "Gospel Acts" of Luke*, BZNW 182 (Berlin: de Gruyter, 2016), 246.

37. See here the very helpful and illuminating essay by Gregory E. Sterling, "'Opening the Scriptures': The Legitimation of the Jewish Diaspora and the Early Christian Mission," in *Jesus and the Heritage of Israel: Luke's Narrative Claim upon Israel's Legacy*, ed. David P. Moessner (Harrisburg, PA: Trinity Press International, 1999), 199–217.

38. Helpful here is Robert L. Brawley, *Luke-Acts and the Jews: Conflict, Apology, and Conciliation*, SBLMS 33 (Atlanta: Scholars Press, 1987), 118–32.

39. Wendel, *Scriptural Interpretation*, 218.

PART ONE: GOD'S ACTS FOR ISRAEL

The majority of the rest of Stephen's speech expands upon the events predicted in 7:2–8. Thus, the Joseph story shows how Abraham's offspring find their way to Egypt (7:9–16), and the Moses story depicts how God leads them out of slavery and judges the Egyptians (7:18–36). Stephen portrays God as one who fulfills the promises made to Abraham as he had described them in Acts 7:2–8. Perhaps this is seen most clearly when Stephen portrays the initial fulfillment of God's promise to Abraham in 7:17, which hearkens back to God's prediction in 7:6, namely, the events of the exodus.[40] Sadly, however, the fulfillment of 7:17 is frustrated by means of the rejection of God's chosen deliverer (Moses) and through worshipping false gods (esp. 7:39–43). Instead of securing the Abrahamic promises and blessings through worshipping God in the land, the people's idolatry blocks the longed-for and promised fulfillment of the Abrahamic blessings.[41]

THE GOSPEL OF JOHN

Abraham only appears in the Fourth Gospel in one passage, and yet the entire back-and-forth between Jesus and his conversation partners centers upon the meaning of Abrahamic paternity (John 8:31–59), initiated by Jesus's audience's retort to his teaching that "we are the seed of Abraham" (8:33a). This stretch of text is notoriously difficult, and its reception history, in particular the reference to "your father the devil" (8:44), has been deplorable.[42] I intend here, however, to primarily focus upon the major themes and exegetical questions raised by the references to Abraham in John 8.

First, I suggest that Jesus's audience should not be understood as "the Jewish people" but rather as "those Jews who had believed in him" (τοὺς πεπιστευκότας αὐτῷ Ἰουδαίους, 8:31). I suggest that the perfect participle should be taken as a reference to those Jews who had professed belief in Jesus but who were no longer following him (cf. also John 11:45–46).[43] This group is

---

40. See further, Dahl, "Story of Abraham in Luke-Acts," 144.

41. Wendel, *Scriptural Interpretation*, 221.

42. There is a host of literature devoted to John and Judaism. Good starting points both broadly and with respect to John 8 are, respectively, Christopher W. Skinner, *Reading John*, Cascade Companions (Eugene, OR: Cascade, 2015), 47–67; Adele Reinhartz, "John 8:31–59 from a Jewish Perspective," in *Remembering for the Future: The Holocaust in an Age of Genocide*, ed. John K. Roth et al. (London: Palgrave, 2001), 2:787–97.

43. On the perfect participle as having the possibility of indicating a state that no longer holds for the action of the main verb, see especially Terry Griffith, "'The Jews Who Had Believed in Him' (John 8:31) and the Motif of Apostasy in the Gospel of John," in *The Gospel*

distinguished, then, from the group referred to in 8:30: "the many who believed in him." This is further justified by means of contextual observations. For example, it is difficult to imagine that within the span of a few verses a group comes to believe in Jesus and then seeks to stone him, referring to him as a Samaritan with a demon (8:48). The audience is, after all, referred to as *not believing* Jesus twice in 8:45-46. Further, given that John 7:1-8:30 focuses on Jesus's discourses articulating the meaning of the Feast of Tabernacles, it is likely that 8:31-59 should be connected with the immediately preceding discourse in 6:60-71. Here John describes many of Jesus's disciples who chafe and grumble at Jesus's difficult bread of life discourse (6:60-61). These disciples are "scandalized" by Jesus's teaching (6:61b), and as a result, many "of his disciples" stopped following Jesus (6:66). This fits more broadly within John's anthropological pessimism and his depiction of faith in Jesus as often lacking or insufficient (see especially John 2:23-25).[44]

Second, it is important to note that within this context, and within the broader narrative of John's Gospel, the devil functions as one who motivates people to commit apostasy. Thus, within the context of disciples who had once believed but are now turning away from Jesus, Jesus refers to Judas as a "devil" (6:70). Later John notes that "the devil" had put it into Judas's heart to betray Jesus (13:2; cf. 13:27).[45] Thus, Jesus's statement in 8:44 that "you are of your father the devil" should not be taken to refer to a polemic against the Jewish people *in toto* but is, rather, a *still remarkably harsh* reference to those fellow Jews who *had at one time believed in Jesus but now having committed apostasy are seeking to murder Jesus*. Griffith notes, then, that "it would be wrong to conclude from 8:44 that John regarded all Jews as children of the devil. The language of *diabolization* is restricted to those who had once been followers of Jesus and is appropriate to them alone."[46]

Third, the debate between Jesus and his audience as to who belongs to their father Abraham centers not upon biological genealogical descent but, rather,

---

of John and Christian Theology, ed. Richard Bauckham and Carl Mosser (Grand Rapids: Eerdmans, 2008), 183-92, here 183-84. See further James Swetnam, "The Meaning of Πεπιστευκότας in John 8,31," *Bib* 61 (1980): 106-9.

44. See Edwyn Clement Hoskyns, *The Fourth Gospel* (London: Faber and Faber, 1947), 338, who notes that this discourse is addressed to "the Jews who believed when they saw His miracles, and to whom Jesus did not trust Himself (ii. 23, 24, cf. vii. 31, xi. 45, xii. 11, 42, 43)."

45. Griffith, "'The Jews Who Had Believed in Him,'" 186-87.

46. Griffith, "'The Jews Who Had Believed in Him,'" 186-91. Griffith further notes that this conclusion fits well with 1 John 3:14-15. See Terry Griffith, *Keep Yourselves from Idols: A New Look at 1 John*, JSNTSup 233 (London: Sheffield Academic, 2002).

upon who does "the deeds of Abraham" (8:39). Jesus shifts the conversation from "seed/offspring" of Abraham to "children of Abraham" and seems to define Abrahamic "paternity [as] strictly a matter of behavior" so that Abraham's children are those who do what Abraham did.[47] Abraham is held up as a model for emulation.[48] I think a strong case can be made here that Jesus's reference to "the deeds of Abraham" (τὰ ἔργα τοῦ Ἀβραάμ, 8:39b) should be understood as a reference to Abraham's extension of hospitality to the divine visitors in Genesis 18. It is well known that Abraham was understood within Jewish tradition as an exemplar of hospitality to strangers, and this portrait of hospitable Abraham was also carried on by early Christian texts as well, for example in James 2:20–26, which also refers to Abraham's deeds.[49]

But hospitality and inhospitality to Jesus and his word also play significant theological roles within John's Gospel. Thus, the prologue notes, "He came to his own and his own did not receive [οὐ παρέλαβον] him, but to as many as did receive him [ἔλαβον αὐτόν], he gave them the right to become children of God [τέκνα θεοῦ], to those who believe [τοῖς πιστεύουσιν] in his name" (John 1:11–12). John's prologue thus characterizes divine paternity in terms of whether or not one provides a welcoming or believing response to Jesus, the divine Word. I have argued that hospitality has a significant theological role in terms of humans welcoming the stranger from heaven who himself extends "redemptive hospitality" (bread, water, wine, foot washing, and entrance into his Father's home).[50] Steven Hunt has also noted that the language of hospitality is "a major motif in the narrative, as the author uses a cluster of words to talk about reception, favoring the word λαμβάνω which gets employed mostly with the sense of receiving Jesus (1:12; 5:43; 6:21; 13:20) or his word (see, e.g., 3:11, 32–33; 17:8)."[51] But instead of doing Abraham's deeds and receiving

---

47. Levenson, *Abraham between Torah and Gospel*, 36.

48. Catrin H. Williams, "Patriarchs and Prophets Remembered: Framing Israel's Past in the Gospel of John," in *Abiding Words: The Use of Scripture in the Gospel of John*, ed. Alicia D. Myers and Bruce G. Schuchard (Atlanta: SBL Press, 2015), 187–212, here 202.

49. There are a host of texts one could set forth here. I have examined them in more detail in my *Divine Visitations* 131–55. On Abraham's deeds in James 2 as inclusive of his mercy and hospitality to strangers, see Roy Bowen Ward, "The Works of Abraham: James 2:14–26," *HTR* 61 (1968): 283–90.

50. Jipp, *Saved by Faith and Hospitality*, chapter 3.

51. Steven A. Hunt, "And the Word Became Flesh—Again? Jesus and Abraham in John 8:31–59," in *Perspectives on Our Father Abraham: Essays in Honor of Marvin R. Wilson* (Grand Rapids: Eerdmans, 2012), 81–109, here 88. Similarly, see Williams, "Patriarchs and Prophets Remembered," 202–5.

Jesus the divine stranger with hospitality, Jesus's audience in John 8 persists in inhospitality to Jesus and his teaching. Thus, they do not continue in Jesus's word (8:31); they seek to kill Jesus because his word does not remain in them (8:37, 45, 46); they have heard divine truth but are trying to kill him (8:40); they do not accept Jesus's word (8:43). They extend inhospitality to Jesus and his word, and thereby they demonstrate that God is not their Father (8:42, 47). One belongs to Abraham, then, if one provides a hospitable response to the heavenly messenger Jesus and his word who, for the author of the Fourth Gospel, has been sent by God. It would seem, then, that for John's Gospel, Jesus's audience is the "offspring of Abraham" (8:33, 37) but not "children of Abraham" (8:39).[52] Both Isaac and Ishmael are the offspring of Abraham, but only Isaac is construed as one of Abraham's children; those who receive Jesus are construed as Abraham's free children who remain in his house forever (8:34–36). Hunt nicely re-paraphrases Jesus's argument: "'If you were Abraham's children, you would be showing the hospitality that Abraham showed when he welcomed me and received my word. In trying to kill me, you are doing the opposite of what Abraham did.'"[53]

Fourth, Abraham was understood in a variety of Jewish traditions as one who saw the glory of God in visions (e.g., Gen 15; *Testament of Abraham*; 4 Ezra 3:14).[54] But Jesus makes the audacious assertion that "Your father Abraham rejoiced that *he saw my day*, and he saw it and rejoiced" (John 8:56). In response to the audience's outrage, Jesus declares, "Before Abraham came into being, I am" (8:58), and they seek to stone him for blasphemy (8:59). Jesus's declaration declares that Abraham is subordinate to him and that he is divine alongside God the Father. If "the works of Abraham" in John 8:39 refer to Abraham's hospitality to the divine visitors in Genesis 18, then the mutual seeing of Jesus and Abraham may further allude to Abraham's seeing the pre-incarnate Word as the divine visitor and extending hospitality to him in his tent. Thus, Abraham is made to conform to John's larger theological vision of Jesus as the focal point of Israel's Scriptures, institutions, and visionary experiences of Israel's heroes.[55]

---

52. So Hunt, "And the Word Became Flesh—Again?" 94.
53. Hunt, "And the Word Became Flesh—Again?" 97.
54. See here John Ashton, *Understanding the Fourth Gospel*, 2nd ed. (Oxford: Oxford University Press, 2007), 300–301.
55. See Williams, "Patriarchs and Prophets Remembered," 205–6.

PART ONE: GOD'S ACTS FOR ISRAEL

Conclusion

My study of Abraham demonstrates that each composition draws upon the figure of Abraham for diverse purposes. Surprisingly, Mark's Gospel shows no serious interest at all in Abraham, as even the singular pericope which refers to Abraham does not actually center upon him in any meaningful way. While it is difficult to make an argument from silence, it may be that Mark's Gospel, as an apocalyptic drama, is simply less interested in making the kinds of salvation-historical claims for continuity between Israel and Jesus as are other NT compositions. Unlike Mark's Gospel, Abraham rises to a consistent theme and even a character within the narrative world of Luke-Acts. Further, the Gospel of Luke is the only text which takes up Abraham into its broader theme of "reversal" in order to show that outcasts, the sick, and the poor are not excluded from the people of God. The Gospel of Matthew draws upon Abraham to make claims of salvation-historical continuity, but the narrative shows little, if any, interest in the moral character of Abraham, whereas in Luke and John one finds allusions to Abraham's hospitality to strangers, his believing response to God, and his being the forefather of the repentant. And John's Gospel seems to be the only text examined which holds up Abraham as one who saw the glory of the pre-incarnate Christ. It is surprising, at least to me, that Abraham's near sacrifice of Isaac (the *Akedah*) in Genesis 22, does not play a more direct role (at least beyond echoes and allusions) in the NT texts examined above, as it does, for example, in James 2:20–26.[56]

There are, however, significant commonalities across the NT compositions in the way in which they draw upon Abraham. Let me conclude by simply noting four of them. First, except for the Gospel of Mark, every text draws upon Abraham to establish continuity between God's election of Israel *and* the person of Jesus and those believing in him as Israel's Messiah. And this claim of continuity is one that would appear to be deeply contested as Jewish believers in Jesus are defining Abrahamic descent through Jesus of Nazareth. This is most obvious in Luke-Acts where, within Luke, the births of John and Jesus are interpreted within the framework of the stories of Abraham and Sarah, and in Acts where the basic kerygma is situated within God's election of Abraham and Israel. But one sees a similar dynamic in John 8 where "children of Abraham" are defined not *only* by genealogical descent but also through doing the deeds of Abraham.

[56]. See, however, L. A. Huizenga, *The New Isaac: Tradition and Intertextuality in the Gospel of Matthew*, NovTSup 131 (Leiden: Brill, 2009).

Second, for these texts, while God may be doing something surprising in the person of Jesus, these events are to be understood within the framework of God's prior promises to, and election of, Israel as his people. But the continuity is also readily apparent in Matthew's genealogy, which refers to Jesus as within the line of Abraham and as Abraham's son. Third, God's covenant with Abraham and his later covenantal promises to David are inextricably bound together in both Matthew's Gospel and Luke-Acts. Thus, they portray the seed of David as the only one who can inherit and bring to fulfillment God's promises to Abraham. Fourth, Abraham is a model for appropriate behavior. Children of Abraham demonstrate their identity through repentance, hospitality, and the sharing of possessions in Matthew, Luke, and John. Fifth and finally, both Mark and Luke portray Abraham as one who already experiences a blessed afterlife and who receives his children into this eschatological fellowship and banquet.

5

"For David Did Not Ascend into Heaven . . ." (Acts 2:34a)

Reprogramming Royal Psalms to Proclaim the Enthroned-in-Heaven King

One of the surprising aspects of Luke's narration of Jesus's ascent into heaven in Acts 1:9–11 is the brevity with which Luke describes this event. While there are some similarities with 2 Kings 2:7–12, the account of Elijah's heavenly rapture is unable to fully explain the meaning of Jesus's ascent into heaven in Acts.[1] Whereas Elijah's heavenly location is no longer mentioned again after 2 Kings 2 and exerts no influence on the rest of the narrative, Jesus's location in heaven continues to exert enormous influence on the rest of Acts.[2] The importance of Jesus's location in heaven is already signaled to the reader through the fourfold repetition in 1:9–11 of Jesus's being "in heaven" (εἰς τὸν οὐρανόν). While Luke clearly places great weight on God's resurrection of Jesus as the royal enthronement whereby God fulfills his promises to David, without the narration of Jesus's heavenly ascent, the reader could potentially fail to understand how the resurrected Messiah continues his work as Israel's enthroned king in

---

1. I emphasize the word "fully" here. See, however, the strong conclusions of Arie W. Zwiep, *The Ascension of the Messiah in Lukan Christology*, NovTSup 87 (Leiden: Brill, 1997), 59–63, 194; Craig S. Keener, *Acts: An Exegetical Commentary*, vol. 1, *Introduction and 1:1–2:47* (Grand Rapids: Baker Academic, 2012), 718–20.

2. See here especially, Matthew Sleeman, *Geography and the Ascension Narrative in Acts*, SNTSMS 146 (Cambridge: Cambridge University Press, 2009); Alan J. Thompson, *The Acts of the Risen Lord Jesus: Luke's Account of God's Unfolding Plan*, NSBT 27 (Downers Grove, IL: InterVarsity Press, 2011).

"For David Did Not Ascend into Heaven..." (Acts 2:34a)

heaven.[3] Thus, making precise distinctions between Luke's interpretation of resurrection and ascension is notoriously difficult.[4] While resurrection and ascension are not interchangeable but rather refer to different chronological moments within Luke's two-volume narrative, they are necessarily integrated into Luke's conception of the Messiah's heavenly exaltation/enthronement.

In this chapter, I will argue that Luke's frequent and programmatic use of royal psalms functions to set forth Jesus's ascension as the event whereby Israel's Messiah is enthroned in heaven and enters into a more powerful rule through which he inaugurates and establishes the kingdom of God.[5] In other words, at the ascension, God completes the process of exalting his son by enthroning him to a position of heavenly rule from where the messianic king reigns over his people, judges his enemies, and extends the sphere of his dominion. As such, Luke's depiction of Jesus's ascension as the event whereby the Messiah enters into his heavenly rule has literary significance beyond the description of the actual event as Jesus is seen as continuing to enact his kingship and establish God's kingdom from heaven. The narration of Jesus's ascent into heaven occurs immediately after Jesus and the disciples have been discussing "the kingdom of God" (τῆς βασιλείας τοῦ θεοῦ, Acts 1:3–4), Jesus's restoration of the "kingdom to Israel" (τὴν βασιλείαν τῷ Ἰσραήλ, 1:6), and the kingdom's expansion to Jerusalem, into the northern and southern kingdoms of Israel, and to the gentiles (Acts 1:8). Thus, the geographical expansion of God's kingdom (1:8) is "produced under a Christological heaven" as the enthroned king establishes

---

3. See Thomas F. Torrance, *Space, Time and Resurrection* (Grand Rapids: Eerdmans, 1976), 111: "It is ultimately in that fusion of resurrection with the ascension in one indivisible exaltation that we are to understanding the continuing ministry of Christ."

4. See similarly, Steve Walton, "'The Heavens Opened': Cosmological and Theological Transformation in Luke and Acts," in *Cosmology and New Testament Theology*, ed. Jonathan T. Pennington and Sean M. McDonough, LNTS (London: T&T Clark, 2008), 60–73, here 64–65. Kevin L. Anderson, *"But God Raised Him from the Dead": The Theology of Jesus's Resurrection in Luke-Acts* (Eugene, OR: Wipf & Stock, 2006), 216: "The Lukan material on resurrection, ascension, and exaltation provides the reader with telescoping or overlapping images. A dynamism exists in the relationship between the three theological concepts that defies precise schematization."

5. Similarly, see Luke Timothy Johnson, *The Acts of the Apostles*, SP 5 (Collegeville, MN: Liturgical Press, 1992), 30: "Luke clearly understands [the ascension] to be Jesus' enthronement as King, and therefore as Messiah. By means of this ascent, Luke enables us to envisage the resurrected Jesus not as a resuscitated corpse or wraith but as one living in power 'at the right hand of God.'"

God's rule (1:9-11).[6] Jesus's ascension into heaven shows how God's messianic king reigns not from the earthly Jerusalem, but from God's right hand.

The Enthroned Davidic King in the Psalter

Perhaps *the* central hope of Israel's royal psalms is the anticipation that God will establish his kingdom and rule over his people through his chosen Davidic king (Pss 89:3, 20; 132:11). This king, often referred to as "the Lord's Anointed" (Pss 2:2; 18:50; 20:6; 89:38; 132:17), was viewed as invested with divine authority and power as God's royal agent.[7] Israel's royal ideology even refers to the Lord's Anointed as "God's Son" as a means of emphasizing God's investiture of him with divine authority and power to rule (Pss 2:6-9; 89:26-28; cf. 2 Sam 7:12-14). The intimate relationship between God and his messiah even allowed the latter to operate as a vessel for God's Spirit (1 Sam 16:13; Isa 11:1-2; 61:1-3; Pss. Sol. 17:22, 37; 18:5-8).[8] Despite the king's favored status by God, he is frequently the target of intense persecution and opposition from those political rebels who refuse to recognize his authority. This is seen throughout the Davidic Psalms where the royal figure's humiliating sufferings are on display (Pss 22:14-18; 38:5-8; 69:16-20). The opposition to the king is established programmatically in Psalm 2 where "the kings of the earth" and "the rulers" attempt to destroy "the Lord and his anointed" (Ps 2:2-3). God's response to the political pretenders is to rescue his son and enthrone him on Zion:[9]

---

6. Sleeman, *Geography*, 79. On the way in which Acts 1:8 reflects a "Davidic map that reflects the theological geography of God's covenant pledge concerning the extent of the Davidic empire," see Scott W. Hahn, *Kinship by Covenant: A Canonical Approach to the Fulfillment of God's Saving Promises*, AYBRL (New Haven: Yale University Press, 2009), 231.

7. Tryggve N. D. Mettinger, *King and Messiah: The Civil and Sacral Legitimation of the Israelite Kings*, CBOT 8 (Lund: Gleerup, 1976), 199.

8. Aubrey R. Johnson, *Sacral Kingship in Ancient Israel* (Cardiff: University of Wales Press, 1967), 114-15.

9. Without endorsing all of the specific proposals for the *Sitz im Leben* of the enthronement Psalms, see the helpful discussions of the royal enthronement ceremony in G. Cooke, "The Israelite King as Son of God," ZAW 73 (1961): 202-25; A. Johnson, *Sacral Kingship*, 24-25; Sigmund Mowinckel, *He That Cometh: The Messiah Concept in the Old Testament and Later Judaism*, trans. G. W. Anderson (Grand Rapids: Eerdmans, 2005), 96-98; John H. Eaton, *Kingship and the Psalms*, SBT 2/32 (London: SCM, 1976), 111-13; Mark W. Hamilton, *The Body Royal: The Social Poetics of Kingship in Ancient Israel*, BibInt 78 (Leiden: Brill, 2005), 60-82; J. J. M. Roberts, "The Old Testament's Contribution to Messianic Expectations," in *The Messiah: Developments in Earliest Judaism and Christianity*, ed. James H. Charlesworth (Minneapolis: Fortress, 1992), 39-51.

"For David Did Not Ascend into Heaven..." (Acts 2:34a)

> "I have set my king on Zion my holy hill."
> I will declare the Lord's decree:
> He said to me, "You are my son; today I have begotten you.
> Ask of me, and I will make the nations your inheritance
> and the ends of the earth your possession."
>
> (Ps 2:6–8)

The decree preserves the installation of the Davidic king who, as God's Son, is granted a share in God's sovereign rule.

In Psalm 110, God enthrones the king above his enemies, shares with him the title of Lord, and invites him to sit at God's right hand:

> The Lord says to my lord, "Sit at my right hand
> until I make your enemies a footstool under your feet."
> The Lord sends out from Zion your mighty scepter.
> Rule in the midst of your enemies.
>
> (Ps 110:1–2)

The messianic king's enthronement results in the king sharing in God's throne and ruling over and shepherding God's people.[10] As such, the king's enthronement results in a period of righteous rule as the people experience peace and prosperity (Pss 72:5–7, 15–16; 144:11–14); alternatively, the king's vindication results in his execution of judgment against his enemies (Pss 2:8–9; 72:8; 89:23; 110:2).

The Psalter's depiction of God's reign through his anointed son stems, of course, from his promise to David in 2 Samuel 7: "I will raise up after you your seed, who will come from your body, and I will establish his kingdom" (2 Sam 7:12; cf. 1 Chr 17:11). The Chronicler frames the Davidic covenant as establishing the closest possible link between God's kingdom and the rule of his Davidic ruler. Thus, even as David declares the supremacy of God's kingship (1 Chr 17:20–21), he also points to God's exaltation of him to a high rank and honor: "You exalt me as someone of high rank, O Lord God [ὕψωσάς με, κύριε ὁ θεός]! And what more can David say to you for glorifying [τοῦ δοξάσαι] your servant?" (1 Chr 17:17b–18).[11] The relationship between the Davidic king and the divine kingdom can be seen in the Chronicler's rendering of the promise to David where there is a clear interrelationship between the two: "I will establish his kingdom" (17:11), "I will establish his

---

10. See Shirley Lucass, *The Concept of the Messiah in the Scriptures of Judaism and Christianity*, LSTS 78 (New York: T&T Clark, 2011), 72.

11. Matthew Lynch, *Monotheism and Institutions in the Book of Chronicles: Temple, Priesthood, and Kingship in Post-Exilic Perspective*, FAT 2/64 (Tübingen: Mohr Siebeck, 2014), 229–30.

PART ONE: GOD'S ACTS FOR ISRAEL

throne forever" (17:12), and "I will confirm him in *my house* and in *my kingdom* forever, and *his throne* shall be established forever" (17:14).[12]

The Resurrection/Ascension as the Messiah's Heavenly Enthronement in Acts

But the Psalter's hope for a righteous king who would reign over Israel's enemies and the Chronicler's idealized depiction of a Davidide sharing God's throne and ruling over Israel had come to frustration through the exile. Psalm 89 states the cognitive dissonance between God's promises to rule the world through an exalted Davidic king (Ps 89:19, 24) and the present reality of exile:

> But you have spurned and rejected him.
> You have become enraged with your anointed.
> You have repudiated the covenant with your servant.
> You have completely dishonored his crown.
> You have broken down all his walls.
> You have reduced his fortified cities to ruins.
> All who pass by plunder him.
> He has become an object of ridicule to his neighbors.
> You have lifted high the right hand of his foes.
> You have made all his enemies rejoice.
>
> (Ps 89:38–42)

God had promised to "establish [David's] line forever, his throne as long as heaven lasts" (Ps 89:29), and yet, as Scott Hahn notes, the exile had "destroyed or damaged most of the fixtures of the Davidic kingdom: the king . . . [was] deposed and exiled, Jerusalem and its Temple destroyed, hope for reunification of Israel and Judah lost, and the Gentiles raised to rulership rather than vassalage with respect to God's people."[13]

Israel's central problem is taken up in the Gospel of Luke, where Jesus is portrayed as the Messiah who will restore David's kingdom to Israel. Gabriel's announcement to Mary activates the Davidic promises of 2 Samuel 7:12–14 and the Psalter in its description of Jesus's royal identity and the promise to bestow

---

12. Similarly, Scott W. Hahn, *The Kingdom of God as Liturgical Empire: A Theological Commentary on 1-2 Chronicles* (Grand Rapids: Baker, 2012), 75–77.
13. Hahn, *Kinship by Covenant*, 202.

"For David Did Not Ascend into Heaven . . ." (Acts 2:34a)

an everlasting kingdom upon him: "He will be great and will be called the son of the Most High. The Lord God will give to him the throne of David his father, and he will rule over the house of Jacob *forever* and his kingdom will have no end" (Luke 1:32–33). Similarly, Zechariah praises God for the redemption, salvation, protection, and mercy this Davidic king will bring "for the house of David" (Luke 1:68–74). While Luke is clear that Jesus is Messiah, Son of God, and Lord from his birth,[14] it is not until Jesus's resurrection and ascension in Acts 1:9–11 that he is enthroned to a position of universal power and actively establishes God's kingdom (cf. 1:8). Both Peter (in Acts 2:22–36) and Paul (in Acts 13:32–37) use the Psalter in order to interpret Jesus's resurrection and ascension as the installation of his Davidic Messiah as powerful king.

Peter at Pentecost (Acts 2:22–36)

There are four significant quotations and allusions to the Psalter in Acts 2:22–36 (Ps 18:4 [LXX 17:5] in Acts 2:24a; Ps 16:8–11 in Acts 2:25–28; Ps 132:11 in Acts 2:30; Ps 110:1 in Acts 2:34–35). Peter's speech immediately draws upon the Psalter to demonstrate the inability of death to keep Jesus underneath its power (οὐκ ἦν δυνατὸν κρατεῖσθαι αὐτὸν ὑπ' αὐτοῦ, 2:24b) when it refers to God as the one who "raised [Jesus] *by loosing the birth pangs of death*" (ἀνέστησεν λύσας τὰς ὠδῖνας τοῦ θανάτου, 2:24a).[15] The emphasized phrase almost certainly stems from Psalm 17:5 (LXX), where "David" cries to God and trusts God to rescue him out of the pangs of death and to exalt him over his enemies (17:49–50; Eng. 18:48–49).[16] The Psalm concludes with the summary, "[God] gives great victories to his king. He shows loyalty to his messiah, to David and his seed forever" (LXX Ps 17:51; Eng. 18:50). In Acts 2:22–36, however, Peter declares that while David is the speaker of the psalms, David is not their referent or subject matter; rather, David spoke in the psalms as a prophet (2:30) who looked forward to the Messiah's resurrection and exaltation into heaven (2:31–33).[17] More precisely, as Matthew Bates has argued, "David was not merely speaking *about*

---

14. See further here C. Kavin Rowe, *Early Narrative Christology: The Lord in the Gospel of Luke*, BZNW 139 (Berlin: de Gruyter, 2006).

15. The emphasized expression is difficult given the complicated relationship between the LXX translation ("pangs of death," in 2 Sam 22:6; Ps 17:5; Ps 114:3) of the Hebrew text (which, depending on its pointing, may be translated as "cord" or "travail.") For an extended discussion, see Anderson, *"But God Raised Him,"* 203–8.

16. Mark L. Strauss, *The Davidic Messiah in Luke-Acts: The Promise and Its Fulfillment in Lukan Christology*, JSNTSup 110 (Sheffield: Sheffield Academic, 1995), 136–37.

17. For the way in which Acts and other Second Temple Jewish sources depict David as a

him, but rather this yet-to-be-revealed Jesus was making an in-character speech at the time of David *through David*."[18] Peter justifies this reading by exploiting the fact that David is dead and buried and his tomb is accessible to the public in Jerusalem (2:29), but the psalms, specifically Psalm 15 (LXX), speak of a figure who is always joyfully living in God's presence, whose body will not experience decay, who will never be abandoned to Hades, and continues to experience the ways of life.[19] Thus, in Acts 2:31b, Peter declares it is the resurrected Messiah who is the referent of Psalm 16:9–10 (LXX 15:9–10) and who "has neither been abandoned into Hades nor has his flesh seen corruption." Peter's most creative interpretive move in his sermon—though one that is common in early Christian discourse—is his interpretation of the Messiah's resurrection from the dead with the fulfillment of God's promise to David: "God swore an oath to him [i.e., David] to seat on his throne [καθίσαι ἐπὶ τὸν θρόνον αὐτοῦ] one from the fruit of his loins" (LXX Ps 132:11; cf. Acts 13:23; Heb 1:5).[20] Luke's association of the Messiah's resurrection with his heavenly enthronement is hinted at by his use of καθίσαι (instead of θήσομαι from Ps 131:11; Eng. 132:11) as it looks forward to Psalm 109:1 (LXX; Eng. 110:1) and indicates "that the enthronement at God's right hand is understood by Luke as the fulfilment of God's promise to David to seat one of his descendants upon his throne."[21] Standing behind Psalm 131:11 (LXX) is obviously God's promise to David in 2 Samuel 7:12: "I will raise up after you your seed, who will come from your body, *and I will establish his kingdom*."[22] Jesus's resurrection, then, must be more than a return to mortal existence, given

---

prophetic figure, see Joseph A. Fitzmyer, "David 'Being Therefore a Prophet...' (Acts 2:30)," *CBQ* 34 (1972): 332–39.

18. Matthew W. Bates, *The Birth of the Trinity: Jesus, God, and Spirit in New Testament and Early Christian Interpretations of the Old Testament* (Oxford: Oxford University Press, 2015), 153.

19. See here especially, Donald Juel, "Social Dimensions of Exegesis: The Use of Psalm 16 in Acts 2," *CBQ* 43 (1981): 543–56; Anderson, *"But God Raised Him,"* 208–9.

20. Dennis C. Duling, "The Promises to David and Their Entrance into Christianity—Nailing Down a Likely Hypothesis," *NTS* 20 (1973): 55–77.

21. Strauss, *Davidic Messiah*, 139. On the interpretation of Psalm 109, see Jacques Dupont, "'Assis á la droite de Dieu.' L'interprétation du Ps. 110, 1 dans le Nouveau Testament," in *Resurrexit: Actes du Symposium International sur la résurrection de Jesus (Rome 1970)*, ed. Edouard Dhanis (Vatican City: Libreria Editrice Vaticana, 1974), 94–148. David P. Moessner, "Two Lords 'at the Right Hand'? The Psalms and an Intertextual Reading of Peter's Pentecost Speech (Acts 2:14–36)," in *Literary Studies in Luke-Acts: Essays in Honor of Joseph B. Tyson*, ed. Richard P. Thompson and Thomas E. Phillips (Macon, GA: Mercer University Press, 1998), 215–32.

22. Timo Eskola, *Messiah and Throne: Jewish Merkabah Mysticism and Early Christian Exaltation Discourse*, WUNT 2/142 (Tübingen: Mohr Siebeck, 2001), 164–65.

"For David Did Not Ascend into Heaven . . ." (Acts 2:34a)

Peter's declaration that the Davidic Messiah now reigns over God's kingdom and shares God's heavenly throne.[23] As Sleeman has noted: "There is an enthroned Davidic king, but one enthroned in heaven."[24]

Psalm 15 (LXX; Eng. 16) suits Peter's purposes nicely as it also speaks of this royal figure as one who is *located at God's right hand* (ἐκ δεξιῶν μου ἐστιν, 2:25b). The spatial placement of God's throne ("God's right hand") next to the messiah is what protects the referent of Psalm 15 from being shaken, and within the context of Acts 2:22–36, this almost certainly refers to God's assistance to sovereignly rescue his messianic son from death (cf. Acts 7:54–60).[25] The prepositional phrase also resonates loudly with the better-known Psalm 109 (LXX; Eng. 110) to which Peter turns in Acts 2:34–35.[26] Again, given that the Father has invited a second Lord to "sit at my right hand" (κάθου ἐκ δεξιῶν μου) until God has triumphed over all their enemies and placed them under the Lord's feet (2:35), this too cannot refer to David who "did not ascend into heaven" (2:34). Obviously, Peter's scriptural interpretation assumes the premise that God has raised Jesus from the dead and located him in a position of heavenly and royal power.[27] And Peter's threefold mention of the Messiah at God's right hand draws emphasis to the heavenly location of the Messiah's powerful rule.[28]

Peter's use of the Davidic psalms functions to establish that Jesus's resurrection and ascension are the means whereby God enthrones his Davidic king to a position of continuing heavenly rule. Peter brings together Psalms 15:11 (LXX) and 109:1 (LXX), in part because of their shared phrase "at the right hand" (ἐκ

---

23. Robert F. O'Toole, "Acts 2:30 and the Davidic Covenant of Pentecost," *JBL* 102 (1983): 245–58: "This promise of an eternal kingdom calls for a king to sit on the throne of that kingdom, this the resurrected Christ who lives forever achieves" (251).

24. Sleeman, *Geography*, 101.

25. Bates, *Birth of the Trinity*, 155: "Moreover, since the Father is in the less-elevated but authoritative station *at the Son's right hand*, the Father is ready to exercise sovereignty *on the Son's behalf*, poised to meet his need speedily by executing the Son's royal command should he so will."

26. Lidija Novakovic, *Raised from the Dead According to Scripture: The Role of Israel's Scripture in the Early Christian Interpretations of Jesus' Resurrection*, T&T Clark Jewish and Christian Texts Series 12 (London: T&T Clark, 2012), 203.

27. Luke Timothy Johnson, *Septuagintal Midrash in the Speeches of Acts*, The Père Marquette Lecture in Theology 2002 (Milwaukee: Marquette University Press, 2002), 40: "It should be obvious, however, that this argument is carried by a premise that few of Peter's hearers and only some of Luke's potential readers will grant: that Jesus the Nazorean is in fact now resurrected from the dead and living as powerful Lord in the presence of God, enthroned 'at his right hand.'"

28. See Zwiep, *Ascension of the Messiah*, 154–55.

PART ONE: GOD'S ACTS FOR ISRAEL

δεξιῶν μου, Acts 2:25b and 2:34b) in order to demonstrate that the resurrected Messiah is currently enthroned in heaven and shares in God's powerful rule at his right hand (τῇ δεξιᾷ . . . τοῦ θεοῦ ὑψωθείς, Acts 2:33).[29] This is why David himself cannot be the referent or subject matter of his own speech—David's death makes it certain that David is not the one who "ascended *into heaven*" (ἀνέβη εἰς τοὺς οὐρανούς, 2:34b).[30] This statement about David, however, reminds the reader of another figure who has ascended "into heaven" (1:10-11).[31] Psalms 15 and 109 (LXX) enable Peter to explain the meaning of Jesus's resurrection as much more than a temporary return to embodied existence and rather as a heavenly royal enthronement.[32] Peter uses the language of the Psalter to make precisely this point in Acts 2:33: the Messiah "who has been exalted to God's *right hand*" is the agent and the cause of the outpouring of the Spirit. The first act of the enthroned king, in other words, is to send God's powerful πνεῦμα as the means for the expansion of God's kingdom (cf. Acts 1:6-11). Peter's use of Psalm 109:1 and its designation of the Messiah also as Lord further enables him to interpret the resurrection as his heavenly enthronement to a position of absolute lordship: "God has made him both Lord and Messiah" (Acts 2:36).[33]

---

29. Novakovic, *Raised from the Dead*, 205-7.

30. David is frequently spoken of as "exalted" (ὑψόω) by God to a position of powerful rule. See O'Toole, "Acts 2:30 and the Davidic Covenant of Pentecost," 248-49.

31. Anderson, *"But God Raised Him,"* 215: "The authorial audience will probably perceive a contrast between Luke's vivid portrayal of Jesus' ascent into heaven and David's continued entombment." Zwiep, *Ascension of the Messiah*, 154-57, tries to demonstrate that Acts 2:32-36 does not understand Jesus's ascension as the Messiah's exaltation to God's right hand but rather suggests that "the heavenly journey type of ascension is reserved for the Easter event" (156). Arie W. Zwiep, "*Assumptus Est in Caelum*: Rapture and Heavenly Exaltation in Early Judaism and Luke-Acts," in *Christ, the Spirit and the Community of God: Essays on the Acts of the Apostles*, WUNT 2/293 (Tübingen: Mohr Siebeck, 2010), 38-67, here 45, suggests that since Luke does not refer to Psalm 110:1 (the "exaltation psalm *par excellence*") in Acts 1:9-11, it is unlikely that he connects Jesus's exaltation with his ascension. This statement carries little weight, however, as it ignores the fact that within Acts, one almost always finds the citations of the Old Testament Scriptures in the discourse (i.e., the speeches of the apostles) and not in the narrative events. Peter's speech in Acts 2:14-36, then, provides the explicit interpretation of the events in 1:9-11 and 2:1-13.

32. Similarly, see Eskola, *Messiah and Throne*, 163.

33. Strauss, *Davidic Messiah*, 144-45: "Only at his exaltation-enthronement, however, is Jesus installed in the full authority as reigning Christ and Lord. . . . Though Jesus was already Christ and Lord by God's divine choice during his earthly ministry, at his resurrection-exaltation he became the reigning Christ and Lord of all."

"For David Did Not Ascend into Heaven . . ." (Acts 2:34a)

Paul in Pisidian Antioch (Acts 13:32–37)

In Paul's synagogue speech in Pisidian Antioch (Acts 13:16–41), Paul's primary focus is on the Messiah's resurrection as the fulfillment of God's promises to Israel (13:32–33a). However, Paul uses biblical enthronement texts to interpret the meaning of Jesus's resurrection as the Messiah's heavenly enthronement (Ps 2:7; Isa 55:3; Ps 16:10 [15:10 LXX]).[34] The fulfillment of the promise for the children comes through "the raising up of Jesus" (ἀναστήσας Ἰησοῦν, 13:33). Most take this phrase to be a direct reference to Jesus's resurrection, but a few have argued that it refers to God bringing Jesus onto the world scene.[35] Arguments for the minority view include: (a) unlike 13:30 and 34, the phrase ἐκ νεκρῶν is omitted; (b) there are at least three places in Acts where ἀνίστημι means something like "to bring into the world" or "to raise up a prophet" (3:22, 26; 7:37); (c) there are no other examples of Psalm 2:7 used to refer to Jesus's resurrection in Luke-Acts; and (d) there is a supposed parallel between 13:33 and the statement that God "brought forth" Jesus to Israel in 13:23.[36] These arguments are not persuasive, however, and the phrase should be interpreted as a direct reference to the resurrection for the following reasons.[37] While it is correct that not every occurrence of ἀνίστημι in Acts refers to the resurrection, the fact that the verb occurs again just a few words later as an explicit reference to the resurrection is significant (ἀνέστησεν αὐτὸν ἐκ νεκρῶν, 13:34). And it is no great argument that the verb occurs without ἐκ νεκρῶν, for Luke uses

---

34. Zwiep, *Ascension of the Messiah*, 158–59; Simon David Butticaz, *L'identite de l'église dans les Actes des apotres de la restauration d'Israel a la conquete universelle*, BZNW 174 (Berlin: de Gruyter, 2011), 286–88; Robert F. O'Toole, "Christ's Resurrection in Acts 13,13–52," *Bib* 60 (1979): 361–72. So also, David W. Pao, *Acts and the Isaianic New Exodus*, WUNT 2/130 (Tübingen: Mohr Siebeck, 2000), 135: "The cluster of these three quotations, together with the explicit mention of David in v. 36, points to the significance of the David tradition for *understanding the status of the exalted Christ*" (emphasis mine).

35. The most comprehensive argument for this position, that I am aware of, is Martin Rese, *Alttestamentliche Motive in der Christologie des Lukas*, SZNW 1 (Gütersloh: Mohn, 1969), 83–84; see also F. F. Bruce, *Commentary on the Book of Acts*, NICNT (Grand Rapids: Eerdmans, 1970), 275–76; C. K. Barrett, *A Critical and Exegetical Commentary on the Acts of the Apostles: In 2 Volumes*, ICC 49 (Edinburgh: T&T Clark, 1998), 645–46; Strauss, *Davidic Messiah*, 164–65.

36. Rese, *Alttestamentliche Motive in der Christologie des Lukas*, 83.

37. Evald Lövestam, *Son and Saviour: A Study of Acts 13, 32–37; With an Appendix: "Son of God" in the Synoptic Gospels*, trans. Michael J. Petry (Lund: Gleerup, 1961), 8–11, 43–47; Darrel L. Bock, *Proclamation from Prophecy and Pattern: Lucan Old Testament Christology*, JSNTSup 12 (Sheffield: JSOT Press, 1987), 244–56.

ἀνίστημι to refer to Jesus's resurrection without ἐκ νεκρῶν in Acts 2:24 and 2:32. While Rese is correct that, in certain passages, ἀνίστημι refers to something other than resurrection, in these instances, the verb is always followed by a title (Luke 1:69—"a horn of salvation"; Acts 3:22 and 7:37—"a prophet"; Acts 13:22—"a king").[38] Further, while Rese is right to claim that Psalm 2:7 is not used elsewhere in Luke-Acts to refer to the resurrection, this does not preclude such a usage here—especially given the similar usage in other early Christian texts (Heb 1:5; 5:5; Rom 1:2–4). Most important, however, is the simple fact that the entire discussion of 13:33-37 focuses upon a scriptural demonstration of Jesus's resurrection as his enthronement as Israel's king. A reference to his earthly ministry would entirely interrupt the flow and logic of Paul's sermon.[39]

Further confirmation that ἀναστήσας Ἰησοῦν should be interpreted as a reference to Jesus's resurrection can be demonstrated on the basis of its connection to Psalm 2:7 in 13:33b. Specifically, ἀναστήσας Ἰησοῦν is said to be according to what "has been written in the second Psalm." Psalm 2 is a Davidic psalm that portrays the victory of God's people through the installation of God's anointed king on Zion.[40] It is necessary that the interpreter of Acts begin with the first reference to Psalm 2 in Acts 4:25-27. In Peter's prayer in Acts 4:25-26, Luke quotes Psalm 2:1-2:

> Our father, through the Holy Spirit, through the mouth of David your servant said: "Why do the nations rage and the peoples plot in vain? The kings of the earth take their stand and the rulers are gathered together for the same purpose against the Lord and against his Christ."

Lest his readers make any mistake, Luke provides the clear interpretation of Psalm 2 through the mouth of Peter in what follows. Luke has linked David with Psalm 2 in two ways: (1) both David and Jesus are referred to as God's

---

38. Also, see Strauss, *Davidic Messiah*, 163.

39. So also, Robert C. Tannehill, *The Narrative Unity of Luke-Acts: A Literary Interpretation*, vol. 2, *The Acts of the Apostles* (Minneapolis: Fortress, 1990), 170–71; Ernst Haenchen, *The Acts of the Apostles* (Philadelphia: Westminster, 1971), 411n3; O'Toole, "Christ's Resurrection in Acts 13,13–52," 366; Jacob Jervell, *Die Apostelgeschichte*, Kritisch-exegetischer Kommentar uber das Neue Testament (Meyer-Kommentar) (Göttingen: Vandenhoeck & Ruprecht, 1998), 358–59; Gerhard Schneider, *Die Apostelsgeschichte: Teil 2* (Freiburg: Herder, 1982), 137.

40. Despite linguistic connections, the Psalm resonates strongly with 2 Samuel 7:12–14, a text we have had occasion to reference already. Within Second Temple Jewish writings, this psalm was interpreted as messianic and brought into intertextual relation with 2 Samuel 7. (See 4QFlor and Pss. Sol. 17:21–32.)

"For David Did Not Ascend into Heaven . . ." (Acts 2:34a)

"servant" (4:25, 27, and 30), and (2) in Luke's interpretation of Psalm 2, Jesus is referred to as the one "whom you [God] anointed" (ὃν ἔχρισας, 4:27). This "whom you anointed" most naturally refers to the coronation of the Davidic king in Psalm 2:6–7. In other words, Jesus is given the same messianic position as that of David in the psalm, the one described as God's "Christ" (2:2). Israel's rulers, Herod, Pilate, and even the people of Israel play the role of the enemies of God and his Christ in Psalm 2 (see Luke 23:12). For Luke, the first part of the drama of Psalm 2 (vv. 1–3) is recapitulated in Herod's, Pilate's, and the Jewish leaders' opposition to the Messiah and the messianic community (Acts 4:24–30; so also 13:27–29). If Luke sees Psalm 2:1–3 as fulfilled in the death of Jesus, then it would only make good sense that Psalm 2:7 would be adduced to indicate God's resurrection and heavenly enthronement of his Son. Thus, what was originally a declaration of God's election of the Davidic dynasty is now fulfilled in the messianic Son of God's resurrection and enthronement.[41]

The most difficult part of Paul's speech is found in the citations of Isaiah 55:3 and Psalm 16:10 (LXX 15:10) in Acts 13:34–35. Paul here argues that Jesus's resurrection from the dead is not a mere resuscitation but is, rather, a promise that Jesus shall "never turn back to decay" (13:34a).[42] The noun διαφθοράν reminds one of Peter's citation of Psalm 16:8–11 (LXX 15:8–11) (in Acts 2:25–29, 31), part of which is quoted by Paul in 13:35. It is important to note the relationship between 13:34a and the quotation of Isaiah 55:3 in 13:34b: *because* (ὅτι) God has raised Jesus from the dead, *so he has spoken* (οὕτως εἴρηκεν) the words of Isaiah 55:3. In other words, it is Jesus's resurrection that activates the gift of "the holy and reliable things of David to you" (Acts 13:34). Paul invokes Isaiah 55:3 as a reference to God's covenantal promises made to David for the benefit of future generations.[43] The genitive Δαυίδ should be viewed, then, as an objective genitive—"the faithful and sure things [promises made to] David."[44] If it is correct that biblical citations frequently recall their larger context, then the citation of Isaiah 55:3 would also recall the context's im-

---

41. L. Johnson, *Septuagintal Midrash*, 42.
42. This is stated nicely by Jervell, *Die Apostelgeschichte*, 359. See also Novakovic, *Raised from the Dead*, 211–12.
43. See here Strauss, *Davidic Messiah*, 170–74; Bates, *Birth of the Trinity*, 74–76.
44. That "David" is to be understood as an objective and not a subjective genitive is also strongly suggested by its Old Testament background. God is the one who demonstrates his "loving-kindness" (though here, of course, the LXX has read it as "holy") and "faithfulness" on behalf of David and his dynasty. This is the case in Isa 55:3 as well as in the Davidic covenantal texts of 2 Sam 7:15; Ps 89:30–34, 49–51; 1 Kgs 3:6; and 2 Chr 6:42. On this, see H. G. M. Williamson, "'The Sure Mercies of David': Subjective or Objective Genitive?," *JSS* 23 (1978): 31–49.

mediate prior wording, "I will make an everlasting covenant with you." In this view, the "holy things of David" could refer either to the promised blessings associated with the Davidic covenant (e.g., an heir, a kingdom, and protection from enemies)[45] or the divine oracles promised to David (cf. 2 Sam 7:12–14).[46] Thus, the relationship between 13:34a and 13:34b would be as follows: *because* God has raised Jesus from the dead (v. 34a) as the fulfillment of his promise to the fathers, *so now* has he bestowed the Davidic covenantal blessings upon the recipients (v. 35).[47] It is a characteristic of the Davidic covenant that it promised salvific blessings to its recipients (2 Sam 7:10–14; Jer 23:5–6; Ezek 34:22–31; 37:24–28; also Luke 1:68–73). The promises are "faithful" (τὰ πιστά) because they depend for their efficacy upon the resurrected and enthroned king who "shall not see corruption" (13:35).[48]

Paul again invokes Psalm 16:10 (LXX 15:10) to support his claim that his audience is the recipients of the blessings of the Davidic covenant. The psalm's promise—that the holy one would not see corruption (13:35)—does not refer to David because David "fell asleep," "was added to his fathers," and "he *did* see corruption." The meaning of "he served the will of God in his own generation" is illuminated by Peter's Pentecost speech. Peter appeals to the obvious fact that David died, was buried, and the place of his tomb is still known (2:29). Given the emphasis on David's role as a prophet in the Pentecost speech (2:29–32), it would seem likely that when Paul refers to David as a servant to his own generation, it is David's role as a prophet to his own generation that is in mind. David's "seeing ahead" (2:31) corresponds neatly with his "serving the will of God" (13:36). David is dead and his body has seen corruption, but Jesus, the object of David's psalms, "the one whom God has raised—this one has not seen corruption" (13:37).

God's Kingdom Established and Expanded by the Heavenly Enthroned King

In this final section, I want to point, all too briefly, to three ways Luke continues to draw upon the Psalter to describe how the risen and ascended Jesus actively exerts his rule and enacts God's kingdom as the enthroned heavenly

---

45. So Joseph A. Fitzmyer, *The Acts of the Apostles*, AB (New York: Doubleday, 1998), 517.
46. So L. Johnson, *Septuagintal Midrash*, 44–45.
47. See Lövestam, *Son and Saviour*, 48–81.
48. My interpretation is somewhat similar to Barrett (*Acts*, 647–48) who paraphrases 13:35: "I will fulfil for you (that is, for the Christian generation) the holy and sure (promises made to) David, by raising up, by not allowing to see corruption, (not David himself but) his greater descendent, who was himself holy."

"For David Did Not Ascend into Heaven . . ." (Acts 2:34a)

king. I will simply illustrate the fact that there is no justification for speaking of an absentee Christology in Acts; rather, the enthroned-in-heaven king actively establishes God's kingdom through pouring out God's Spirit, vindicating his witnesses, and procures Israel's repentance and salvation.

The Enthroned King Pours out the Spirit (Acts 1:7-8; 2:29-36)

Peter interprets the first act of the ascended and enthroned Messiah as making good on his promise (Luke 24:49; Acts 1:4, 8) to pour out the Holy Spirit (2:14-36). Peter's speech, using the exaltation language of Psalm 110:1 (LXX 109:1), makes a precise connection between the Messiah's heavenly exaltation to God's right hand (τῇ δεξιᾷ οὖν τοῦ θεοῦ ὑψωθείς, 2:33) and the Spirit's descent.[49] That the sending of the Spirit should be viewed as a royal act of the enthroned Davidic king is demonstrated in a variety of ways. First, as we have already seen, Peter draws upon four royal psalms (Pss 15, 17, 109, and 131 LXX) in order to justify his claim that God has fulfilled his promises to David to seat one of his descendants on God's throne in the resurrection and ascension of Jesus. Second, we have also seen that the Lord's anointed Davidic ruler was often seen as an agent of God's Spirit and, therefore, there was a traditional association between Messiah and Spirit (1 Sam 16:13; Isa 11:1-2; 61:1-3). Third, while the Prophets do not use the language of "the kingdom of God," they do frequently associate the sending of God's Spirit as the time when God would restore Israel to his people, forgive their sins, dwell among them, and ingather the nations (Joel 3:1-5 in Acts 2:16-21; cf. Isa 32:15; 44:1-4; Ezek 36:26-27; 37:14).[50] Finally, in Acts 1:4-8, the risen Jesus makes a close association between his sending of the Spirit, who will empower the disciples in their missionary task (1:4b, 5, 8), and the kingdom (1:3b, 6).[51] While Jesus redirects the disciples from concerns with timing (1:6), he does go on to "describe the means by which the kingdom will be restored, namely, through the Spirit-inspired witness of the Apostles throughout the earth (v. 8)."[52] Thus, it is significant that the very next event Luke narrates is Jesus's ascension into heaven (1:9-11), and in this way, Luke establishes the closest possible connection between Jesus's royal enthronement, the outpouring of the Spirit, and the inauguration and expansion of God's kingdom.

---

49. The underlined inferential conjunction highlights the fact that the sending of the Spirit stems from the ascended Messiah. So Thompson, *Acts of the Risen Lord*, 130.
50. Pao, *Acts and the Isaianic New Exodus*, 115-16.
51. See Butticaz, *L'identite de l'eglise dans les Actes des Apotres*, 72-75.
52. Hahn, *Kinship by Covenant*, 231. See also Thompson, *Acts of the Risen Lord*, 126-31.

PART ONE: GOD'S ACTS FOR ISRAEL

The Enthroned King Vindicates and Establishes His Witnesses (Acts 4:23–31; 7:54–60)

In Acts 4:23–28, the apostles come together in prayer after their harassment from the Jerusalem priests and elders. In Peter's prayer, they use the language of Psalm 2 to interpret Jesus as the anointed Davidic king who is persecuted by the agents of Psalm 2:1–2, namely, Israel's rulers, Herod, and Pilate. In 4:29–30, their prayer demonstrates that the early Christians are enacting the role and pattern of the Anointed One as they too are now suffering at the hands of Israel's leaders.[53] Their prayer, however, demonstrates their belief that the vindicated Anointed One of Psalm 2 is still alive and is powerfully able to empower them to perform healings, signs, and wonders through the name of Jesus (4:30). And as God vindicated his messianic son (Acts 13:32–36), so he answers their prayer by sending forth the Spirit to further empower their mission (4:31). One sees a similar dynamic in Acts 7:54–60 where Stephen is martyred as a result of his vision of the ascended and enthroned Christ: "Being filled with the Holy Spirit, and gazing *into heaven*, he saw God's glory and Jesus standing *at God's right hand*. And he said: 'Behold I see *heaven opened up* and the Son of Man *standing at God's right hand*'" (7:55–56). The vocabulary of the Holy Spirit, heaven, divine glory, and the Psalm 110 language of God's right hand converge to indicate that Stephen encounters a proleptic vision of the full glory of the enthroned Messiah (cf. Luke 9:22; 21:27).[54] While the risen Lord does not save Stephen from death, he does (a) receive Stephen's spirit (7:59) and (b) use Stephen's death to expand the kingdom into the rest of Judea and Samaria (8:1–4; cf. Acts 1:8).[55] Thus, both Acts 4:23–31 and 7:54–60 use the language of the Psalter to show how the enthroned-in-heaven Messiah of Acts 1:6–11 answers the prayers of his people and establishes God's kingdom through empowering the testimony of his witnesses.

The Enthroned King Gives Restoration Blessings (Acts 3–5)

In Acts 3:1–10, Peter and John heal the lame man sitting at the gate of the temple. The obvious parallels between this account and Jesus's healing of the

---

53. I have discussed this in more detail in Joshua W. Jipp, "Luke's Scriptural Suffering Messiah: A Search for Precedent, a Search for Identity," *CBQ* 72 (2010): 255–74, here 272–73.
54. Eskola, *Messiah and Throne*, 180–81.
55. Especially insightful for relating the spatial location of the heavenly Messiah and the geographical expansion of the Messiah's witnesses is Sleeman, *Geography*, 163–71.

"For David Did Not Ascend into Heaven..." (Acts 2:34a)

paralytic suggest that the healing ministry of Jesus continues through his witnesses (see Luke 5:17-26).[56] But Peter is emphatic that the healing derives not from Peter's abilities (3:12), but rather takes place "by *the name* of Messiah Jesus of Nazareth" (Acts 3:6b; cf. 4:9-10). Peter's speech declares that it is the resurrection power of the God of Israel (3:13a) that has "glorified his servant Jesus" (ἐδόξασεν τὸν παῖδα αὐτοῦ Ἰησοῦν, 3:13b) that is responsible for the healing of the lame man. The language of God glorifying Jesus probably draws upon the Psalter's frequent promise that God would exalt his anointed Davidic servant (e.g., Ps 89:20-21; cf. Isa 52:13).[57] Thus, the enthroned king is able to continue his healing ministry on earth by means of his witnesses.[58] This is further emphasized by the notoriously difficult statement in 3:19-21, where Peter exhorts the people to repent so that they might experience "times of refreshment from the face of the Lord" (καιροὶ ἀναψύξεως ἀπὸ προσώπου τοῦ κυρίου, 3:19-20). These times of refreshment come from the glorified heavenly figure (3:21) who grants signs of his favor, presence, and healing to those who turn to him as a foretaste of his "time of universal restoration" (3:21a). The parallels between 3:20-21 and 1:6-11 (times and seasons, restoration, heaven, Jesus's return, Spirit/refreshment) suggest the heavenly enthroned king is actively responsible for pouring out blessings upon his repentant people in anticipation of his return.[59]

In Acts 5:30-31, Peter uses the language of Psalm 109:1 (LXX) to ground Israel's repentance in God's exaltation of Jesus: "God has exalted this one to his right hand (ὕψωσεν τῇ δεξιᾷ αὐτοῦ) as prince and savior in order to provide repentance to Israel and the forgiveness of sins."[60] Thus, Acts 3:19-21 and 5:30-31 indicate that God's enthronement of Jesus to his right hand stands behind the mass conversions of the Jews in Jerusalem who turn to God and experience divine forgiveness (2:41; 4:4; cf. 13:38-39).

In Acts 4:10, Peter declares that the rejected but now resurrected Messiah is the one who has healed the lame man (4:10b), and Peter quotes Psalm 117:22 (LXX) to identify him as "the stone that was despised by your builders, this one has become the head stone" (4:11).[61] The claim that "there is no other name

---

56. L. Johnson, *Acts of the Apostles*, 71.
57. Jipp, "Luke's Scriptural Suffering Messiah," 264-65.
58. Sleeman, *Geography*, 109.
59. Anderson, "But God Raised Him," 228.
60. Eskola, *Messiah and Throne*, 177-78.
61. On the significant role that Psalm 118 plays throughout Luke and Acts, see J. Ross Wagner, "Psalm 118 in Luke-Acts: Tracing a Narrative Thread," in *Early Christian Interpretation of the Scriptures of Israel: Investigations and Proposals*, ed. Craig A. Evans and James A.

under heaven" that can procure humanity's salvation links Jesus's ascended and enthroned status with his ability to continue his healing ministry. Given Peter's direct quotation of the psalm, it is also likely that the frequent invocation of the name of Jesus as the powerful agent of healing (3:6, 16; 4:7, 10, 12, 17, 30) stems from Psalm 117 (LXX) where the king embodies "the name of the Lord" (v. 26a) and triumphs as the result of "the name of the Lord" (vv. 10, 11, 12). Thus, in Acts 3-4, Luke continues to use the Psalter (Ps 117 directly and Ps 88 and the language of royal enthronement indirectly) to show how the resurrected and enthroned-in-heaven Messiah sends forth healing (3:1-10; 4:10-11), forgiveness of sins and times of restoration (3:20-21), and salvation (4:12) to those who turn to the Lord (3:19).

With more space and time, one could further argue that the enthroned Messianic ruler engages in judgment and defeat of his enemies (Acts 1:15-26 citing Ps 69:26; 109:8; Acts 5:1-11; 12:20-23),[62] creates a unified community in Jerusalem that fulfills the prophetic expectations and hopes for Israel as God's people (2:42-47; 4:32-35; 5:12-16), and challenges false conceptions of sacred space (7:44-45; 17:24-25).[63] But, hopefully, enough small gestures have been made to make the point that Luke uses the Psalter not only to narrate God's enthronement of Israel's resurrected Messiah to his right hand, but to also demonstrate the way in which the ascended king continues to rule and establish God's kingdom from heaven.

Sanders, JSNTSup 148, SSEJC 5 (Sheffield: Sheffield Academic, 1997), 154-78; Thompson, *Acts of the Risen Lord*, 160-61.

62. L. Johnson, *Septuagintal Midrash*, 14-15; Jipp, "Luke's Scriptural Suffering Messiah," 266-69; Jacques Dupont, "La Destinée de Judas Prophétisée par David (Actes 1,16-20)," *CBQ* 23 (1961): 41-51, here 50-51.

63. See here Walton, "'The Heavens Opened,'" 71-73.

Part Two

God's Acts for Gentiles

6

Does Paul Translate the Gospel in Acts 17:22–31?

A Critical Engagement with C. Kavin Rowe's One True Life

The suggestion that Luke's Paul employs themes, scripts, and vocabulary that resonate powerfully with Hellenistic philosophy, and particularly that of Stoicism, in his Areopagus speech is not controversial.[1] Stoics would have been not only familiar with, but deeply sympathetic to a theology which emphasized (a) the singularity of God/monotheism (Acts 17:24), (b) a philosophical critique of religion with critical consequences for temples and sacrifices (17:24b–25), (c) the unity of humanity (17:26a), (d) providence (17:26b), and (e) humanity's union with God (17:28–29).[2] The notion that Paul is inviting his audience to consider his theology in light of Stoicism seems to me to be banal and uncontroversial for at least three reasons: (1) the obvious similarities between Paul's speech and Stoicism just noted, (2) Stoic and Epicurean philosophers are explicitly mentioned as comprising part of the audience for Paul's sermon (Acts 17:18), and (3) Paul's direct appeal to the pagan poets, which includes a direct citation from the Stoic Aratus's *Phaenomena* 5 ("for we are his offspring," Acts 17:28).[3]

---

1. References to Paul throughout this essay refer to Luke's portrait of Paul in Acts.
2. Numerous specific studies and commentaries demonstrate the similarities between Stoic philosophy and Paul's speech. See especially David L. Balch, "The Areopagus Speech: An Appeal to the Stoic Historian Posidonius against Later Stoics and the Epicureans," in *Greeks, Romans, and Christians: Essays in Honor of Abraham J. Malherbe*, ed. David L. Balch et al. (Minneapolis: Fortress, 1990), 52–79; Eckhard J. Schnabel, "Contextualising Paul in Athens: The Proclamation of the Gospel Before Pagan Audiences in the Graeco-Roman World," *R&T* 12 (2005): 172–90, here 178–80.
3. C. Kavin Rowe, *World Upside Down: Reading Acts in the Graeco-Roman Age* (Oxford:

PART TWO: GOD'S ACTS FOR GENTILES

These observations, of course, do not mean that Paul's speech *is* Stoic, only that significant portions of Paul's address share recognizable commonalities with Stoicism and thereby functions as *one* critical context for making sense of Paul's sermon.[4] To recognize Stoic themes, scripts, and vocabulary does not yet tell us *their meaning within Paul's speech or the purpose of the speech*, but it would seem at the least to indicate that Luke crafted the speech with a view to inviting comparisons between Paul's message and Stoic philosophy.

Recently, however, C. Kavin Rowe has argued that readings of Acts 17 that "argue for a deep theological *Anknüpfungspunkt* between pagan philosophical thinking and Paul's proclamation" are entirely wrong, and this *despite the fact* that, as he acknowledges, this "long history of reading Acts 17 . . . constitutes a relatively stable and coherent hermeneutical tradition."[5] Again, Rowe emphasizes the misguided history of the interpretation of Acts 17:22-31: "Given the power and longevity of this way of thinking, it is really no less remarkable that this is not what Acts 17 actually argues." By "this way of thinking" Rowe refers to the view that Paul's sermon is "a paean of the Greek intellectual or spiritual achievement."[6] Paul's sermon is, rather, "the presentation of an alternative pattern of life."[7] Rowe presents five arguments suggesting that Paul's message ("Christianity") and Stoicism are incongruous: (a) the narrative frame of the speech emphasizes conflict and misunderstanding between Paul and the philosophers (17:16-21); (b) Paul's commendation of his audience's religiosity could just as well be understood as a charge of superstition based on the semantic domain of δεισιδαιμονέστερος (17:22); (c) Paul's reference to their veneration of the unknown god emphasizes *ignorance* in Athenian worship (17:23); (d) Paul's reference to Aratus and his audience's poets does not show

---

Oxford University Press, 2009), 33-39, demonstrates more, albeit still limited, interest in some of these similarities than in C. Kavin Rowe, "The Grammar of Life: The Areopagus Speech and Pagan Tradition," NTS 57 (2011): 31-50, and C. Kavin Rowe, *One True Life: The Stoics and Early Christians as Rival Traditions* (New Haven: Yale University Press, 2016).

4. The history of the interpretation of this speech has oscillated back and forth between those who view it as a placid and conventional affirmation of monotheism and natural theology and those who see it as a strong critique of gentile religiosity. For the former, see Martin Dibelius, *Studies in the Acts of the Apostles*, trans. Mary Ling (London: SCM, 1951), 53-56. For the latter, see Bertil Gärtner, *The Areopagus Speech and Natural Revelation*, trans. Carolyn Hannay King, ASNU 21 (Uppsala: Gleerup, 1955).

5. Rowe, "Grammar of Life," 34.

6. For both quotes, see Rowe, "Grammar of Life," 35. Rowe's view of the history of Acts 17 is lacking some important nuance here, as interpretations of this speech are often remarkably incongruous. See n. 4 and the differences between Dibelius and Gärtner.

7. Rowe, "Grammar of Life," 35.

theological commensurability, since "in Luke's text the pagan philosophical vocabulary has been incorporated into a radically different overall interpretative framework: the biblical story that stretches from Adam to the return of Jesus Christ;"[8] and (e) Paul's sermon situates humanity with the story of Adam and the resurrected Jesus (17:26, 31).[9] Paul does not translate his message into Stoic philosophy. Rather, the speech provides evidence for "the conflict and confrontation that occurs when irreducibly particular patterns of life offer irreducibly different ways of being."[10]

Rowe's study of Acts 17 previews his more recent methodological and comparative study of Stoicism and Christianity in *One True Life*, where he argues that at every point of significance Stoicism and Christianity are rival traditions that offer visions of life that are incompatible and *incommensurable*. One cannot, then, be both a Stoic and a Christian, for these traditions require two entirely different kinds of lives and, as Rowe has said, we only have a single life to live. Since Christianity and Stoicism are both *traditions,* in the thick sense of the term, *comparison can only be carried out,* for Rowe, as "an exploration in the conflict of traditions."[11] Rowe's argument is dependent upon Alasdair MacIntyre's three notions of inquiry (i.e., encyclopedia, genealogy, and tradition). Since Stoicism and Christianity are *traditions* of inquiry, this means that one's knowledge is "inescapably tied to the inculcation of habits in the life of the knower and to the community that originates and stewards the craft of inquiry through time."[12] Even where one finds near identical themes, scripts, and vocabulary, such as in Acts 17, these elements only make sense within their particular tradition.

But biblical scholars have not, says Rowe, recognized the implications of Stoicism/Christianity as traditions and have, instead, approached the texts according to the encyclopedic way of knowing, a way of knowing that operates with a single form of unitary knowledge which, through the accumulation of religious parallels, confidently *advances* to explain everything. Operant within the encyclopedic form of knowing is the belief that all texts and traditions can be intelligibly translated into different frameworks. When it comes to comparing the Christians and Stoics on God, death, humanity, salvation, and the like, one finds that they do not "share the sort of agreements that are necessary for

---

8. Rowe, "Grammar of Life," 43.
9. Rowe, "Grammar of Life," 35–43.
10. Rowe, "Grammar of Life," 49–50.
11. Rowe, *One True Life*, 205.
12. Rowe, *One True Life*, 184.

substantive conceptual translation." Further, this shows that one cannot isolate "similar words or phrases from each corpus of texts" in order to show "the synonymy of the common terms."[13] Paul, therefore, was not translating the gospel message at all precisely because translation itself is impossible, for no "amount of linguistic innovation, augmentation, or enrichment could make it possible to live rival traditions in one life at the same time. In this precise and extraordinarily significant sense, the disagreement does go all the way down."[14]

If I understand Rowe rightly here, then there is no possibility of overlap or continuity between Christianity and non/pre-Christian cultures and religions. What then should we do with the obvious allusions within the speech to Stoic themes, scripts, poets, and even Stoic philosophers in Acts 17? If the relationship between Christianity and Stoicism *can only be one of a conflict of traditions,* per Rowe, why does Paul use *this* kind of discourse in Acts 17? Rowe devotes one sentence to this question in his "Grammar of Life" and suggests that since Paul is on trial at the Areopagus, he cannot make his Christian commitments too explicit lest he "lose his life," and so he uses vocabulary that resonates with both "Christian and pagan tradition alike" but only "enough to save Paul's life."[15] Rowe has illuminated the *conflict* between Paul's gospel and Stoicism, but a more plausible explanation of the *similarities* between his speech and Stoicism is necessary for both a convincing interpretation of Acts 17 and an explanation for the relationship between Christianity and Stoicism. Again, I emphasize that I think Rowe is right to emphasize conflict between Paul and his audience in Acts 17 and that Christianity and Stoicism are different traditions, but I do not think he has successfully accounted for the way in which Paul (and missionary proclamation more broadly) translates his message into language that resonates deeply with Stoic philosophy as a means of showing that the Christian message is a superior philosophy.

If the history of interpretation of Acts 17 is as stable and coherent as Rowe himself claims it to be, it would be truly remarkable if it was this misguided, awaiting Alasdair MacIntyre's philosophy to set us back on the right track. Rowe is hard on NT scholars for their "typical neglect of rigorous philosophical thinking," but given that Paul is engaged in missionary proclamation as he seeks to persuade the Athenians and Hellenistic philosophers of the gospel message, I suggest that Rowe's study could benefit from some basic insights offered from missiological studies and intercultural hermeneutics. In other

13. Rowe, *One True Life,* 234.
14. Rowe, *One True Life,* 246.
15. Rowe, "Grammar of Life," 50.

Does Paul Translate the Gospel in Acts 17:22–31?

words, how do religious devotees communicate with those who have competing religious commitments? Does the history of Christian mission and the communication and understanding that take place between different cultures illuminate Paul's speech to the Athenians? This would seem to be closer to the function of Acts 17, which is *not* primarily a philosophical reflection upon two distinct traditions but is rather a communicative attempt to persuade those with competing theological commitments of the truth of the gospel. Worthy of additional consideration as well is the history of the relationship between Stoicism and Hellenistic Judaism. As Rowe knows well, Philo and a wealth of other Jewish texts testify to the encounter between Stoicism and Judaism. If the best way of describing the relationship between Christianity and Stoicism is, per Rowe, one of theologically incommensurate and rival traditions, then I would expect we should find the same to be the case for Judaism and Stoicism. In what follows I want to suggest that a kind of "both/and" reading of Acts 17—one that emphasizes *both* cultural and religious convergence *and* conflict—makes much better sense of Paul's sermon as intercultural missionary proclamation.

Before returning to Paul's speech in Acts 17, then, I want to take two brief forays into (a) some missiological studies that help us understand what happens when the gospel encounters new cultures and territories, and (b) the relationship between Stoicism and Hellenistic Judaism. My hope is that we will be able to return to Paul's Areopagus speech with fresh methodological and historical insights.

Cross-Cultural Transmission of the Gospel in the History of Christianity

Given that, in my view, Paul's proclamation in Acts 17 seeks to convince his audience of the truth of the gospel *by* appealing to their own religious/philosophical history, the histories of the encounters between Christianity and non/pre-Christian cultures are worth examining in more detail. The gospel has no *pure* form apart from its particular linguistic and cultural expression.[16] The gospel is *always* articulated within culture, though it is not *identified* with any

---

16. "The simplest statement of the gospel, 'Jesus is Lord,' depends for its meaning on the content which that culture gives to the word 'Lord.' What kind of thing is 'lordship' in the culture in question?" Lesslie Newbigin, *The Gospel in a Pluralist Society* (Grand Rapids: Eerdmans, 1989), 144.

particular local culture.[17] Since Christianity does not sacralize any particular language or culture, every new culture is, thereby, destigmatized as well as relativized.[18] Rowe's portrait of Christianity and Stoicism seems to present both as *pure* and *idealized* philosophical/religious traditions, with the result that he fails to appreciate the significance of how Christianity has appropriated and drawn its language from non-Christian cultures.[19]

The history of Christianity bears this point out as the gospel has spread through a multiplicity of languages and cultures different from those of its founder.[20] Lamin Sanneh has emphasized the significance of the fact that the earliest Christians did not spread the gospel message through diffusion or cultural adoption, but rather through translation—which "rests on the persuasive nature of the idioms adopted in religious practice."[21] The contents of the Christian proclamation, then, were "received and framed in the terms of its host culture; by feeding off the diverse cultural streams it encountered, the religion became multicultural. The local idiom became the chosen vessel."[22] Translation proceeds with the belief that "the originating language is . . . inadequate, inappropriate, . . . a hindrance, or at any rate ineffective *for the task at hand* [italics mine]."[23] The history of Christian mission manifests in not only how peoples have been encountered by the gospel but how people have appropriated and translated the gospel into their local cultural idioms. Thus, "Christian history is not lineal and singular and reducible to the course of a simple institution. Christian history, following the path of conversion, is constituted by a series of cross-cultural encounters and the local appropriations

---

17. John G. Flett, *Apostolicity: The Ecumenical Question in World Christian Perspective* (Downers Grove, IL: InterVarsity Press, 2016), 246–47.

18. Flett, *Apostolicity*, 276–77.

19. See here the criticism of Rowe by Elizabeth Agnew Cochran, "Bricolage and the Purity of Traditions: Engaging the Stoics for Contemporary Christian Ethics," *JRE* 40 (2012): 720–29. I am obviously in agreement with her claim that "Rowe's critique of a piecemeal retrieval of Stoicism implicitly constructs a binary that assumes that Stoic thought can only be entirely embraced or entirely rejected—it is impossible to be influenced meaningfully by Stoicism unless one becomes a Stoic oneself" (724).

20. See Andrew F. Walls, *The Missionary Movement in Christian History: Studies in the Transmission of Faith* (Maryknoll, NY: Orbis, 1996), 3–54.

21. Lamin Sanneh, *Translating the Message: The Missionary Impact on Culture*, 2nd ed. (Maryknoll, NY: Orbis, 2009), 33–34.

22. Lamin O. Sanneh, *Disciples of All Nations: Pillars of World Christianity*, Oxford Studies in World Christianity (Oxford: Oxford University Press, 2008), 26.

23. Sanneh, *Translating the Message*, 36.

of the gospel. It encompasses many histories, all of which contribute to the full stature of Christ."[24]

Thus, the history of Christianity testifies that the transmission of the gospel entails both discontinuity *and* continuity between the gospel and the local culture. On the one hand, the gospel divinizes no culture or language; it critiques idolatry and polytheism; it calls into question all kinds of patterns of life which do not produce human flourishing in accordance with the life and pattern of Jesus. On the other hand, the transmission of the gospel in new cultural frontiers invariably shows significant levels of continuity with the local culture. When the gospel of Christ has encountered new cultures, it has not only critiqued but also used and engaged the specific cultural forms and expressions of the people.[25] Andrew Walls has argued that this encounter results not in the rejection of the culture's pre-Christian history but, rather, its conversion to Christ.[26]

Numerous theologians and missiologists have provided extensive examples of how the message of Jesus Christ has been translated into local languages and idioms.[27] But here I want to mention briefly some of the insights of the Ghanaian theologian Kwame Bediako. Bediako is concerned with charting a way forward for African theology that moved beyond Western theological categories and theologians who generally underestimated "the African knowledge and sense of God."[28] Bediako draws upon the writings and insights of the Kenyan theologian John Mbiti and the Nigerian Bolaji Idowu, who both argue for continuity between pre-Christian African religion and Christianity, for example, with respect to belief in the oneness of God.[29] Bediako appeals to Desmond Tutu, who encourages African theologians to turn to their own "African religious experience and heritage" as "the vehicle for conveying the Gospel verities to Africa." For Africans, Tutu argues, "have had a genuine

24. Flett, *Apostolicity*, 270.
25. See Andrew F. Walls, "The Rise of Global Theologies," in *Global Theology in Evangelical Perspective: Exploring the Contextual Nature of Theology and Mission*, ed. Jeffrey P. Greenman and Gene L. Green (Downers Grove, IL: InterVarsity Press, 2012), 19–34.
26. Walls, "Rise of Global Theologies."
27. See especially, Sanneh, *Translating the Message*; Sanneh, *Disciples of All Nations*.
28. Kwame Bediako, "Understanding African Theology in the Twentieth Century," in *Jesus and the Gospel in Africa: History and Experience* (Maryknoll, NY: Orbis, 2004), chap. 4, esp. 52.
29. See, for example, John S. Mbiti, *New Testament Eschatology in an African Background: A Study of the Encounter between New Testament Theology and African Traditional Concepts* (Oxford: Oxford University Press, 1971); Kwame Bediako, *Theology and Identity: The Impact of Culture upon Christian Thought in the Second Century and in Modern Africa* (Oxford: Regnum, 1992), 303–46.

knowledge of God and . . . have had our own ways of communicating with deity, ways which meant that we were able to speak authentically as ourselves and not as pale imitators of others. It means that we have a great store from which we can fashion new ways of speaking to and about God, and new styles of worship consistent with our faith."[30]

Thus, for these African theologians, Bediako describes the "task of African theology" as consisting in "letting the Christian Gospel encounter, *as well as be shaped by, the African experience.*"[31] Since the gospel *is* Jesus Christ, one can, then, explore new languages and theological idioms and expressions without sacrificing any Christian content.[32] Bediako sees this dynamic as rooted deeply in the NT, particularly, the book of Acts, where the mighty acts of God are proclaimed in the local languages, vocabulary, idioms, and cultural expressions of the languages of every nation under heaven (Acts 2:1–13).[33]

The proclamation of the gospel involves critique, as we have noted, but Bediako claims that it also "brings up to fulfilment all the highest religious and cultural aspirations of our heritage."[34] Christ is the solution or answer to the longings and needs of Africans and their world. For example, Bediako examines the depiction of Christ's ancestral function in the letter to the Hebrews in order to show

> more fully how Jesus Christ is the only real and true Ancestor and Source of life for all mankind, fulfilling and transcending the benefits believed to be bestowed by lineage ancestors. . . . No longer are human horizons bounded by lineage, clan, tribe or nation. For the redeemed now belong within the community of the living God, in the joyful company of the faithful of all ages and times. They are united through their union with Christ, in a fellowship infinitely richer than the mere social bonds of lineage, clan, tribe or nation that exclude the stranger as a virtual enemy.[35]

---

30. Desmond Tutu, "Whiter African Theology?" in *Christianity in Independent Africa*, ed. E. Fashole-Luke et al. (London: Collings, 1978), 364–69, quoted in Bediako, "Understanding African Theology," 50.

31. Bediako, "Understanding African Theology," 55.

32. Kwame Bediako, "How Is Jesus Christ Lord? Evangelical Christian Apologetics amid African Religious Pluralism," in Bediako, *Jesus and the Gospel in Africa*, chap. 3, esp. 43–44.

33. See further Amos Yong, *Hospitality and the Other: Pentecost, Christian Practices, and the Neighbor* (Maryknoll, NY: Orbis, 2008).

34. Kwame Bediako, "Jesus in African Culture: A Ghanaian Perspective," in *Jesus and the Gospel in Africa*, chap. 2, here 21.

35. Bediako, "Jesus in African Culture," 31–32.

Does Paul Translate the Gospel in Acts 17:22–31?

Others have shown how the Buhaya people of Tanzania understand Christ through the metaphors of "King" and "Lord," which makes sense with their social history of feudal administration that was administered through a large and complex structure of royal power. Christ is understood within this frame of reference as *the King* who rules over his subjects, unites the clan within his person, and cares for all people—even the weak, the poor, and the sick.[36] Wrogemann notes that the African "metaphors for Christ reflect the social structures of each individual ethnic group," and "the titles used for Christ evidently convey the specific experiences of these people groups" as "the process of appropriation clearly takes place on the basis of the self-evidence of ethnic-cultural lifeworlds."[37] I hasten to emphasize that these are, of course, just a few examples among many more that could be offered for how Jesus Christ is situated and understood within the language, social structures, and theological idioms of a particular people and their culture.

One of Bediako's primary contributions to the conversation has focused upon the similarities between modern African Christianity and the rise of Hellenistic Christianity in the second century CE.[38] Both contexts have faced the challenge of Christian identity and its particular relation to its pre-Christian history. In particular, they have asked, "How did the Gospel relate to the Hellenistic past? What was the nature of the saving activity of the one Living God through the centuries prior to the Incarnation of the Saviour and inauguration of the Christian era?"[39] Was it possible to be both "Christian" and "Greek," or in contemporary terms could one be both "Christian" and "African"? Bediako argues that the early church fathers, even those who emphasized cultural discontinuity, used the language and themes of Hellenistic culture and philosophy to articulate the gospel. As is well known, Justin and Clement identified Jesus with the Greek/Hellenistic philosophical concept of the *logos*. It would be tedious and unnecessary here to try to detail all of the ways in which the early church fathers appropriated aspects of their Hellenistic philosophical heritage *within* their *Christian* theological frameworks. While the *logos* concept now means something *new* within their theology—it is after all no longer a concept or an idea but a person!—it

---

36. I am entirely dependent here upon the description from Henning Wrogemann, *Intercultural Hermeneutics*, trans. Karl E. Böhmer, vol. 1 of *Intercultural Theology* (Downers Grove, IL: InterVarsity Press, 2016), 216.

37. Wrogemann, *Intercultural Hermeneutics*, 219.

38. See here Kwame Bediako, *Theology and Identity*; Bediako, "Africa and the Fathers: The Relevance of Early Hellenistic Christian Theology for Modern Africa," in Bediako, *Jesus and the Gospel in Africa*, chap. 5.

39. Bediako, "Africa and the Fathers," 69.

enables them to "provide a . . . Christ-centered interpretation of Hellenistic tradition of the past."[40] Justin and Clement did not, then, shy away from their complete commitments to the truth of the Scriptures and Christianity, and yet they did not see "Christianity" and aspects of the Greek philosophical heritage as "mutually exclusive systems."[41] Andrew Walls describes Bediako's insight in this way: "We cannot abandon or suppress our past or substitute something else instead, nor can our past be left as it is, untouched by Christ. Our past, like our present, has to be converted, turned toward Christ. The second-century quest was the conversion, not the suppression or replacement, of Hellenistic culture, and in that case conversion had led to cultural renewal."[42]

Similarly, Flett argues that mission is *christologically* grounded, and therefore the "Gentiles are to turn to Christ, which means a turning of their own religious and historical heritage, which, by extension, takes a different shape."[43] Thus, the diverse expressions of "Jesus is Lord" are not reducible to a singular culture or form,[44] *even though* the confession "Jesus is Lord" produces a plurality of cultural expressions of Christianity as a particular way of life.

Stoicism and Philo of Alexandria on the Law

Before Paul gave his Areopagus speech, Jews had a long history already of encountering, criticizing, and appropriating Stoic philosophy. John Barclay speaks, for example, of a variety of textual "examples of cultural convergence" whereby Hellenistic Jews situated "their national traditions within Hellenistic moral, historical, philosophical and theological frameworks."[45] I cannot here give a detailed description of the interactions between Hellenistic Jewish texts and Stoic philosophy, but the ways in which the former drew upon and interacted with Stoic ideas is relevant for understanding the nature and meaning of the convergences between Paul's gospel message and Stoic philosophy in Acts 17. We could

---

40. Bediako, *Theology and Identity*, 148.
41. Bediako, "Africa and the Fathers," 70.
42. Andrew F. Walls, "Kwame Bediako and Christian Scholarship in Africa," *International Bulletin of Missionary Research* 32 (2008): 188–93, esp. 189.
43. Flett, *Apostolicity*, 314.
44. Flett, *Apostolicity*, 321–22.
45. John M. G. Barclay, *Jews in the Mediterranean Diaspora: From Alexander to Trajan (323 BCE–117 CE)* (Berkeley: University of California Press, 1996), 127. Relevant here also is Gregory E. Sterling, *Historiography and Self-Definition: Josephos, Luke-Acts and Apologetic Historiography*, NovTSup 64 (Leiden: Brill, 1992).

Does Paul Translate the Gospel in Acts 17:22-31?

examine with profit the texts and authors of 4 Maccabees, the *Letter of Aristeas*, Aristobulus, and others, but here I want to simply make a few brief comments on the way in which Philo drew upon Hellenistic philosophy, and particularly Stoicism, to portray the law of Moses as the rational and universal divine law. In my view, the cultural convergences between Hellenistic Judaism and Stoic philosophy problematizes depicting them as static binary traditions.

As is well known, Philo considers himself a follower of "the philosophical school of Moses" (*Mut.* 223) and expounds the law of Moses and Jewish beliefs about God with explicit assistance from Hellenistic philosophy. On occasion Philo even refers to Judaism as a philosophy (e.g., *Mos.* 2.216; *Legat.* 156, 245). Philo does not see any conflict between Judaism and the best aspects of Hellenistic philosophy, though he indicates that the best aspects of Greek and Hellenistic philosophy received guidance from Moses (e.g., *Prob.* 57; *Mos.* 1.1-3).[46] His exposition of the Jewish philosophy, however, is attained through his exegesis of the Torah.[47] And yet his exegesis of the Torah and Stoic philosophy converge in their harmonious understanding of the divine and particularly the divine law. Philo states this clearly in *Virt.* 65: "For what comes to the adherents of the most esteemed philosophy, comes to the Jews through their laws and customs, namely the knowledge of the highest and most ancient Cause of all and the rejection of the deception of created gods."[48] Thus, Philo posits the Jewish people's knowledge of the true God positions themselves as devoted to "the most esteemed philosophy" and having a superior constitution (*Conf.* 141). It should be noted here that in Philo's commitment to the "most ancient Cause of all," he simultaneously appropriates Hellenistic philosophical discourse *and* rejects pagan worship of idols (see also *Spec.* 2.163-167).

Philo's appropriation of Stoic philosophy is seen most clearly in his depiction of the law of Moses as rational, universal, and eternal. Christine Hayes summarizes the relationship in this way: Philo "labors to demonstrate that

---

46. In this regard, Philo can be characterized as eclectic as he makes use of a variety of Hellenistic philosophical traditions. See Gregory E. Sterling, "'The Jewish Philosophy': Reading Moses via Hellenistic Philosophy according to Philo," in *Reading Philo: A Handbook to Philo of Alexandria*, ed. Torrey Seland (Grand Rapids: Eerdmans, 2014), 129-54, here 137.

47. See here especially Peder Borgen, *Philo of Alexandria: An Exegete for His Time*, NovTSup 86 (Leiden: Brill, 1997); Gregory E. Sterling, "The Interpreter of Moses: Philo of Alexandria and the Biblical Text," in *A Companion to Biblical Interpretation in Early Judaism*, ed. Matthias Henze (Grand Rapids: Eerdmans, 2012), 415-35.

48. For further expansion of this point and for the translation, see Sterling, "'Jewish Philosophy,'" 153-54. On Philo's engagement with Stoic physics, see Anthony A. Long, "Philo on Stoic Physics," in *Philo of Alexandria and Post-Aristotelian Philosophy*, ed. Francesca Alesse, Studies in Philo of Alexandria 5 (Leiden: Brill, 2008), 121-40.

PART TWO: GOD'S ACTS FOR GENTILES

the Torah of Moses possesses *all* of the properties and qualities of Greek natural law: it is self-identical with universal truth, which entails its rationality, its immutability, and its unwritten character."⁴⁹ Thus, the law of Moses is a written copy of the prior and universal divine law. So those who examine the particular laws of Moses will find "that they seek to attain to the harmony of the universe and are in agreement with the principles of eternal nature" (*Mos.* 2.52 [Colson, LCL]). This is why Moses penned the creation account *before* giving the particular laws, namely, to show that "the ... maker of the world was in the truest sense also its Lawgiver" and "that he who would observe the laws will accept gladly the duty of following nature and live in accordance with the ordering of the universe" (*Mos.* 2.48 [Colson, LCL]). The resonances with Stoicism are obvious. Note the obvious resonances, for example, with Cicero's description of the natural law (*Rep.* 3.22 [Keyes, LCL]):

> True law is right reason in agreement with nature; it is of universal application, unchanging and everlasting; it summons to duty by its commands, and averts from wrongdoing by its prohibitions ... but one eternal and unchangeable law will be valid for all nations and all times, and there will be one master and ruler, that is, God, over us all, for he is the author of this law, its promulgator, and its enforcing judge.

Philo's appropriation of Stoic philosophy is obvious when he argues that Moses's creation account implies "that the world is in harmony with the Law, and the Law with the world, and that the person who observes the law is constituted thereby as a loyal citizen of the world, regulating his doing by the purpose and will of Nature, in accordance with which the entire world itself also is administered" (*Opif.* 3 [Colson and Whitaker, LCL]). Philo's statement resonates clearly with the Stoic belief that the world is providentially administered through rationality or "the will of nature" and that those who live according to nature are cosmopolitans.⁵⁰ Thus, Philo claims that the specific laws of the Torah have a universal and cosmic character and should be observed not just by Jews but by all people.⁵¹

How should one think of Philo's relationship to Stoicism and Judaism? Rowe does not engage this question, but I wonder, Do the categories Rowe

---

49. Christine Hayes, *What's Divine about Divine Law? Early Perspectives* (Princeton: Princeton University Press, 2015), 111.

50. On Stoic cosmopolitanism, see Cicero, *Nat. d.* 154.

51. John W. Martens, "The Meaning and Function of the Law in Philo and Josephus," in *Torah Ethics and Early Christian Identity*, ed. Susan J. Wendel and David M. Miller (Grand Rapids: Eerdmans, 2016), 27–40, esp. 29.

Does Paul Translate the Gospel in Acts 17:22–31?

uses for Christianity and Stoicism work here, namely, theologically incommensurate traditions? I doubt many scholars who would claim that Philo's appropriation of Stoic discourse invalidates or compromises his genuine devotion to Judaism and the law of Moses. Philo's appropriation of Stoic ideas by no means results in the loss of his Jewish identity. Philo is representative of a variety of Hellenistic Jews (and Christians) who

> entered into a vigorous process of reciprocal exchange on all levels—social, material, and intellectual . . . result[ing in] a kind of cultural "hybridity" provided that we understand that distinct cultures were not lost or transformed beyond recognition in a syncretistic melting pot. Rather, members of different cultures mutually assimilated to one another while continuously constructing differences in practice and thought.[52]

Thus, to recognize that Judaism and Stoicism are distinct traditions is, in one sense, accurate so long as this does not result in portraying either of them as static, binary traditions that are capable of obtaining some level of perfect purity.

At the same time, it would be foolish and irresponsible to try to interpret Philo without some basic knowledge of Stoicism.[53] Philo does indeed work *within a tradition*, but this tradition is not a binary one of "Judaism" or "Stoicism" but rather a tradition of philosophically oriented Jewish exegetes who see deep convergences between Torah/Judaism and the best of Hellenistic philosophy, with the former being superior as it contains the truest and best aspects of the latter. Erich Gruen describes the matter in this way: "The Jews were not so much permeated by the culture of the Greeks as they were an example of it. This made it all the more important to exhibit the features of their own legacy in the terms and language of their adopted one."[54] Thus, at the hands of Philo, Judaism is not compromised or left behind but is rather redefined through his appropriation of Hellenistic philosophy.[55] Philo's appropriation of Hellenistic divine-law discourse to the Jewish Torah invites his audience to compare Judaism with the best of Hellenistic philosophy to see which one is superior, but it does so precisely through showing convergences and differences.

---

52. M. David Litwa, *IESUS DEUS: The Early Christian Depiction of Jesus as a Mediterranean God* (Minneapolis: Fortress, 2014), 32.
53. So Sterling, "'Jewish Philosophy,'" 142.
54. Erich S. Gruen, *Heritage and Hellenism: The Reinvention of Jewish Tradition* (Berkeley: University of California Press, 1998), 292.
55. More broadly, Gruen, *Heritage and Hellenism*, 293–94.

PART TWO: GOD'S ACTS FOR GENTILES

Paul's Effort to Surpass Hellenistic Philosophical Critiques of Superstition

It is time now to return to our question, What is the relationship—if any—between Paul's Areopagus sermon and Stoic philosophy? I want to suggest that Rowe's response of "theologically incommensurate traditions" is one important part of the answer but that it ultimately fails to convince as an explanation for both the details of Acts 17 itself as well as the way in which Paul's sermon functions as a piece of intercultural missionary communication. Rowe is right to draw attention to Acts 17:22–31 and its narrative introduction as a critique of Greco-Roman religiosity, especially as it pertains to polytheism and idolatry.[56] But he has not successfully accounted for the ways in which Paul's speech draws upon some of the best features of Hellenistic philosophy, especially Stoic traditions, as a means of exalting the Christian movement as a legitimate, even superior philosophy. The fairly obvious overlap between Paul's speech and Stoic philosophy, then, is not accidental nor incidental to Paul's sermon. The topics of monotheism, the critique of temples and sacrifices, the deity's providential arrangement of the seasons, and the unity of humankind resonate quite clearly with Stoic philosophy. These similarities function to call the Athenians to turn from their ignorant worship of the deity by showing them that the Christian movement is the fulfillment of the *best* aspects of *their* history and traditions.[57] What we have learned from our studies of the encounter between the gospel and pre-Christian African religion as well as what we have seen in Philo's application of *Greco-Roman divine law traditions* to his articulation of the meaning of the *Jewish law* is applicable here. Our brief forays into the nature of missional interreligious communication and Philo as one representative of Hellenistic Judaism suggest that theological/religious "traditions" are not static systems of ideas that do not and *cannot* influence *and* be influenced by other traditions. Paul's sermon shows intentional overlap with Stoic philosophy as Paul connects his gospel message with Stoic notions of deity and humanity as a means of calling his audience to embrace the truth of the gospel as the superior and true philosophy.

Some scholars of Acts have recognized that Paul's sermon resonates with Hellenistic philosophical critiques of superstitious religion, a critique which

---

56. I have articulated my strong agreement with Rowe on this matter in Joshua W. Jipp, "Paul's Areopagus Speech of Acts 17:16–34 as *Both* Critique *and* Propaganda," *JBL* 131 (2012): 567–88.

57. My argument throughout this section has been articulated in more detail throughout Jipp, "Paul's Areopagus Speech."

centers upon human ignorance of the gods. One of the primary characteristics of superstition is the false belief that the gods should be feared and that one must pacify them lest they harm the one who has failed to give them their due worship.[58] Paul's opening salvo, then, while standing before the Areopagus, "I perceive that you are in every way ὡς δεισιδαιμονεστέρους" (17:22b), could possibly commend the Athenians for being "religious" or, alternatively, "superstitious."[59] Given that Luke has noted for the reader that Paul's spirit was "provoked" during his tour of the Athenian idols (17:17), his note about Athenian curiosity and novelty (often related to superstition, 17:21),[60] and the ensuing content of Paul's sermon, there are good reasons for seeing Paul's comment as indicating his intention to criticize polytheistic Athenian religion as superstitious.

I suggest that Paul is attempting to "one-up" the Stoics and Epicureans and beat them at their own game, so to speak, given that the Stoics and Epicurean philosophers were some of the primary critics of superstitious religion in the ancient world. The Epicureans engaged in the study of the natural world in order to alleviate the populace's superstitious fear that the gods controlled the world (see esp. Lucretius, *De rerum natura*). Stoics were known for their claim that temples and altars were not necessary for the gods (e.g., Diogenes, *Lives* 7.33). Seneca criticizes excessive religious devotion when he argues that cultic worship, sacrifices, and images are not necessary given that the deity is present everywhere and is accessible to all people (*Ep.* 95.47). Superstition, for Seneca, is religion without knowledge (*Ep.* 95.35). Since the gods are self-sufficient and need nothing from humans, the god is better worshipped by "those who know him" rather than through sacrifices.

Further, it is well known that the Stoics argued that humanity was the offspring of the deity, and, therefore, since the world and especially humanity are kin of the gods, humanity worships god through rational means rather than through sacrifice. Cleanthes says in his *Hymn to Zeus*, "We are your [i.e., Zeus's] offspring and we alone of all mortal creatures . . . bear a likeness to you" (*SVF* 1:537). Epictetus repeatedly emphasizes that humans are kin of Zeus and that they carry him about within themselves. For example, "Remember never

---

58. See here especially Dale B. Martin, *Inventing Superstition: From the Hippocratics to the Christians* (Cambridge: Harvard University Press, 2004), esp. 1–35.

59. This point is recognized by most commentators. For the potential for deliberate ambiguity here and beyond, see Mark D. Given, "Not Either/Or but Both/And in Paul's Areopagus Speech," *BibInt* 3 (1995): 356–72.

60. See Jipp, "Paul's Areopagus Speech," 574–75; Patrick Gray, "Athenian Curiosity (Acts 17:21)," *NovT* 47 (2005): 109–16.

to say you are alone, because you are not; god is inside and your own divine spirit too" (*Diatr.* 1.14.14). And again:

> You are a fragment of God; you have within you a part of him. Why, then, are you ignorant of your own kinship? . . . You are bearing God about within you, you poor wretch, and know it not! Do you suppose I am speaking of some external God, made of silver and gold? It is within yourself that you bear Him (Epictetus, *Diatr.* 2.8 [Oldfather, LCL]; cf. 1.12.26; 2.5.13; 4.7.6-7; 2.8.10-117).[61]

The Fourth Epistle of Pseudo-Heraclitus also testifies to the uselessness of temples for god since the entire world and humanity in particular contains the presence of the deity (*Ep.* 4):

> Where is god? Is he shut up in temples? You are a fine sort of pious men, who set up god in darkness! A man takes it as an insult if he is said to be stony; but is a god truly spoken of whose honorific title is "he is born from crags?" You ignorant men, don't you know that god is not wrought by hands, and has not from the beginning had a pedestal, and does not have a single enclosure? Rather the whole world is his temple, decorated with animals, plants, and stars.[62]

Further, god does not need sacrifices because he is completely self-sufficient: "God confers on us the greatest and most important favors without any thought of return. He has no need for anything to be conferred, nor could we confer anything on him" (Seneca, *Ben.* 4.9.1). If humanity is god's kin and likeness, and if the deity is autonomous and self-sufficient, then it is ignorant at best, superstitious at worst, for humans to suppose that they should worship him through temples, sacrifices, and priestly rituals. This connection between god's nearness to humanity and the resultant uselessness of statues, images, and sacrifices is further emphasized by Seneca: "We do not need to uplift our hands towards heaven, or to beg the keeper of a temple to let us approach his idol's ear, as if in this way our prayers were more likely to be heard. *God is near you, he is with you, he is within you*" (Seneca, *Ep.* 41.1 [Gummere, LCL]). Of course, Aratus, quoted by Paul in Acts 17:28, himself states the pervasive presence among the world and especially humanity:

---

61. On which, see A. A. Long, *Epictetus: A Stoic and Socratic Guide to Life* (Oxford: Oxford University Press, 2002), 180-206.

62. Translation here is taken from Harold W. Attridge, *First Century Cynicism in the Epistles of Heraclitus*, HTS 29 (Missoula, MT: Scholars Press, 1976), 58-59; further, see Abraham J. Malherbe, "Pseudo-Heraclitus, Epistle 4: The Divinization of the Wise Man," *JAC* 21 (1978): 42-64, esp. 51-54.

Does Paul Translate the Gospel in Acts 17:22-31?

> From Zeus let us begin; him do we mortals never leave unnamed; full of Zeus are all the streets and all the market-places of men; full is the sea and the havens thereof; always we all have need of Zeus. For we are also his offspring. (*Phaen.* 5 [Mair, LCL])

The similarities between the topics of Paul's sermon and basic Stoic beliefs about the nature of the deity, humanity, and proper worship are hard to miss. Like the Stoics, Paul too proclaims that the *singular* God (a) is the creator of all things and, therefore, does not dwell in human-made temples (οὐκ ἐν χειροποιήτοις ναοῖς κατοικεῖ, Acts 17:24); (b) is not rightly worshipped through human priestly sacrifices since he is the creator of everything (17:25); (c) has implanted internally within humans a desire to seek him (17:27); (d) and cannot be imaged through idols or created material since humanity alone is the offspring and likeness of God (17:28-29). Not only the topics themselves but the similarity of their internal logic and reasoning demonstrate close similarities to Stoic thinking. And again, the fact that the Stoic philosophers make up the dramatic audience of the sermon (17:18), along with Paul's explicit quotation from the well-known Stoic Aratus (17:28b) and the general reference to the Athenian poets (17:28a), suggests that Luke has crafted the sermon in such a way as to invite both the dramatic audience of the Athenians *and* readers of Acts to engage in comparison between Hellenistic philosophy and Paul's proclamation of the gospel.

On the one hand, Rowe is right that Stoicism and Christianity/Paul's gospel are distinct "traditions" and cannot be subsumed under a broader category. We have seen, as Rowe has helpfully emphasized, that the narrative introduction to Paul's speech prepares the reader for conflict between Paul's gospel and his audience. Further, if Paul is to be understood as chastising his audience for being "excessively superstitious" (17:22b), which makes good sense in light of his reference to having encountered an altar to "an unknown god" (17:23), then Paul is charging his audience of engaging in *irrational worship*. The motivation for establishing altars to unknown gods stems from anxiety that one has not placated every god possible.[63] Thus, when Paul declares that he will now proclaim to them the one "whom they have worshipped *in ignorance*" (17:23b), he turns the table on the Athenians by declaring that *they are the superstitious ones who worship in ignorance.*[64] Rowe is absolutely right here that Paul's proc-

---

63. See Hans-Josef Klauck, *Magic and Paganism in Early Christianity: The World of the Acts of the Apostles* (Edinburgh: T&T Clark, 2000), 82-83.
64. Paul refers to their worship as "ignorant" or "without knowledge" three times in his speech (17:23 twice; 17:30).

lamation of this "unknown god" is not the materialistic deity of Stoicism but is the God revealed in Israel's Scriptures and Messiah. And, of course, Paul's invocation of the Stoic poets and Aratus functions to make the point that *the singular human* Jesus of Nazareth, the one who died and has been raised from the dead, is God's appointed judge of the world (17:31)—a point which most of the audience finds absurd (17:32).

But on the other hand, Paul's sermon engages Stoic scripts, vocabulary, and even authors as a means of proclaiming God to his audience.[65] Paul enters into the cultural and religious logic of Stoicism, then, and presents the Hellenistic philosophers as capable of rightly responding to Paul's God even out of their own philosophical commitments.[66] Paul's proclamation, "What you worship in ignorance, I proclaim this one to you" (17:23), indicates that the Creator God has been present within Athens before the arrival of the gospel.[67] Paul shows cultural convergence here between his message and the philosophers by seeking to portray the Christian movement as a superior philosophy. God is the creator of the universe who is self-sufficient and autonomous and does not need sacrifice or cultic worship from humans. On this, the Stoics and Paul are agreed; but Paul states that despite this convergence, the Athenians have remained ignorant of the true God, and this is demonstrated by the fact that they still continue to engage in *irrational* cultic worship. Thus, there is indeed criticism and conflict between Paul's God and the Stoics, but Paul is portrayed as one who works within—even as he disrupts and criticizes—the philosophical commitments of his audience in order to call them to repentance to the true God and conversion to the gospel of Christ.[68] While there is much more that could be said, a reading

---

65. In this regard, I think Rowe's criticism of Abraham Malherbe is misguided (see Rowe, *One True Life*, 184–89). Malherbe's work often posits similarity when comparing Christian texts and Hellenistic philosophy, but one of Malherbe's important contributions was to show how Hellenistic philosophers *and* Christian authors used *similar* topoi for *similar* ends albeit within *different* contexts or traditions. Malherbe's work is not characterized by an inability to differentiate between Christianity and Stoicism.

66. See here the important work of Luke Timothy Johnson, *Among the Gentiles: Greco-Roman Religion and Christianity*, AYBRL (New Haven: Yale University Press, 2009), who draws attention to some of the deep similarities between ancient pagans and Christians in terms of religious impulses, convictions, and practices.

67. Rowe, *World Upside Down*, 34, seems to me to show greater recognition of some of the convergences than does "Grammar of Life" or *One True Life*. The emphasis is still almost entirely upon that of "conflict" and "cultural destabilization."

68. I have made a similar argument for Paul among the Maltese in Joshua W. Jipp, "Hospitable Barbarians: Luke's Ethnic Reasoning in Acts 28:1–10," *JTS* 68 (2017): 23–45, here 40–44, which appears as chapter 7 of this volume.

of Acts 17 that draws attention to *both* cultural and religious convergence *and* conflict in Paul's sermon makes much better sense of Acts 17 *and* makes better sense of Paul's sermon as intercultural missionary proclamation.

As Kwame Bediako argued for the conversion rather than replacement and complete rejection of pre-Christian African cultural and religious sensibilities to Christ, so Paul's gospel seeks to do the same with the Stoic philosophers. In both cases, this "conversion" toward Christ involves critique and at times rejection due to ignorance of the one true God, but it also involves the cultural appropriation of the language, categories, and beliefs of pre-Christian religion and culture. In other words, rather than conceptualizing Paul's missionary strategy as *mission as replacement* (with which Rowe's analysis fits well),[69] Paul's sermon fits better with a model of mission as *appropriation* whereby non-Christian cultures appropriate the gospel within their own culture; thus, the gospel both *transforms* culture and takes new forms and shapes as it is articulated and expressed through different cultures and languages.[70] All too briefly, I have suggested that certain Hellenistic Jews, most obviously Philo, provide a precedent for this as they consciously appropriated and adapted Greco-Roman philosophy, particularly divine law traditions, in their portrait of Judaism and the Torah.[71]

A moment's thought, I think, indicates that Luke does the same thing throughout Luke-Acts as he adapts scripts, themes, and traditions from Greco-Roman culture as a means of communicating the gospel. In addition to Paul's appropriation of Stoic philosophy in his proclamation in Athens, I think of the following as indicating Luke's adaptation of the gospel to Greco-Roman cultural patterns and traditions: Luke's literary prefaces and their similarities to Hellenistic historiography (Luke 1:1-4; Acts 1:1-2), the portrait of Jesus as participating in four symposia (Luke 5:27-30; 7:36-50; 11:37-54; 14:1-24),[72] the transformation of the traditions of Jesus's crucifixion into that of noble death (Luke 23; cf. Acts 4:29; 5:29),[73] the shaping of Jesus's resurrection appearance

---

69. Wrogemann describes this sense of mission as making "a radical break with the old religion: the old must be replaced by the new because light has nothing in common with darkness, because God has nothing in common with the devil and his accomplices, and because the true faith has nothing to do with reprehensible paganism" (*Intercultural Hermeneutics*, 235).

70. Wrogemann, *Intercultural Hermeneutics*, 291-310.

71. See here Wolfgang Nauck, "Die Tradition und Komposition der Areopagrede," *ZTK* 53 (1956): 11-52.

72. Dennis E. Smith, "Table Fellowship as a Literary Motif in the Gospel of Luke," *JBL* 106 (1987): 613-38.

73. Gregory E. Sterling, "*Mors philosophi*: The Death of Jesus in Luke," *HTR* 94 (2001): 383-402.

PART TWO: GOD'S ACTS FOR GENTILES

in the literary guise of a theoxeny (Luke 24:13–35; cf. Acts 28:1–10),[74] the use of philosophical friendship language to exalt the Jerusalem church's common life (Acts 2:41–47; 4:32–35), God's validation of the Christian movement as exemplified in the apostles' prison escapes (Acts 5:19–20; 12:1–17; 16:25–34),[75] and the depiction of the Christian movement's power and success as validated through victorious turf wars against its competitors (8:14–25; 13:5–12; 19:11–20; 28:3–6). If the gospel of Jesus Christ is best understood as a tradition, then it is a tradition that is able to continually both adapt to and criticize the culture and religion within which it takes root.

---

74. Joshua W. Jipp, *Divine Visitations and Hospitality to Strangers in Luke-Acts: An Interpretation of the Malta Episode in Acts 28:1–10*, NovTSup 153 (Leiden: Brill, 2012).

75. John B. Weaver, *Plots of Epiphany: Prison-Escape in Acts of the Apostles*, BZNW 131 (Berlin: de Gruyter, 2004).

7

"Hospitable Barbarians"

Luke's Ethnic Reasoning in Acts 28:1–10

In his *The Christian Imagination: Theology and the Origins of Race*, Willie James Jennings narrates "Christian identity from within the Gentile-Jewish relational matrix" in order to show how "a supersessionist sensibility coupled with visions of life from within white supremacist imaginings" have contributed to a diseased Christian social imagination.[1] Christianity's diseased social imagination is wed to the colonial dominance whereby "other peoples and their ways of life had to adapt, become fluid, even morph into the colonial order of things, and such a situation drew Christianity and its theologians inside habits of mind and life that internalized and normalized that order of things."[2] According to Jennings, this diseased Christian social imagination has underestimated the significance of God's election of Israel and has thereby failed to grasp the biblical "scandal of particularly."[3] Jennings's use of the language "Israel" and Israel's "particularity" is often problematic, both from a broader historical standpoint and from the evidence of the author of Acts (see especially Acts 2:5–11), for the suggestion that Israel is *one dis-*

---

1. Willie James Jennings, *The Christian Imagination: Theology and the Origins of Race* (New Haven: Yale University Press, 2010), 291–92.
2. Jennings, *Christian Imagination*, 8. On the processes whereby African countries were divided into tribes with a native elite, under the direction of European colonial dominance, who enforced so-called "customary" laws upon the majority of the population as a means of assimilation, see Mahmood Mamdani, *Citizen and Subject: Contemporary Africa and the Legacy of Late Colonialism* (Princeton: Princeton University Press, 1996).
3. Jennings, *Christian Imagination*, 160.

tinct ethnic group.[4] Rather, as Cynthia Baker, Shaye Cohen, and others have demonstrated, it would be more historically accurate to admit that Jews were frequently depicted as a multiethnic people who often "embody multiple (often dual) lineages of birth, land, history, and culture."[5] Certain scholarly descriptions, then, of the peoples of Israel, as *particular* do not do justice to the way in which the author of Acts uses the multiethnic diversity of Israel as a precedent and anticipation for the incorporation of non-Jewish peoples into the *already* multiethnic people of Israel.[6] I speak of Israel, then, as an ethnic group—with its own *claims* to a shared ancestry, kinship, geographical land, and deity—but with the recognition that Israel must not be thought of as a particular or monolithic ethnic group.[7]

Nevertheless Jennings is right that the failure to attend to God's election of Israel has proved disastrous for Christian theology by failing to understand the way in which the non-Jewish peoples are incorporated into the *peoples* of Israel "through the body of Jesus," such that Christian theology lacks "patterns of communion" whereby it can understand and enter into relationship with "the cultural inner logics of peoples."[8] A healed social imagination, for Jennings, must reckon with the fact that Christian theology exists *within* the peoples of Israel and Israel's God: "Israel's house is a space where people are joined in worship and where ways of life come into the communion of the common, of eating, sleeping, and living together."[9] Only through the election of Israel and Israel's Messiah is Christian theology provided with the resources that enable communion between peoples.[10] J. Kameron Carter also notes that

---

4. See here especially Cynthia M. Baker, "'From Every Nation Under Heaven': Jewish Ethnicities in the Greco-Roman World," in *Prejudice and Christian Beginnings: Investigating Race, Gender, and Ethnicity in Early Christianity*, ed. Elisabeth Schüssler Fiorenza and Laura Nasrallah (Minneapolis: Fortress, 2009), 79–99. See also Shaye J. D. Cohen, *The Beginnings of Jewishness: Boundaries, Varieties, Uncertainties* (Berkeley: University of California Press, 1999), 135–39; Laura Salah Nasrallah, *Christian Responses to Roman Art and Architecture: The Second-Century Church Amid the Spaces of Empire* (Cambridge: Cambridge University Press, 2010), 107–10. While Jennings consistently speaks of "Israel," when appropriate I refer to the peoples of Israel to highlight the fact that Israel *is a multiethnic people*.

5. Baker, "From Every Nation Under Heaven,'" 81.

6. Again, see Baker, "'From Every Nation Under Heaven,'" 91–99.

7. On the concept of ethnicity in the Greco-Roman world, see Jonathan M. Hall, *Hellenicity: Between Ethnicity and Culture* (Chicago: University of Chicago Press, 2002), 9–18.

8. Jennings, *Christian Imagination*, 154.

9. Jennings, *Christian Imagination*, 160.

10. See now, however, among others, Robert W. Jenson, "Toward a Christian Theology of Israel," *Pro Ecclesia* 9 (2000): 43–56; R. Kendall Soulen, *The God of Israel and Christian*

"Hospitable Barbarians"

it is modernity's dispensing with Christ's Jewishness that results in a portrait of Christ who "is not a figure who disrupts and draws us out of the reality that whiteness crafts for itself."[11] Jesus, in fact, is frequently reinscribed with the social and political structures of a non-particular and unmarked order of whiteness.[12] The ability to heal Christianity's diseased social imagination, then, resides not in some grand theological universalizing principle that denies or minimizes the significance of cultural and ethnic identities;[13] rather, the embrace of bodies, lands, customs, and languages of non-Jewish peoples resides in remembering that non-Jewish Christian existence resides in the deep connection between Jesus and Israel.[14] Only when this connection is made will Christians be able to "recognize the grotesque nature of a social per-

---

Theology (Minneapolis: Fortress, 1996); R. Kendall Soulen, *Distinguishing the Voices*, vol. 1 of *The Divine Name(s) and the Holy Trinity* (Louisville: Westminster John Knox, 2011).

11. J. Kameron Carter, *Race: A Theological Account* (Oxford: Oxford University Press, 2008), 117. On the way in which popular images and depictions of Jesus have been inscribed within racial agendas, see Edward J. Blum and Paul Harvey, *The Color of Christ: The Son of God and the Saga of Race in America* (Chapel Hill: University of North Carolina Press, 2012), 154: "The white Jesus could be found far and wide in the culture of militant expansion, and his presence cloaked particular national, racial, and economic interests under a sacred canopy of universal care and compassion. As imperialism stretched from the American West to overseas ventures, the white Christ became a big brother figure who sanctified concepts of white racial adulthood and nonwhite racial childhood. He was made into a supposedly universal savior, but one who privileged white authority and dominance."

12. Carter, *Race*, 89. Relevant here is also Halvor Moxnes, Ward Blanton, and James G. Crossley, *Jesus Beyond Nationalism: Constructing the Historical Jesus in a Period of Cultural Complexity* (London: Routledge, 2014).

13. On modernity's development of racialized ideologies which are hostile to particularity (often linked with Judaism), see Shawn Kelley, *Racializing Jesus: Race, Ideology and the Formation of Modern Biblical Scholarship* (London: Routledge, 2002); Michael Mack, *German Idealism and the Jew: The Inner Anti-Semitism of Philosophy and German Jewish Responses* (Chicago: University of Chicago Press, 2003); Denise Kimber Buell, *Why This New Race: Ethnic Reasoning in Early Christianity* (New York: Columbia University Press, 2005), 28–29; Carter, *Race*, 39–121. Often with the best of professed intentions, the significance of Jesus's Jewish identity has often been minimized in order to present him as a universal savior for all people. See here again, Blum and Harvey, *Color of Christ*, 151–54; Susannah Heschel, *The Aryan Jesus: Christian Theologians and the Bible in Nazi Germany* (Princeton: Princeton University Press, 2008), 26–65.

14. Jennings, *Christian Imagination*, 259–65. See also Carter, *Race*, 13, who draws a parallel between modernity and ancient Gnostic attempts to eradicate "all things Jewish from the Christian imagination," 13: "My claim is that this concerted effort to overcome Judaism is what binds the racial imagination at work in the forms and systems of thought marking modernity and the anthropological imagination at work in the forms and systems of thought marking the ancient Gnostic movements."

formance of Christianity that imagines Christian identity floating above land, landscape, animals, place, and space, leaving such realities to the machinations of capitalistic calculations and the commodity chains of private property."[15]

A healed Christian imagination must work for "the emergence of spaces of communion that announce the healing of the nations through the story of Israel bound up in Jesus," and this will mean the ability to "discern the ways [peoples'] cultural practices and stories both echo and contradict the divine claim on their lives" rather than a vision of "a Creator bent on eradicating peoples' ways of life and turning the creation into private property."[16] Modern interpretations of the Acts of the Apostles—with its narration of the Christian movement's expansion from Jewish territory into non-Jewish peoples and lands—is fertile ground for exploring the exegetical and theological tactics interpreters have used to deny the significance of Israel's election for Christian existence *and* the concomitant devaluation of the particular ethnic identities and cultural practices of the peoples who dot the landscape of Acts.[17] The consequences of these readings of Acts have deleterious consequences both with respect to Israel *and* for non-Jewish peoples. For example, Shawn Kelley, among others, has demonstrated how F. C. Baur's historical reconstruction of Christian origins is thoroughly racialized as Christianity is seen as breaking free from the stultifying particular rites and ordinances of Judaism into a higher form of religious consciousness.[18] Martin Heidegger's discourse of temporality, primordiality, authenticity, fallenness, and "the They" has exerted enormous weight (often unwittingly) on interpretations of Luke-Acts.[19] Thus, the conflict between the Hebrews and Hellenists in Acts 6 is seen as centering upon—despite what the text itself says—the Hebrews' attachment to national

---

15. Jennings, *Christian Imagination*, 293.

16. Jennings, *Christian Imagination*, 292–93.

17. Defining ethnicity is a highly controversial and contested task. See John Hutchinson and Anthony D. Smith, eds., *Ethnicity* (Oxford: Oxford University Press, 1996). Hutchinson and Smith argue that there are in varying degrees six common features of ethnicity: a common proper name, a myth of ancestry, shared memories, some elements of a common culture, a homeland, and a sense of solidarity (6–7).

18. In this vein, one can see how the dominant notion of Luke-Acts as participating in the "early Catholic" tendencies of early Christianity is a thoroughly racialized notion. Kelley, *Racializing Jesus*, 150–54.

19. See Kelley's conclusion where he argues for the discarding of these racialized constructs. See Kelley, *Racializing Jesus*, 211–15. See also the critique of biblical scholarship's quest for the "pure essence" of Christian origins by Jonathan Z. Smith, *Drudgery Divine: On the Comparison of Early Christianities and the Religions of Late Antiquity* (Chicago: University of Chicago Press, 1990), 1–35.

"Hospitable Barbarians"

Judaism and the Hellenists' deeper grasp of the spiritual and universal context of Jesus's preaching.[20] Even for those who position themselves as critics of Baur's reconstruction of Christian origins, most interpreters operate within this racialized framework.[21] Albeit unwittingly, then, modern and contemporary history of scholarship on Acts is filled with racialized judgments and interpretive strategies that frequently deny or minimize the significance of Israel and Israel's election, fail to reckon with Paul's adamant and repeated claims to have never moved away from historic Judaism (Acts 22–26),[22] and valorize the Hellenists for breaking away from a cramping Judaism that is too closely wed to Torah, land, and temple.[23]

If Jennings is right that a more loving, welcoming appreciation of the cultural logics of various ethnicities depends upon recovering Israel's election as the means whereby the non-Jew is joined to God's people through the body of Jesus, then these racialized interpretations of Acts have disastrous consequences not only for understanding Judaism but also for the way in which Acts envisions non-Jewish peoples *and* the patterns of communion shared between the Jew and non-Jew who belong to God's people.[24] In this chapter,

---

20. Kelley, *Racializing Jesus*, 64–75.

21. Defining "race" and "racism" is notoriously difficult. Attempting to steer a middle way between offering an essentializing definition of race and race as an illusory ideological construct, Michael Omi and Howard Winant define race as "a concept which signifies and symbolizes social conflicts and interests by referring to different types of human bodies. . . . Thus, we should think of race as an element of social structure rather than as an irregularity within it; we should see race as a dimension of human representation rather than as an illusion." See their "Racial Formation," in *The New Social Theory Reader*, 2nd ed., ed. Steven Seidman and Jeffrey C. Alexander (London: Routledge, 2008), 405–6.

22. Interpreters often see James's statement (a slanderously false rumor according to Acts) that Paul teaches the Diaspora Jews to abandon Moses as corresponding to reality (Acts 21:21). See further the common view that James and the Jerusalem church are setting up Paul for an ambush in Acts 21:15–29 and that this accounts for the Jerusalem church's failure to help Paul during his custody. On scholarly disbelief that Paul would engage in the purification mentioned in Acts 21:20–27, see those scholars mentioned by Reidar Hvalvik, "Paul as a Jewish Believer—according to the Book of Acts," in *Jewish Believers in Jesus: The Early Centuries*, ed. Oskar Skarsaune and Reidar Hvalvik (Peabody, MA: Hendrickson, 2007), 121–53, here 141–43.

23. See here Wayne A. Meeks, "Judaism, Hellenism, and the Birth of Christianity," in *Paul Beyond the Judaism/Hellenism Divide*, ed. Troels Engberg-Pedersen (Louisville: Westminster John Knox, 2001), 17–28; Dale B. Martin, "Paul and the Judaism/Hellenism Dichotomy: Toward a Social History of the Question," in *Paul Beyond the Judaism/Hellenism Divide*, 29–61.

24. For example, the Institute for the Study and Eradication of Jewish Influence on German Church Life sought to redefine Christianity as a Germanic religion precisely through

PART TWO: GOD'S ACTS FOR GENTILES

I suggest that a reading of Acts 28:1–10 that attends to the narrative's use of ethnic reasoning may help provide a window into broader Lukan ethnic reasoning that will help to recover a more compelling and embracing Christian social imagination. By "ethnic reasoning" I refer to Luke's use of "culturally available understandings of human difference, which we can analyze in terms of our modern concepts of 'ethnicity,' 'race,' and 'religion.'"[25] While I examined the literary and socio-cultural function of hospitality to strangers and its bearings on Acts 28 in a previous study, I did not recognize the extent to which the episode contains significant *Lukan* language related to ethnic discourse: Paul's characterization as an emissary of Israel's God, Maltese islanders, the other-ing language of barbarians, the religious dispositions of the Maltese, and the dynamics of ritualized friendship/hospitality.[26] Rather than rejecting or transcending ethnicity through a universal form of "Christian-ness",[27] Luke uses ethnic discourse to show the possibility of hospitable encounters and "patterns of communion" between the God of Israel and non-Jews and in such a way that does not demand the non-Jew to eradicate his/her particular ethnic identity.[28] I will suggest that Luke's reversal of ethnic stereotyping, his use of the social-cultural dynamic of ritualized friendship between Jew and non-Jew, and respect for the spaces of non-Jewish peoples suggests a broader Lukan strategy of ethnic reasoning that may hold some promise for healing a racially diseased Christian social imagination. This episode of Paul's travel to Malta and his encounter with the Maltese islanders provides one small but significant instance of how Luke conceptualizes patterns of communion between Jew and non-Jew in a way that both maintains the centrality of Israel's election *and* does not force non-Jews to assimilate in such a way as to eradicate or minimize their ethnic identity.[29]

---

racializing strategies. See Heschel, *Aryan Jesus*, 21: "Eliminating the Jewish from Christianity constituted a renewed racialization, Christianity's reassertion of itself as a racial religion."

25. Buell, *Why This New Race*, 2.

26. Buell, *Why This New Race*, 2, further speaks of ethnic reasoning in early Christianity as "the rhetorical situations in which early Christian texts use ideas about peoplehood to communicate and persuade readers about Christianness."

27. The assumption by many (historically white European) NT scholars that Acts projects a universal vision of Christian identity that transcends ethnicity is, in my opinion, almost certainly intertwined with their own white identity as unmarked, unnamed, and normative. See here Ruth Frankenberg, *White Women, Race Matters: The Social Construction of Whiteness* (Minneapolis: University of Minnesota Press, 1993).

28. Similarly, see Eric D. Barreto, *Ethnic Negotiations: The Function of Race and Ethnicity in Acts 16*, WUNT 2/294 (Tübingen: Mohr Siebeck, 2010).

29. See also Nasrallah, *Christian Responses*, 111, who notes that many of Paul's travels

"Hospitable Barbarians"

ETHNIC STEREOTYPING

When Paul and his crew wreck on the coast of Malta, Luke refers twice to the islanders as οἱ βάρβαροι (28:2, 4). This is surprising given that Luke uses this language nowhere else in his narrative and in light of the fact that he typically uses the term τὰ ἔθνη to describe non-Jews.[30] I do not find the notion that Luke uses the term to indicate the inability of the Maltese to verbally communicate with Paul especially in light of the very Roman sounding name of Publius—"the first man of the island" (28:7a).[31] While βάρβαρος is most frequently used to distinguish between Greek and non-Greek and is, therefore, an othering term, it is not always used in a pejorative manner to engage in negative ethnic stereotyping.[32] Plutarch, as is well known, referred to Herodotus as a "barbarian-lover" (*Her. Mal.* 857a), and while this overstates the matter, it is not difficult to find both critique and appreciation for the Persian "barbarians" in Herodotus's *Histories*.[33] Xenophon wrote an entire volume detailing his appreciation for the Persian ruler in his *Cyropaideia*. Arnoldo Momigliano and Erich Gruen more recently have shown how many Greeks appreciated the wisdom of the barbarians *and* that scholarly emphasis on the Greeks' and Romans' denigrations of others is often overdone.[34] With this caveat firmly in mind, it is not difficult to find plentiful examples of Greeks using the language of "barbarian" to engage in ethnic and cultural stereotyping

---

are described as "narrative distillations of issues of ethnicity, proper practice of religion, *paideia*, and relations with Rome."

30. So Joshua W. Jipp, *Divine Visitations and Hospitality to Strangers in Luke-Acts: An Interpretation of the Malta Episode in Acts 28:1–10*, NovTSup 153 (Leiden: Brill, 2012), 39.

31. On the use of "barbarian" by Greeks to describe the speech of non-Greek speakers, see Herodotus, *Hist.* 2.57; Ovid, *Tristia* 5.10.37; 1 Corinthians 14:11. Archaeological evidence suggests that the Maltese spoke Punic. See Colin J. Hemer, *The Book of Acts in the Setting of Hellenistic History*, WUNT 49 (Tübingen: Mohr Siebeck, 1989), 152–53.

32. Henry J. Cadbury, *The Book of Acts in History* (London: Adam and Charles Black, 1955), 32, states that the word is "the exact term by which the ancient Greeks distinguished all people outside their own circle."

33. E.g., see the Persians' constitutional debate where they deliberate about the best form of government and constitutional structure (3.80–82). Also see Herodotus's appreciation of some Persian characteristics in 1.136–138. See François Hartog, *The Mirror of Herodotus: The Representation of the Other in the Writing of History*, trans. Janet Lloyd (Berkeley: University of California Press, 1988).

34. Arnoldo Momigliano, *Alien Wisdom: The Limits of Hellenization* (Cambridge: Cambridge University Press, 1975); Erich S. Gruen, *Rethinking the Other in Antiquity* (Princeton: Princeton University Press, 2011); Patrick J. Geary, *The Myth of Nations: The Medieval Origins of Europe* (Princeton: Princeton University Press, 2002), 42–46.

PART TWO: GOD'S ACTS FOR GENTILES

whereby the language, customs, religion, land, and ancestry of another people is the polar opposite of the ideal civilized Greek.[35] Thus, Stamenka E. Antonova is right to say that even when the term "refers merely to a foreign ethnicity or foreign tongue, it is laden with negative connotations that go beyond the original meaning of the word in Greek."[36]

A fairly frequent topos, in fact, and one that I suggest is almost certainly activated by the depiction of Paul and his crew shipwrecking on an unfamiliar island is the inhospitable, impious, and uncivilized barbarian who kills shipwrecked strangers.[37] Given that Greeks see themselves as civilized practitioners of hospitality to strangers, they frequently project the barbarian other as inhospitable and as those who corrupt or subvert hospitality protocols.[38] More particularly, one finds this theme with respect to the shipwrecked Odysseus throughout Homer's *Odyssey* as Odysseus encounters new lands in his voyage: "Alas, to the land of what mortals have I now come? Are they insolent, wild, and unjust? Or are they hospitable to strangers and fear the gods in their thoughts?"[39] In other words, Odysseus, who recognizes his vulnerable position as a stranger as he approaches new lands and peoples, wonders if he will encounter civilized hospitable peoples or Cyclopes who impiously break

---

35. See here especially Edith Hall, *Inventing the Barbarian: Greek Self-Definition through Tragedy* (Oxford: Clarendon, 1989); Paul A. Cartledge, *The Greeks: A Portrait of Self and Others*, 2nd ed. (Oxford: Oxford University Press, 1997), 38-39, 51-77. Even if the use of βάρβαρος stressed, in the first instance, an inability to speak the Greek language, there is a close connection between the Greek's perception of speech, culture, reason, and virtue. See E. Hall, *Inventing the Barbarian*, 199-200.

36. Stamenka E. Antonova, "Barbarians and the Empire-Wide Spread of Christianity," in *The Spread of Christianity in the First Four Centuries: Essays in Explanation*, ed. W. V. Harris, Columbia Studies in the Classical Tradition 27 (Leiden: Brill, 2005), 69-85, here 69. Geary, *Myth of Nations*, 42, describes the two categorizations of peoples in classical and biblical antiquity as follows: "The one was *constitutional*, based on law, allegiance, and created by a historical process. The other, standing largely outside the process of historical change was *biological*, based on descent, custom, and geography. Crudely, one can characterize the difference as 'us' and 'them'; 'civilized' and 'barbarian.'" Cf. the numerous examples in Hans Windisch, "βάρβαρος," *TDNT*, 546-553.

37. Of the reasons for Luke's use of the term "barbarian" in 28:2, 4 has remained a problem, in my view, due to the lack of recognition of this literary motif. See, for example, Ronald H. van der Bergh, "Insiders or Outsiders: The Use of the Term βάρβαρος in the Acts of the Apostles: A *Problemanzeige*," *Neotestamentica* 47 (2013): 69-86. Cf. Jipp, *Divine Visitations*, 39-44.

38. Paris: Aeschylus, *Agamemnon* 60-62, 362-363, 395-402, 525-527, 701-704, 745-749; Euripides, *Trojan Women* 865-866; the Egyptian king Teucer: Euripides, *Helen* 155; Lycaon: Ovid, *Metamorphoses* 1.197-198.

39. Homer, *Odyssey* 6.119-121; 9.172-176; 13.200-202.

"Hospitable Barbarians"

every hospitality protocol and violently attack strangers who approach their land (9.252–370). Similarly, in Virgil's *Aeneid*, Ilioneus asks Dido if Carthage is "a country of barbarians" based on the inhospitable treatment the Trojans receive when they shipwreck (1.538–539). Herodotus says the Tauric "barbarians" sacrifice those who shipwreck on their land (*Hist.* 4.103), and the "barbarian gates" of the Egyptians do the same in Euripides's *Helen* (789). Cicero notes that it is both "inhumane" and "barbaric" to refuse hospitality to a stranger (*Verr.* 2.4.25). Alternatively, Seneca (*On Benefits*) and Dio Chrysostom ("The Hunter," 6.51–54) speak of hospitality to the shipwrecked stranger as the pinnacle of virtue since the one who bestows benefits upon the vulnerable shipwrecked has little hope of receiving a return on his benefaction.

Thus, Luke has prepared the reader for an impending inhospitality episode. Paul is unknown to the Maltese; there is no description of "brothers" (Acts 21:7–17; 28:12–15) or "friends" (27:3) on the island; and the term "barbarian" others the islanders by activating social, cultural, and ethnic differences between Paul and the Maltese. Henry Cadbury is right, then, when he notes that the socio-cultural expectations of the passage forebodes "to any Greek unfriendly treatment, especially shipwrecked strangers."[40] Luke surprises the reader, however, by describing the Maltese as kindly bestowing care and hospitality upon Paul and the vulnerable prisoners who shipwreck on the island.[41] Rather than those who kill the shipwrecked, Luke's language of "they showed us no insignificant kindness" (παρεῖχον οὐ τὴν τυχοῦσαν φιλανθρωπίαν ἡμῖν, 28:2a) and "they welcomed all of us" (προσελάβοντο πάντας ἡμᾶς) by building a fire to provide warmth from the cold (28:2b) portray the Maltese as exemplars of the civilized custom of hospitality to strangers. At the very least, the Maltese are kind and hospitable hosts; but given Luke's consistent use of the practice of hospitality to strangers to mark out characters who embrace God's visitation of his people, the Maltese are placed with characters like the so-called sinful woman (Luke 7:36–50), Mary (Luke 10:38–42), Zacchaeus (Luke 19:1–10), Cornelius (Acts 10:1–48), and Lydia (Acts 16:11–15). Their extraordinary kindness is extraordinary precisely because as those who are shipwrecked, Paul is not only entirely vulnerable to the actions of the Maltese but he also has nothing with which to reciprocate for any kindness he might receive. This is why au-

---

40. Cadbury, *Book of Acts in History*, 25.
41. John Chrysostom notes the incredible fact that the Maltese are practitioners of the early Christian virtue of hospitality to the incarcerated (*Hom. Act.* 1–55). See here Ronald H. van der Bergh, "The Missionary Character of Paul's Stay on Malta (Acts 28:1–10) according to the Early Church," *Journal of Early Christian History* 3 (2013): 83–97, here 90.

PART TWO: GOD'S ACTS FOR GENTILES

thors frequently use stories of kindness to shipwrecked sailors as examples of pure piety given that the vulnerable are destitute and unable to make a return for any benefits they might receive.[42] Luke's pairing, then, of βάρβαρος with φιλανθρωπία is intentionally jarring. Barbarians, stereotypically, do not show hospitable kindness to shipwrecked strangers. But Luke deliberately rejects this stereotype by juxtaposing "barbarian" and "love for humanity." The text challenges one to put together two impossible (or at least incredibly unlikely based on cultural conventions) descriptions for the same people—"barbarian" and "extraordinarily hospitable"—and in so doing works to subvert and deconstruct the validity of engaging in ethnic stereotyping as a valid means of making sense of the cultural worth and value of other ethnicities.

This is not at all unlike how Luke employs other ethnic and cultural stereotypes, namely, raising the stereotype only in order to subvert it. For example, as John Dominic Crossan has noted in the so-called parable of the good Samaritan, "The literal point of the story challenges the hearer to put together two impossible and contradictory words for the same person: 'Samaritan' (10:33) and 'neighbor' (10:36).... The story demands that the hearer respond by saying the contradictory, the impossible, the unspeakable."[43] As the hearer struggles to make sense of the *seemingly* contradictory terms, Luke effectively renders the stereotype entirely deficient to make sense of human characters. Luke may be doing something similar with his descriptions of Roman centurions. Within Luke-Acts, centurions recognize and submit to Jesus's authority (Luke 7:2–10), confess Jesus's innocence (Luke 23:46–47), are pious and give alms (Acts 10:1–6), and show great kindness toward Paul (φιλανθρώπως, Acts 27:3; cf. 21:37–40). Luke's centurions behave contrary to the majority socio-cultural expectations of the readers in that these Roman military leaders are not brutish, thuggish, violent, or shaking down and conscripting local citizens. Rather, as Laurie Brink has demonstrated, Luke's "portrait invites the authorial audience to recognize that even a soldier possesses the possibilities of conversion and commitment."[44] Luke's description of the "Ethiopian" (8:27) "eunuch" (8:27, 34, 38, 39) neither activates stereotypes of Ethiopians as symbols of vice or sexual passion nor tropes of eunuchs as salacious, hybrid/ambiguous monstrosities.[45]

---

42. E.g., Seneca, *Ben.* 1.5.4; 3.9.3; 3.35.4; 4.11.1–3; Lucian, *True Story* 1.28–29; 2.46; Petronius, *Satyricon* 114.

43. John Dominic Crossan, *In Parables: The Challenge of the Historical Jesus* (New York: Harper and Row, 1975), 64.

44. Laurie Brink, *Soldiers in Luke-Acts: Engaging, Contradicting, and Transcending the Stereotypes*, WUNT 2/362 (Tübingen: Mohr Siebeck, 2014), 166.

45. There are, of course, a variety of descriptors for ancient Ethiopians. See Rebecca F.

"Hospitable Barbarians"

Rather, the eunuch is a "model of virtue": he is silent and humble as he listens to the interpretation of Isaiah, receives baptism, and rejoices.[46] Thus, the Malta episode provides us with a window into Luke's disrupting and subverting cultural and ethnic stereotypes as a means of making sense of human relations as the Maltese "barbarians" execute hospitality protocols as appropriately and beneficently as any other character or group within Luke-Acts.

Ritualized Friendship—ξενία

Readers of Acts invariably recognize its universalizing impulses. God's salvation is for "all peoples" (Luke 2:31) and "all flesh" (Luke 3:6); the apostles are Christ's witnesses to "the ends of the earth" (Acts 1:8); the message is for "all the nations" (Luke 24:47); God shows no partiality to any people group (Acts 10:34–35). Clearly, Luke is concerned to demonstrate that God's salvation and its implications are for all peoples. But this creation of a people oriented around Israel's Messiah does *not* demand people to assimilate in such a way so as to *eradicate* peoples' ethnic or cultural identity, even if it does result in some transformation of one's collective ethnic consciousness.[47] Luke does not, in other words, present "Christians" as a new race or ethnicity into which non-Jews must assimilate.[48] Neither does Luke's universal impulses result in

---

Kennedy, C. Sydnor Roy, Max L. Goldman, trans., *Race and Ethnicity in the Classical World: An Anthology of Primary Sources in Translation* (Indianapolis: Hackett, 2013), 179–201. On the eunuch as a representative example of the outcast, see David W. Pao, *Acts and the Isaianic New Exodus*, WUNT 2/130 (Tübingen: Mohr Siebeck, 2000), 140–42. On scholarship's tendency to downplay the significance of the man's ethnic identity, see Clarice J. Martin, "A Chamberlain's Journey and the Challenge of Interpretation for Liberation," *Semeia* 47 (1989): 105–35.

46. See here Gay L. Byron, *Symbolic Blackness and Ethnic Difference in Early Christian Literature* (London: Routledge, 2002), 108–15.

47. After all, a non-Jew that joins the Way is situated within a movement that worships the God of Israel, is the recipient of the promises of Israel, and confesses a Jewish Messiah as Lord. See especially Denise Kimber Buell, "Early Christian Universalism and Modern Forms of Racism," in *The Origins of Racism in the West*, ed. Miriam Eliav-Feldon, Benjamin Isaac, and Joseph Ziegler (Cambridge: Cambridge University Press, 2009), 109–24, especially, 124–29. With respect to Paul's treatment of his non-Jewish converts as simultaneously Jewish and *not-Jewish*, see Caroline Johnson Hodge, "The Question of Identity: Gentiles as Gentiles—but Also Not—in Pauline Communities," in *Paul Within Judaism: Restoring the First-Century Context to the Apostle*, ed. Mark D. Nanos and Magnus Zetterholm (Minneapolis: Fortress, 2015), 153–73.

48. Buell, *Why This New Race*, demonstrates that many early Christians *did* use ethnic

PART TWO: GOD'S ACTS FOR GENTILES

the denial or eradication of the continuing significance of Israel's election. Rather, non-Jews experience God's salvation and are brought into a kinship relationship with those who worship the God *of Israel* in such a way that simultaneously affirms Israel's election *and* in a way that does not empty the ethnic and cultural significance of the non-Jew. Non-Jews are, to use Jennings's language, related to the peoples of Israel through the body of Jesus. However, while Luke's commitment to the promises of the God of Israel as the means whereby non-Jews join the Way certainly allow for the potential for readers to read Acts as requiring one to change their ethnic identity, Luke insists that non-Jews do not become Jews in order to join the Way.[49]

More specifically, Luke employs the social-cultural ritual of *xenia* (ritualized friendship) to show the creation of a fictive kinship relationship between those who worship Paul's God (the God of Israel) and the Maltese islanders. Whereas the author of Acts often uses *xenia* to show how non-Jews are joined to "the Way," Acts 28:1–10 is remarkable for its absence of apostolic proclamation and any indication of whether Paul sought to make converts. The open-endedness of Acts 28:1–10 allows for competing interpretations of Paul's relationship with the Maltese islanders, given that Luke is not explicit about whether the act of *xenia* results in the Maltese joining the early Christian movement—as is clearly the case with Cornelius (10:23–48) and Lydia (16:11–15). It is difficult to tell here whether Luke intends the reader to *assume* that Paul preached to the islanders,[50] or that Luke is showing the possibility

---

reasoning in order to portray the Christian movement as a superior race/ethnicity. I do not contest this claim, and certainly Luke's universalizing elements are susceptible to later readings that would suggest one must alter one's ethnic identity to join the Christian movement. But I do not think this is how Luke's ethnic reasoning operates. See here especially the work of Barreto, *Ethnic Negotiations*, 28–29: "Specifically, Acts aims not to eradicate ethnic and racial differences under a homogenizing Christian identity but to demonstrate how the flexibility of ethnic identities played a critical function in the spread of the Jesus movement." On the processes involved in the use and adoption of the label "Christian," see Judith M. Lieu, "The Christian Race," in *Christian Identity in the Jewish and Graeco-Roman World* (Oxford: Oxford University Press, 2004), 239–68.

49. Striking the appropriate balance here can be difficult. For example, Luke does expect that the non-Jews join the people of God through allegiance to the God of Israel whereby they reject their own ethnic deities. See especially Buell, "Early Christian Universalism," 120–29. But Luke's opposition to non-Jews *converting to Judaism* through circumcision would seem to indicate that non-Jewish adherents to the Way retain their ethnic identity. See Matthew Thiessen, *Contesting Conversion: Genealogy, Circumcision, and Identity in Ancient Judaism and Christianity* (Oxford: Oxford University Press, 2011).

50. Foreshadowing numerous contemporary commentators on Acts here is John Chrysostom, *Homilies in the Acts of the Apostles* (*NPNF* 1–32).

"Hospitable Barbarians"

of positive encounters between the Christian movement and broader general culture,[51] or that he intentionally left the episode open-ended to encourage future missionary endeavors.[52] While Luke does not indicate that the Maltese joined "the Way," the positive relations between Paul and the Maltese and the use of the script of ritualized hospitality suggest Luke portrays the initiation of a kinship relation between the islanders and Paul.

If one reads Paul's shipwreck on Malta in light of the literary context of Acts, especially chapters 21–27, the reader is abundantly aware that Paul has been characterized as the emissary of Israel's God, and this ethnic-specific characterization of Paul is crucial for Luke's ethnic reasoning.[53] We, of course, are not told anything explicit about what the Maltese think or know (except for vv. 4–6). But the reader knows that Paul is a Pharisaic Jew who is zealous for God and is Torah observant (21:20–26; 22:1–3; 23:1, 5; 26:4–5); Paul believes everything that is written in the Law and the Prophets (24:14–15; 26:22–23); Paul stands on trial out of his loyalty to the hope made by "God to our ancestors, the promise our twelve tribes hope to obtain" (26:6–7; cf. 28:20).[54] Paul, however, is not simply an orthodox, loyal, and Torah-observant Jew; rather, he *is* the faithful emissary of Israel's God who embodies the powerful presence of Israel's Messiah *and* proclaims God's fulfillment of his promises for Israel in God's resurrection of the Messiah from the dead. Throughout Acts 22–28 Paul emphasizes that he is on trial for "the hope of Israel" (28:20), namely, God's resurrection of the Messiah.[55] Paul speaks of his entire mission as obedient

51. See here Richard I. Pervo, *Acts*, Hermeneia: A Critical and Historical Commentary on the Bible (Minneapolis: Fortress, 2009), 674; Robert C. Tannehill, *The Narrative Unity of Luke-Acts: A Literary Interpretation*, vol. 2, *The Acts of the Apostles* (Minneapolis: Fortress, 1990), 340–41.

52. So Jipp, *Divine Visitations*, 270–87.

53. Luke uses a variety of strategies to characterize Paul as a Jesus-like emissary. For example, Paul's trial before the Sanhedrin, his testimony, and rejection echoes Jesus's trial in Luke 22–23. See Walter Radl, *Paulus und Jesus im lukanischen Doppelwerk: Untersuchungen zu Parallelmotiven im Lukasevangelium und in der Apostelgeschichte* (Bern: Lang, 1975), 211–25. On Paul's extension of hospitality on the ship as recalling Jesus's meal scenes in the Gospel of Luke, see Bo Reicke, "Die Mahlzeit mit Paulus auf den Wellen des Mittelmeers Acts 27,33–38," *TZ* 4 (1948): 401–10.

54. On Paul's trial narratives in Acts 22–28 as a defense of his Jewish orthodoxy, see Jacob Jervell, *Luke and the People of God: A New Look at Luke-Acts* (Minneapolis: Augsburg, 1972), 153–83; Hvalvik, "Paul as a Jewish Believer," 145–51. For these reasons, namely, Luke's presentation of Paul as a Jewish Christian who is Torah-observant, Philipp Vielhauer thinks there is little continuity between the Paul of Acts and the Paul of the Epistles. See Philipp Vielhauer, "On the 'Paulinism' of Acts," in *Studies in Luke-Acts*, ed. Leander E. Keck and J. Louis Martyn (Philadelphia: Fortress, 1968), 33–50.

55. See further Klaus Haacker, "Das Bekenntnis des Paulus zur Hoffnung Israels nach

PART TWO: GOD'S ACTS FOR GENTILES

testimony to what the God of Israel has done through the risen Christ, and this makes sense of Paul's frequent recounting of instances where the resurrected Messiah appears to Paul and demands that Paul testify about Christ (22:3-6, 9-11, 13; 23:11; 26:15-18; 27:20-26).[56] Again, the simple point here is that when Paul encounters the Maltese islanders, he has been repeatedly characterized as the Jesus-like emissary and representative of Israel's God.

Thus, when Publius—who as "the first man of the island" (28:7a; cf. 13:50; 17:4; 25:2; 28:17) is the representative of the people of Malta—takes the initiative to bestow hospitality upon Paul, the scene functions to portray the initiation of a kinship relation between Paul and Publius through the socio-cultural practice of ritualized friendship (ξενία). This institution was, according to the definitive study by Gabriel Herman, conducted "between persons who originated from different, and at times, drastically dissimilar social systems, and who had no previous record of social intercourse. Intimacy was established not through a lengthy interaction, but abruptly, as in marriage, through a ritual act."[57] This ritualized process often involved the practice of hospitality within the host's home, the exchange of gifts, and mutual sharing in worship in the domestic sphere. In every instance, the one initiating the relationship "always had a group identity distinct from that of his partner."[58] The enactment of ritualized friendship has the purpose of creating kinship relations between these two distinct groups or individuals and was, in fact, one of the very few ways of creating kinship relations between strangers outside of the institution of marriage.[59] Given that the institution initiates strangers into a position of friends and family it is no surprise that one frequently encounters related vocabulary, particularly terms such as ξένος and φίλος.[60]

Thus, the scene between Paul and Publius in 28:7-10 conforms nicely to the convention of ritualized friendship. After their initial display of hospitality to Paul (28:1-2) and their recognition of Paul's embodiment of the powerful

---

der Apostelgeschichte des Lukas," *NTS* 31 (1985): 437-51; Robert F. O'Toole, *Acts 26: The Christological Climax of Paul's Defense (Ac 22:1-26:32)*, AB 78 (Rome: Pontifical Biblical Institute, 1978).

56. See further Daniel Marguerat, *The First Christian Historian: Writing the "Acts of the Apostles,"* trans. Ken McKinney, Gregory J. Laughery, and Richard Bauckham, SNTSMS 121 (Cambridge: Cambridge University Press, 2002), 197-200.

57. Gabriel Herman, *Ritualised Friendship and the Greek City* (Cambridge: Cambridge University Press, 1987), 29-30.

58. Herman, *Ritualised Friendship*, 11.

59. Herman, *Ritualised Friendship*, 34-40; M. I. Finley, *The World of Odysseus* (London: Chatto and Windus, 1977), 99-102.

60. See Jipp, *Divine Visitations*, 110-11; Herman, *Ritualised Friendship*, 16-34.

"Hospitable Barbarians"

presence of God (28:3-6), Publius initiates guest-friendship with Paul: "He welcomed and for three days extended friendly hospitality to us" (ὃς ἀναδεξάμενος ἡμᾶς τρεῖς ἡμέρας φιλοφρόνως ἐξένισεν, 28:7b). Luke's use of hospitality lexemes (δεχ- and ξεν-) and friendship language (φιλοφρόνως, cf. φιλανθρωπία, 28:2) suggests that Publius's hospitality initiates a kinship/friendship relationship between Publius (representative of Malta) and Paul (representative of Israel's God). The friendship language further reminds the reader of the Jerusalem church that was similarly portrayed as a kinship group through its meals and sharing (2:42-47; cf. 6:1-6). Paul's Jesus-like healing of Publius's father (28:8; cf. Luke 4:38-39) and subsequent healing of "the rest of those on the island who had sicknesses" (28:9a; cf. Luke 4:40-41; 10:8-9) is Paul's guest-gift or reciprocation to his guest-friend Publius for his hospitality.[61] The episodes concludes with the Maltese islanders further confirming their hospitality-friendship relation with Paul by giving Paul their own guest-gifts as they grant him many honors (πολλαῖς τιμαῖς ἐτίμησαν) and all that they need (τὰ πρὸς τὰς χρείας) for their voyage (28:10). Thus, for the following reasons, the scene in 28:7-10 should be understood as the enactment of ritualized friendship that functions to bind the two ethnic groups into a perpetual kinship/family-like relationship.

1. The relationship takes place between two distinct ethnic groups.
2. Simple hospitality gives way to a more formalized and lengthier bestowal of hospitality upon recognition of Paul's identity.
3. Paul receives hospitality from Publius the representative of the Maltese, while Paul is characterized as the Jesus-like emissary of Israel's God.
4. Paul reciprocates Publius's hospitality by healing Publius's father and the rest of the sick Maltese.
5. The honors and supplies given to Paul by the Maltese function as guest-gifts and provide a reminder of the binding relationship between the ethnic groups.

While the Malta episode is indeed surprising for any reader in that the scene contains no mention of Paul's proclamation, baptisms, or conversions, the passage would seem to suggest some type of initiation of kinship incorporation between Paul and the Maltese. It may be that Luke uses the institution of ξενία to show how the islanders, perhaps as Gentile representatives of the

---

61. Herman, *Ritualised Friendship*, 60: "It was as important to give such gifts as to receive, and refusal to reciprocate was tantamount to a declaration of hostility. Mutual acceptance of the gifts, on the other hand, was a clear mark of the beginning of friendship."

"ends of the earth" (Isa 40:15; 49:1–6), are brought into a kinship-like relationship with Paul, as the emissary of Israel's God, albeit in such a way that their ethnic identity is not eradicated but rather retained.[62]

Luke uses ritualized friendship as a means to establish a new social order for the Christian movement that results in surprising forms of communion and hospitality between distinct ethnicities. This new social order is established programmatically in the ritualized friendship that takes place between Peter (representative of Israel's God and Messiah) and Cornelius (representative of non-Jewish peoples). God establishes communion between Jew and non-Jew through initiating alternating extensions of hospitality between Peter and his companions and Cornelius and his companions in each other's homes (Acts 10:23–27, 48).[63] The non-Jew is joined to Israel's God and people through incorporation into the story of Jesus, hence the necessity of Peter's recounting the kerygma in 10:36–43, and a family/friendship relationship is thereby established through mutual hospitality between Jew and non-Jew. The practice, which again I emphasize takes place between two distinct ethnic groups and preserves their ethnic identity, allows for both social parity and ethnic differentiation. Parity between Jew and non-Jew is seen in (a) Peter's statement that God shows no partiality (10:34; cf. Lev 19:15–19; Deut 10:17–19), (b) the evidence that both receive the same guest-gift of the Spirit (10:44–48; 11:15),[64] (c) the statement that Israel's Messiah is "the Lord of *all*" (10:36) as evidenced in the fact that both groups are incorporated into the story of Jesus and thereby receive God's covenantal blessings of forgiveness of sins and baptism from Israel's Messiah (10:43–48),[65] and (d) the claim that God is the hospitable host who "welcomes" (δεκτός, 10:35b) all who fear him from "among every ethnicity" (ἐν παντὶ ἔθνει, 10:35).[66] Thus, non-Jews are joined to the peoples of Israel and Israel's Messiah but in such a way that the non-Jew remains a non-Jew and is

---

62. On islands as symbolizing Gentile lands, see Loveday C. A. Alexander, *Acts in Its Literary Context: A Classicist Looks at the Acts of the Apostles*, LNTS 298 (New York: T&T Clark, 2005), 214.

63. See here especially Walter T. Wilson, "Urban Legends: Acts 10:1–11:18 and the Strategies of Greco-Roman Foundation Narratives," *JBL* 120 (2001): 77–99, here 91–93. Peter's speech essentially provides a summary of the Gospel of Luke. So Ulrich Wilckens, "Kerygma und Evangelium bei Lukas (Beobachtungen zu Acta 10,34–43)," *ZNW* 49 (1958): 223-37.

64. On guest-gifts as an important component of the initiation of ritualized friendship, see Herman, *Ritualised Friendship*, 58–69.

65. Wilson, "Urban Legends," 93, states this nicely: "Above all, this means that the basis, terms, and purpose of the community are grounded in a story about Jesus."

66. See here Andrew Arterbury, *Entertaining Angels: Early Christian Hospitality in Its Mediterranean Setting*, New Testament Monographs 8 (Sheffield: Sheffield Phoenix, 2005), 169.

not forced or encouraged to assimilate or transform one's ethnicity.[67] In Luke's vision of relationship between Jew and non-Jew joined to Israel's Messiah, new patterns of communion, the ability to enter into meaningful relationships in order to understand the cultural and ethnic logic of others, and new spaces of hospitality emerge through the ritualized friendship that takes place between Jew and non-Jew.

Paul, the Maltese's Guest

Unlike his role as the hospitable host who shares a Jesus-like meal with his fellow prisoners in Acts 27:33–38, here Paul occupies the role of guest as he enters into the space, territory, and houses of the Maltese. I suggest that in his role not as host but as guest, Paul, as portrayed by Luke, enters into the cultural and religious logic of the Maltese. Luke does not present Paul mocking or demonizing the Maltese but rather operating within the cultural and religious logic of the islanders. It is worth noting that despite the adventure of the episode in Acts 28, Luke does not overplay the Maltese as exotic; after all, as Loveday Alexander has noted, the head of the island has the Roman name "Publius" (28:7), and an Alexandrian ship is available on the other side of the island (28:11).[68] Luke is not, in other words, projecting fantastic stereotypes of the exotic islanders.[69] This is not to say that Luke works with a contemporary sanitized, tolerant, pluralist ideology of religious belief; nor is it to say that Luke translates the Christian message into ideas and practices amenable to Greco-Roman paganism (or vice versa).[70] But it *is* to say that Luke does not

---

67. So Wilson, "Urban Legends," 91, who notes that "the elements of the Christian cult introduced to Caesarea are described in terms that essentially duplicate those used earlier in Acts to describe Jewish Christian institutions."

68. Alexander, *Acts in Its Literary Context*, 212–14.

69. Acts' portrait of "the other" should not, in other words, be seen as contributing to the legacy of "Orientalism." See here the famous work of Edward W. Said, *Orientalism* (New York: Vintage Books, 1979).

70. See here especially the convincing work of C. Kavin Rowe, "The Grammar of Life: The Areopagus Speech and Pagan Tradition," *NTS* 57 (2011): 31–50. Jennings, *Christian Imagination*, 160, also criticizes the concept of religious translation due to its disarming "Christian particularity of its central scandal, the election of Israel and through Israel the election of Jesus." Jennings is criticizing the notion of translation as propagated by Lamin Sanneh, *Translating the Message: The Missionary Impact on Culture*, 2nd ed. (Maryknoll, NY: Orbis, 2009); Andrew F. Walls, *The Missionary Movement in Christian History: Studies in the Transmission of Faith* (Maryknoll, NY: Orbis, 1996), 26–42.

demonize the religion of non-Jews, and in fact presents non-Jews as capable of rightly responding to the emissaries of the risen Christ even out of their own Greco-Roman cultural and religious dispositions. We have already noted that on three separate occasions Luke presents non-Jews showing disinterested kindness or friendliness to Paul (φιλανθρώπως, 27:3; φιλανθρωπίαν, 28:2; φιλοφρόνως, 28:7). Given the literary function of sharing possessions and showing hospitality to strangers as highly positive symbolic depictions of one's acceptance of God's visitation of his people, it is striking that the Maltese are portrayed exemplarily as engaging in both of these activities (28:2, 7, 10).[71]

Perhaps most remarkable to interpreters is the fact that when the Maltese see Paul's immunity to the viper attack, they go from thinking that Paul is receiving retributive justice to "changing their mind and declare him to be a god" (ἔλεγον αὐτὸν εἶναι θεόν, 28:6b). Given that Luke (and his literary characters) clearly do not agree with the belief that exceptional humans are divine (e.g., Acts 10:25-26; 14:8-18), why does Paul do nothing to correct the remark?[72] Some interpreters think Luke is portraying the barbarians as superstitious and thereby stresses their inferior intellectual faculties;[73] others suppose that Luke is poking fun or having some humor at the expense of the Maltese;[74] and still others recognize the positive characterization of the Maltese but claim that their actions "occur in a context of spiritual failure" due to their "spiritual blindness."[75] These proposals that essentially mark Luke as engaging in negative ethnic stereotyping (barbarian = superstitious, inferior reasoning abilities, good for a laugh) fail to reckon with Luke's subversion of ethnic stereotyping here and elsewhere (barbarian = *philanthropia*) and the highly positive depiction of these hospitable, possession-sharing barbarians.

---

71. On the role of sharing possessions in Luke-Acts, see Luke Timothy Johnson, *The Literary Function of Possessions in Luke-Acts*, SBLDS 39 (Missoula, MT: Scholars Press, 1977).

72. In this regard, those interpreters who suggest that the reader clearly knows Luke's beliefs on the matter and therefore the narrator does not need to correct the barbarians' statement in 28:6 are partially correct. E.g., Jacob Jervell, *Die Apostelgeschichte*, Kritisch-exegetischer Kommentar uber das Neue Testament (Meyer-Kommentar) (Göttingen: Vandenhoeck & Ruprecht, 1998), 616.

73. C. K. Barrett, *A Critical and Exegetical Commentary on the Acts of the Apostles: In 2 Volumes*, ICC 49 (Edinburgh: T&T Clark, 1998), 2:1224.

74. I. Howard Marshall, *The Acts of the Apostles* (Sheffield: Sheffield Academic, 1992), 417; F. F. Bruce, *Commentary on the Book of Acts*, NICNT (Grand Rapids: Eerdmans, 1970), 523; Colin J. Hemer, *The Book of Acts in the Setting of Hellenistic History*, WUNT 49 (Tübingen: Mohr Siebeck, 1989), 153.

75. Christoph W. Stenschke, *Luke's Portrait of Gentiles Prior to Their Coming to Faith*, WUNT 2/108 (Tübingen: Mohr Siebeck, 1999), 236.

"Hospitable Barbarians"

Perhaps more importantly, these interpretations have failed to grasp Luke's use of *theoxenia* (i.e., hospitality to a deity/divine agent), a trope that functions here to simultaneously portray Paul's characterization as a powerful-Jesus-like figure and the piety of the Maltese. Thus, while the reader knows that Paul is not a god, Paul's immunity to the snake does show that he is protected by and is an emissary of God (cf. Luke 10:17–20). Further, as Richard Pervo has noted, those interpreters who think Luke is mocking the barbarians underestimate that within Luke-Acts there is a highly positive relationship between Jesus's healings and exorcisms and the elicitation of faith in individuals.[76] The Maltese are not, then, superstitious for supposing that divine presence is in their midst, for they rightly recognize the powerful work of God in the person of Paul.[77] Acts 28:1–10 is, in other words, one discrete episode with three scenes that comprise the three constituent parts of hospitality to a god/divine agent: (a) the barbarian's show hospitality to Paul, (b) Paul's identity, as one who embodies the powerful presence of Jesus, is unveiled to the Maltese, and (c) the Maltese receive the rewards of Jesus-like healing from Paul and cement their relationship through ritualized friendship.[78] Given that accounts of *theoxenia* are literary symbolizations of piety and impiety, the barbarians are further characterized as pious, even if they do not yet have all the critical theological information about the identity of Paul. While the reader still wonders why there is no mention of christological proclamation or conversion, it is hard to escape the conclusion that Luke intends the reader to remember the Maltese's kindness, hospitality, and openness to the power of God at work within Paul when s/he encounters Paul's final words: "God's salvation has been sent to the Gentiles; they will listen" (Acts 28:28).

Again, the primary point I am trying to establish is that Paul does not engage in demonizing the religious and cultural logic of the Maltese. Nor does he show them to be superstitious, naïve, fickle, or worthy of being mocked for their inferior rationality. Interpretations that go this route unwittingly engage in ethnic stereotyping by failing to understand the logic of the admittedly

---

76. Pervo, *Acts*, 674. Or as Luke Timothy Johnson has stated (*Acts of the Apostles*, 462): "Once more the logic is sound enough once the premise is granted: if someone can withstand deadly serpents, then some divine *dynamis* must be at work in him (compare Mark 16:18)."

77. Interpreters who label the barbarians as superstitious due to their perception of divine power in their midst may do well, as Averil Cameron warns, to "be a little careful about importing the ethnocentric assumption that we ourselves inhabit a world of reason." See Cameron, *Christianity and the Rhetoric of Empire: The Development of Christian Discourse* (Berkeley: University of California Press, 1991), 42.

78. See further Jipp, *Divine Visitations*, 256–70.

difficult and surprising text. Instead, Luke's Paul is a guest who works within—even as he disrupts their beliefs and allegiances—the cultural and religious logic of the Maltese, a logic that enables them to show *philanthropia* to the incarcerated, to recognize the powerful presence of God at work within Paul, to initiate the kinship making practice of ritualized friendship, and to engage in sharing their possessions with Paul and his crew. I am not claiming that Luke valorizes Greco-Roman religion. He clearly does not, and he presents significant episodes where his characters criticize aspects of Greco-Roman religiosity (e.g., 12:20–23; 14:8–18; 19:8–40). He does, however, make abundant use of Greco-Roman religious discourses in order to show that the early Christian movement embodies supremely the superior elements of Greco-Roman religiosity and philosophy.[79] The "Christian" characters, then, both disrupt the cultural and religious dispositions of the pagan audience even as they call them to exclusive allegiance to Israel's Messiah, *even as* they work within their religious and cultural logics.[80]

A Window into Luke's Ethnic Reasoning

The insights into the ethnic reasoning presented in the Malta episode suggests that Luke does not present a vision of ethnic distinction and cultural difference as a problem in need of a solution. Luke's so-called universalism whereby the risen Jesus is *Lord of all* (Acts 10:36), in other words, does not result in a theological enterprise that negates ethnic and cultural difference. Luke's subversion of ethnic and cultural stereotyping disrupts any form of racial reasoning that would view the "other"—whoever that might be for the particular reader of Acts—as a source of fear, anxiety, or pollution.[81] The theological and ethnic significance of Israel's election as God's people, albeit mediated particularly

---

79. Though in my view there is not enough emphasis on *disruption and critique*, a marked advance in examining early Christianity's relationship to paganism has been offered now by Luke Timothy Johnson, *Among the Gentiles: Greco-Roman Religion and Christianity*, AYBRL (New Haven: Yale University Press, 2009).

80. I recognize that I have made some forceful and probably controversial assertions here that are in need of justification, and I hope to remedy this lack in future writings. I am thinking here, for example, of Luke's use of miraculous turf wars/battles to narrate the superior power of Israel's God, the role of prison escapes in founding and establishing the early Christian movement, and the use of philosophical utopian friendship language to portray the early Christians. See here also Joshua W. Jipp, "Paul's Areopagus Speech of Acts 17:16–34 as *Both* Critique *and* Propaganda," *JBL* 131 (2012): 567–88.

81. See Baretto, *Ethnic Negotiations*, 184: "Ethnic difference ultimately was not an obstacle

> "Hospitable Barbarians"

and highly controversially through Israel's resurrected Messiah, is seen in the manner in which *all* peoples are incorporated into God's people in such a way that their ethnic and cultural identity is not eradicated. Luke's use of ritualized hospitality, as seen in the Malta episode, the Cornelius-Peter interaction, *and* in Paul's second missionary journey (Acts 16–18), is a particularly significant cultural practice as it allows members from different ethnic groups to enter into kinship-like relations but without eradicating their particular cultural and ethnic identity. The valorization of the practice of hospitality further creates patterns of communion and new spaces of communion between groups that allow them to enter into and understand the cultural, ethnic, and religious logic of one another. While the Malta episode provides only a brief window into Luke's ethnic reasoning, I have hinted at the likelihood that a broader examination would largely confirm rather than call into question these insights.

---

but an opportunity, a resource in theological reflection on the expansion of the followers of Jesus in the diverse lands ringing the Mediterranean."

8

Paul's Areopagus Speech of Acts 17:16–34
as *Both* Critique *and* Propaganda

Interpretations of Paul's Areopagus discourse in Acts 17:16–34 are often radically incongruous. They range from seeing it as a placid pantheistic sermon on natural theology all the way to seeing it as a scathing demonization of gentile religion.[1] Interpreters who emphasize the speech's similarities to Greco-Roman philosophy incline toward the former view, while those attuned to the Jewish context incline toward the latter. Both types have a significant amount of supporting evidence and are able to provide strong readings for their argument, given that the speech does indeed utilize Hellenistic philosophical concepts *and* Jewish critiques of idolatry. I suggest, however, that matters are more complex than an either/or interpretation of the Areopagus discourse and that Luke's purposes are more subtle than either "accommodation" or "critique/resistance" would allow.[2]

Special thanks to David W. Pao and especially Carl R. Holladay for providing detailed feedback on earlier versions of this chapter.

1. The classic representation of the former view is Martin Dibelius, "The Speeches in Acts and Ancient Historiography," in Dibelius, *Studies in the Acts of the Apostles*, trans. Mary Ling (London: SCM, 1951), 138–85; for the latter view, see Bertil Gärtner, *The Areopagus Speech and Natural Revelation*, trans. Carolyn Hannay King, ASNU 21 (Uppsala: Gleerup, 1955). On the speeches in Acts as Lukan creations that utilize speech-in-character, see H. J. Cadbury, "The Speeches in Acts," in *The Beginnings of Christianity: Part 1, The Acts of the Apostles*, ed. F. J. Foakes Jackson and Kirsopp Lake (London: Macmillan, 1933), 5:402–27.

2. Virginia Burrus notes that interpreters have seen Acts as "radically subversive" and some as "skillfully accommodationist" in its relation to majority culture ("The Gospel of Luke and the Acts of the Apostles," in *A Postcolonial Commentary on the New Testament Writings*, ed. F. F. Segovia and R. S. Sugirtharajah, Bible and Postcolonialism 13 [London: T&T Clark, 2007], 133–55, here 133). On this, see now C. Kavin Rowe, *World Upside Down: Reading Acts in the*

Paul's Areopagus Speech of Acts 17:16–34 as Both Critique and Propaganda

I suggest, rather, that Luke has crafted a sermon that invokes *both sets of traditions* and that this corresponds to two Lukan intents for the Areopagus speech. Luke has (at the least) a twofold agenda in Acts 17:16–34: (1) to narrate the complete incongruity between the Christian movement and gentile religion—an incongruity exemplified by the speech's critique of Greco-Roman religiosity, anti-idolatry polemic, and its theologically exclusive claims; and (2) to exalt the Christian movement as comprising the best features of Greco-Roman philosophical sensibilities and therefore as a superior philosophy. The speech is, then, simultaneously both radical and conventional, and a dualistic construct of "accommodation" *or* "resistance" is too simplistic to describe the purposes of the speech. It is conventional in that the topics of monotheism, critiques of temples and sacrifices, the unity of humankind, and the like would have resonated with Greco-Roman philosophical sensibilities. The speech is radical in that it co-opts—one might say takes over and transforms the cultural script—the best aspects of Hellenistic philosophy and claims that they can be found *only* in the Christian movement.[3] The speech is most radical in its insistence that the resurrected Jesus is *the Lord* of heaven and earth (17:24) who will judge everyone everywhere (17:31), a claim that results in the speech's anti-idol polemic. In order to accomplish these goals, Luke hellenizes Jewish traditions of monotheism, anthropology, and anti-idol polemic to show that the best and most consistent Greco-Roman philosophical religion is contained within the Christian movement.[4] The Areopagus discourse illustrates, therefore, *both* the critique of pagan religiosity and the exaltation of the Christian movement within the Mediterranean world.

Graeco-Roman Age (Oxford: Oxford University Press, 2009). See also Rowe, "The Grammar of Life: The Areopagus Speech and Pagan Tradition," *NTS* 57 (2011): 31–50, in which Rowe argues against "the long tradition of reading Paul's Areopagus speech as a 'translation' of Christian theological convictions into pagan philosophical terms" (49). Rowe's exegesis is impeccable, and I am in full agreement with his argument that the pagan traditions found in Paul's speech find their meaning only within the larger narrative logic and hermeneutical framework of Paul's speech—a framework that "reveals a fundamentally Christian grammar" (49). But to my mind Rowe has not fully explained *why and for what reason* Paul's speech utilizes pagan traditions to the extent that it does—he states only briefly that Paul could not make his criticism of Athenian religion *too explicit* if he hoped to save himself from the trial (50).

3. On minority peoples appropriating the cultural public transcripts of their oppressors (or the majority culture) as a form of strategic resistance, see James C. Scott, *Domination and the Arts of Resistance: Hidden Transcripts* (New Haven: Yale University Press, 1990).

4. On Luke as hellenizing his ethnic and religious traditions, see Gregory E. Sterling, *Historiography and Self-Definition: Josephos, Luke-Acts, and Apologetic Historiography*, NovTSup 64 (Leiden: Brill, 1992).

Before proceeding to demonstrate this contention through a detailed exegetical examination of the speech, it is worth noting that similar arguments have been set forth with respect to other portions of the Acts of the Apostles. Gary Gilbert has shown that the list of nations in Acts 2:5-11 is an echo of lists that celebrated Rome's rule over the inhabited world in order to declare that the true empire belongs to Jesus and not Caesar.[5] Laura Salah Nasrallah has suggested that Paul's travels to Greek cities are best understood in light of cultural discourses of Greek cities under Roman rule and that Acts produces its own version of Hadrian's Panhellenion.[6] Thus, Acts "configures a Christianity that fits within the superior aspects of Greek culture and cities under the Roman Empire."[7] Loveday C. A. Alexander has argued that Luke's portrait of Paul's sea voyage in Acts 27 mimics other Greco-Roman accounts of sea journeys over the Mediterranean and constitutes an act of narrative aggression by claiming that the "Greek Sea" belongs to the emissaries of the gospel. Paul is presented as "laying claim to a cultural territory which many readers . . . would perceive as inherently 'Greek.'"[8] And Todd Penner has suggested that the characters of Acts embody "the array of appropriate and moderate responses demanded of individuals in the *polis*."[9] They are model Roman citizens who engage in public declamations defending and propagating their polity.

With these scholars, I argue that in the Areopagus discourse Luke takes over the topics, tools, and scripts of Greco-Roman philosophy, particularly matters of true worship and piety, and mimics them to persuade his readers that the Christian movement contains the best aspects of Greco-Roman philosophy and embodies them more consistently than other movements. The speech is a bold attempt to claim as its own the superior aspects of Greco-Roman philosophical traditions. In so doing, Luke simultaneously exalts his movement and criticizes competing movements.[10]

---

5. Gary Gilbert, "The List of Nations in Acts 2: Roman Propaganda and the Roman Response," *JBL* 121 (2002): 497-529.

6. Laura Salah Nasrallah, *Christian Responses to Roman Art and Architecture: The Second-Century Church amid the Spaces of Empire* (Cambridge: Cambridge University Press, 2010), 87-118.

7. Nasrallah, *Christian Responses*, 88.

8. Loveday C. A. Alexander, "'In Journeyings Often': Voyaging in the Acts of the Apostles and in Greek Romance," in *Acts in Its Ancient Literary Context: A Classicist Looks at the Acts of the Apostles*, LNTS 298 (London; T&T Clark, 2005), 69-96, here 85.

9. Todd C. Penner, "Civilizing Discourse: Acts, Declamation, and the Rhetoric of the *Polis*," in *Contextualizing Acts: Lukan Narrative and Greco-Roman Discourse*, ed. Todd C. Penner and Caroline Vander Stichele, SBLSymS 20 (Atlanta: Society of Biblical Literature Press, 2003), 65-104, here 82.

10. Rowe (*World Upside Down*, 27-41) provides a strong reading of the Areopagus dis-

Paul's Areopagus Speech of Acts 17:16-34 as Both Critique and Propaganda

The Trial of Paul as Socrates Redivivus: Acts 17:16-21

The narrative framework of the Areopagus discourse contradicts those who interpret Paul's speech as a placid philosophical discourse over shared conceptions of deity.[11] Rather, Luke's narrative frame prepares his reader for a conflict between the Christian movement's conception of God and that of the Athenian philosophers. However, Luke characterizes Paul as Socrates redivivus, the great Athenian philosopher, and thereby casts Paul as hero and the philosophers as narrative antagonists. Paul, as Socrates redivivus, is the knowledgeable philosopher, while those who oppose him, the Stoics and Epicureans, are misguided and ignorant in their antagonism to Paul. Three elements of the introduction point to conflict.

Athens as a Luxuriant Forest of Idols (17:16)

First, Paul's first impression of Athens is one of provocation due to the fact that "he was seeing the city was full of idols" (θεωροῦντος κατείδωλον οὖσαν τὴν πόλιν, 17:16).[12] As a result of the idols, "his spirit was provoked [παρωξύνετο] within him." That Luke uses παροξύνω to stress that Paul's spirit is *negatively* provoked is clear in view of the use of the noun in 15:39 to refer to the "sharp contention" (παροξυσμός) over John Mark. Furthermore, by now in the narrative Luke's readers know his negative stance toward idolatry (e.g., 14:8-20). Thus, while Athens was famous for its temples and monuments,[13] Luke's decision to highlight Athens as filled with idols indicates that the subject of Paul's speech will contain a polemic against idolatry.[14] Whereas Cicero sees Rome as the cultural heir of the august Athens "from which education, science,

---

course, and I am in agreement with Rowe on numerous points. I differ with him in my emphasis on the speech as a subversive attempt to co-opt the best aspects of Greco-Roman philosophy and place these aspects within the Christian movement.

11. Dibelius, by starting with the speech proper, underestimates the importance of the speech's introduction and thereby concludes that the author's tone is one of enlightening his audience ("Paul on the Areopagus," 53-56). See, however, Rowe, *World Upside Down*, 27-33.

12. On the adjective κατείδωλος, see R. E. Wycherley, "St. Paul at Athens," *JTS* 19 (1968): 619-21, who argues that the prefix means something to the effect of "luxuriant with."

13. For more detail, see David W. J. Gill, "Achaia," in *The Book of Acts in Its First Century Setting*, vol. 2, *The Book of Acts in Its Graeco-Roman Setting*, ed. David W. J. Gill and Conrad Gempf (Grand Rapids: Eerdmans, 1994), 443-45.

14. This is confirmed by the fact that Luke's depiction of Athenian religion anticipates Paul's introduction to his sermon in 17:22-23, where the city's idols form the starting point for his message. On this, see Gerhard Schneider, *Die Apostelgeschichte*, 2 vols., HTKNT 5 (Freiburg: Herder, 1982), 2:235.

belief in the gods, agriculture, justice, and law derives" (*Flac.* 62), the Lukan attribute of Athens is that it is "a luxuriant forest of idols."

Paul Introducing New Gods (17:17-20)

It has been observed that Luke depicts Paul as a Socrates figure who "argues ... in the agora everyday with *whoever happens to be present*" (v. 17: διελέγετο ... ἐν τῇ ἀγορᾷ κατὰ πᾶσαν ἡμέραν πρὸς τοὺς παρατυγχάνοντας).[15] Socrates was, of course, that pesky philosopher who never left Athens and spent his time in the agora conversing with philosophers and sophists.[16] Not unlike Luke's depiction of Paul as "reasoning" (διελέγετο, v. 17a) with those in the agora, Socrates's favorite weapon was his dialectical technique of *elenchus*. Karl Olav Sandnes notes that this rhetorical tool is often described with the verb διαλέγομαι (Diogenes Laertius, *Lives* 2.20, 45, 122), the same verb used to describe Paul's "reasoning" in the agora.[17] The most important parallel, however, is that, as Socrates was charged with introducing foreign deities to Athens (ἕτερα δαιμόνια καινά; Plato, *Euthyphr.* 1C; 2B; *Apol.* 24B; Xenophon, *Mem.* 1.1.1), so is Paul charged with the same infraction in 17:18b-20 (v. 18b: ξένων δαιμονίων δοκεῖ καταγγελεὺς εἶναι, ὅτι τὸν Ἰησοῦν καὶ τὴν ἀνάστασιν εὐηγγελίζετο). That Luke refers to Paul as "introducing" (εἰσφέρεις, v. 20) foreign deities also echoes the Socratic tradition, as this verb was used to depict the charge against Socrates (Xenophon, *Apol.* 10-11; Justin, *1 Apol.* 5.4; *2 Apol.* 10.5).[18] Another echo of Socratic tradition lies in the narration of Epicurean and Stoic philosophers who were "arguing with him" (συνέβαλλον αὐτῷ, v. 18a).[19] Luke depicts Paul as Socrates, however, not for the purpose of narrating a philosophical conversation between Hellenistic philosophical

---

15. E.g., Karl Olav Sandnes, "Paul and Socrates: The Aim of Paul's Areopagus Speech," *JSNT* 50 (1993): 13-26; Eckhard Plümacher, *Lukas als hellenistischer Schriftsteller: Studien zur Apostelgeschichte*, SUNT 9 (Göttingen: Vandenhoeck & Ruprecht, 1972), 97-99; Loveday C. A. Alexander, "Acts and Ancient Intellectual Biography," in *Acts in Its Ancient Literary Context: A Classicist Looks at the Acts of the Apostles*, LNTS 298 (New York: T&T Clark, 2005), 43-68, here 61-68; Rowe, *World Upside Down*, 31-33.

16. Plato, *Apol.* 1.17C; 17.30B; Xenophon, *Mem.* 1.1.10; Diogenes Laertius, *Lives* 2.21; Dio Chrysostom, *Or.* 54.3.

17. Sandnes, "Paul and Socrates," 21. Luke describes the apostles with reminiscences of Socratic tradition in Acts 4:19 and 5:29 (see Plato, *Apol.* 29D).

18. Sandnes, "Paul and Socrates," 21-22.

19. On the Epicureans and Stoics, see A. A. Long, "Hellenistic Ethics and Philosophical Power," in *Hellenistic History and Culture*, ed. Peter Green, Hellenistic Culture and Society 9 (Berkeley: University of California Press, 1993), 138-56.

schools, but rather in order to depict the event as a kind of mock trial between early Christianity and the epicenter of pagan philosophy and culture. The echoes of Socrates's trial before the Athenians function, therefore, to establish a confrontation over the competing conceptions of God that exist between Paul and the philosophers. Luke's goal here is both *apologetic*—namely, to show that the early Christian movement is no crude superstition but contains within it the best of Greek philosophy and religion—and *criticism* of pagan religiosity—namely, that Greek culture has failed, primarily through idolatry, to attain knowledge of God. There are four clues that indicate that this event is a mock trial scene between Christianity and Hellenistic philosophy.

First, the initial response of the philosophers to Paul is one of intellectual contempt as some ask, "What would this *unmethodical scavenger* [σπερμολόγος] be trying to communicate?" (v. 18). The word σπερμολόγος refers to the kinds of scavenger birds that pick up seeds and scraps.[20] The slur against Paul refers to the philosophers' perception of him as a philosophically untrained novice who spouts forth bits of street philosophy.[21]

Second, the most obvious relationship between Paul and Socrates is the similar accusation brought against them. Both are charged with introducing foreign deities into Athens. According to Xenophon, the formal charge against Socrates is that he "does evil, for he does not acknowledge the gods whom the state acknowledges, while introducing other, novel divine beings" (*Mem.* 1.1.1). Likewise, of Paul, the philosophers claim that he "seems to be a herald of foreign deities [ξένων δαιμονίων]" (17:18b) and that he is bringing forth "some foreign things [ξενίζοντα γάρ τινα] into our ears" (17:20a). The seriousness of this charge must not be underestimated, and the resonances of this story with the last days of Socrates should be enough to remind Luke's reader of this fact.[22] While it is true that Athens took an active role in promoting new cults throughout the Greek world, one must not underestimate the sense in which Athens could be hostile to foreign deities.[23] Josephus, for example, commends the Athenians for their punishment of those who propagate new cults. He

---

20. See Plutarch, *Demetr.* 902; Demosthenes, *Or.* 18.127; Dionysus of Halicarnassus 19.5.3.

21. Jacob Jervell captures the ironic pejorative tone of the philosophers well by referring to their perception of Paul as a "Quatschkopf" (*Die Apostelgeschichte*, Kritisch-exegetischer Kommentar uber das Neue Testament [Meyer-Kommentar] [Göttingen: Vandenhoeck & Ruprecht, 1998], 443).

22. Bruce Winter wrongly portrays the Athenians as mildly questioning Paul as to whether they should set up a cult center for Paul's new gods. See "On Introducing Gods to Athens: An Alternative Reading of Acts 17:18-20," *TynB* 47 (1996): 71-90.

23. See Richard I. Pervo, *Acts*, Hermeneia: A Critical and Historical Commentary on the

PART TWO: GOD'S ACTS FOR GENTILES

claims that the Athenians inflict "an inexorable penalty on any who uttered a single word about the gods contrary to their laws" (*Ag. Ap.* 2.262). Anaxagoras barely escaped being executed by the Athenians because of his belief that the sun was a god (2.265). Josephus's most interesting claim is that the Athenians did not spare the priestess Ninus from death:

> Someone accused her of initiating people into the mysteries of foreign gods [ξένους ἐμύει θεούς]; this was forbidden by their law and the penalty decreed for any who introduced a foreign god was death [τιμωρία κατὰ τῶν ξένον εἰσ αγόντων θεὸν ὥρισατο θάνατος]. Those who had such a law evidently did not believe that the gods of other nations were gods; else they would not have denied themselves the advantage of increasing the number of their own. (*Ag. Ap.* 2.266-268)

Furthermore, even with respect to the *successful* introductions of new deities into cities, a standard trope in the narratives that depict their transfer is opposition and the putting to death of the deity's representative.[24] For example, when Cybele was introduced into Athens, the Athenians killed her priest, upon which a plague occurred in the city. The Athenians then built a temple to the Mother and the plague subsided (Julian, *Or.* 5.159). Likewise, in Euripides's *Bacchae*, one of the fundamental themes is the resistance and opposition that the cult of Dionysus encountered when it was introduced into Greece.[25] Note Pentheus's chastisement of Teiresias: "You want to introduce [ἐσφέρων] this new divinity to mankind.... If you weren't protected by your gray hair, you would be sitting in prison surrounded by bacchants for introducing these wicked rites" (256-259). To read Acts 17:17-20, therefore, as though it were an innocuous philosophical discussion between the Athenians and Paul is to misread the narrative and the evidence regarding the introduction of new gods into Greek cities. The evidence points, rather, in the direction of a conflict, more specifically in the direction of the Athenians putting Paul on trial.

Third, the philosophers "grasped him [ἐπιλαβόμενοί τε αὐτοῦ] and brought him before the Areopagus" (v. 19a). Given that Luke uses the verb ἐπιλαμβά-

---

Bible (Minneapolis: Fortress, 2009), 427; see also Robert Garland, *Introducing New Gods: The Politics of Athenian Religion* (London: Duckworth, 1992), 10.

24. See Elizabeth R. Gebhard, "The Gods in Transit: Narratives of Cult Transfer," in *Antiquity and Humanity: Essays on Ancient Religion and Philosophy, Presented to Hans Dieter Betz on His 70th Birthday*, ed. Adela Yarbro Collins and Margaret M. Mitchell (Tübingen: Mohr Siebeck, 2001), 455.

25. See Anne Pippin Burnett, "Pentheus and Dionysus: Host and Guest," *CP* 65 (1970): 15-29.

Paul's Areopagus Speech of Acts 17:16-34 as Both Critique and Propaganda

νομαι throughout the latter portions of Acts to indicate the forceful seizure of the apostles (16:19; 18:17; 21:30, 33), one is justified in translating ἐπιλαβόμενοί τε αὐτοῦ as "arresting him."[26]

Finally, the role of the Areopagus as the Athenian tribunal provides confirmation for a judicial setting. While there is ambiguity as to whether Luke understands the Ἄρειον πάγον to be the hill of Ares or the official Athenian committee, a few factors in Acts lead me to concur with Timothy D. Barnes that Luke refers to "the effective government of Roman Athens and its chief court."[27] First, the echoes of Socrates and the charge brought against Paul, suggest that readers would associate the Areopagus with the Athenian tribunal. Second, Luke notes that among those receptive to Paul's message was Διονύσιος ὁ Ἀρεοπαγίτης (17:34). The epithet describing Dionysius suggests that he is a member of the Athenian committee.[28] Third, it makes more sense to imagine Paul speaking "in the midst of an assembly," not on the middle of a hill, based on 17:22a: Σταθεὶς δὲ ὁ Παῦλος ἐν μέσῳ τοῦ Ἀρείου πάγου. The same insight holds for 17:33: οὕτως ὁ Παῦλος ἐξῆλθεν ἐκ μέσου αὐτῶν.[29] Most important, however, are the popular resonances that the Areopagus carried of being the primary governing council over Athens, a council invested with the role of being the caretaker of religious, cultural, and political matters.[30] Cicero, for example, states that "if someone says that the Republic of Athens is governed by the Council, we must understand him to mean, by the Council of the Areopagus" (*Nat. d.* 2.74; cf. *Att.* 1.5; 5.6). By placing Paul before the Areopagus, the text evokes respect for ancient venerable religions. Paul is truly among the

---

26. So Rowe, *World Upside Down*, 29. Note, however, Hans Conzelmann ("The Address of Paul on the Areopagus," in *Studies in Luke-Acts: Essays Presented in Honor of Paul Schubert*, ed. Leander E. Keck and J. Louis Martyn [Mifflintown, PA: Sigler, 1966], 219), who claims that "this does not mean . . . that the Areopagus, to which Paul is led is the *court* rather than the well-known historical location, Mars' Hill; that ἐπιλαμβάνεσθαι . . . means to arrest, and that the events starting with vs. 19 are to be interpreted as a court trial rather than as a philosophical discussion." See also Timothy D. Barnes, "An Apostle on Trial," *JTS* 22 (1969): 413; Pervo, *Acts*, 428.

27. Barnes, "Apostle on Trial," 413; also Pervo, *Acts*, 428.

28. So Hans-Josef Klauck, *Magic and Paganism in Early Christianity: The World of the Acts of the Apostles* (Edinburgh: T&T Clark, 2000), 79.

29. Pervo (*Acts*, 428n35) notes that the phrase ἐν μέσῳ means "among" in Luke (2:46; 4:30; 22:27; 24:36) and Acts (1:15; 2:22; 4:7; 17:33).

30. See Gill, "Achaia," 447-48; Hubert H. Martin Jr., "Areopagus," *ABD* 1:370-72. Martin writes, "The council of the Areopagus was a body hallowed by its unique origins, and as such it exercised certain functions deeply rooted in religious tradition as to be virtually sacrosanct" (371).

PART TWO: GOD'S ACTS FOR GENTILES

most ancient and venerable of councils in the ancient world. However, the Areopagus's association with bringing miscreants and religious innovators to justice also would have rung in the ears of Luke's readers. The founding myth of the Areopagus was, after all, that it was the council established by Athena for those who violated Athens's laws (Aeschylus, *Eumenides* 470–489, 680–684). In Diogenes Laertius, the Areopagus is what Aristippus is saved from appearing before for violating the mysteries (*Lives* 2.101), the tribunal before which Stilpo is brought for denying Athena's divinity (2.116), and the setting for Cleanthes's trial over suspicions of his new wealth (7.168–169).[31]

Since the Areopagus functioned as the Athenian tribunal and Paul is reported as introducing new deities, it seems best to translate 17:19b not as a polite request to hear about Paul's interesting beliefs but rather as informing Paul of the council's right to question and, if necessary, put him on trial. I translate v. 19b, then, as follows: "We have the right to know what this new teaching is of which you are speaking" (δυνάμεθα γνῶναι τίς ἡ καινὴ αὕτη ἡ ὑπὸ σοῦ λαλουμένη διδαχή).[32] And v. 20 indicates that the Areopagus must form a decision regarding these "certain strange [ξενίζοντα] things" that Paul is proclaiming.

Paul's speech before the Areopagus is, then, not a placid discourse over mutually shared conceptions of the divine *even though* he appeals to much that they share in common; rather, Luke portrays Paul, like Socrates, on trial before the most revered tribunal in the ancient world to demonstrate the incongruity that exists between the Christian movement's understanding of God and the polytheism that characterized the ancient world. Paul's speech will *both* apologetically legitimate the movement as philosophically superior *and* criticize pagan conceptions of the divine.

Athenian Obsession with Novelty (17:21)

One final component of Luke's introduction to Paul's speech must not be underestimated, namely, the stereotype in v. 21 of "all Athenians and foreigners who travel there" as obsessed with τι καινότερον. Luke plays on a well-known stereotype, namely, Athens's fabled curiosity. Thucydides refers to the Athenians as "despisers of what is familiar, [while] worshippers of every new extravagance" (*Hist.* 3.38.5). The pirate in Chariton's *Chaereas and Callirhoe*

---

31. See Robert Parker, *Polytheism and Society at Athens* (Oxford: Oxford University Press, 2005), 102, 133–35.
32. Further support for this translation is provided by Winter, "On Introducing Gods to Athens," 81–83.

exclaims, "[Have] you not heard what busybodies the Athenians are? They are a talkative lot and fond of litigation.... The Areopagus is near at hand and their officials are sterner than tyrants."[33] Luke's depiction of the Athenian philosophers and the Areopagus council takes on a negative valence in view of the criticism of obsessive curiosity in the Hellenistic moralists. Cicero commends the pursuit of knowledge but claims that one must avoid "excessive devotion and effort" on that which is novel (*Off.* 1.19). Plutarch devoted an essay to the matter and claims that such vices as envy, malice, and gossip characterize the overly curious (*Curios.* 513D–518B).[34] One of the most interesting points for our purposes is the relationship in the moralists between curiosity and superstition. For example, Apuleius warns his audience against the dangers of curiosity by depicting the misfortunes that Lucius encounters as a result of his superstitious dabbling in magic (*Metam.* 11). Throughout *On Superstition*, Plutarch connects the excessively curious about religion with the superstitious. In this light, Acts 17:21 depicts Paul's audience as obsessively curious and even superstitious. Luke has deftly taken a jab at the Athenian elite. By drawing on popular stereotypes of "Athenian curiosity" and its relationship to superstition, Luke has set forth a critique of Athens's religiosity.

The scene is set for a dramatic encounter between Paul and the Athenian elite. I have argued that there are indicators that suggest that Luke intends us to read this scene as one of conflict. Paul's provocation over idolatry (v. 16), the philosophers' criticism of Paul and inability to understand his message (vv. 18–19), the echoes of Socrates's trial (vv. 17–20), the judicial function of the Areopagus, and the stereotype of the Athenians as curious (v. 21) prepare the reader for a conflict between Paul and Athens. Is this what we find in the speech?

The Function of the Speech as Both Critique and Propaganda: Acts 17:22–31

One reason for the scholarly tradition of interpreting Paul's speech as a foreign intrusion of Hellenistic philosophy into the NT has been the failure to take the literary context (17:16–21) seriously, but an equally important reason is

---

33. For further references to the fabled Athenian love of novelty, see Pervo, *Acts*, 429n42.
34. See Patrick Gray, "Athenian Curiosity (Acts 17:21)," *NovT* 47 (2005): 109–16. On the critique of curiosity, Gray refers to Seneca, *Ep.* 88.36–38; Plutarch, *Superst.* 171F; Apuleius, *Metam.* 5.6.3; 6.20.5.

that much of what Paul says in the speech truly does resonate with Hellenistic philosophy and religious sensibilities.[35] If Luke is not to be charged with utter inconsistency, a reason must be given as to why the context of his speech emphasizes anti-idol polemic but the speech resonates with Hellenistic philosophy. In what follows, I suggest that Paul engages in critique of his audience with respect to superstition and idolatry by using Hellenistic philosophical tools and by hellenizing biblical traditions. In so doing, he demonstrates that his movement's beliefs about God not only demonstrate it to be legitimate but even prove it to be a superior form of religion. The Christian movement embodies the philosophically elite's ideals better *and more consistently* than do the Athenians. Luke thereby fuses Septuagintal traditions with Hellenistic philosophy regarding monotheism, worship of images, and anthropology both to critique *and* to legitimate.

The Superstitious or Pious (17:22-23)

It is customary to label 17:22-23 as the *captatio benevolentiae*, as Paul, from the standpoint of the audience, expresses his good will by commending them as δεισιδαιμονεστέρους.[36] Luke's rhetorical skill is highlighted by a deliberate use of ambiguity in this characterization of the Athenians.[37] The term was used on some occasions in a positive sense to mean piously religious.[38] The overwhelming use of this term and its cognates by the end of the first century, however, tilts toward the negative connotation of "superstition." Plutarch and Theophrastus both devoted essays to critiques of superstition. The essential characteristic of superstition is *a false conception of the gods*, a mistaken notion, or passion, that one must continually placate the gods, which is motivated by fear of the gods.[39] While the semantic range of δεισιδαίμων allows for a positive interpretation such as "religious," and while rhetorical convention demands that Paul *not* begin his speech by insulting his audience, there are good

---

35. So Dibelius, *Acts of the Apostles*, 47-58; Conzelmann, "Address of Paul," 224.
36. So Pervo, *Acts*, 433; Ernst Haenchen, *The Acts of the Apostles: A Commentary* (Philadelphia: Westminster, 1971), 520; Schneider, *Die Apostelgeschichte*, 2:237-38.
37. So Rowe, *World Upside Down*, 33-35.
38. BDAG, (s.v. "δεισιδαίμων") lists the following as using the term in a positive manner: Aristotle, *Pol.* 5.11; Xenophon, *Cyr.* 3.3.58; Pausanias 24.3.
39. More broadly, see Dale B. Martin, *Inventing Superstition: From the Hippocratics to the Christians* (Cambridge: Harvard University Press, 2004).

reasons for translating this word as "superstitious."[40] Given that the occasion of the speech is criticism of idolatry (17:16), the pejorative meaning seems likely.[41] When one considers these facts, along with Luke's final criticism of Athenians in v. 21 as obsessed with novelty about religion—one of the prime examples of superstition according to the moralists—it is hard to avoid the conclusion that Paul's speech begins with a criticism of polytheism as superstitious.[42] This is why the presence of the Stoic and Epicurean philosophers is so ironic and striking, *for they are stereotypically the primary critics of superstitious religion.*[43] The impetus for the study of the natural world was, for the Epicureans, the alleviation of the superstition that the gods controlled the world. Lucretius refers to the multitude who assigns all causes to the gods:

> Unhappy human race, to attribute such behavior, and bitter wrath too, to the gods! What lamentations did they lay up for themselves in those days, what wounds for us, what tears for our descendants! It is no piety to be seen with covered head bowing again and again to a stone and visiting every altar, nor to grovel on the ground and raise your hands before the shrines of the gods, nor to drench altars in the blood of animals, nor to utter strings of prayers. (*On the Nature of the Universe* 5.1194–1203)

Note that which is criticized: attributing wrong characteristics to the gods, bowing to stones, visiting altars, and offering sacrifices.[44] Numerous quotations from Epicurus, Lucretius, Plutarch, and Cicero could be reproduced that identify the Epicureans' primary philosophical motivation as bringing forth tranquility (ἀταραξία) by alleviating humanity's superstitious fear of the gods.[45] Despite opposition between the two groups on key doctrines, the Stoics shared with the Epicureans an abhorrence of superstition. This is seen in the Stoics' claim, particularly Zeno and Seneca, that temples and altars should not

---

40. On the distinction between the implied reader and dramatic audience, see Mark D. Given, "Not Either/Or but Both/And in Paul's Areopagus Speech," *BibInt* 3 (1995): 356–72.

41. However, see Dibelius, *Acts of the Apostles*, 66–67.

42. So Jervell, *Die Apostelgeschichte*, 445–46.

43. This was suggested by C. K. Barrett, "Paul's Speech on the Areopagus," in *New Testament Christianity for Africa and the World*, ed. M. Glasswell and E. Fashole-Lake (London: SPCK, 1974), 74–75. See also Patrick Gray, "Implied Audiences in the Areopagus Narrative," *TynB* 55 (2004): 205–18.

44. Opposition to traditional cultic practices can be seen also in Lucian, *Alex.* 17, 25, 38, 61; Cicero, *Nat. d.* 1.20.55; 2.65.162; Diogenes Laertius, *Lives* 10.135.

45. See Gisela Striker, "*Ataraxia*: Happiness as Tranquility," in *Essays on Hellenistic Epistemology and Ethics* (Cambridge: Cambridge University Press, 1996), 183–95.

be built for the gods (e.g., Diogenes, *Lives* 7.33; Seneca, *Superst.*; cf. Plutarch, *Stoic. abs.* 1034b). The justification for this is their belief that the cosmos and humanity were pervaded by and even kin of the gods.[46] As Cleanthes says in his *Hymn to Zeus*, "We are your [Zeus] offspring and we alone of all mortal creatures... bear a likeness to you" (*SVF* 1:537). Or Epictetus:

> You are a fragment of God; you have within you a part of him. Why, then, are you ignorant [ἀγνοεῖς] of your own kinship? Why do you not know the source from which you have sprung?... You are bearing God about within you, you poor wretch, and know it not! Do you suppose I am speaking of some external God, made of silver and gold [ἀργυροῦν τινα ἢ χρυσοῦν]? It is within yourself that you bear him. (*Diatr.* 2.8)

Epictetus and Cleanthes provide exactly the kind of argument one might expect from the Stoics regarding the religious insignificance of temples, altars, and images. Given that humanity is God's kin and image, what could possibly be the purpose of external images of the divine? It is a striking fact, however, that the sources depict the Stoics and Epicureans as continuing in the practice of cultic worship. It is an odd fact, for example, that Diogenes Laertius reports Epicurus as stating, "[The wise man] will take more delight than other men in state festivals. The wise man will set up votive images [εἰκόνας τε ἀναθήσεν]" (*Lives* 10.120). And Cotta mocks the Epicureans: "I have known Epicureans who reverence every little image of a god... so as not to offend the Athenians" (Cicero, *Nat. d.* 1.85). Paul's declaration of his audience as "superstitious" functions as an ironic reversal whereby the religiosity of the Athenian philosophers is demonstrated as an inferior superstition when compared to the philosophically superior and consistent Christian movement.

It is unsurprising, then, that Luke should portray Paul inspecting Athens's "objects of cultic worship" (τὰ σεβάσματα, 17:23) and finding an "altar upon which it was engraved: Ἀγνώστῳ θεῷ." The existence of altars to unknown gods is known from literary and epigraphic sources as a real phenomenon (Pausanias 1.1.4; 5.14.8; Diogenes Laertius, *Lives* 1.110).[47] What is important for this chapter is the *reason* why Paul refers to this altar. Paul's reference to the altar to the unknown god serves again to convict the philosophers as being

---

46. On Epictetus's theology, see A. A. Long, *Epictetus: A Stoic and Socratic Guide to Life* (Oxford: Clarendon, 2002), 180–206.

47. The evidence is examined by Pieter W. van der Horst, "The Altar of the 'Unknown God' in Athens (Acts 17:23) and the Cult of 'Unknown Gods' in the Hellenistic and Roman Periods," *ANRW* 2.18.2 (1990): 1426–56.

superstitious. The motivation for establishing altars to unknown gods arises out of a fear that one has not placated every god possible. As Hans-Josef Klauck states, "If gods are continually overlooked, they react in anger by punishing the human beings who refuse them the sacrifice that is their due."[48] Establishing altars and sacrificing to unknown gods fit perfectly with the superstitious activity described, for example, by Plutarch. Pieter W. van der Horst agrees, stating that behind this motivation for establishing altars is a "sense of fear or anxiety that by naming one god instead of another their acts of worship would not yield the results desired. To be on the safe side, a Greek could use the formula, 'unknown god.'"[49] Furthermore, one of the core critiques of superstition offered by the Hellenistic moralists was that superstitious individuals worshiped in ignorance (Plutarch, *Superst.* 164EF; 165C; Cicero, *Nat. d.* 1.117; Diogenes Laertius, *Lives* 2.91–92). Luke turns the tables on his audience. That which the Athenians "worship ignorantly" (ὅ . . . ἀγνοοῦντες εὐσεβεῖτε), Paul will proclaim to them. Already we see that Paul's speech will be along the lines of propaganda and criticism. Luke stresses their ignorance as he refers to it twice in v. 23 and again in v. 30, characterizing the Athenians' past as τοὺς . . . χρόνους τῆς ἀγνοίας. The altar functions as a means for Paul to introduce his audience's ignorance and superstition regarding deity, and as a transition into a proclamation of this God's identity.

The Creator of the World Does Not Dwell in Temples (17:24–25)

Paul's first description of the identity of this unknown God is twofold. First, God is the *singular* creator of the world and all that is in it: ὁ θεὸς ὁ ποιήσας τὸν κόσμον καὶ πάντα τὰ ἐν αὐτῷ (17:24a). Second, "he gives to everyone life and breath and all things" (αὐτὸς διδοὺς πᾶσι ζωὴν καὶ πνοὴν καὶ τὰ πάντα, 17:25b). The two statements about God likely derive from LXX Isa 42:5:

οὕτως λέγει κύριος ὁ θεὸς ὁ ποιήσας τὸν οὐρανὸν καὶ πήξας αὐτόν, ὁ στερεώσας τὴν γῆν καὶ τὰ ἐν αὐτῇ καὶ διδοὺς πνοὴν τῷ λαῷ ἐπ' αὐτῆς καὶ πνεῦμα τοῖς πατοῦσιν αὐτήν,

Thus says the Lord God who created the heaven and stretched it out, who spread out the earth and everything in it and who gives breath to the people upon it and spirit to those who walk in it.[50]

---

48. Klauck, *Magic and Paganism*, 82–83.
49. Van der Horst, "Altar of the 'Unknown God,'" 1449.
50. Luke uses κόσμος instead of γῆ to refer to the material world, and Pervo (*Acts*, 434)

PART TWO: GOD'S ACTS FOR GENTILES

Three points about Isaiah 42 and its possible influence on Luke's speech should be noted.[51] First, one of the primary themes of Isaiah 42 is the revelation of the knowledge of God *to the pagans*. Thus, God's servant will bring forth "justice to the nations" (42:1) and will be a "light to the nations" (εἰς φῶς ἐθνῶν, 42:6). Second, given that Paul is confronting a polytheistic audience, it is striking that he draws from such a monotheistic portion of the LXX. To cite two examples: "I am the Lord God, that is my name" (42:8a), and "I am God and there is no one else who saves except me" (43:11). Third, Isaiah draws the same conclusion as does Paul in Acts 17:24b, namely, because the *one God is creator of everything*, "he does not inhabit temples made by human hands" (οὐκ ἐν χειροποιήτοις ναοῖς κατοικεῖ). Israel's belief that their God is creator of everything and that he *alone* is God, is precisely the reason why God does not dwell in things "made by human hands." The word χειροποίητος, which Paul uses in 17:24, occurs fourteen times in the LXX, seven of which are found in Isaiah.[52] In each instance, the adjective is a pejorative reference to idolatry. For example, Isaiah 46:6 states, "They hire a goldsmith, who makes it into a handmade idol [ἐποίησαν χειροποίητα]; they fall down and worship." Isaiah 66:1-2a, quoted by Stephen in Acts 7:49-50, is explicit: "Heaven is my throne and earth is my footstool. What kind of house will you build for me, and what will be my resting place? For all of these things my hands have made."[53]

That this creator God is self-sufficient is emphasized by the fact that "he is not served by human hands" (οὐδὲ ὑπὸ χειρῶν ἀνθρωπίνων θεραπεύεται, 17:25). In two verses, Paul has managed to criticize both temples and cultic service as useless in humanity's search for God. Two citations from the LXX also speak to God's self-sufficiency and its relationship to temples and cultic

---

suggests that this may be a "concession to Greek philosophical language." One should note also the following texts as similar to Acts 17:24-25: Wis 9:1, 9; Tob 7:17; Ps 146:5; Exod 20:11.

51. On the allusion to Isaiah 42:5, see David W. Pao, *Acts and the Isaianic New Exodus*, WUNT 2/130 (Tübingen: Mohr Siebeck, 2000), 194-95; Rowe, *World Upside Down*, 36; Haenchen, *Acts*, 522; Pervo, *Acts*, 434n81.

52. Isaiah 2:18; 10:11; 16:12; 19:1; 21:9; 31:7; 46:6; Lev 26:1, 30; Jdt 8:18; Wis 14:8; Dan 5:4; 5:23.

53. That Stephen's speech levels the same criticism against the Jerusalem temple ("made by human hands") as Paul does against pagan images and temples (Acts 17:24-25) is significant. While the claim cannot be further substantiated here, I take it that every other space or place that claims to house deity is challenged and exposed as theologically counterfeit by the revelation of Christ as the one exalted "into heaven" and at "the right hand of God" (7:55-56), and the one who is "Lord of heaven and earth" (17:24), and "the man whom [God] has appointed to judge the world in righteousness having presented proof by raising him from the dead" (17:31). Suggestive here is Matthew Sleeman, *Geography and the Ascension Narrative in Acts*, SNTSMS 146 (Cambridge: Cambridge University Press, 2009), esp. 160-69.

worship. In 2 Maccabees 14:35 and 3 Maccabees 2:9 it is emphasized that God needs nothing, but both passages draw the conclusion that God, in his beneficence, has graciously chosen to dwell in Israel's temple. The God whom Paul proclaims, however, cannot be housed in human-made structures, nor can he be ministered to through human hands.

While it is important to note that Luke draws on Isaiah as a means of polemicizing against polytheism, one must also keep in mind the evidence from Hellenistic philosophical sources that criticize temple worship, sacrifices, and images as superstitious.[54] For example, Seneca states,

> We should like to forbid the morning levee and sitting at the temple gates: human pride lets itself be ensnared by such exercises of religious duty. The god is worshipped by those who know him. We should like to forbid offering linen garments and a stiff brush to Jupiter, and holding up a mirror to Juno: the god needs no domestic servants. And why is this so? Because he himself serves the human race, he is present everywhere and to everyone. . . . It is the gods who direct the course of the world, who order the universe with their power, and maintain the human race in existence. (*Ep.* 95.47-50)[55]

Note how Seneca justifies his revision of cultic worship of the gods. The gods are self-sufficient; they do not need anything from humans; the gods order the cosmos and provide for humans. Similarly, the Fourth Epistle of the Stoic-Cynic Heraclitus:

> Where is god? Is he shut up in temples [ἐν τοῖς ναοῖς]? You are a fine sort of pious men, who set up god in darkness! A man takes it as an insult if he is said to be stony; but is a god truly spoken of whose honorific title is "he is born from crags?" You ignorant men, don't you know that god is not wrought by hands [οὐκ ἔστι θεὸς χειρότμητος], and has not from the beginning had a pedestal, and does not have a single enclosure? Rather the whole world is his temple [ὅλος ὁ κόσμος αὐτῷ ναός ἐστι], decorated with animals, plants, and stars.[56]

---

54. Scholarship on the Areopagus speech is filled with examples of those who account for only one religious-tradition background. So Dibelius states, "The fact that, with the exception of 17.31, he [i.e. Luke] makes such little use, and then only incidentally, of phrases found in the LXX shows how little the Old Testament influenced the content of his sermon" (*Acts of the Apostles*, 36n24).

55. Quoted from Klauck, *Magic and Paganism*, 84.

56. Translation and text taken from Harold W. Attridge, *First-Century Cynicism in the Epistles of Heraclitus*, HTS 29 (Missoula, MT: Scholars Press, 1976), 58-59.

The similarities between this text and Paul's argument in 17:24–25 are striking. By virtue of his transcendence, God cannot be housed in structures made by human hands, for the entire cosmos is the theater of God's presence.[57]

The question arises, therefore, as to what the reader is to make of Paul's critique of temples and cultic worship, given that this critique resonates with *both* Septuagintal anti-idolatry polemic *and* Hellenistic philosophical critiques. Scholars who see Luke as drawing only on Septuagintal critiques of idolatry read the speech as a critique of pagan polytheism, whereas those who emphasize the Hellenistic philosophical background find little that would be offensive to Luke's dramatic audience.[58] Again, Luke has a twofold purpose that encompasses both concerns. On the one hand, Paul's speech *is* a real criticism of pagan religiosity as idolatry. Temples and human-made structures cannot house the divine. Temples, sacrifices, and images are useless in humanity's quest for God. On the other hand, in appealing to Hellenistic philosophical critiques of temples and cultic worship, Luke presents his movement as a superior philosophy in terms of its beliefs and its consistent religious practices. Do the Stoics and Epicureans reject cultic veneration as superstition for the masses? So does Paul. But whereas the Hellenistic philosophers continued to engage in cultic worship, Luke's movement disengages from what it believes to be false belief about God. Luke crafted Paul's speech such that it both critiques pagan religiosity from a Septuagintal context and does so in such a way as to legitimate the early Christian movement as a philosophical repudiation of superstition. This new religious movement is, then, no crass superstition but rather represents a superior and more consistent form of philosophical knowledge of the divine.

The Unity of Humanity (17:26–27)

Luke's skill in hellenizing biblical traditions is perhaps nowhere more evident than in these verses, as the differing views of Martin Dibelius and Bertil Gärtner have demonstrated. For example, when Paul states that God ἐποίησέν τε ἐξ ἑνὸς πᾶν ἔθνος ἀνθρώπων κατοικεῖν ἐπὶ παντὸς προσώπου τῆς γῆς (17:26a), the interpreter may take ἐξ ἑνός as referring to the biblical story of God's creation of humanity in Genesis 1. The plausibility of this interpretation

---

57. On this text, see Abraham J. Malherbe, "Pseudo-Heraclitus, Epistle 4: The Divinization of the Wise Man," *JAC* 21 (1978): 42–64, esp. 51–54.

58. Gray ("Implied Audiences," 213) also recognizes that Luke has combined philosophical criticism with Jewish attacks on idolatry.

Paul's Areopagus Speech of Acts 17:16-34 as Both Critique and Propaganda

gains weight when one sees that the latter phrase echoes LXX Gen 2:6 (πᾶν τὸ πρόσωπον τῆς γῆς).[59] Some manuscripts intend to erase any ambiguity by inserting αἵματος after the phrase ἐξ ἑνός, thereby producing a reading that unambiguously refers to humanity. Or the interpreter may interpret the phrase in the Stoic sense whereby all humanity originates in and is a part of, Zeus.[60] The unity of humanity was certainly a significant doctrine of the Hellenistic philosophers (e.g., Cicero, *Leg.* 22–39; *Off.* 3.28).

Susceptible to dual interpretations, likewise, are the phrases in 17:26b. Does the phrase ὁρίσας προστεταγμένους καιρούς refer to the biblical historical periods of the nations (e.g., Deut 32:8; Dan 8), or does it refer to the philosophical divine ordering of the seasons (e.g., Acts 14:15–17)? Again, should the phrase τὰς ὁροθεσίας τῆς κατοικίας αὐτῶν be translated in terms of the biblical concept of "the boundaries of their [nations'] habitations" or the philosophical rendering of "the boundaries [of the season's geographical zones] for their habitation"?[61] I suggest that convincing answers to these questions are impossible, precisely because Luke has crafted this sentence in such a manner as to resonate with both biblical and philosophical traditions. Two translations of 17:26 are, therefore, available to the interpreter, both the biblical and the philosophical. Again, it is important to see that Luke has portrayed the early Christian movement as affirming the best of Hellenistic philosophy, in this case Stoicism, and has rendered its biblical traditions in Hellenistic terms. Luke exploits the overlap between biblical and Stoic traditions: both affirm that God is one, that the human race is unified and originates in God, and that God orders the seasons and humanity's habitations.[62]

The reason for God's beneficent and providential care for humanity is set forth in the purposive infinitival clause: ζητεῖν τὸν θεόν εἰ ἄρα γε ψηλαφήσειαν αὐτὸν καὶ εὕροιεν, καί γε οὐ μακρὰν ἀπὸ ἑνὸς ἑκάστου ἡμῶν ὑπάρχοντα (17:27). The conditional contrary-to-fact clause, however, indicates the gap

---

59. "Face of the earth" occurs throughout the LXX (e.g., Gen 4:14; 6:7; 7:4, 23).

60. The first interpretation takes the phrase ἐξ ἑνός as masculine, which would correspond to ἀνθρώπων, whereas the second interpretation takes the disputed phrase as neuter. The D Text, E, and Majority Text took the phrase in the former sense by adding the noun αἵματος, which necessitates the biblical interpretation.

61. Dibelius ("Paul on the Areopagus," 27–37) suggests that interpretations of the Areopagus speech must begin with 17:26–27, which, he argued, evidences a reliance on the Stoic view of the world (see, e.g., Wis 7:18; Dio Chrysostom, *Or.* 40; and Acts 14:17). Gärtner (*Areopagus Speech and Natural Revelation*, 147–52) argues that 17:26b refers to "historical epochs" (e.g., 1 En. 2:1; Dan 2:21).

62. Similarly, see Barrett, "Paul's Speech on the Areopagus," 73.

between humanity and God and suggests the failure of this quest for Paul's gentile audience. In the LXX, the verb ψηλαφάω bears the negative connotation of a person fumbling and stumbling after something (see also Homer, *Od.* 9.416; Plato, *Phaed.* 99b). So, for example, the verb is often applied to a blind person trying to feel out something with great difficulty (Gen 27:21-22; Deut 28:29; Judg 16:26; Job 5:14; Isa 59:10).[63] Intriguingly, in two instances the verb is used to describe pagan idols that have human body parts engraved on them but who cannot feel anything (LXX Pss 113:15; 134:17). Yet this unknown God that Paul proclaims is not far from humanity. Again, Paul echoes Isaiah: ζητήσατε τὸν θεὸν καὶ ἐν τῷ εὑρίσκειν αὐτὸν ἐπικαλέσασθε ἡνίκα δ' ἂν ἐγγίζῃ ὑμῖν (Isa 55:6). This unknown God has made himself known through his creative and providential acts and through the implanting of the divine within humanity. The Septuagintal language resonates with Hellenistic philosophical thought. So Seneca: "One need not lift one's hands to heaven nor implore the temple guardian to give us access to the ear of the divine statue, as though our prayer would be better heard there: the god is near you, he is with you, he is in you" (*Ep.* 41.1-2; cf. Dio Chrysostom, *Or.* 12.27-30). While Seneca is a prime example of one who opposes statues and images, it is precisely the human search for God that leads to the establishment of cultic images. So Dio:

> All human beings are oriented towards the divine, so that they are driven by a powerful yearning to venerate the god from close at hand, serving him, drawing close to him, touching him with full conviction, sacrificing to him and decking him with garlands. For human beings behave towards the gods in exactly the same way as little children who are separated from their father or mother: these experience an irresistible longing for their parents and stretch out their hands yearningly to them in dreams, although the parents are not in fact present. (*Or.* 12.60-62)

Paul agrees with Seneca, Dio, and Isaiah, that God is near humanity and has implanted within humanity the desire to search after God. Unlike Dio and Seneca, however, Paul states that, despite God's nearness and beneficence to humanity, the Athenians have remained ignorant of this God and are like the blind groping after the divine.

---

63. Pervo (*Acts*, 437n115) notes that in Greek literature the verb often has the connotation of groping after an object in the dark.

Paul's Areopagus Speech of Acts 17:16–34 as Both Critique and Propaganda

The Images of God (17:28–29)

Both the reason why humanity has been created with the purpose of seeking God (17:27a) and the justification for God's nearness to humanity (17:27b) are explained in vv. 28–29 by Paul's citation of two lines of Greek poetry. The first line has no clear parallel to any known Greek text: ἐν αὐτῷ γὰρ ζῶμεν καὶ κινούμεθα καὶ ἐσμέν (17:28a). The sentiment fits well with a Stoic or Platonic cosmology. So Epictetus states, "If our souls are so bound up with God and joined together with him, as being parts and portions of his being, does not God perceive their every motion [κινήματος] as being a motion of that which is his own and of one body with himself?" (*Diss.* 1.14.6). Plato writes in the *Timaeus*: "And when the Father that engendered it perceived it in motion and alive [κινηθὲν καὶ ζῶν] [i.e., the soul] . . . he rejoiced" (37c6–7).[64]

Regardless of the background, more important is Paul's claim that he is referencing "some of your own poets" (τινες τῶν καθ' ὑμᾶς ποιητῶν) as proof that humanity is related to God.[65] The second line derives from Aratus's *Phaenomena* (v. 5) and states, τοῦ γὰρ καὶ γένος ἐσμέν (for even we are his offspring, 17:28b).[66] The fact that Aratus was an early-fourth-century BCE Stoic poet who studied under Stoicism's founder, Zeno, provides evidence that the philosophers from 17:18 are still in Paul's purview, as he uses their own religious-philosophical traditions to explain the identity of the unknown God. The resonances with Stoicism are clear. Cleanthes's *Hymn to Zeus* is relevant as context for 17:28b: "Zeus, lord of nature, who governs the universe according to law, all hail! It is fitting to praise you, *for we are indeed all your offspring*, and we alone, of all that *lives and moves* here on earth, are endowed with speech."

---

64. The reference to Plato's *Timaeus* is supported by H. Hommel, "Platonisches bei Lukas: Zu Acta 17.28a," *ZNW* 48 (1957): 193–200. Some have suggested that the phrase derives from Epimenides; see Kirsopp Lake, "Your Own Poets," in Lake and Cadbury, *Additional Notes to the Commentary*, 246–51.

65. Klauck (*Magic and Paganism*, 88) suggests that the plural poets "may be nothing more than a conventional stylistic device." So Pervo, *Acts*, 439n126.

66. This quotation was likely mediated to Luke through the Hellenistic Jew Aristobulus. So Mark J. Edwards, "Quoting Aratus: Acts 17,28," *ZNW* 83 (1992): 266–69. Both figures invoke the Stoic poet in the context of proclaiming God as the beneficent and providential creator of the universe. Both toy with a relationship between the God of Israel and Zeus (Acts 17:22–23; Aristobulus, frag. 4b). That Luke had Hellenistic-Jewish predecessors who were negotiating the relationship between their biblical traditions with respect to many of the themes mentioned in the Areopagus speech has been argued by Wolfgang Nauck, "Die Tradition und Komposition der Areopagrede: Eine Motivgeschichtliche Untersuchung," *ZTK* 53 (1956): 11–52.

PART TWO: GOD'S ACTS FOR GENTILES

Paul, thus, invokes the Athenians' poets, with a Stoic emphasis, to support his claim that humanity's desire for God has been implanted within them.

Two factors, however, suggest that the interpreter of this speech should be wary of assimilating Paul's speech too snugly within this Stoic outlook. First, it bears reminding that the Stoic view of God was decidedly materialistic and pantheistic. All of materiality, the world and humanity, derived from this kind of fiery pneumatic world principle—most often identified by the Stoics as Zeus. God is, thus, an inner-worldly force, and humanity is literally part of God as it derives its pneumatic materiality from this principle.[67] Paul is, it is true, assimilating his message regarding the God of Israel and Jesus Christ to the philosophical and religious ethos of his audience, but given the obvious differences between the conception of God in the overall narrative of Acts and that of the Stoics and Epicureans we should be careful of interpretations that see Paul as completely assimilating his message to Greek philosophy. Second, Gärtner has shown that the three verbs used in 17:28a (ζῶμεν, κινούμεθα, and ἐσμέν) occur in Septuagintal anti-idolatry polemic.[68] In other words, idols do not live, do not move, and have no existence. Again, I draw attention to Isaiah. Human-made images must be nailed in place so that "they will not be moved" (οὐ κινηθήσονται, Isa 41:7). The maker of the idol sets it up where he wants, and "it will not be moved" (οὐ μὴ κινηθῇ, Isa 46:7). The Assyrians make gods "which are no gods" (οὐ γὰρ θεοὶ ἦσαν, Isa 37:19a). Daniel explains why he does not worship the Babylonians' gods: "I do not worship idols made by human hands but, rather, the living God" (οὐ σέβομαι εἴδωλα χειροποίητα ἀλλὰ τὸν ζῶντα θεόν, Bel 5). More texts could be added,[69] but here I emphasize that Luke has hellenized his Septuagintal critique of idolatry. He has advanced his claims that God is near humanity (Acts 17:27–28) and has prepared for his anti-idol polemic (17:29) by invoking the Greek poets that resonate with Septuagintal teaching on God.

Paul draws the conclusion from humanity's relatedness to God that "we ought not to suppose that God would be like gold, silver, stone, imaged by the craft and imagination of humanity" (οὐκ ὀφείλομεν νομίζειν χρυσῷ ἢ ἀργύρῳ ἢ λίθῳ, χαράγματι τέχνης καὶ ἐνθυμήσεως ἀνθρώπου, τὸ θεῖον εἶναι ὅμοιον, 17:29). The language here is again Septuagintal. For example, Isa 40:18–20 states,

> To whom will you liken God, or with what likeness will you compare him?
> A craftsman casts forth an image [εἰκόνα], and the goldsmith overlays it

---

67. See Klauck, *Magic and Paganism*, 88–89.
68. Gärtner, *Areopagus Speech and Natural Revelation*, 219–23.
69. Especially relevant are Jer 10:19; 16:19; Wis 13:6–19; 15:16–17; Jub. 12:5; 20:7–8.

Paul's Areopagus Speech of Acts 17:16-34 as Both Critique and Propaganda

with gold [χρυσίον] and makes silver chains for it. . . . He seeks a skilled craftsman to set up an image that will not be moved.

The logic of Paul's argument is important for the conclusion of his speech. Since humanity is God's offspring, one should not suppose that anything other than humanity—such as golden, silver, or wooden idols—can represent God. Underlying 17:28-29 is something akin to an *imago Dei* theology.[70] Paul has claimed in 17:26 that humanity derives from a single source (ἐξ ἑνός), which the implied audience would recognize as a reference to Adam (Gen 1:26-27; 2:7). The verbs of 17:28 "to live," "to move," and "to have one's being" are not true for idols, but they are true of humanity. In Genesis 2:7 humanity is given by God "the breath of life" (πνοὴν ζωῆς) and becomes a "living entity" (ψυχὴν ζῶσαν). Humanity is "like God" (ἄνθρωπον κατ' εἰκόνα ἡμετέραν καὶ καθ' ὁμοίωσιν, Gen 1:26a); idols are not like God (οὐκ . . . τὸ θεῖον εἶναι ὅμοιον, Acts 17:29b).

I have presented numerous texts above both from the Septuagint and from Hellenistic philosophy that criticize temples and idols. Two points are worth summarizing. First, whereas Stoics and Epicureans criticized temples and human-made images, both groups continued to engage in this form of civic religion (Plutarch, *Stoic. abs.* 1034B; Dio Chrysostom, *Or.* 12).[71] Paul presents the Christian movement as a superior form of philosophical reflection on God by demonstrating the movement's consistency in both its theological reflection and its practical worship of God apart from images. Second, by criticizing temples (v. 24), cultic service (v. 25), and idols (v. 29), Paul shows his dramatic audience their failure to attain a true knowledge of God. This unknown God has revealed himself to them in creation (v. 24), history (v. 26), and humanity (vv. 28-29). It is with respect to God's revealing himself in humanity that Paul's speech now takes its crucial turn.

The Resurrected "Man" Is Judge of the World (17:30-31)

Having demonstrated his audience's failure to attain knowledge of God, Paul declares, τοὺς μὲν οὖν χρόνους τῆς ἀγνοίας ὑπεριδὼν ὁ θεός (17:30a). The interpreter should not soften Paul's bluntness: Athenian religion is characterized by lack of knowledge (17:23b, 30a).[72] God has remained "the unknown god"

---

70. See Nasrallah, *Christian Responses*, 114-15; Nauck, "Die Tradition und Komposition der Areopagrede," 22-23.

71. See also David L. Balch, "The Areopagus Speech: An Appeal to the Stoic Historian Posidonius against Later Stoics and the Epicureans," in *Greeks, Romans, and Christians: Essays in Honor of Abraham J. Malherbe*, ed. David L. Balch et al. (Minneapolis: Fortress, 1990), 52-79, here 67-72.

72. So Jervell, *Die Apostelgeschichte*, 450.

(ἄγνωστος θεός) until now. The plethora of idols (17:16), their obsession with religious novelty (17:21), the altar to the "unknown god" (17:22), their building of temples (17:24), their cultic worship (17:25), and their forming gods out of earthly material (17:29) testify that Athenian religiosity is characterized by ignorance.[73] The resonance between lack of knowledge and idolatry in the LXX is precisely what one would expect given the critique of idolatry in Paul's speech. Isaiah 45:20 states, for example, that the gentiles who engage in worship of idols "have no knowledge" (οὐκ ἔγνωσαν). More emphatic is Wisdom of Solomon, which repeatedly draws the connection between ignorance and idolatry. Idolatry, to cite one instance, results from the fact that the gentiles have "failed to know the one who formed them" (ἠγνόησεν τὸν πλάσαντα αὐτόν, Wis 15:11; cf. 13:8–19; 14:1–31). The Athenians' lack of knowledge is, therefore, exemplified in their idolatry. However, because they have worshiped in ignorance "God now is commanding *all* of humanity *everywhere* [τοῖς ἀνθρώποις πάντας πανταχοῦ] to repent" (Acts 17:30b). The universality of Paul's claim is striking. Because this God is the single God who created the world (17:24), controls and maintains history (17:26–27), and has made humanity to seek him (17:27–29), he has authority to "command" all humanity to repent. Paul's command "to repent" calls the Athenians to turn away from their religiosity. Lukan repentance does not consist, as Philipp Vielhauer suggests, "in the self-consciousness of one's natural kinship to God."[74] Humanity's natural kinship to God is precisely that which testifies that they have not found God (17:26–29). Rather, the command to repent calls for a rejection of their cultic worship and an acceptance of Paul's christological claim in 17:31.

Finally, in 17:31 there is an explicit return to the speech's introduction of 17:16–21. With the eschatological shift in Paul's claim that God "has established a day in which he will judge the inhabited world in righteousness" (ἔστησεν ἡμέραν ἐν ᾗ μέλλει κρίνειν τὴν οἰκουμένην ἐν δικαιοσύνῃ, 17:31a) the tables have been turned. Whereas the Athenians originally stood in judgment of Paul and placed him on trial for his introduction of the new gods Ἰησοῦς καὶ Ἀνάστασις (17:18–19), Paul now declares that this deity is the judge of the entire world.[75] The agent of this judgment is precisely the deity whom the Athenians wanted to put on trial, namely, "the human whom God has appointed, having presented proof to everyone by raising him from the dead" (ἐν ἀνδρὶ ᾧ ὥρισεν, πίστιν παρασχὼν

---

73. Dibelius (*Acts of the Apostles*, 55–61) underestimates the extent to which Paul's references to "ignorance" speak to a criticism of Athenian religion.

74. Philipp Vielhauer, "On the 'Paulinism' of Acts," in *Studies in Luke-Acts*, ed. Leander E. Keck and J. Louis Martyn (Philadelphia: Fortress, 1968), 36.

75. On the resurrected Jesus's displacement of other gods, see Pao, *Acts and the Isaianic New Exodus*, 209–12; Rowe, *World Upside Down*, 39.

Paul's Areopagus Speech of Acts 17:16-34 as Both Critique and Propaganda

πᾶσιν ἀναστήσας αὐτὸν ἐκ νεκρῶν, 17:31b). It is at this point that Paul's speech is interrupted by his audience. Paul's preaching of the resurrection is precisely that which led to misunderstanding and contempt in 17:18, and here again it is Paul's mention of Jesus's resurrection that brings forth mocking (17:32). It is not uncommon to find claims that 17:30-31 is the generic Christian appendage to the real Hellenistic philosophical sermon of 17:23-29. This kind of statement, however, can be accepted only when critical facts are ignored. First, Luke often indicates the climactic portion of his speeches through interruptions of the high point of the speech (e.g., 7:53-54; 10:43-44).[76] Second, it ignores the foregrounding of the *inclusio* of "What would this babbler have to say?" (17:18) and "Some mocked" (17:32), which are both in response to Jesus's resurrection.[77] Finally, the claim that Jesus's resurrection is insignificant in the Areopagus speech ignores the role that the resurrection has in the larger narrative. Scholarly attention to the Areopagus speech has too often failed to integrate this speech within the rest of Acts.[78] The claim that God has "appointed" (ᾧ ὥρισεν) this man finds parallels in other speeches. Perhaps most important is 10:42, where Peter proclaims that this Jesus "has been appointed by God as judge of the living and dead" (οὗτός ἐστιν ὁ ὡρισμένος ὑπὸ τοῦ θεοῦ κριτὴς ζώντων καὶ νεκρῶν). In both 10:42 and 2:23-24 it is God's appointing of Jesus through the resurrection that procures the fulfillment of God's plan and establishes Jesus with ultimate power. Even more importantly, throughout Acts one can discern numerous places where the power of the risen Messiah challenges false religion. For example, in Acts 19:11-20 the power of the "name of the Lord Jesus" (19:13) exposes the futility of religious competitors. In 19:23-41 Paul's preaching of the risen Jesus gives Demetrius concern for Artemis. Likewise, Jesus's resurrection undergirds the calls to Jews to repent (2:37-41; 3:11-26; 5:27-32). Luke has bracketed the speech (17:18, 32) and ended Paul's discourse with references to the resurrection in order to foreground the challenge that the risen Jesus presents to pagan religion.

The Results of Mocking and Believing: Acts 17:32-34

Two points need to be made here regarding these verses. First, Paul's preaching of the resurrection, as typical in Luke-Acts, results in division. The μὲν ...

---

76. See, e.g., Haenchen, *Acts*, 212; Pervo, *Acts*, 635.
77. Given, "Not Either/Or but Both/And," 358-59.
78. See, however, Paul Schubert, "The Place of the Areopagus Speech in the Composition of Acts," in *Essays in Divinity*, vol. 6, *Transitions in Biblical Scholarship*, ed. J. Coert Rylaarsdam (Chicago: University of Chicago Press, 1968), 235-61.

δέ clause typifies the split to which the preaching of the resurrection leads.[79] When Paul spoke of the resurrection from the dead "some mocked" (οἱ μὲν ἐχλεύαζον, 17:32) and some shrugged off the matter, but "some of the men believed and were joined together with him" (τινὲς δὲ ἄνδρες κολληθέντες αὐτῷ ἐπίστευσαν, 17:34).[80] As is so often the case in Luke-Acts, it is Jesus's resurrection that produces division (e.g., Acts 2:12–13 with 2:37–41; Acts 13:15 with 13:45). Paul's discourse should be viewed not as an atypical account of the gospel's failure, but rather as an example showing that the Christian movement gains converts even in pagan Athens. Second, that among those who believed were "even Dionysius the Areopagite and his wife named Damaris and others with them" (17:34b) functions to legitimate Paul's message as even this high-standing Athenian was persuaded.

In this chapter I have argued that an approach to Acts 17:16–34 must account for the resonances of both Septuagintal and Hellenistic philosophical texts. While I have pointed to only a few of the many pertinent texts that form the context for understanding the speech, I have attempted to demonstrate that Luke's invoking these dual sets of texts corresponds to the dual purpose of the speech. On the one hand, the speech invokes Septuagintal critiques of idolatry, which corresponds to one of Luke's purposes, namely, anti-idol polemic. Ultimate power—or, one might say, God—resides with the resurrected Jewish Messiah, and the power of this Resurrected One exposes pagan religion as counterfeit. Additionally, however, the speech has been construed as a form of legitimation or propaganda. The Christian movement is not only *not* a crude superstition but is a superior form of philosophical knowledge of God. Do the Stoics and Epicureans challenge superstition? So does the early Christian movement. But these philosophers do not live out these beliefs in practice; the early Christians, Luke suggests, live them out and do so consistently.

---

79. So Barrett, "Paul's Speech on the Areopagus," 70–71.
80. Scholars often claim that Luke intends his readers to identify the Epicureans with those who mocked and the Stoics with those who gave a polite response. For example, see N. Clayton Croy, "Hellenistic Philosophies and the Preaching of the Resurrection (Acts 17:18, 32)," *NovT* 39 (1997): 21–39. While the Stoics did believe in a providential deity and future conflagration, it is hard to believe that the Jewish belief of resurrection from the dead would have been any more palatable to the Stoics than to the Epicureans.

9

Why Did Gentiles Convert to Christianity?

Storytelling and the Rise of Christianity

How did the early Christian movement persuade gentiles that its God, its gospel message centering upon a crucified and resurrected Messiah, and its attendant way of life were superior to competing Greco-Roman ways of worship and piety toward their gods?[1] Some of the most illuminating works that explore this (or related) question have seemed to me to be characterized by an interesting tension. On the one hand, powerful arguments have been mustered that demonstrate early Christian distinctiveness among ancient Mediterranean religions. Kavin Rowe, for example, has made a powerful argument that Christianity and ancient philosophy, particularly Stoicism, are traditions that offer distinct and rival ways of life—ways of life that are incompatible and incommensurable.[2] Larry Hurtado has argued that the Christian movement in the first three centuries "was a different, even distinctive, kind of religious movement in the cafeteria of religious options of the time. . . . In fact, in the eyes of many in the Roman era, Christianity was very odd, even objectionably so."[3] The rejection of the worship of the traditional gods, its "bookish" nature, its distinction between

---

1. See the recent posing of this question by Larry W. Hurtado, *Why on Earth Did Anyone Become a Christian in the First Three Centuries?* (Milwaukee: Marquette University Press, 2016).

2. C. Kavin Rowe, *One True Life: The Stoics and Early Christians as Rival Traditions* (New Haven: Yale University Press, 2016). See also C. Kavin Rowe, *World Upside Down: Reading Acts in the Graeco-Roman Age* (Oxford: Oxford University Press, 2009) where he argues that the early Christian proclamation of Jesus as the messianic king results in conflict and cultural destabilization throughout ancient Mediterranean cities.

3. Larry W. Hurtado, *Destroyer of the Gods: Early Christian Distinctiveness in the Roman World* (Waco, TX: Baylor University Press, 2016), 183.

one's religious and ethnicity identity—these features and more distinguished Christianity as something new and distinctive. J. B. Rives has argued that Christianity is historically innovative precisely because "it represents the growth of a *new social and conceptual system, a new ideology of religion.*"[4]

On the other hand, other fine scholars have convincingly pointed to the ways in which early Christianity bears remarkable similarities to Greco-Roman religiosities in its ways of being religious. For example, Luke Timothy Johnson has demonstrated how the primary ways of being religious are shared between pagans and early Christians. That is to say, they share with one another the religious convictions or impulses that would look to religion for divine benefits, as an aid for moral transformation, or as a way of stabilizing (or alternatively escaping) the world.[5] With respect to early Christology, many have demonstrated that Jesus is often depicted in ways reminiscent of Greco-Roman deities. To give one recent example, Michael Bird states, "Jesus is, then, a bit like a Jewish Hercules, an apotheosized Augustus, or an archangel, but he is a lot like the Jewish deity Yahweh."[6] I have also tried to demonstrate how Paul used ancient Greco-Roman kingship discourses in his depiction of Jesus as Israel's messianic ruler.[7]

This does not seem to be a situation of an "either/or," but rather one where both distinctiveness and similarity, tension and continuity, characterize early Christianity's relationship to Greco-Roman religions their practices, discourse, and religious sensibilities. And perhaps this is not too surprising given that the Christian movement's persuasiveness was dependent upon its ability to present its God and way of life as the superior alternative that brooks no competitors but participates in the cultural and religious logic of its competitors.

This chapter asks the question: How did the early Christian movement persuade others that its God and attendant way of life was superior to competing Greco-Roman religions? I propose the book of Acts and its engagement with Greco-Roman religion provides a significant window into answering this question *and* establishes a defining feature of Christian identity throughout its history. Acts makes abundant use of Greco-Roman religious discourses

---

4. J. B. Rives, "Christian Expansion and Christian Ideology," in *The Spread of Christianity in the First Four Centuries: Essays in Explanation*, 15–42, ed. William V. Harris (Leiden: Brill, 2005), 16. Italics mine.

5. Luke Timothy Johnson, *Among the Gentiles: Greco-Roman Religion and Christianity*, AYBRL (New Haven: Yale University Press, 2009).

6. Michael F. Bird, *Jesus Among the Gods: Early Christology in the Greco-Roman World* (Waco, TX: Baylor University Press, 2022), 3. See also M. David Litwa, *IESUS DEUS: The Early Christian Depiction of Jesus as a Mediterranean God* (Minneapolis: Fortress, 2014).

7. Joshua W. Jipp, *Christ Is King: Paul's Royal Ideology* (Minneapolis: Fortress, 2015).

Why Did Gentiles Convert to Christianity?

in order to show that the early Christian movement embodies supremely the superior elements of Greco-Roman religiosity and philosophy. Acts portrays its characters and movement as working within the cultural and religious logic of a variety of aspects of Greco-Roman religiosity as a means of simultaneously criticizing and disrupting pagan beliefs, allegiances, and ways of life, *and* using said Greco-Roman cultural scripts to portray Christianity as *the* superior Greco-Roman religion. Christianity—or at least Christian discourse—emerges out of intense conflict with Greco-Roman religiosity. But its employment of Greco-Roman religious scripts, themes, and philosophy results in deep cultural convergences between Christianity and pagan religion as the former emerges out of the latter. The Acts of the Apostles provides significant testimony to this dynamic as it both adapts to and criticizes aspects of the culture within which it takes root.

CHRISTIAN RHETORIC AND IDEOLOGY

Those historians who have sought to explain the success and expansion of Christianity have not often emphasized the stories, the discourses, the beliefs, and ideologies of the Christian movement as a primary reason for its success.[8] Historians of Christian origins have not, at least to my knowledge, sufficiently engaged Averil Cameron's *Christianity and the Rhetoric of Empire*. In an earlier work, I drew briefly upon Cameron to help me make the claim that the apostle Paul's depiction of Christ as a good king is an act of world construction whereby Paul strategically reworks and applies royal scripts to Christ such that this king now stabilizes Paul's assemblies and is the focal point for their symbolic world.[9] Cameron is helpful for her argument that the rise of Christianity cannot be explained solely through social and economic observations. Rather, much of Christianity's success is due to its invention of a totalizing Christian discourse which established itself "in the hearts and minds of people."[10] That is to say, Christian discourse told the types of stories that people understood, wanted to hear, and were persuaded by.[11] Christianity was effective in large part due to its literary abilities to draw upon the secular intellectual imagina-

---

8. But now more recently, Hurtado, *Why on Earth Did Anyone Become a Christian*, 108–29.

9. See Jipp, *Christ Is King*, 11–16.

10. Averil Cameron, *Christianity and the Rhetoric of Empire: The Development of Christian Discourse* (Berkeley: University of California Press, 1991), 27.

11. Cameron, *Christianity and the Rhetoric of Empire*, 92–93.

tion and familiar pagan rhetorical devices in order to persuade others of the superiority of the Christian God and way of life. Cameron perceptively notes the paradox of Christian discourse.[12] On the one hand, its stories are marked by "openness and multiplicity" with respect to pagan precedents; on the other hand, Christian discourse produced a totalizing worldview "with no room for dissenting opinion."[13] Rives has argued that Christian totalization resulted in a situation where Christian teachers could "monopolize access to the divine among adherents of the Christian god: they alone possessed a true knowledge of the divine world, they alone could distinguish the right path from the wrong, they alone could mediate the power of the god."[14]

In what follows, I want to offer only a *brief sketch*, often drawing upon some of my claims in the previous chapters, to show how Acts offers an example of appealing and powerful stories and rhetorical discourses that depict the Christian movement as a superior cult, philosophy, and community. Acts does this by simultaneously drawing upon Greco-Roman precedents and using them to make the totalizing claim that the Christian movement, its deity, and its way of life are exclusively superior to its competitors.

A Superior Deity

In the ancient world the divine benefits of the pagan gods were understood to be offered in tangible ways for humans in exchange for their worship. Power is the single most important and essential aspect of a god. So Xenophanes: "For this is 'god' and the power of god: to rule and not to be ruled, and to be the mightiest of all" (Ps.-Aristotle, *Xen.* 977a).[15] Luke Timothy Johnson describes this well when he notes that divine benefits were given in such forms as "revealing through prophecy, healing through revelation, providing security and status through Mysteries, enabling and providing for the daily successes of individuals, house-

---

12. One should also see the fascinating essay by Todd Penner, "Civilizing Discourse: Acts, Declamation, and the Rhetoric of the Polis," in *Contextualizing Acts: Lukan Narrative and Greco-Roman Discourse*, ed. Todd Penner and Caroline Vander Stichele, SBLSymS 20 (Atlanta: Society of Biblical Literature Press, 2003), 65–104. Penner argues, for example, that Luke "presents Christianity as the model *politeia* with an exemplary constitution and leadership. Theological themes are therefore deeply embedded in, and in principle indistinguishable from, these more expansive sociocultural and political emphases" (90).

13. Cameron, *Christianity and the Rhetoric of Empire*, 222.

14. Rives, "Christian Expansion and Christian Ideology," 38.

15. Quoted from Jennifer Eyl, "Divination and Miracles," in *T&T Clark Handbook to the Historical Paul*, ed. Ryan S. Schellenberg and Heidi Wendt (London: T&T Clark, 2022), 215–32, here 224.

holds, cities, and empires."[16] Demonstration of true divinity was dependent upon the god's powers and benefits to humans in the empirical world—again, healing, prophecy, and answering prayers for safety and security.[17] Itinerant soothsayers, healers, and wonder-workers (so-called religious freelance experts) frequently mediated these divine benefits and, at times, even established cults to their patron deities.[18] Aelius Aristides consistently gives devout worship to the healing god Asclepius who, as his patron deity, has frequently healed him of illnesses and thereby made possible the continued use of his rhetorical abilities.[19] Lucian of Samosata tells the story, albeit in order to satirize and debunk it as fraudulent, of a man named Alexander who established a cult in honor of the oracular snake-deity named Glycon (Lucian, *Alexander the False Prophet*).

The Acts of the Apostles too demonstrates the superiority of the Christian cult by telling stories that depict the God of Israel and Jesus the Messiah as having unrivaled and superior power to the pagan gods, magicians, and rulers as this superior power is revealed through the apostles. The telling of these stories in early Christian discourse, as Ramsay MacMullen has noted, "made physically (or dramatically) visible the superiority of the Christian's patron Power of all others. One and only one was God. The rest were *daimones* demonstrably, and therefore already familiar to the audience as nasty, lower powers that no one would want to worship anyway."[20] The offering of worship and allegiance to the Christian God was motivated, in large part, by the expectation for divine benefits and alleviation of fear in the face of divine judgment.[21] We can note three types of stories that show that the Christian deity is singularly supremely powerful over and against other competitors.

Turf Wars

Acts narrates a variety of episodes which pit the emissaries of the Christian deity against other soothsayers and magicians. The episodes function most

---

16. L. Johnson, *Among the Gentiles*, 46.
17. Ramsay MacMullen, *Paganism in the Roman Empire* (New Haven: Yale University Press, 1981), 94–112.
18. See here especially Heidi Wendt, *At the Temple Gates: The Religion of Freelance Experts in the Roman Empire* (New York: Oxford University Press, 2016).
19. Aelius refers to Asclepius repeatedly throughout the six orations that make up his *Sacred Tales*, but see in particular "Oration Regarding Asclepius." For helpful commentary, see L. Johnson, *Among the Gentiles*, 50–63.
20. Ramsay MacMullen, *Christianizing the Roman Empire: A.D. 100–400* (New Haven: Yale University Press, 1984), 28.
21. MacMullen, *Christianizing the Roman Empire*, 29, 73.

basically as a contest between deities and, according to Acts, result in the conversion of many to the Christian movement. Often these stories depict the movement of the gospel into new geographical regions—places which are often beholden to the power of Satan at work in magicians, soothsayers, exorcists, and false gods.[22]

The Samaritans are depicted as deceived and beholden to Simon—a practitioner of black magic (8:9-13). Acts sets the story up as a competition. On the one side is Philip who proclaims the Messiah to the Samaritans and performs signs, wonders, and exorcisms (8:5-8). His opponent refers to himself as "someone great" (8:9b) and receives the confession "this one is the power of God which is called great" (8:10b). And yet the contest is anticlimactic as Simon recognizes the superior power of "the kingdom of God and the name of Jesus Christ" at work in Philip (8:13). There is more to the story, but it is sufficient for my purposes to note that the power of God at work in Philip results in joy and receptivity to the word among the Samaritan villages (8:8, 25). In Cyprus, Paul and Barnabas proclaim "the word of God" by the power of the Holy Spirit (13:4-5), and this results in a contest with "a certain Jewish magician and false prophet whose name is Bar-Jesus" (13:6). When Bar-Jesus opposes the success of the word of God, Paul proclaims something of a curse upon the man: "Now the hand of the Lord is against you and you will be blind, unable to see the sun for some time" (13:11). The presence of Jesus is powerfully at work in Paul when, in Ephesus, he performs incredible works of healings and exorcisms (19:11-17). The demonstrable superiority of Paul's God leads to many turning away from magic and sorcery through burning their magic books and materials (19:18-19). In Malta, when Paul is apparently attacked by a viper—a symbolic enemy of the Christian movement in Luke-Acts (e.g., Luke 3:7; 10:18-19; 11:11-12)—Paul "shook off the beast into the fire and he suffered no evil" (Acts 28:5). Paul's immunity to the viper marks him as God's prophetic emissary who is protected by God and is able to triumph over evil (see Luke 10:19). The Maltese islanders acclaim Paul as divine and, while readers of Acts know their claim is imprecise, there is much to commend in their perception of Paul. Paul's immunity to the snake, whereby he conquers the demonic, demonstrates that Jesus's resurrection power is at work in Paul. They rightly respond to Paul by extending extraordinary hospitality and sharing their possessions with him for his ongoing voyage to Rome (28:7-10).

---

22. On which see Susan R. Garrett, *The Demise of the Devil: Magic and the Demonic in Luke's Writings* (Minneapolis: Fortress, 1989).

God-Fighters

Acts contains a variety of stories whereby enemies of God's people receive harsh and visible payment for their wicked deeds. The reader will likely remember how Gamaliel warned his fellow members of the Sanhedrin to leave the Christian movement alone "lest you be found to be fighting against God" (μήποτε καὶ θεομάχοι εὑρεθῆτε, 5:39). The notion of "god-fighting" likely originates from early Greek stories, such as Euripides's *Bacchae*, that use a "plot of divine punishment" to refer to what happens when deities are resisted and opposed.[23] Here the king of Thebes refuses to offer cultic worship to Dionysus and is, as a result, referred to as a "god-fighter" (θεομαχεῖ, *Bacch.* 45–46). The god punishes the king's hubris by inflicting him with a shameful and violent death.

Luke shares a variety of stories whereby God brings a violent end as judgment against those who fight against him and his people. Surprisingly, Judas is depicted as a god-fighter who opposes the Messiah and his people. Luke notes that "Satan entered into Judas the one called Iscariot" (Luke 22:3), and his conspiracy against Jesus indicates that he is an ally of "the authority of darkness" (22:53b). Judas's motivation to betray Jesus due to greed is an obvious Lukan indication that Judas is one of the text's primary antagonists (so too Acts 5:1–11; 8:18–23; 16:16–18). It is with a certain amount of irony, then, that Judas leaves behind his ministry in order to "acquire a field as the payment for his wickedness" (Acts 1:18a). And it is on his acquired land that Judas dies a violent death: "Falling headfirst, he burst open in the middle and all his intestines spilled out" (1:18b CEB).

When Ananias and Saphira hold back some of the profits from their sale of the land, their deceit marks the first potential threat to the unity of the church—a unity marked through the generous sharing of possessions with one another. As a result, Peter declares to Ananias, "You have not lied to humans but to God" (οὐκ ἐψεύσω ἀνθρώποις ἀλλὰ τῷ θεῷ, 5:4). Immediately, Ananias drops dead (5:5). When Peter receives a deceitful response from Saphira, she is rebuked for "testing the Spirit of the Lord" (πειράσαι τὸ πνεῦμα κυρίου, 5:9). She immediately drops dead at the feet of the Peter. The narrator emphasizes the emotions of fear, amazement, and dread that come upon the church as a result (5:5b, 11). It's difficult to resist the conclusion that the scene provides a powerful warning that the true God is not to be taken lightly and that he is willing and powerful enough to mete forth justice against those who actively resist and oppose him.

---

23. Anne Pippin Burnett, "Pentheus and Dionysus: Host and Guest," *CP* 65 (1970): 15–29, here 15.

PART TWO: GOD'S ACTS FOR GENTILES

The most surprising variation of this story takes place when the reader encounters an enemy of the church who "ravages the church" and goes from "house to house to drag off both men and women and put them in prison" (8:3). Saul "breathes threats and murder against the disciples of the Lord" (9:1). The identification between the Lord and his people is clear as the risen Lord asks Saul, "Why are you harassing *me*?" (9:4b). God's response to Saul surprises the reader's expectations as he defeats this violent enemy and transforms him into his star witness to take the Lord's "name to gentiles, kings, and Israelites" (9:15).

Prison Escapes

Related to the theme of "god-fighting" are the three narrations in Acts of prison escapes (5:17–26; 12:1–25; 16:25–34).[24] In each of these episodes, opposition to the success of the Christian movement is responded to with the incarceration of the disciples by the Sanhedrin, Herod Agrippa I, and the local authorities in Philippi. The imprisonment of the agents of the Christian deity are ironic and resonate with stories where "god-fighters" oppose the appearance of a god in a new location (as noted with the *Bacchae*). God's implacable plan to establish the gospel in Jerusalem (and beyond) is summarized well when the angel simply unlocks the prison doors, leads the apostles to the temple, and declares, "Go, take your place in the temple, and tell the people everything about this new life" (5:20 CEB). And finally, Luke makes sure the readers know that Herod Agrippa I, the one who harassed the Jerusalem church, murdered the disciple James, and imprisons Peter (12:3–5)—this Herod dies the death of a god-fighter. The angel of the Lord strikes him down, and "he was eaten by worms and died" (12:23).

All of these episodes in Acts could be illuminated in much more detail through comparing them with Greco-Roman stories of the gods. Here I have simply attempted to make the point that one of the ways that Luke's narrative appeals to its audience is through the recounting of stories that portray the Christian deity as the supremely powerful God against all of his competitors. The disciples are able to make the beneficent power of God known through healings and exorcisms. The Christian deity, while not sparing his people from suffering, protects his church from those who would seek to exterminate or harm it.

---

24. The prison-escape stories and their literary precedents have been illumined by John B. Weaver, *Plots of Epiphany: Prison-Escape in Acts of the Apostles*, BZNW 131 (Berlin: de Gruyter, 2004).

Why Did Gentiles Convert to Christianity?

A SUPERIOR COMMUNITY

Another way that ancient Greeks and Romans defended or argued for the superiority of their ethnic, civic, or political community was through telling stories and making arguments for the superiority of their rulers, their laws or way of life, and their virtues. In what follows, I note how Luke depicts the earliest Christian movement as a superior people based on their king who has created a unified people and in their commitment to hospitality, fellowship, and philanthropy.

A Unified Family

Friendship was one of the most popular topics for reflection in ancient philosophy as exemplified by the serious reflection given to the topic by the likes of Cicero, Seneca, Plutarch, and Epicurus.[25] But no text was more influential than Aristotle's books 8 and 9 of the *Nicomachean Ethics*. Aristotle argues that humans are inherently social and that flourishing thereby requires friendship (*NE* 1169b18–23). A friend shares all things with another, so much so that a friend will even "lay down his life in their behalf" (1169a18–22). Friendships predicated on shared character and virtue are such that "a friend is another self" (1166a31–32).

Acts also depicts the early Christians as a unified and diverse community of friends who are capable of and willing to resolve conflict. While the idyllic depictions of the Jerusalem church resonate with a variety of conceptual precedents, few can ignore the echoes of the ancient moralists on friendship. The community as marked by "fellowship" (2:42), having "all things in common" (2:44; 4:32b), and "one heart and soul" (4:32) draws from the world of philosophical friendship. Luke's claim that they are breaking bread together with joyful and sincere hearts (2:42, 46), and sharing their possessions (2:44–45; 4:32–35), indicates that their practice of hospitality and table fellowship has resulted in a fictive family. Plutarch frequently referred to "the friend-making nature of the dining table" (e.g., *Table-Talk* 612 D–E), but what is surprising here is Luke's expansion of the scope of friendship to include all types of people—rich and poor, Hebrew and Hellenist, and men and women.[26] Douglas

---

25. See throughout David Konstan, *Friendship in the Classical World* (Cambridge: Cambridge University Press, 1997).

26. See Alan C. Mitchell, "The Social Function of Friendship in Acts 2:44–47 and 4:32–37," *JBL* 111 (1992): 255–72.

PART TWO: GOD'S ACTS FOR GENTILES

Hume states this well: "By sharing meals together, the believers are enacting a practice of friendship that forms a kind of family, a fictive kinship group that meets their needs for nourishment, social interaction, and joy."[27]

One of the primary ways that rulers and constitutions were evaluated in the ancient world was with respect to their ability to secure unity for the people.[28] Herodotus, for example, links together successful military exploits with the unity created by the victorious ruler whereas a peoples' defeat in battle is linked to the discord of the people (e.g., *Hist.* 5.3). The assumption that good kings produced harmony and unity for a people stands behind the propagandistic claims for Alexander the Great and the Roman Empire (e.g., Plutarch, *Alex. Fort.* 323; Dionysius of Halicarnassus, *Ant. Rom.* 2.2.2; 2.11.2). The same relationship between a good king (or constitution) and a unified community is seen in biblical Jewish traditions. So, for example, Chronicles shows how "all Israel" is of "one mind" to exalt David and then Solomon to kingship (1 Chr 12:38; 29:21–24). And there are numerous prophetic texts which anticipated a time when a messianic king will unify God's people (e.g., Ezek 34:5–23; 37:15–28; Isa 11:10–13).

So Acts also expresses the unity of the people of God as something predicated upon their common submission to the exalted Davidic Messiah. Luke's glowing even idyllic depiction of the church's unity in 2:42–47 stems from the outpouring of the Spirit who has been sent from the exalted Messiah (see Acts 2:33). A mark of a good ruler is that he is capable of maintaining the peoples' harmony in the face of potential division. The abundance of Greco-Roman rhetorical orations on concord and harmony demonstrate that it was believed that a fundamental trait of victorious kings and peoples was their shared unity (e.g., Dio Chrysostom, *Or.* 13, 38, 39, 40, and 41). Alan Thompson summarizes: "Politicians boast in their ability to bring concord and dispense with strife. Cities, rulers and statesman are praised according to their ability to bring concord and to dispense with strife."[29] Thus, it is within this context that we should situate the threat to the unity of God's people due to the grumbling between the Hellenist and Hebraic widows over the food distribution and how it is overcome as the twelve disciples call forth the seven Hellenists to "wait on tables" (Acts 6:2)—in remembrance of Jesus's manner of table fellowship in

---

27. Douglas A. Hume, *The Early Christian Community: A Narrative Analysis of Acts 2:41–47 and 4:32–35*, WUNT 2/298 (Tübingen: Mohr Siebeck, 2011), 110.

28. For what follows, see Alan J. Thompson, *One Lord, One People: The Unity of the Church in Acts in Its Literary Setting*, LNTS 359 (London: T&T Clark, 2008), 19–56.

29. Thompson, *One Lord, One People*, 120.

the Gospel of Luke (see Luke 22:24-30).[30] All of the major earliest Christian leaders are depicted as engaging in public speeches and councils when there are disputes, the result of which is unity and shared commitment to their mission (see Acts 1:15-26; 11:1-18; 15:1-29). And even the division between "Asia" and "Europe" is overcome by means of "the Spirit of Jesus" (Acts 16:7) who bridges the divide through Paul's ministry.

A Virtuous People

Acts depicts the earliest Christians as proclaiming and embodying shared values related to virtue and piety. While there are a variety of shared values related to piety that could be discussed, here I will focus on how the growth of the earliest Christian movement stems from their commitment to hospitality and philanthropy. The earliest Christians are repeatedly portrayed as committed to extending hospitality (as host) and receiving it (as guest) from different ethnic groups and thereby incorporating mixed populations into its people.[31] Cicero is representative of those Roman citizens who praise Rome for welcoming foreigners. He states that justice should be shown to foreigners so as not to "tear apart the common fellowship of the human race" a fellowship which was "established by the gods" (Cicero, *Off.* 3.28). Failure to show hospitality to a foreigner is, Cicero notes, both "inhumane and barbaric" (*Verr.* 2.4.25). I have commented frequently enough already on the way in which hospitality and philanthropy were prized values in the Greco-Roman world and how, in fact, hospitality was held up as a mark of civilized peoples (e.g., Homer, *Od.* 4.30-37; 7.159-166; Virgil, *Aen.* 1.538-543; Ovid, *Metam.* 1.163-252; 8.617-724; Dio Chrysostom, "The Hunter").

Luke uses the practice of "ritualized friendship"—the practice of shared hospitality between different ethnic groups—to show how the earliest Christians incorporate various ethnicities into a fictive kinship group (see here Acts 10:1-48 and 28:1-10).[32] Those gentiles who respond positively to the gospel proclamation often mimic the behavior of the Jerusalem church (2:42-47

---

30. See here Todd C. Penner, *In Praise of Christian Origins: Stephen and the Hellenists in Lukan Apologetic Historiography* (New York: T&T Clark, 2004).

31. See here David L. Balch, "ΜΕΤΑΒΟΛΗ ΠΟΛΙΤΕΩΝ—Jesus as Founder of the Church in Luke-Acts: Form and Function," in *Contextualizing Acts: Lukan Narrative and Greco-Roman Discourse*, ed. Todd Penner and Caroline Vander Stichele, SBLSymS 20 (Atlanta: Society of Biblical Literature Press, 2003), 139-88.

32. See Walter T. Wilson, "Urban Legends: Acts 10:1-11:18 and the Strategies of Greco-Roman Foundation Narratives," *JBL* 120 (2001): 77-99.

PART TWO: GOD'S ACTS FOR GENTILES

and 4:32-35) in terms of their extension of hospitality to the traveling missionaries (see 16:15, 40; 17:1-9; 18:1-11; 28:1-2, 7-10). Toward the end of Acts, Luke draws the reader in the Hellenistic territory of sea travel, adventures, storms and shipwrecks. Homer's *Odyssey* and Virgil's *Aeneid*, among other sea voyage stories, functioned to increase the sense of adventure and worked symbolically to present a lasting impression of the hero's identity.[33] So Luke expends forty-four verses (27:1-44) to depict Paul as one who receives philanthropic kindness (see 27:3) and shows mercy and hospitality to those on the ship—through encouraging and prophetic exhortations (27:9-12, 13-20, and 24-26) and through sharing table fellowship (27:33-38).[34] When Paul lands on the island of Malta, despite Luke's reference to the Maltese islanders as "barbarians," we find them to be a pious people who bestow *philanthropia* on Paul and the shipwrecked strangers (Acts 28:1-2). Their embrace of Paul is seen climactically in the hospitable reception by "Publius the first man of the island" who "welcomed and for three days extend[ed] friendly hospitality to us" (28:7). Undergirding their commitment to hospitality, philanthropy, and shared fellowship is the conviction that their God is one who is committed to impartiality and welcomes any ethnicity who seeks justice (10:35). God is the creator of peoples; all of humanity is "God's offspring" (17:29). While much more could be said to unpack this theme, it should be clear that Luke draws upon the shared virtues of hospitality, philanthropy, and shared fellowship among the earliest Christians—values that would have appealed to Greco-Roman sensibilities.

A SUPERIOR PHILOSOPHY

Finally, Acts draws upon a variety of discourses to depict its movement as a superior philosophy. Given that I have devoted two chapters to this theme already, I will be brief. The Jerusalem apostles are described with echoes of the true philosophers, even Socrates, as they speak the truth to the religious authorities with "boldness of speech" (παρρησία, Acts 2:29; 4:13, 29, 31), and like Socrates they claim that they will obey God rather than humans (4:19;

---

33. See Daniel Marguerat, *The First Christian Historian: Writing the "Acts of the Apostles,"* trans. Ken McKinney, Gregory J. Laughery, and Richard Bauckham, SNTSMS 121 (Cambridge: Cambridge University Press, 2002), 231-56.

34. I have written on this in more detail in Joshua W. Jipp, *Divine Visitations and Hospitality to Strangers in Luke-Acts: An Interpretation of the Malta Episode in Acts 28:1-10*, NovTSup 153 (Leiden: Brill, 2013), 254-56.

Why Did Gentiles Convert to Christianity?

5:29; compare with Plato, *Apol.* 29D; Epictetus, *Diatr.* 1.30), and who use their voice to challenge and resist tyrannical power (see Dio Chrysostom, *Or.* 78.45). In their willingness to speak truth to power, they demonstrate the integrity of their convictions and they suffer as a result (4:21, 29; 5:33).[35] Many have noted how Acts frequently narrates how their teaching, despite their lack of education and rhetorical training (4:13), results in conversions of those with at least some level of status, education, or wealth (e.g., priests [6:7]; the Ethiopian official [8:26–40]; a Roman centurion [10:1–48]).

The main plank in this argument, of course, is Paul's Areopagus speech in Acts 17:16–34, and so I refer to the reader to chapter 8, where I demonstrate that this text not only narrates the incongruity between the Christian movement and gentile religiosity but also exalts the Christian movement as comprising the best features of Hellenistic and Roman philosophical sensibilities and therefore as a superior philosophy. Luke depicts Paul as a Socrates-like teacher who proclaims philosophical ideas that resonate with Stoicism but only in order to make the claim that true piety and worship is only found in the Christian movement. Paul is no street philosopher who peddles his philosophy upon the gullible ("babbler," σπερμολόγος, 17:18) but is, rather, one who demonstrates the rhetorical and educational skills necessary to hold his own with the Athenian philosophers.

In Paul's last will and testament to the Ephesian elders in Miletus (Acts 20:18–35), Paul's review of his life and ministry resonates with ancient moral philosophers in his claims to have shared the full breadth of truth to his audience in both public and private (20:20–21, 26–27). Paul's emphasis on the public nature of his proclamation and non-sectarian nature of the Christian movement resonates powerfully with the conduct of the good philosopher. As Paul says to Festus, "Indeed the king knows about these things, and to him I speak freely [παρρησιαζόμενος]; for I am certain that none of these things has escaped his notice, for this was not done in a corner" (26:26). Paul is also a true philosopher in that he did not receive payment for his services and did not covet anyone's wealth or possessions (20:33). As a good philosopher, he practiced self-sufficiency by working with his hands to provide for himself and his companions (20:34–35). Likewise, in chapters 22–26 Paul is depicted as giving rhetorically crafted forensic speeches to rulers. Paul speaks regularly with Felix regarding "justice, self-control [δικαιοσύνης καὶ ἐγκρατείας], and the coming

---

35. Excellent here is Ruben R. Dupertuis, "Bold Speech, Opposition, and Philosophical Imagery in the Acts of the Apostles," in *Engaging Early Christian History: Reading Acts in the Second Century*, ed. Ruben R. Dupertuis and Todd Penner (Durham: Acumen, 2013), 153–68.

PART TWO: GOD'S ACTS FOR GENTILES

judgment" (24:25), and Paul refuses to pay a bribe in exchange for his freedom (24:26). With respect to Paul's speech to Herod Agrippa II, Malherbe notes that "Luke has Paul, like the moral philosophers, claim divine guidance (26:16–17, 22), deny that his activity has been confined to a corner (26:26), speak fearlessly to rulers (26:26), and offer himself as an example to all (26:29). Luke's apologetic aim . . . [is] to present Christianity in Paul's person as philosophical."[36]

A FINAL WORD

Acts wants its readers to accept the claim that their God has supreme power and is a benevolent and generous gift-giver to humanity, that their resurrected and cosmic king has brought into existence a unified and philanthropic community of friends, and that Christianity is the true philosophy. In contrast to the Christian community, the reader encounters jealous and petty leaders in the temple (4–5), wicked tyrants (12:20–23), weak and incompetent civic officials who are unable to stop mobs (18:12–17; 19:28–41), and Roman governors looking for bribes (24:25). The reader knows that Lysias, Festus, and Agrippa are not practitioners of justice, for they all know that Paul is innocent and yet do nothing to procure his freedom (23:29; 25:25; 26:31–32).[37] As Todd Penner states, Acts wants its readers to accept the claim that "the great civic traditions of antiquity are manifested . . . in the Christian community, which has God as its king."[38]

In making these claims and attempting to communicate their way of life, Acts provides insight into one of the ways the earliest Christians attempted to convert pagans, namely through telling recognizable and compelling stories to show that the Christian way of life—in terms of its community, philosophy, and virtue—is superior to all of its competitors. Acts recounts the growth and the identity of the Christian movement through drawing upon an abundance of cultural scripts shared with Greco-Roman religion, philosophy and politics. To what we have seen here,[39] I might add Luke's literary prefaces and their

---

36. Abraham J. Malherbe, "'Not in a Corner': Early Christian Apologetic in Acts 26:26," in *Light from the Gentiles: Hellenistic Philosophy and Early Christianity: Collected Essays, 1959–2012*, NovTSup 150 (Leiden: Brill, 2014), 209–26, here 222.

37. On these episodes, see Rowe, *World Upside Down*, 53–89.

38. Penner, "Civilizing Discourse," 94.

39. For the sentence that follows and the scholarship that supports it, see Joshua W. Jipp, "The Acts of the Apostles," in *The State of New Testament Studies: A Survey of Recent Research*, ed. Scot McKnight and Nijay K. Gupta (Grand Rapids: Baker Academic, 2019), 359–60.

similarities to Hellenistic historiography (Luke 1:1–4; Acts 1:1–2),[40] the table of nations in Acts 2:5–11 as mimicking Rome's rule over the known world,[41] the transformation of the traditions of Jesus's crucifixion into a story of noble death (Luke 23),[42] the shaping of Jesus's resurrection appearance in the guise of a theoxeny,[43] and the apostles' speeches as powerful declamations that discuss topics related to virtue, piety, and ethnicity.[44] Acts uses these cultural, religious, and political scripts in order to set forth the claim that the Christian movement is superior to its competitors in terms of its God, virtue, and community.

Of interest for further research would be the exploration of the way these scripts are used throughout the history of Christian missionary activity. I suggest that one would find that adaptation of Greco-Roman scripts to portray Christianity as the superior religion and philosophy, similar to the adaptation found in the book of Acts, continues in the second through fourth centuries CE as the early Christians work to articulate the identity of Christianity and its relation to non-Christian religion.

---

40. See the important work of David P. Moessner, *Luke the Historian of Israel's Legacy, Theologian of Israel's "Christ": A New Reading of the "Gospel Acts" of Luke*, BZNW 182 (Berlin: de Gruyter, 2016).

41. Gary Gilbert, "The List of Nations in Acts 2: Roman Propaganda and the Roman Response," *JBL* 121 (2002): 497–529.

42. Gregory E. Sterling, "*Mors Philosophi*: The Death of Jesus in Luke," *HTR* 94 (2001): 383–402.

43. Rick Strelan, "Recognizing the Gods (Acts 14.8–10)," *NTS* 46 (2000): 488–503.

44. Laura S. Nasrallah, *Christian Responses*, 87–118.

Part Three

God's Acts for Christians

10

The Beginnings of a Theology of Luke-Acts

Divine Activity and Human Response

Whereas NT theology has been the subject of a large amount of sophisticated analysis, the lack of methodological reflection regarding what it means to speak of the theology of a distinct NT text is surprising, especially given that the task is foundational, one would suppose, for the larger project. One should begin, then, by asking the methodological question: What does it mean to speak of a theology of a distinct NT text? Related, what is theology, and how does it, or how should it, determine the task of writing a theology of Luke-Acts? What sets apart a theology of Luke-Acts from, say, a literary analysis, a motif-oriented study, or a historiographical examination? And what is the relationship between theology and genre, in this instance, theology and narrative?

My basic claim is that a "theology of Luke-Acts" should render the kerygmatic intention of Luke in such a way to explicate the epistemological, existential, and theological claims that Luke's narrative makes on the reader. It is odd that so little work has been devoted to exploring how Luke's narrative challenges his readers to encounter God and make decisions for or against God.[1] To read Luke-Acts rightly is to listen to the claims it makes about God's activity not only on the lives of the first-century readers (descriptive) but also

---

1. See the lament of Joel B. Green, in the afterword of *Reading Luke: Interpretation, Reflection, Formation*, ed. Craig G. Bartholomew, Joel B. Green, and Anthony C. Thiselton (Grand Rapids: Zondervan, 2005), 446. Despite many fine treatments of the theological content of Luke-Acts, there is a glaring omission of the self-involving nature of the narrative in most treatments. For example, see Jacob Jervell, *The Theology of the Acts of the Apostles* (Cambridge: Cambridge University Press, 1996); I. Howard Marshall and David Peterson, eds., *Witness to the Gospel: The Theology of Acts* (Grand Rapids: Eerdmans, 1998); Darrell L.

upon our lives and to render responses and decisions to these claims. To *understand* Luke-Acts and its theology is to understand oneself in light of, and to be shaped by, the God that is revealed in the narrative.

The subject of Luke-Acts is the living God as revealed in Jesus Christ *and*, as Acts would have us affirm, within his church. Therefore, to speak of theology, and more specifically a theology of Luke-Acts, presumes that God is known and experienced within the lives of his people through these writings. A theology of an NT composition, then, should include both rigorous attention to the text and attention to the way the biblical text elicits human faith, knowledge of God, humanity's right relation to God, and the experience of his power in the lives of its readers. To justify my proposal, I want to reflect on two necessary aspects of anything that would go by the name *A Theology of Luke-Acts*, namely, the nature of theology and the nature of narrative.

The Nature of Theology as Intrinsically Self-Involving

Because the subject matter of Luke-Acts is God as he has revealed himself to humanity in Jesus and through the Spirit-gifted church, a theology of Luke-Acts is inescapably self-involving. The interpreter of Luke-Acts is constantly engaged in theology given that the subject matter she or he is engaging is a form of proclamation or address to humanity about God that is constantly pressing the reader to make personal responses and decisions in light of the God narrated in the text.

One voice that can aid us in charting a way forward here is that of Adolf Schlatter, particularly from his programmatic essay, "The Theology of the New Testament and Dogmatics."[2] On the one hand, Schlatter affirms the importance of the descriptive and historical task of New Testament theology whereby our work "is not concerned with the interests which emerge from the course

---

Bock, *A Theology of Luke and Acts: God's Promised Program, Realized for All Nations*, Biblical Theology of the New Testament Series (Grand Rapids: Zondervan, 2012).

2. Adolf Schlatter, "The Theology of the New Testament and Dogmatics," in *The Nature of New Testament Theology: The Contribution of William Wrede and Adolf Schlatter*, ed. and trans. Robert Morgan (London: SCM, 1973). In this section of the chapter, page numbers in parentheses in the main text refer to this essay. The promise of Schlatter for current NT studies has been highlighted by Peter Stuhlmacher, "Adolf Schlatter's Interpretation of Scripture," *NTS* 24 (1978): 433–46. See also Robert W. Yarbrough, "Modern Reception of Schlatter's New Testament Theology," in Adolf Schlatter, *The Theology of the Apostles: The Development of New Testament Theology*, trans. Andreas Köstenberger (Grand Rapids: Baker, 1998), 2:417–31.

The Beginnings of a Theology of Luke-Acts

of our own life, but directs its attention quite deliberately away from ourselves and our own contemporary interests, back to the past. . . . We keep [our convictions] out of the investigation so that we can see the subject matter as it was" (118). Required of the NT interpreter is the historical and literary work that "rests entirely on observation and demands wide open eyes and the sort of whole-hearted surrender which perceives that with which it is presented" (121). Schlatter is no "postmodern" or "reader-response" reader of the NT who advocates for the reader's playful construction of textual meaning. No, for Schlatter, the theologian who "no longer observes" but engages in "free construction, is at best a poet and at worst a dreamer" (121). The fundamental beginning point for the reader of the NT, Schlatter was fond of saying, begins and ends with "observation," namely, "seeing what is there" (136).[3] The method of science as well as historical research, Schlatter argued, is "first seeing and secondly seeing and thirdly seeing and again and again seeing."[4] Thus, NT theology is, in part, inescapably descriptive in character.

On the other hand, Schlatter also affirms that the theological nature of the NT texts does not allow a neutral or detached engagement precisely because the NT "by its very nature . . . demand[s] a response of its readers and thus also of the scholar."[5] The reader of the NT cannot avoid or try to escape the fact that she or he is constantly addressed by the subject matter of the text, namely, God as he has revealed himself in Jesus Christ. The Scriptures are, then, constantly pressing on humans to faith and decision for or against God. Any interpretation of the NT that does not convey its form of proclamation and address to humanity is thereby untrue to its subject matter. Thus, "the word with which the New Testament confronts us intends to be believed, and so rules out once and for all any sort of neutral treatment" (122).[6] Given that "the attitude to which the New Testament calls us and leads us is faith,"

---

3. On Schlatter's warning regarding using contemporary philosophy to dictate the meaning of the NT, see Roy A. Harrisville and Walter Sundberg, *The Bible in Modern Culture: Baruch Spinoza to Brevard Childs*, 2nd ed. (Grand Rapids: Eerdmans, 2002), 183, 186–89; Robert W. Yarbrough, *The Salvation Historical Fallacy? Reassessing the History of New Testament Theology* (Dorset, UK: Deo, 2004), 96–100.

4. Werner Neuer and Adolf Schlatter, "Adolf Schlatter on Atheistic Methods in Theology," trans. David R. Bauer, in Werner Neuer, *Adolf Schlatter: A Biography of Germany's Premier Biblical Theologian*, trans. Robert W. Yarbrough (Grand Rapids: Baker, 1996), 211–25, here 218.

5. Hendrikus Boers, *What Is New Testament Theology? The Rise of Criticism and the Problem of a Theology of the New Testament* (Philadelphia: Fortress, 1979), 69.

6. Boers (*New Testament Theology*, 70) describes "the relationship between historical investigation of the New Testament and dogmatics, thus, according to Schlatter, [as] not one of dependence but of dialectical interaction."

it is necessary that the NT and our own will "enter into discussion and come to terms" (131). The NT witnesses to a God whose relationship to humanity "moves us totally, and so it gives us certainty of God, that we should believe him, serve him, live through him and for him" (162).

Given that the NT and particularly Luke-Acts witnesses to a God once engaged and *still engaged* within history to accomplish his purposes, to a reign of the resurrected and exalted Messiah that spans the apostolic age and into our age, and to the Holy Spirit who *once and still* mediates divine knowledge and power to the believer, the interpreter of the NT is invited to understand his or her own life, will, and history in continuity with the history and theology of the NT writings.[7] For the NT constantly claims to describe the reader's own human situation and need for God. For this reason, the NT interpreter is constantly pressed to engage in asking: What does this text, statement, or claim mean for me, for humanity? For Schlatter, a person can only "become clear about the course of his own life by seeing the past as it exercises its power upon us" (119).[8] Thus, the interpreter of the NT has no neutral ground on which to stand, for the NT claims that the history to which it witnesses has determined the very life of the interpreter by the God revealed in the NT. It claims to witness to "God's creating and giving [to] penetrate man's existence and consciousness" (152).

Schlatter rejects, then, the legacy of J. P. Gabler, which would make a clear demarcation between the interpretation of Scripture and the theological task.[9] Given that the historian is repeatedly confronted with theological address that demands belief or rejection, "the historian's neutrality becomes a fiction when it leads to insistence on a complete separation between these two distinct functions [history and theology]" (126). There is no two-stage process whereby the NT interpreter hands over the purely descriptive "what it meant" raw materials to the theologian who then constructs and arranges them into a systematic theology to determine "what it means." This sort of view ignores the religious power of the texts and the fact that the interpreter is constantly addressed

---

7. See also C. Kavin Rowe, *World Upside Down: Reading Acts in the Graeco-Roman Age* (Oxford: Oxford University Press, 2009), 174.

8. For a similar proposal to Schlatter's, see Nicholas Lash, *Theology on the Way to Emmaus* (London: SCM, 1986), 75-92.

9. Gabler's programmatic essay can be found in John Sandys-Wunsch and Laurence Eldredge, "J. P. Gabler and the Distinction between Biblical and Dogmatic Theology: Translation, Commentary, and Discussion of His Originality," *SJT* 33 (1980): 133-58. On Gabler's program, with which he is supportive, see Heikki Räisänen, *Beyond New Testament Theology: A Story and a Programme*, 2nd ed. (London: SCM, 2000), 11-13.

The Beginnings of a Theology of Luke-Acts

by God through these writings.[10] In order to understand the existential and theological claims of the NT—claims having to do with life, suffering, death, human freedom, and love—it is necessary that the interpreter already has some knowledge of the "fundamental features of the human predicament to which those texts were constructed as an element of response."[11] Further, given that all theology is historical, Schlatter engages in no Gablerian enterprise of distinguishing eternal truths from the contingent (e.g., 135). One cannot describe the theology of the NT writings in terms of a "series of abstract statements and models," for this fails to capture the unity between "thinking and willing" (133). Pure intellectualism, seen in an encyclopedic form of knowledge that produces doctrinal concepts or catalogs vast amounts of descriptive information about the NT, is fundamentally opposed, then, by the very theological and self-involving nature of the NT writings.[12]

I suggest, then, that a theology of Luke-Acts that is true to the subject matter of the text is not only descriptive or historical, but is inherently self-involving as it summons the reader to believe, confess, obey, and understand the entirety of one's existence—both her or his thinking and willing—in light of the God revealed in the text.[13] Though the NT theologian must engage in the descriptive task of observing what is there, the NT writings do not, as Schlatter states, "let hovering on the fence go on indefinitely" (129). The subject matter of Luke-Acts is the living God who once and still presses on readers of the narrative to respond to him by understanding every aspect of human life as influenced and determined by God.[14] The successful articulation of the theology of Luke-Acts will be, then, the one that "ask[s] what claim or truth about man, his world, and transcendence we hear from these texts."[15]

---

10. For a persuasive critique of Gabler, see Joel B. Green, "Scripture and Theology: Failed Experiments, Fresh Perspectives," *Int* 56 (2002): 5–20; Lash, *Theology*, 75–92.

11. Green, "Scripture and Theology," 80.

12. See Boers, *New Testament Theology*, 74; Yarbrough, *Salvation Historical Fallacy*, 83–87. For a critique of the encyclopedic epistemology, see Alasdair MacIntyre, *Three Rival Versions of Moral Enquiry: Encyclopaedia, Genealogy, and Tradition* (Notre Dame: University of Notre Dame Press, 1990).

13. An overly intellectual definition of theology is advanced by Scott Shauf, *Theology as History, History as Theology: Paul in Ephesus in Acts 19*, BZNW 133 (Berlin: de Gruyter, 2005), 42.

14. More broadly, see Luke Timothy Johnson, "Fragments of an Untidy Conversation: Theology and the Literary Diversity of the New Testament," in *Biblical Theology: Problems and Perspectives, In Honor of J. Christiaan Beker*, ed. Steven J. Kraftchick et al. (Nashville: Abingdon, 1995), 276–89, here 282.

15. Peter Stuhlmacher, *Historical Criticism and Theological Interpretation of Scripture: Towards a Hermeneutics of Consent*, trans. Roy A. Harrisville (Philadelphia: Fortress, 1977), 85.

PART THREE: GOD'S ACTS FOR CHRISTIANS

The Nature of Narrative as Intrinsically Self-Involving

Various proposals for determining the theology of Luke-Acts have been advanced. Isolating Lukan redactional elements, the interpretation of the so-called kerygma, setting forth the most important theological themes and convictions that drive the narrative (often found in Luke's speeches), and uncovering Luke's theological presuppositions—these are a few of the most prominent.[16] All of these proposals, however, operate according to the logic that Luke's theology must be extracted from the narrative which functions as a repository for Luke's theology.[17] Because form and genre are irreducibly constituent for content and meaning, the most appropriate interpretation of Luke's theology will be the one that most honors it as narrative. It is questionable that the proposals above, then, do justice to the nature of Luke's writing as narrative, and particularly a theological διήγησις, that is, a "narrative about the events that have been fulfilled among us" (διήγησιν περὶ τῶν πεπληροφορημένων ἐν ἡμῖν πραγμάτων, Luke 1:1). Interpreters agree that the passive participle is a divine passive and, indeed, one finds that the verb διηγέομαι is used five times for the narration of divine activity (Luke 1:1; 8:39; 9:10; Acts 9:27; 12:17). Thus, Luke preaches and interprets the actions of God to the reader through his narrative history.[18] Luke's preface is a hermeneutical key that indicates that the narrative is theological in that it depicts and interprets the actions of God so that the reader may have knowledge or *perception* (ἵνα ἐπιγνῷς, Luke 1:4a) of God's activity.[19] Thus, the audience is invited to participate in Luke's narrative and so discern divine activity and respond accordingly.[20]

It is Luke's narrative that renders the identity and actions of God, and hence *prima facie* is most likely to aid the interpreter in determining the theology of Luke-Acts. If Luke's theology is mediated through narrative, then it is imperative that the interpreter understands *how* narrative produces meaning. The elements of biblical narrative that make up its internal logic, organization, and structure

---

16. On the failure of these attempts to get at the theology of Acts, see Beverly Roberts Gaventa, "Toward a Theology of Acts: Reading and Rereading," *Int* 42 (1988): 146–57.

17. See Gaventa, "Toward a Theology of Acts," 150.

18. See Richard J. Dillon, "Previewing Luke's Project from His Prologue (Luke 1:1–4)," *CBQ* 43 (1981): 205–27, here 208–9; Joel B. Green, *The Theology of the Gospel of Luke* (Cambridge: Cambridge University Press, 1995), 19.

19. See Joel B. Green, *The Gospel of Luke*, NICNT (Grand Rapids: Eerdmans, 1997), 38–39.

20. See David P. Moessner, "Reading Luke's Gospel as Ancient Hellenistic Narrative: Luke's Narrative Plan of Israel's Suffering Messiah as God's Saving 'Plan' for the World," in *Reading Luke: Interpretation, Reflection, Formation*, ed. Craig G. Bartholomew, Joel B. Green, and Anthony C. Thiselton (Grand Rapids: Zondervan, 2005), 125–54, here 124–32.

The Beginnings of a Theology of Luke-Acts

are here assumed, that is, what might be referred to as the "sense" of the text. But the theologian, the one concerned with the text's reference, with what it is really *about*, must move from explanation to understanding, and therefore to the hermeneutical question: *How* does narrative produce meaning, and more specifically, how does the narrative of Luke-Acts produce theological meaning?

First, narratives construct and project possible worlds. Through its construction of a plot, narrative imitates reality and thereby creates new worlds, a certain ordered way of seeing reality, including human life and experience.[21] Emplotment vitiates, then, against timeless doctrinal concepts or propositions and rather creates a new world, a new way of interpreting the world through its representation of time, characters, and action.[22] Thus, narrative is a form of reconfiguring the apprehensible world into a new world that gives structure to human experience.[23] Furthermore, narrative is intrinsically moralizing in that it produces an ordered world, in conformity to the author's viewpoint, and thereby confers meaning on reality.[24] The same is true for all narrative representations of history, for before the creation of the work the author has selected the narrative strategies, mode of emplotment, closure of story, and meaning of the events that will make up the narrative.[25] Thus, narratives not *only* describe what happened, but given that emplotment is a matter of a narrator's judgment and represents a point of view, narratives also explain why it happened.[26] Every narrative, then, has a "moralizing impulse" in that it claims something like, "This is what the world is like," or "Imagine if the world looked like this."[27]

---

21. Paul Ricoeur, "Philosophical Hermeneutics and Theological Hermeneutics," *SR* 5 (1975): 14–33, here 26; Paul Ricoeur, *Time and Narrative*, vol. 1, trans. Kathleen McLaughlin and David Pellauer (Chicago: University of Chicago Press, 1984), 33. On Ricoeur and narrative, see Kevin J. Vanhoozer, *Biblical Narrative in the Philosophy of Paul Ricoeur: A Study in Hermeneutics and Theology* (Cambridge: Cambridge University Press, 1990).

22. Ricoeur, *Time and Narrative*, 33–37. The concept of *mythos*, which is often translated or rendered as emplotment by Ricoeur, is used to refer to the narrative's organization of events, which is the result of the author's making a representation in terms of time and action.

23. Ricoeur, *Time and Narrative*, 54, refers to this as Mimesis 1: "The composition of the plot is grounded in a pre-understanding of the world of action, its meaningful structures, its symbolic resources, and its temporal character."

24. Hayden White, "Narrativity in the Representation of Reality," in *The Content of the Form: Narrative Discourse and Historical Representation* (Baltimore: Johns Hopkins University Press, 1987), 1–25, esp. 12–15, 20–25.

25. Elizabeth A. Clark, *History, Theory, Text: Historians and the Linguistic Turn* (Cambridge: Harvard University Press, 2004), 99; White, "Narrativity," 24; Ricoeur, *Time and Narrative*, 91–94.

26. See Ricoeur, *Time and Narrative*, 154; see also 178–79; Clark, *History, Theory, Text*, 90–91.

27. Roger Lundin, Clarence Walhout, and Anthony C. Thiselton, *The Promise of Hermeneutics* (Grand Rapids: Eerdmans, 1999), 82.

Second, a true understanding of a narrative only occurs when the reader understands her world in light of the narrative. Narratives have a mediating role in that they reconfigure the "real world" for the purpose of transforming "the world of the reader."[28] Narratives are, then, inherently participatory in that they redescribe the world and invite the reader to inhabit this new world, to accept its premises as true, and to be addressed and transformed.[29] Narrative makes meaning when the reader enters into a dialogue with the text and responds to its discourse by reflecting on the "fit" between her world and the world projected by the text.[30] "Meaning, in a work of narrative art, is a function of the relation between two worlds: the fictional world created by the author and the 'real' word, the apprehensible universe. When we say we 'understand' a narrative, we mean that we have found a satisfactory relationship or set of relationships between these two worlds."[31] For example, I can claim to understand Dostoevsky's *The Brothers Karamazov* when I reflect on what it would mean for me to live in a world where there is no God and, therefore, where murder and all else is permitted and goes unpunished. I thereby participate in the narrative by understanding myself, my situation, and the world in the light of the author's projected world. This is stated well by Ricoeur: "To understand, therefore, is to understand oneself before the text.... This implies that the reader does not submit the meaning of the text to his own finite capacity of understanding, but that he lets himself be exposed to the text in order to receive from it ... the 'thing' of the text."[32] Meaning is produced, then, when the reader's understanding of himself and his world is transformed through dialogue with and participation in the world of the narrative. The reader's participation in the reconfigured world of the narrative is, in this regard, revelatory and transformative. For example, by choosing to identify with a character or reject the character's way of being in the world, humans are led to more fully understand their own identity and situation.[33] Narratives are, then, inherently formational and press the reader to make decisions, to accept or reject its premises regarding how the world works, to identify with characters, and so on. Narratives invite readers to "a fundamental acceptance of its premises,

---

28. Ricoeur, *Time and Narrative*, 53–54.
29. Ricoeur, *Time and Narrative*, 81.
30. Ricoeur, "Philosophical Hermeneutics," 29.
31. Robert Scholes and Robert Kellogg, *The Nature of Narrative* (New York: Oxford University Press, 1966), 82.
32. Ricoeur, "Philosophical Hermeneutics," 30.
33. Vanhoozer, *Biblical Narrative*, 103–4.

an adjustment of vision according to its perceptions, and a decision to act as though these premises and perceptions were not only real but valid."[34]

Luke-Acts is, however, different from a novel and different from narrative representations of history, for its narrative creates a world that is universalizing in that its vision claims to constitute the world of the reader.[35] Given that the subject matter of Luke-Acts is the one God who has intervened within history through Jesus to fulfill the promises he made to Israel, and for the salvation of the world, the narrative makes a totalizing claim on every reader. The narrative of Luke-Acts and the world of the reader, then, "do not exist in isolation, but constitute one world and one story."[36] Thus, the reader is internal to, is included within the world projected by Luke-Acts. The world that is created by the narrative, in this instance, claims to define all of reality, the situation of all of humanity, and all of our human experiences.[37] Again, the reason that the world of Luke-Acts is universalizing is due to the fact that it is the one God's identity and activity that define the narrative. Given that God and God's activity define the narrative, to read Luke-Acts is "to be addressed by a claim on one's life from this God."[38] The world of Luke-Acts, taken on its own terms, *is* the real world, and the appropriate response of the reader is "to see his disposition, his actions and passions, the shape of his own life as well as that of his era's events as figures of that ... world."[39] Through the reader's inclusion within the narrative and the reality depicted, she is called to participate within the narrative and make decisions in response to it.[40] Like a musical score or a Shakespearean script, the very nature of the Scriptures and the readers it projects (i.e., its implied audience) calls for a self-involving performance by its readers.[41] Understanding occurs when readers actually

---

34. Luke Timothy Johnson, "Imagining the World Scripture Imagines," *Modern Theology* 14 (1998): 165–80, here 166.

35. The difference between biblical narrative and Homer's *Odyssey* and the claims the former makes on the reader is stated in a justly famous passage in Erich Auerbach, *Mimesis* (Princeton: Princeton University Press, 1968), 15–16.

36. Michael Root, "The Narrative Structure of Soteriology," in *Why Narrative? Readings in Narrative Theology*, ed. Stanley Hauerwas and L. Gregory Jones (Eugene, OR: Wipf & Stock, 1997), 263–78, here 266.

37. See William C. Placher, *The Domestication of Transcendence: How Modern Thinking about God Went Wrong* (Louisville: Westminster John Knox, 1996), 189.

38. Placher, *Domestication of Transcendence*, 189.

39. Hans W. Frei, *The Eclipse of Biblical Narrative: A Study in Eighteenth and Nineteenth Century Hermeneutics* (New Haven: Yale University Press, 1974), 3.

40. Frei, *Eclipse of Biblical Narrative*, 24.

41. So Lash, *Theology*, 38–46.

use the script and perform it. A theology of Luke-Acts, then, that is true to its form as narrative should explicate how the identity and activity of God and the reader are brought together into a single story that highlights humanity's knowledge of God, alienation from and restored relation to God, and human speech about God.[42]

My argument so far is that the character of theology and the nature of narrative as self-involving and inherently participatory converge such that the reader of Luke-Acts is drawn into a relationship with God.[43] The reader finds that she too is implicated within the same human problem and vices that plague the characters of the narrative, and conversely is invited to identify with Jesus and those characters who identify with God's plan. Thus, a successful theology of Luke-Acts will be one that—since its subject matter is God as known through the mediation of a theological narrative that gives definition to the experiences of the world, humanity, and all of history—seeks to articulate how the narrative shapes our lives and world. It will not only pass on information about what happened or what Luke thinks about a topic; rather, it will draw the readers of Luke-Acts into participating and interacting with the world projected by Luke, the world that *is* and *defines* the real world.[44]

God Acting, Humans Responding in Luke-Acts

Whatever else it may be, Luke-Acts is all about God. As the prologue makes clear with its claim to recount "the things that have been fulfilled among us" (Luke 1:1), Luke-Acts is from beginning to end a narrative construal of God and God's activity.[45] Characters respond to and reject divine activity, Luke draws on Israel's Scriptures to give witness to God's acts, the Spirit enables characters to prophesy regarding God's plan, characters respond with praise when God's activity is discerned, and Luke uses the language of "the will/purpose of God" and divine necessity to express God's plan.

---

42. Similarly, see Root, "Narrative Structure," 275. Cf. Nicholas Wolterstorff, "Living within a Text," in *Faith and Narrative*, ed. Keith E. Yandell (Oxford: Oxford University Press, 2001), 202–13.

43. See Trevor Hart, *Faith Thinking: The Dynamics of Christian Theology* (Downers Grove, IL: InterVarsity Press, 1995), 161–62.

44. Green, *Theology of the Gospel of Luke*, 23–24.

45. See Michael A. Salmeier, *Restoring the Kingdom: The Role of God as the "Ordainer of Times and Seasons" in the Acts of the Apostles*, Princeton Theological Monograph Series 165 (Eugene, OR: Pickwick, 2011), 1–2.

The Beginnings of a Theology of Luke-Acts

Surprising, then, is that God's acts and plans are rarely obvious to characters within the narrative. God and his purposes are frequently misunderstood; human "ignorance" of God and his purposes are at the heart of the story's conflicts; when God's activity *is* recognized it is frequently a lengthy and painful process for the characters; and God's purposes remain hidden to most and are often rejected. And yet God's plans are accomplished *through* human participation in his purposes and response to his acts. Especially in Acts, one finds that God's purposes come to fruition only when the church rightly interprets and aligns itself with what God has done. Thus, Luke narrates God's acts *not only* for the purpose of describing past events but also with the aim of forming an audience that sees, rightly interprets, and responds to God's ongoing activity in the world through the work of the Spirit of the exalted Christ. Luke-Acts seeks to form a people who continue performing Luke-Acts through their ongoing discernment of and response to what God continues to do through Christ's presence in the world. Readers are invited to identify with a perspective internal to the narrative and thereby become people who can see and rightly interpret what God is doing.

Given the abundance of divine activity that oozes forth from every page of Luke-Acts, it is surprising that God never directly enters into the narrative. Only through a voice from heaven does God make an appearance (Luke 3:22; 9:35). In other words, Luke preserves God's transcendence as God's presence and activity are never immediately obvious but must be interpreted and discerned through human characters who respond to what they see and hear. In his narration of divine activity, Luke seeks to form his audience to be the kind of people who align themselves with God's plan in Jesus, to see God's kingdom operant in Jesus's ministry, and to interpret God's continuing work in their lives. Those characters who recognize divine activity at work in Jesus (in the Gospel) are then able to discern, interpret, and *give witness* to God's continuing activity through the exalted Christ despite his physical absence (in Acts).

DIVINE ACTIVITY AND HUMAN RESPONSE IN THE GOSPEL OF LUKE

Luke presents a number of characters who *see and hear* divine activity at work in Jesus and immediately *respond by praising and giving glory to God*.[46]

---

46. On the role of praise as a Lukan tactic to portray the unfolding of God's visitation, see Kindalee Pfremmer De Long, *Surprised by God: Praise Responses in the Narrative of Luke-Acts*, BZNW 166 (Berlin: de Gruyter, 2009).

PART THREE: GOD'S ACTS FOR CHRISTIANS

Throughout the Gospel, there is an interweaving of the theme of sight and hearing, that is, the ability to discern divine activity in the person of Jesus and the appropriate verbal response of praise to God. Luke's model characters sensibly perceive God at work in Jesus and respond with praise and rejoicing in God.[47] The numerous Lukan additions of character responses of praise and rejoicing where Mark has no such reaction (e.g., cf. Luke 5:25 with Mark 2:12; Luke 18:43 with Mark 10:52) suggests that Luke intends to emphasize a verbal response to divine activity. The infancy narrative, in fact, programmatically sets up the response of joyous praise and confession of God's activity as the correct way to respond to the divine activity that is seen and heard.[48] In response to Elizabeth's blessing on Mary for believing "the things spoken to her by the Lord" (1:45), Mary sings a hymn exalting God for his acts (1:46-55). Despite his initial disbelief, when Zechariah's speech is restored he immediately "speaks to bless God" (ἐλάλει εὐλογῶν τὸν θεόν, 1:64b) and praises God for visiting his people (1:68-79). So also the shepherds respond to the news of Jesus's birth by "giving glory and praise to God [δοξάζοντες καὶ αἰνοῦντες τὸν θεόν] for all the things they had heard and seen [ἐπὶ πᾶσιν οἷς ἤκουσαν καὶ εἶδον]" (2:20). When Simon *sees* the child Jesus, he "blesses God" (εὐλόγησεν τὸν θεόν, 2:28) and says, "My eyes have seen your salvation" (εἶδον οἱ ὀφθαλμοί μου τὸ σωτήριόν σου, 2:30). Thus, when the characters encounter God through angels, the Spirit, and the infant Jesus, they are described as able to hear and/or see, and in each instance, they respond by praising God.

The crowds are absolutely right, then, when they encounter Jesus's healings and give glory and ascribe the activity to God. When the healed paralytic picks up his mat and "gives glory to God" (δοξάζων τὸν θεόν, 5:25), the crowd rightly responds by "giving glory to God" (ἐδόξαζον τὸν θεόν) and confessing, "We have *seen* incredible things today" (εἴδομεν παράδοξα σήμερον, 5:26). Given that Jesus's healing enacts God's kingdom (e.g., 7:18-23; 10:1-16), the crowd's response is exactly right in that it sees Jesus's healings as the work of God. Readers are meant to identify with the crowd who encounter the resurrection of the dead child and "give glory to God [ἐδόξαζον τὸν θεόν], saying 'a great prophet has been raised up for us and God has visited his people'" (ἐπεσκέψατο ὁ θεὸς τὸν λαὸν αὐτοῦ, 7:16b). When the bent woman is healed, her first response is to give glory to God (ἐδόξαζεν τὸν θεόν, 13:13), and this

---

47. See Brian E. Beck, *Christian Character in the Gospel of Luke* (London: Epworth, 1989), 61-65.
48. This is nicely stated by John R. Donahue, "A Neglected Factor in the Theology of Mark," *JBL* 101 (1982): 563-94, here 568.

The Beginnings of a Theology of Luke-Acts

again results in the "entire crowd rejoicing over all the glorious things he was doing" (13:17b). When the ten Samaritan lepers are healed, only one returns to Jesus "to give glory to God" (δοῦναι δόξαν τῷ θεῷ, 17:18). Jesus's healing of the blind man near Jericho nicely encapsulates this motif. The man's single desire is "to see" (ἵνα ἀναβλέψω, 18:41). Jesus's granting of sight (ἀνάβλεψον, 18:42; ἀνέβλεψεν, 18:43) to the blind man results in the man's "giving glory to God" (δοξάζων τὸν θεόν, 18:43a), and the crowd in turns "gives praise to God" (ἔδωκεν αἶνον τῷ θεῷ, 18:43b).

Jesus himself establishes the necessity of giving praise to God for his work and revelation as he bursts forth in praise to God for the disclosure of his identity to the disciples.[49] In response to the seventy's rejoicing in God's work, so also Jesus "rejoiced within himself with the Holy Spirit" (10:21a). A more explicit statement concerning the disclosure of Jesus's identity cannot be found than within this prayer where Jesus addresses as "Father" the one who is "the Lord of heaven and earth" (10:21b). Further, Jesus declares himself to be the singular embodiment of God's visit. Not everyone is able to see Jesus as the agent of divine activity, however, as this is hidden from the eyes of "the wise and understanding" but is "disclosed to the infants," that is, "to those whom the son desires to reveal it" (10:21, 22). Jesus therefore pronounces a blessing on his disciples: "Blessed are the eyes that see what you see" (οἱ ὀφθαλμοὶ οἱ βλέποντες ἃ βλέπετε, 10:23b).

Therefore, the crowd of disciples is right to respond to the journeying Jesus by "praising God and rejoicing with a great voice for all the mighty displays of power they had seen [εἶδον]" (19:37b). Again, seeing the divine power at work in Jesus leads to the verbal response of rejoicing and praising God. The disciples' cry fulfills Jesus's promise that "you will not *see* me until *you say*, 'Blessed is the one who comes in the name of the Lord'" (13:35), and marks them as those who see Jesus's entrance into Jerusalem as the Lord's coming. Notable, however, is the absence of priests, scribes, and temple leaders (19:47). Indeed, some Pharisees try to silence the disciples' praise (19:39) and thereby function as exemplars of those who are blind to the things that make for peace (19:42) and fail to recognize the time of their visitation (19:44b).

The ability to see God at work in the person of Jesus is brought to the fore in Jesus's crucifixion. Throughout the narration of his death, Luke notes those who "see" the fulfillment of Jesus's messianic task in the cross but fail to perceive the event as constitutive of divine activity. When Pilate sends Jesus to Herod,

---

49. See David Michael Crump, *Jesus the Intercessor: Prayer and Christology in Luke-Acts*, WUNT 2/49 (Tübingen: Mohr Siebeck, 1992), 49–75, here 56.

PART THREE: GOD'S ACTS FOR CHRISTIANS

for example, Luke notes Herod's desire to use Jesus for sport: "When Herod saw Jesus [ἰδὼν τὸν Ἰησοῦν] he rejoiced greatly, because for a long time he had wanted *to see* him [θέλων ἰδεῖν αὐτόν] for he had heard about him and he hoped he might see [ἰδεῖν] a sign performed by him" (23:7-8; cf. 10:23-24). The identity of Jesus is concealed from Herod who construes Jesus's task in terms of entertainment and not the cross.[50] Herod is not alone, however, for Jesus's teaching to the disciples that the Messiah must be handed over to the authorities, suffer, and be crucified has remained "hidden from them so they could not perceive it" (9:45). The emphasis on sight continues in the crucifixion account. Luke notes that all "the people were watching" (ὁ λαὸς θεωρῶν, 23:35), "the entire crowd had assembled together at the spectacle to watch the things happening" (ἐπὶ τὴν θεωρίαν ταύτην, θεωρήσαντες τὰ γενόμενα, 23:48), and all Jesus's companions "watched these things" (ὁρῶσαι ταῦτα, 23:49).

There is no hint, despite their "seeing" the crucified one, that Herod, the crowds, the people, or even Jesus's companions comprehend the meaning of the crucifixion. Ironically, it is the Roman centurion who, on "seeing . . . the event" (ἰδὼν . . . τὸ γενόμενον), namely, Jesus's last breath, gives glory to God (ἐδόξαζεν τὸν θεόν) and declares Jesus righteous (23:47).

In contrast to the centurion, Luke emphasizes the disciples' incomprehension. When Peter runs to the tomb and departs marveling after "he sees" the linen clothes in the tomb (24:12), the reader is also left wondering if the disciples will be given sight into God's activity. The theme comes to a head when the disguised, resurrected Jesus journeys with two disciples, but "their eyes were kept from recognizing him" (24:16). When Luke presents the disciples on the road "seeing" Jesus but "not recognizing him" (24:16), he draws attention to their inability to understand divine activity through Jesus's death. Through shared hospitality, however, "their eyes were opened and they recognized him" (24:31). Their ability now to *see* the identity of the stranger leads to the disciples' confession of God's raising (24:34) Jesus from the dead and their *narration* (αὐτοὶ ἐξηγοῦντο, 24:35) of Jesus's disclosure of his identity to them. The Gospel concludes with Jesus's exaltation to heaven and the disciples' response of worshiping Jesus "with great joy" and "blessing God" (24:52-53).

I suggest that Luke's narrative pattern whereby characters move from sight and recognition of divine activity to giving praise and glory to God is meant to form his audience to be people who recognize God's activity at work in the crucified, resurrected Jesus and to respond by giving praise to God and testimony to what God is doing. The reader is led to identify with those characters who

50. Green, *Gospel of Luke*, 804.

are able to see God at work in Jesus; they are invited to align their speech with the speech of those characters and adopt a liturgical response of rejoicing in, giving glory to, and praising God for what God has done. The reader who has formed these habits is then taught in the book of Acts to continue the practices of discerning, interpreting, and rightly aligning with God's continued activity through the exalted Christ.

Divine Activity and Human Response in the Acts of the Apostles

The characters who have learned to see God at work in the person of Jesus, who have accepted Jesus's manner of being in the world, and who have learned to praise God in response for his acts are then led in Acts to discern, interpret, and testify to God's *continuing* work. Acts is, in fact, all about how God's plan is "willed, initiated, impelled, and guided by God through the Holy Spirit."[51] Despite this, however, the narrator rarely *directly* refers to God doing something, and God never appears directly and obviously.[52] Rather, identifying, naming, and interpreting God's work in the world is usually left to the characters who are responsible to discern God's activity through various media. The narrator speaks of many events such as healings and exorcisms, prison escapes, ecstatic speech, and visions. But Luke's tendency is to have the characters discern that God is the one acting through these events and to have them interpret their theological significance. Divine activity is, then, never obvious, often ambiguous, and, hence, mandates human interpretation.[53] Luke's account of divine action intersects the fabric of human lives so as to respect the importance of human decisions and preserve God's transcendence. Thus, within Acts one finds an interplay between event and interpretation, that is, between God's interventions in history *and* the characters' directly naming God. I suggest that Acts not only recounts God's acts within history but that it does so in order to teach its readers to discern, interpret, and testify to God's continuing work.[54] The reader who has aligned herself with Jesus in the Gospel of Luke

---

51. Luke Timothy Johnson, *The Acts of the Apostles*, SP 5 (Collegeville, MN: Liturgical Press, 1992), 15.
52. Daniel Marguerat, *The First Christian Historian: Writing the "Acts of the Apostles,"* trans. Ken McKinney, Gregory J. Laughery, and Richard Bauckham, SNTSMS 121 (Cambridge: Cambridge University Press, 2002), 86–92.
53. So Shauf, *Theology as History*, 299.
54. Marguerat, *First Christian Historian*, 91.

PART THREE: GOD'S ACTS FOR CHRISTIANS

and then identifies with the apostles' interpretation of God's acts learns how to respond to divine activity in her own world. Allow me to illustrate this with two examples.

(1) *Jesus's death and resurrection.* Within the Gospel of Luke, there are no explicit references to *God's* willing Jesus's death or to his act of raising him from the dead. Quite simply, θεός is never the explicit subject of any statement regarding Jesus's death and resurrection in the Gospel. The reader does ascertain, however implicitly, that the events of the passion belong to God's plan. But while this plan may be clear to the reader familiar with Luke's narrative, the indications that Jesus's death is the will of God remain implicit. So, for example, the relation between God's plan and Jesus's death is hinted at through the use of δεῖ (Luke 9:22; 13:33; 17:25; 22:37), through possible but ambiguous divine passives (5:35; 9:44; 18:32; 22:37), through the testimony of the Scriptures (18:31; 20:17; 22:37), and through the comment that Jesus was discussing "his exodus which was about to be fulfilled in Jerusalem" (9:31). Not once is God named as the initiator of the events of the passion in Luke 22–23, and there are no direct references to divine activity within these chapters.[55] The overwhelming sense of these chapters, in fact, is that the active agents in Jesus's death are Satan and Jesus's human enemies (22:2, 3, 31, 48, 53).[56] And, in fact, often it is "the will" or "the plan" of Jesus's opponents as initiating Jesus's sufferings that is emphasized (e.g., 23:25, 51). One may infer that God's refusal to answer Jesus's prayer, "Father, if you are willing, take this cup from me, but not my will but yours be done" (22:42), is an indication that Jesus's death is God's will, but it is not yet obviously so. Again, Jesus foretells the *necessity* of his resurrection, but its relation to divine activity is not explicit (9:22; cf. 24:26, 44). Jesus declares that "he will rise up on the third day" (18:33) as part of the "fulfillment of all the things written by the prophets about the Son of Man" (18:31b), but God is not mentioned directly. And even the angels' use of the passive in their response to the women, "He has been raised" (ἠγέρθη, 24:6), does not state that *God* has raised Jesus. Despite hints, there are, then, no direct unambiguous statements regarding God's role in Jesus's death and resurrection in the Gospel.

There is a distinct shift in the theological discourse in Acts, then, when the apostles directly refer to Jesus's death and resurrection as the result of God's activity.[57] Peter's statements that Jesus's death was the result of "God's deter-

---

55. Note John T. Squires, *The Plan of God in Luke-Acts,* SNTSMS 76 (Cambridge: Cambridge University Press, 1993), 56.
56. See Hans W. Frei, *The Identity of Jesus Christ* (Philadelphia: Fortress, 1975), 121.
57. On this aspect of Luke's theological discourse, see Robert L. Mowery, "Lord, God,

mined will and foreknowledge" (Acts 2:23), that "God has fulfilled all he foretold through the mouth of all the prophets regarding the suffering of his Christ" (3:18), and that Jesus's enemies in crucifying him accomplished all "your hand and will had determined" (4:28) declare explicitly what the Gospel had only indicated implicitly. The statements regarding God's agency in raising Jesus from the dead are even more explicit where the apostles make numerous statements where θεός is the subject, followed by a verb for resurrection, and Jesus as the object: "God raised him" (ὃν ὁ θεὸς ἀνέστησεν, 2:24), "God raised this Jesus" (τοῦτον τὸν Ἰησοῦν ἀνέστησεν ὁ θεός, 2:32), "God raised him from the dead" (ὃν ὁ θεὸς ἤγειρεν ἐκ νεκρῶν, 4:10), "God raised him on the third day" (τοῦτον ὁ θεὸς ἤγειρεν ἐν τῇ τρίτῃ ἡμέρᾳ, 10:40; cf. 3:15; 5:30; 13:30, 33, 34, 37; 17:31).

By withholding direct statements regarding God's activity in the events surrounding Jesus's death and resurrection, Luke moves the reader from the event to its interpretation, from apparent human activity in the passion narrative to its theological meaning. The apostles are portrayed, then, as moving from ignorance to discernment, interpretation, and testimony. How does Luke narrate the apostles' transition from the implicit to the explicit, or, in this case, from misunderstanding God's plan to being faithful witnesses and interpreters of it? First, the apostles have aligned themselves with Jesus's understanding of God's plan. Jesus's declarations regarding the necessity of his sufferings, death, and resurrection have been internalized by the witnesses and are now proclaimed directly. Second, the witnesses have undergone a transformation in their ability to read Israel's Scriptures as finding their fulfillment in the Messiah's death and resurrection (Acts 2:24–35; 4:10–11, 25–28; cf. Luke 24:24–27, 44–49). Third, the outpouring of the Spirit has empowered them to interpret and testify to God's acts (Luke 24:48–49; Acts 2:33–35). And fourth, their experience of the empty tomb and the living Christ has enabled them to see the events of the passion as divine activity (Luke 24:8–12, 28–35, 36–43; Acts 1:1–8).

(2) *Cornelius and the inclusion of the Gentiles.* Luke narrates the foundational event of the gentiles' inclusion within God's people through a lengthy and alternating process of divine event and human interpretation. While the reader knows God has willed the gentiles' inclusion with the people of God, Luke is at pains to show *how* the church comes to discern and recognize this as God's will.[58] Luke narrates this event by showing how a difficult and ambiguous event is rightly interpreted as divine activity by the characters in the narrative.

---

and Father: Theological Language in Luke-Acts," *SBLSP* (1995): 82–101, here 95–101; also, see Squires, *Plan of God*, 57–58.

58. For an interpretation of the Cornelius-Peter episode that is attuned to the relation-

PART THREE: GOD'S ACTS FOR CHRISTIANS

The story begins with two accounts of human experience of divine activity: Cornelius's vision of "God's angel" who commands him to call for Peter (10:3-6) and Peter's subsequent vision while he is praying (10:9). In Peter's vision, he is commanded to eat clean and unclean food. In response to Peter's refusal, the voice speaks a second time: "That which God has cleansed, you shall not [consider] common" (10:15b). *God* is the one who has rendered insignificant the social divisions between Jew and gentile, and his command requires that Peter's understanding of God undergo transformation. Luke again portrays the nonobvious nature of divine activity by emphasizing Peter's confusion over the vision.[59] Thus, as Cornelius's men arrive at Simon's home, "Peter was greatly perplexed over the vision that he had seen" (10:17; cf. 10:19). The repetition of Peter's perplexity over the meaning of the vision invites the audience to participate in construing its meaning. Though he does not yet understand its meaning, Peter obeys the voice: "Now get up, go down, and go with the men with no discrimination, for I have sent them" (10:20). Peter's guests declare that they have come as a result of a divine revelation to Cornelius (10:22), and that they have been "sent to bring you into his house and to listen to your words" (10:22b). Peter, still not yet understanding the meaning of the event, responds with initial obedience in that he invites the gentiles in to receive hospitality (10:23a).

The rest of the story narrates Peter's progressive growth in his ability to interpret God's activity within these events. So, finally within Cornelius's home, Peter declares that though it is not permissible for a Jew to associate with a gentile, "*God* has shown [ὁ θεὸς ἔδειξεν] me that I should not call any person defiled and unclean" (10:28b). Through the shared visions and the shared hospitality with one another, Peter goes further in his declaration of divine identity: "Truly I now perceive that God [ὁ θεός] shows no partiality" (10:34). Peter's statement can be understood as an insight into Israel's Scriptures (e.g., Lev 19:15-19; Deut 10:17-19) where God is described as impartial. But never had this axiom been used as the basis to provide for full inclusion of the non-Jew *qua* non-Jew within the people of God. Further, when the gentiles experience the same outpouring of the Spirit that inspires ecstatic declaration of God's deeds (10:44-46), Peter rightly baptizes them because they have experienced the Spirit of God "just as even we had" (10:47). Thus, through his

---

ship between divine activity and human response, see Luke Timothy Johnson, *Scripture and Discernment: Decision Making in the Church* (Nashville: Abingdon, 1983), 89-108.

59. See Beverly Roberts Gaventa, *From Darkness to Light: Aspects of Conversion in the New Testament*, OBT (Philadelphia: Fortress, 1986), 109.

The Beginnings of a Theology of Luke-Acts

encounter of gentiles gifted with the Spirit, Peter recognizes divine activity. In his report to the Jerusalem church, Peter has no doubt that God has acted in these events: "God had given to them [ἔδωκεν αὐτοῖς ὁ θεός] the same gift just as he gave us" (11:17). The story ends with the church responding by "giving glory to God [ἐδόξασαν τὸν θεόν], saying 'indeed, then, God [ὁ θεός] has granted to the gentiles repentance unto life'" (11:18).

Note that the narrator has not entered into the story to say "God did" and "God said" but, rather, has allowed Peter to discern, interpret, and name God's activity in the surprising events.[60] Further, Peter's affirmation of God's activity has been the result of a process of *experience and encounter* of divine work: visions from heaven, hospitality with strangers, and the work of the Spirit. Though the event is surprising to Peter, Luke presents the inclusion of the gentiles as aligning with the testimony of Israel's Scriptures (Acts 15:14–18), Jesus's own inclusion of outcasts within God's people (e.g., Luke 5:27–32; 7:36–50), Jesus's commission to preach "to all the nations" (Luke 24:47), and the initiative of the Holy Spirit (Acts 10:44–46; 11:15–17; 15:11).

Performing Luke-Acts

If the God rendered by Luke-Acts is the same God of the contemporary audience's world, then Luke's narration of divine activity should bear continuity with our experience of God's acts as we inhabit the world of Luke-Acts and continue the story in our lives and communities. And our theological engagement with the meaning of Luke-Acts will not be complete until *we* have understood ourselves in light of the world of the text. Albeit too briefly, I conclude with three theses to this end.

First, human life, its fundamental meaning and purpose, is established by God's past acts as narrated in Luke-Acts. In fact, the narrative portrays a God whose interventions in the world constitute the fundamental shape of human history, including the nature of ultimate reality, human identity and personhood, matters of race and ethnicity, the meaning of suffering, and life after death. The reader who accepts the text's claims about God and his acts is pressed and shaped to affirm that all of human history is authored by the God of Israel, the father of Jesus Christ, and that the meaning of all reality and human identity and personhood is determined through God's acts. If it is true, as Schlatter intimates, that clarity regarding the meaning of human life now

60. Marguerat, *First Christian Historian*, 102.

PART THREE: GOD'S ACTS FOR CHRISTIANS

depends on understanding how the past exercises power on humanity, then the reader of Luke-Acts cannot engage the text neutrally, for the text witnesses to God's decisive acts to shape human existence.

God's activity through Jesus's death and his raising him from the dead constitutes our identity, for example, just as it did the identities of the first witnesses, as those whose "repentance for the forgiveness of sins" is made possible (Acts 5:31; cf. 8:32–33), whose identity follows the same messianic pattern of "suffering and then vindication" (7:55–60; 14:22), as recipients of the fulfillment of God's promised salvific blessings (13:30–39), as members of "God's church which he purchased through his own blood" (20:28), and as those who will be judged by God's appointed man (17:31). God's resurrection of the Messiah from the dead (2:22–32; 3:13–15; 5:30; 13:3–37) and his vindication of Stephen (7:55–60) are not merely remarkable past events; rather, they call us to trust and hope in God for the same resolution of the problem of death (4:2; 26:6–8, 22–23). God's act of exalting Messiah Jesus at his right hand establishes us as recipients of the blessings of the messianic kingdom: the promised Spirit (2:17–36; 5:30–32), healings and salvation (3:11–26), forgiveness of sins (5:31), and justification (13:38–39). God's outpouring of the Holy Spirit on Jews (2:1–13), Samaritans (8:14–17), and gentiles (10:44–46) establishes our identity as those empowered for mission and enabled to testify to God's mighty acts. God's inclusion of outcasts (8:14–17, 26–40), enemies (9:1–19), and gentiles (10:1–11:18) within his people has determined our existence as people who are part of one global, multiethnic, people of God. Thus, a theological engagement of a text that witnesses to divine acts that claim to define our life, and even that of all of human history, cannot remain at the level of pure description but must, rather, demonstrate how God's acts have reconfigured our lives and world. For the text invites its readers to undergo a mental and dispositional transformation, whereby their own narrative world is reconfigured to align with the things that God has done.

Second, Luke-Acts witnesses to a God who *continues* to act within human history and who calls people to discern, interpret, and respond to divine activity. One of the calls of Luke-Acts is to invite its readers to continue discerning and witnessing to what God is doing in the church and the world. One of the implications, then, is that the readers of Luke-Acts must be attentive to their own human experience of God within their own world.[61] There is nothing within the narrative that would suggest that God's acts are singularly isolated to the past. The constant irruptions of divine activity from heaven, actions

---

61. See L. Johnson, "Imagining the World Scripture Imagines," 177.

The Beginnings of a Theology of Luke-Acts

that stem from God's rule over his people through the exalted Christ, lead the audience to anticipate continued divine activity in its own world. In other words, the God who *once* ruled and acted in the life of his people is the same God who *even now* continues to act—whether through dreams and visions, healings, prayer, proclamation of the word, or whatever the specific media. And the amount of time spent detailing the witnesses' discernment and interpretation of divine activity indicates that God's new deeds will continue to require human interpretation. Thus, theological understanding of Luke-Acts takes place when its readers see their own world as a continuation of the narrative world.

The patterned process whereby Luke narrates the event, where the narration of the act of God is ambiguous and indirect, to its direct and explicit theological interpretation exercises a teaching function by showing us how to talk about God and discern God's activity in the world and the church. Understanding, in the sense articulated by Ricoeur, takes place when the narrative's configuration of divine activity is taken up and reconfigured by its readers.[62] The narrative rendering of a God who always moves ahead of and beyond the characters, and often in remarkably surprising ways (e.g., Acts 2:1–13; 8:26–40; 9:1–19; 10:1–11:18), but whose deeds are discerned and interpreted by human characters creates a pattern of "divine act"/"human response" that is to be continued by Luke's audience as it reads and names the divine activity in its own world. Given that the most frequent title for followers of the risen Lord in Acts is "witness," the task of interpreting and testifying to God's mighty acts is indispensable if the contemporary church is to retain continuity of identity and mission with the earliest church.[63]

Third, I suggest that Luke's narration of *how* characters come to recognize and then interpret divine activity should function (loosely) as a model for *our* ability to recognize and respond to God's acts. In other words, not only does Luke-Acts call its audience to continue the process of discerning God's acts, but it also provides a pattern for successful recognition and interpretation. There are four characteristics that govern the Lukan characters' interpretation of divine activity. God's acts (1) are discerned through religious experiences within human lives, (2) align with the teachings and actions of Jesus in the Gospel of Luke, (3) conform to the testimony of Israel's Scriptures, and (4) are worked out and understood within the context of the ecclesial community. I do not suggest that every act of God within the pages of Luke-Acts conforms to a

---

62. See Marguerat, *First Christian Historian*, 91.
63. See Luke 24:48–49; Acts 1:8; 1:22; 2:32; 3:15; 5:32; 7:58; 10:39, 41; 13:31; 22:15; 26:16.

simple model but only that the four characteristics listed above are the primary elements that govern the interpretation of divine activity.

For example, the characteristics of divine activity at Pentecost involve a powerful religious experience of ecstatic speech and miraculous understanding (Acts 2:5–11), which is aligned with promises Jesus made to his disciples (Luke 24:44–49; Acts 1:4–8) and coheres with the testimony of the prophet Joel (Acts 2:16–21). God's conversion of Saul involves his experience of a vision of the risen Lord (9:3–7), his commission stemming from the words of Jesus (9:15–16; 22:17–21; 26:15–23), and his inclusion within the Christian community and validation of the authenticity of his faith through the community's representatives (9:17–18, 26–30). The story of Peter and Cornelius is, again, divinely initiated through religious experience: visions from God's angel (10:3, 9), prayer (10:9b), and ecstatic speech (10:44–46). The event coheres with Jesus's commission to Peter and the disciples (Luke 24:47) and Peter's understanding of Jesus as "Lord of everyone" (Acts 10:36; cf. 10:42–43) whose mission was one of benefaction and healing for "everyone afflicted by the devil" (10:38). Peter's speech invokes the maxim from Israel's Scriptures—"God shows no partiality" (e.g., Deut 10:17)—and later James ratifies the gentiles' full inclusion within God's people, in part, through his claim that "this agrees with the words of the prophets" (Acts 15:15; citing Amos 9:11). The decisive choice to include the gentiles as full members is, then, worked out in the Jerusalem community who, after hearing Peter's story, concludes together, "So God has granted to the gentiles the repentance that brings life" (Acts 11:18b).

The audience that would inhabit the world of Luke-Acts, that would live as though its world and its premises were true and constitutive of human history and all reality, must first be open to the God of Luke-Acts continuing to manifest himself and act within the fabric of human life. Christian identity, according to Luke-Acts, depends on the ability of humans to discern, interpret, and testify to God's acts. Luke does not provide a how-to-manual for human interpretation of divine activity, but it does suggest that faithful discernment of God's work in the world will take seriously human experience of divine activity.

11

The Migrant Messiah and the Boundary-Crossing Messianic Community in Luke-Acts

Does Luke's narration of the story of Jesus (in the Gospel of Luke) and his foundation story of the rise of the messianic community—what we refer to as the church (in the Acts of the Apostles)—address our most pressing contemporary social and ethical concerns?[1] To answer this question, at least two challenges must be addressed: one concerning the antiquity of our texts (i.e., "historical distance") and the other having to do with their genre as narratives. For example, Luke narrates prison escapes and speaks of Jesus engaging in liberation for the captives, but of course he knows nothing of the 2.3 million persons incarcerated in the United States. Luke is well acquainted with how ethnic and cultural stereotypes harm and stigmatize minority peoples (e.g., think Samaritans, eunuchs, barbarians), but of course he does not directly address America's history of race-based slavery, Jim Crow, or contemporary manifestations of white nationalism. With respect to this chapter's theme, Luke knows that the history of Israel is one of migration, that the God of Israel is a God who demands hospitality for the vulnerable, that Jesus was an itinerant wanderer dependent upon hospitality from others, and that the early church too was a migrant people pursuing mission on the move and creating all kinds of unusual and surprising friendships for the sake of the gospel. And yet Luke, of course, says nothing about public policy, legislative proposals, or questions related to borders and modern nation-states.

To clarify then: The first challenge in drawing upon Luke-Acts for contemporary social and ethical matters is that it is an ancient text which does

---

1. There are a variety of helpful ways of reading Luke and Acts. On my decision to read them as *Luke-Acts*, see Joshua W. Jipp, *Reading Acts* (Eugene, OR: Cascade, 2018), 1–13.

not know of and, therefore, is not able to speak with the degree of directness to our situation that we might desire. The second hermeneutical challenge is that of genre: Luke and Acts are narratives. They tell stories about Jesus and the church. Any contemporary use of these narratives, therefore, cannot be simply an extraction of universal rules or laws; neither will it be a simplistic replication or imitation of the characters in the stories.

I will suggest that these two potential objections are easily overcome. I highlight them, however, precisely because they have been used as a means of avoiding the robust, prophetic, and unsettling contemporary call to practice the moral and social vision of Luke-Acts (and other Christian Scriptures) as it pertains to discerning how the church responds to the contemporary challenge of migration (among many other matters). Let me say it this way: the correspondences between our contemporary situation and that of the ancient world of the Bible will always be inexact.[2] Searching for laws, policies, and patterns to replicate cannot be the way forward, then, for moving from Scripture to the contemporary world, from biblical narrative to ethics. Instead, those of us wanting to practice theology do better to "learn again how to live in the world Scripture produces."[3] Given that Luke-Acts witnesses to a God once engaged *and still engaged* with the world he created, to a reign of an enthroned messianic king who is present in our world through the Holy Spirit, our reading of Luke-Acts is inherently self-involving as it invites us to believe, confess, and act in ways that are congruent with its literary and theological imagination.[4] The world that is imagined by Luke-Acts claims to give definition to all of reality, the situation of all of humanity, and the purpose of God's messianic people. The world of Luke-Acts, then, is not merely story; it is a totalizing vision that claims to constitute the world of its readers.[5] In what follows, then, I intend to read Luke-Acts with attention to how its scriptural vision can call us to faithful practice in our world. I read Luke-Acts, in the words of Eric Barreto, "searching for a theological imagination that can encourage prophetic action,

---

2. This is rightly noted by Robert W. Heimburger, *God and the Illegal Alien: United States Immigration Law and a Theology of Politics* (Cambridge: Cambridge University Press, 2018), 5–10.

3. Luke Timothy Johnson, "Imagining the World Scripture Imagines," *Modern Theology* 14 (1998): 165–80, here 165.

4. I have articulated this approach in much more detail in Joshua W. Jipp, "The Beginnings of a Theology of Luke-Acts: Divine Activity and Human Response," *JTI* 8 (2014): 24–43.

5. See throughout here the similar theological reflections in the important work of C. Kavin Rowe, *World Upside Down: Reading Acts in the Graeco-Roman Age* (Oxford: Oxford University Press, 2009). My way of stating this is also obviously indebted to the likes of Hans Frei.

The Migrant Messiah and the Boundary-Crossing Messianic Community

compassionate care, and a communal identity open to God's transformative activity among and with us."[6]

Developing a Theological Imagination

How then do we develop such a theological imagination that will enable us to respond with compassion, hospitality, and humility as the people of God? I examine three important literary and theological threads of Luke-Acts that, I hope, will help us do exactly that.

Thesis #1: God's saving presence is embodied in the vulnerable stranger-guest Jesus. In other words, Jesus is the king and savior of strangers precisely because he himself is the stranger-guest par excellence. Jesus's identity as a vulnerable and poor stranger corresponds precisely to the identity of his followers.[7]

The early chapters of Luke make it emphatically clear that Jesus is the singular agent of God's saving visitation of his people. Luke's birth narrative has three epiphanies where angelic messengers come *from heaven* to earth and announce a coming figure from heaven (Luke 1:5–25; 1:26–38; 2:8–20). Zechariah's hymn twice praises God for making good on his promise to visit his people. Zechariah declares, "Blessed is the Lord the God of Israel for he has *visited* his people and brought redemption for them" (1:68); and "from the compassionate mercy of our God, the dawn from on high *will visit us*" (1:78).[8] The language of divine "visitation" connotes a downward spatial movement of God from heaven to earth.

Stories of divine visitors—God or the gods—descending to earth to make a test of peoples and societies are pervasive in antiquity. The plot is fairly simple. God, or the gods, descend wearing the guise of impoverished travelers. The reason for their descent and disguise is that they have come to test the piety of the peoples and lands they visit. Quite obviously, the appropriate response to the disguised deity will be one of hospitality, and conversely, inhospitality to the seemingly vulnerable strangers will reveal the impiety of the people. And, of course, the peoples' response will have significant consequences: blessings

---

6. Eric D. Barreto, "A Gospel on the Move: Practice, Proclamation, and Place in Luke-Acts," *Int* 72 (2018): 175–187, here 176.

7. Foundational here is David P. Moessner, *Lord of the Banquet: The Literary and Theological Significance of the Lukan Travel Narrative* (Minneapolis: Fortress, 1989).

8. Here and throughout, the translation is the author's.

and rewards vs. curses and punishment. The stories are quite obviously moralizing as they function as literary symbolizations of piety versus impiety.[9]

In the Gospel of Luke, Jesus, of course, is the singular agent of God's visitation whose identity as the Son of God is hidden—even disguised—from the people he visits.[10] Luke presents Jesus as an itinerant wanderer, with little connection to family ties, with no home, and even birthed away from home during a journey and spending the night in the open air (Luke 2:1–7).[11] Luke Timothy Johnson notes this Lukan dynamic well: "[Jesus] does not have a fixed abode. He does not occupy a cult center. Instead, Luke shows him constantly on the move."[12] In the words of René Padilla, "[Jesus's] whole ministry is marked by a constant identification with the destitute—an identification that won him the title 'Friend of tax collectors and sinners.'"[13] While this theme pervades the entirety of Luke, it is highlighted most powerfully in Luke's travel narrative. Luke repeatedly describes Jesus as an itinerant journeyer, a wandering stranger (e.g., 9:51–62; 10:38; 13:22, 33; 14:25; 18:31, 35–37; 19:1, 11, 28). Jesus's journey begins with an opening vignette indicating that Jesus's journey will be marked by inhospitality and vulnerability. When his disciples go on ahead to find places for him to lodge in Samaritan villages, Luke narrates, "They did not receive him" (9:53a). Thus, in the very next scene, when a would-be disciple declares his desire to travel with Jesus on his journey ("I will follow you wherever you go," 9:57b), Jesus's response ("the Son of Man has nowhere to lay his head"; 9:58b) is a direct reference to the Samaritan villagers' refusal to show hospitality to him and his disciples, a situation that will characterize his journey as a whole. In other words, the rejection of Jesus and his mission is quite literally evident in Jesus's current homeless state. Ensuing inhospitality scenarios will take place between Jesus and Israel's religious leaders who consistently break hospitality protocols as they use meals as opportunities to criticize and insult the journeying guest (11:37–44; 14:1–6; cf. 7:36–50).

---

9. See here also John B. Weaver, *Plots of Epiphany: Prison-Escape in Acts of the Apostles*, BZNW 131 (Berlin: de Gruyter, 2004).

10. E.g., Jesus's identity is disclosed to infants but is hidden from the wise and powerful (10:21–24). A blind beggar "sees" (18:41–43), while his identity as the suffering Son of Man is "concealed" from his disciples (18:34).

11. Henry J. Cadbury, "Lexical Notes on Luke-Acts: III. Luke's Interest in Lodging," *JBL* 45 (1926): 305–22, here 317–19.

12. Luke Timothy Johnson, *Prophetic Jesus, Prophetic Church: The Challenge of Luke-Acts to Contemporary Christians* (Grand Rapids: Eerdmans, 2011), 100–101.

13. René Padilla, "Mensaje biblico y revolucion," *Certez* 10 (1970): 197. Quoted in Samuel Escobar, *In Search of Christ in Latin America: From Colonial Image to Liberating Savior* (Downers Grove, IL: InterVarsity Press, 2019), 169.

The Migrant Messiah and the Boundary-Crossing Messianic Community

The theme of inhospitality to Jesus during his journey gradually builds and leads to the sad climax, occurring at the end of the journey narrative, where Jesus weeps for God's people who have "not recognized the time of its [divine] visitation" (19:41–44). While this scene foreshadows Jesus's ultimate rejection in Jerusalem, not all is bleak, however. Jesus will experience hospitality, kindness, and welcome—e.g., from women (Mary and Martha in Luke 10:38–42), sinners (5:27–32; 7:36–50), and tax collectors (19:1–10). The inhospitality Jesus receives as a journeying guest is, of course, deeply related to the company he keeps in his own hospitality encounters. As is well known, one of the major marks of Jesus's table practices is his indiscriminate and non-calculating offer of hospitality to all people. Jesus eats with tax collectors (5:27–32; 19:1–10), a sinful woman (7:36–50), two women (10:38–42), and the poor and ritually unclean (9:11–17). Jesus is tangibly extending God's welcome to those who, in the eyes of others, are unrighteous, have a low status, and are viewed as unworthy of friendship with God. Jesus is rejected because he eats with the "wrong people," thereby incorporating them into God's family.[14]

Why do some extend hospitality to Jesus, seemingly recognizing him and his message as God's saving visitation of his people, whereas others treat him with inhospitality? It seems to me that Jesus's identity as stranger-guest functions as something of an embodied parable of his teaching. Jesus is the stranger par excellence precisely because he is the king and savior of strangers. In his poverty, homelessness, vulnerability, and dependence upon others Jesus reveals—to those who are able to see—that God himself is in the deepest solidarity with the poor, the sojourner, the vulnerable refugee, and the journeying immigrant. Just as Jesus portrays himself in the parable of the sheep and the goats in Matthew 25 as "the hungry, thirsty, naked, homeless migrant" and as a "king who comes to the unsuspecting disciples as a beggar," so also Luke makes the deepest connection between Jesus's identity as stranger-guest and the recipients of God's saving visitation.[15] Jesus himself declares, "The Spirit of the Lord is upon me, for he has anointed me to proclaim good news to the poor; he has sent me to preach release to the captives, sight to the blind, to bring release to the oppressed, to proclaim the year of the Lord's favor" (4:18–19); "blessed are the poor for yours is the kingdom of God" (6:20); and "when you give a feast, invite the poor, the maimed, the lame, and the blind"

---

14. See my *Saved by Faith and Hospitality* (Grand Rapids: Eerdmans, 2017), 22–24; Barreto, "Gospel on the Move," 182.

15. The language here comes from Mark W. Hamilton, *Jesus, King of Strangers: What the Bible Really Says about Immigration* (Grand Rapids: Eerdmans, 2019), 129.

(14:13). Again, Jesus is the king of strangers, the poor, and the humble, and as such he takes to himself the identity of the poor, vulnerable stranger guest.

Thesis #2: The church continues the ministry of Jesus and enacts God's mission precisely through crossing borders, settling in new lands, and engaging in deeply surprising, even unsettling, friendships.

Luke's Gospel repeatedly makes it clear that God's salvation is universal in scope. It is "for all people" (e.g., Luke 2:10, 32; 3:4–6; 24:44–49). As such, God's salvation—like the journeying Jesus—is constantly on the move in the book of Acts. One of the fabulous aspects of this book consists in the reader's entering into new lands and encountering all kinds of peoples. As Barreto rightly notes, "The gospel cannot stay in one place, for it is God's uncontainable grace that propels witnesses to every corner of the world."[16]

Throughout the book of Acts, God's mission is propelled forward by means of God's Spirit. Peter's initial Pentecost sermon declares what attentive readers of Luke's Gospel already know: the Spirit is the Spirit of the resurrected and enthroned-in-heaven Messiah Jesus. Peter declares that with God's exaltation of Jesus to his right hand, this resurrected Jesus has now poured out the Spirit upon those dwelling in Jerusalem (Acts 2:33; cf. Luke 24:47–48; Acts 1:4–5). In other words, the risen Jesus is responsible for the incredible event at Pentecost, whereby the pilgrim Jews in Jerusalem are able to hear the proclamation of God's mighty acts in their native language.

If the Spirit poured out upon God's people at Pentecost flows from the very person of Jesus, now enthroned in heaven, we should expect that this Spirit will enable God's people to embody the mission, character, and very marks of Jesus. In fact, we find God's Spirit throughout Acts enabling God's people to share in his mission in surprising ways, in ways that require movement and engagement in unusual friendships. This theme is foreshadowed in Acts 2:1–13, when the Spirit's powerful presence is manifested in the ability to speak in unlearned languages. The emphasis on speech is obvious as tongues like fiery flames descend upon the community, enabling them to speak in different languages "just as the Spirit gave them the ability to proclaim" (2:4). The Diaspora Jews are perplexed as they are enabled to hear these Galilean Jews speaking in their own dialects (2:8). Luke's listing of the virtual table of nations from Genesis 10, the emphasis upon language and hearing, and the note that

---

16. Barreto, "Gospel on the Move," 182.

the content was "the mighty deeds of God" (2:11) indicate that the function of the Spirit is to enable God's people to engage in cross-cultural testimony. It seems likely that Luke has alluded to both the Table of Nations (Gen 10) and the Tower of Babel (Gen 11) to show that the multiplication of languages will serve God's purposes to reach all peoples.

Just as the journeying Jesus extended God's salvation and hospitality to surprising people in the Gospel of Luke, so the Spirit of the risen Jesus is constantly pressing and pushing God's people to share God's blessing through crossing borders and developing unusual friendships. Before we look at some of these border crossings, note how Stephen's speech, strategically placed right before the gospel's movement beyond the borders of Jerusalem in Acts 8, prepares us to share Luke's conviction that God's presence is not bound to one geographical locale. In fact, Stephen portrays Israel and its patriarchs as a migrant people, a people who are on the move and who encounter both God's presence outside the land of Israel as well as the challenges and vulnerabilities common to migrants and refugees. Willie James Jennings says it well: "God took hold of Abraham and made him new by turning him into a sojourner and making in him something new, creating a people who were sojourners."[17] Thus, God's glory appears to Abraham in Mesopotamia (Acts 7:2); God is with Joseph in Egypt (7:9); Moses is raised in Egypt where he receives an Egyptian education (7:22–23); God visits Moses in the burning bush at Sinai and refers to the place as "holy land" (7:30–33); God is present with the wilderness generation in a moveable tent (7:44–45). God's people, however, also experience the vulnerabilities of a migrant people: leaving behind of family and friends (7:1–5), imprisonment (7:9–10), movement due to famine (7:11–12), the violent rage of tyrants (7:19), and the abuse and exploitation that stems from Pharaoh's fear (7:19–29). Stephen rightly understands that numerous portions of the biblical tradition, specifically the Torah, have inscribed a migrant identity into Israel such that the experience of being an immigrant—both the vulnerabilities and the possibilities for experiencing God's presence—is built into the very fabric of Israel's identity (see also Lev. 25:23; Deut. 26:1–11; 1 Chron 29:15; Ps 39:13).[18]

The death of Stephen results in a great persecution against the church in Jerusalem such that the believers are forced to leave Jerusalem and are "scat-

---

17. Willie James Jennings, *Acts*, Belief (Louisville: Westminster John Knox, 2017), 70–71.
18. See further *DOTP*, s.v. "Alien, Foreign Resident." I have written more on this in my *Divine Visitations and Hospitality to Strangers in Luke-Acts: An Interpretation of the Malta Episode in Acts 28:1–10*, NovTSup 153 (Leiden: Brill, 2013), 151–56.

tered" throughout the regions of Judea and Samaria (8:1–4). Thus begins the move of the gospel to new lands and peoples. Without analyzing the historical intricacies and literary texture of Luke's storytelling here, we simply note the following surprising boundary crossings.

Samaritans: The persecution of the believers in Jerusalem leads to some traveling into Samaria, where the gospel message of Christ is proclaimed (8:4–5). Luke's repeated references to "Samaria" (Acts 8:1, 5, 14, 15, 25), along with the concluding narrative summary in Acts 9:31 ("So then all the church in the entirety of Judea, and Galilee, and Samaria had peace"), draws attention to Luke's concern to show the surprising friendship and the eradication of the long-seated hostility between Jews and Samaritans.[19]

Ethiopians (Eunuch): The surprises continue as Philip now meets up with an Ethiopian eunuch. That this is a divinely ordained encounter is clear from the fact that God sends an angel to tell Philip to "go south to the road that goes down from Jerusalem to Gaza" (8:26) and concludes with the Spirit snatching Philip away (8:39). Jennings again: Philip "witnesses a God whose love expands over every road and transgresses every bordered identity. The Spirit is Lord of the road."[20] Why is an Ethiopian eunuch portrayed as an ideal or model convert? A few things stand out. First, while there are a variety of descriptors for ancient Ethiopians including some positive ones, more frequently references to them are as symbols of vice and sexual desire. Second, Luke repeatedly refers to the man as a "eunuch" (8:27, 34, 36, 38, 39). Eunuchs often served as royal officials, just as this man does, in part so that there would be no worries of sexual liaisons with the nobility. Despite this, eunuchs were frequently stereotyped as salacious and sexually ambiguous monstrosities.[21] The Torah speaks of eunuchs as excluded from the "assembly of the Lord" and from worshipping God in the temple (e.g., Deut 23:1; Lev 21:16–23). The eunuch is, in short, a symbol of an outcast, one who conjures up exotic cultural, gender, and ethnic stereotypes.[22] Luke activates none of these potentially negative stereotypes. Instead, the eunuch recognizes the God of Israel as the true God; he is reading the prophet Isaiah; he responds with

---

19. I have learned much here from David W. Pao, *Acts and the Isaianic New Exodus*, WUNT 2/130 (Tübingen: Mohr Siebeck, 2000), 127–29.

20. Jennings, *Acts*, 82.

21. Jennings, *Acts*, 83: "His difference is marked by his origin in Ethiopia, the outer limits of the known world, and is even signified by his blackness. His difference is also marked by his sexuality, neither unambiguously male nor female."

22. See here especially Brittany E. Wilson, *Unmanly Men: Refigurations of Masculinity in Luke-Acts* (Oxford: Oxford University Press, 2015), 113–49. See also Pao, *Acts and the Isaianic New Exodus*, 140–42.

The Migrant Messiah and the Boundary-Crossing Messianic Community

belief and enthusiasm to Philip's teaching of the gospel; and he presses Philip for baptism (8:26–40). Luke's point is clear: Nothing like physical disability, or exotic ethnicity, or geographical distance can exclude one from encountering the powerful presence of Christ who meets this man through Philip.

Pagans: The proclamation of the gospel has now expanded beyond the borders of Jerusalem through new witnesses in surprising ways and to unexpected peoples. God has used the Greek-speaking Hellenists Stephen and Philip to bring the gospel to the Samaritans and outcasts. Luke's narration of the movement of the gospel into new territories "stokes confidence about venues the gospel has yet to find. Even the places that the book's original readers might consider new, unfamiliar, distant, or curious await the gospel."[23] We should not be shocked if God continues to use surprising people to bring the gospel to new places and widen the expansiveness of those included in the people of God. This prepares us for the biggest shock: the narration of the foundational event whereby gentiles are included within the people of God. Luke uses a lot of words, even repeating the Peter-Cornelius encounter three times, to indicate its central importance. Here I only point to the experiential process whereby Peter is led to recognize the surprising act of God in his encounter with the Roman centurion Cornelius.[24] The story begins with two accounts of the human experience of divine activity: Cornelius's vision of the angel of God who commands him to call for Peter, and Peter's subsequent vision while he is praying. Peter is deeply unsettled as the voice from heaven commands him to eat both clean *and* unclean food. Peter is perplexed by the vision (10:17, 19). Peter obeys the voice of the Spirit, who tells him to go without discrimination to the home of Cornelius (10:23). The rest of the story narrates Peter's progressive growth in his ability to interpret God's activity within these events. Finally, within Cornelius's home, Peter declares that even though it is not permissible for a Jew to associate with a gentile, "God has shown me that I should not call any person defiled and unclean" (10:28b). Through reflection on the visions, through the shared hospitality, Peter goes even further and claims, "Truly I now perceive that God shows no partiality" (10:34). Further, when the Spirit comes upon Cornelius and the other gentiles and inspires ecstatic declaration of God's deeds (10:44–46), Peter rightly declares that they belong to the people of God since they have

---

23. See here Matthew L. Skinner, *Intrusive God, Disruptive Gospel: Encountering the Divine in the Book of Acts* (Grand Rapids: Brazos, 2015), 65.

24. I am indebted here to Luke Timothy Johnson, *Scripture and Discernment: Decision Making in the Church* (Nashville: Abingdon, 1996); Beverly Roberts Gaventa, *From Darkness to Light: Aspects of Conversion in the New Testament*, OBT (Minneapolis: Fortress, 1986).

PART THREE: GOD'S ACTS FOR CHRISTIANS

received the Spirit of God "just as even we had" (10:47). Peter's affirmation of God's surprising activity is the result of a process of *experience and encounter* of divine work: visions from heaven, hospitality with strangers, and the work of the Spirit. Luke's narration of God's inclusion of the gentiles marks a new point in the narrative of Acts. If Greek-speaking Jews (Stephen and Philip), Samaritans, Ethiopian eunuchs, and now pagans are part of God's people, then there are no limitations in terms of peoples or geographical locales to which God's gospel can move. Jesus is, in fact, as Peter had declared, "Lord of all" (10:36).

The crossing of boundaries, the unusual friendships, and the diverse cast of characters and lands continues throughout Acts: the ethnic diversity in the church in Antioch (13:1), Lydia the Philippian God-fearer (16:11–15), the Philippian jailer (16:25–34), Athenian intellectuals (17:16–34), barbarian islanders on Malta (28:1–10)—all of this helps us grasp that, according to the witness of Acts, the church is a multiethnic people engaged in mission, crossing borders, embracing ethnic and cultural differences as gifts from God, and being attentive to God's ongoing work to establish new and surprising friendships.[25] The Spirit is the Spirit of cross-cultural testimony who enables people to cross geographical borders and transgress cultural stigmas.

Thesis #3: Luke's ethnic reasoning subverts the popular belief that ethnic and cultural differences are problems to be overcome. Rather, Luke disrupts notions of the other as a source of fear, pollution, or inferiority. He does this through the subversion of ethnic and cultural stereotypes and through working within rather than demonizing the cultural and religious logics of non-Jewish peoples.

To support my third thesis, I want to examine two aspects of Luke's ethnic reasoning. By "ethnic reasoning" I refer to Luke's use of "culturally available understandings of human difference, which we can analyze in terms of our modern concepts of 'ethnicity,' 'race,' and 'religion.'"[26] First, I suggest that Luke consistently overturns and subverts common stereotypes, so much so that one can suggest this is an intentional Lukan strategy whereby ethnic, gender, and cultural difference is seen as a gift of God rather than a problem. Second, I look at how Luke appropriates diverse religious and cultural scripts and stories to proclaim the gospel.

---

25. See Barreto, "Gospel on the Move," 185: "Counter to this racialized way of thinking, Acts can help us imagine that our differences are gifts from God, not problems to overcome or obstacles on the way to becoming God's church."

26. Denise Kimber Buell, *Why This New Race: Ethnic Reasoning in Early Christianity* (New York: Columbia University Press, 2005), 2.

The Migrant Messiah and the Boundary-Crossing Messianic Community

One of the defining features of God's hospitality in Jesus for his people is that this welcome does not correspond to some prior existing social worth of the individual.[27] God's welcome is for male and female, Jew and gentile, Pharisees and sinners, rich and poor, apostles and outcasts. By frequently raising a negative cultural stereotype only then to reject or subvert it, Luke shows that God's friendship is for all people and not predicated upon social and cultural norms. A few examples suffice. I have written at length about how Paul's shipwreck on Malta plays on the stereotypes of the supposedly exotic islanders as uncivilized barbarians. Only here does Luke use the language "barbarian" (Acts 28:2, 4), and it seems this is almost certainly his intention to raise the stereotype of the barbarian, the non-Greek, as one who is prone to prey on shipwrecked strangers and who lacks the civilized custom of hospitality.[28] The reader is prepared, then, for an impending *inhospitality* scenario as Paul and his fellow prisoners wreck on the island. But Luke raises this stereotype only to reject it as a poor means of making sense of the Maltese. Luke pairs "barbarian" together with *philanthropia* (philanthropy), and this is intentionally jarring for the reader. The Maltese execute hospitality protocols as well as any of the other characters throughout Luke-Acts. They make a fire to warm the prisoners (28:1–2); Publius, the leading man of the island, receives Paul into his home with a friendly and hospitable welcome (28:7–9); and the Maltese provide Paul with what he needs for his journey as they grant honors to him (28:9–10).

Luke does something similar, of course, with the parable of the good Samaritan in Luke 10. One aspect of Luke's genius is seen in his forcing the lawyer and reader, to use the insights of John Dominic Crossan, "to put together two impossible and contradictory words for the same person: 'Samaritan' (10:33) and 'neighbor' (10:36).... The story demands that the hearer respond by saying the contradictory, the impossible, the unspeakable."[29] The story packs the punch that it does precisely because the reader struggles to say, "The *Samaritan* was the neighbor to the man," and maybe even harder, "The *Samaritan* obeyed and fulfilled the commands of the law of Moses."

We have already noted that Luke's transformation of stereotypes occurs in his portrait of the Ethiopian eunuch, a man considered a sexual deviant by most ancient standards. The Torah forbids castrated men from full partici-

---

27. Readers will note that I have also reused this argument for a different purpose in chapter 12.

28. See here Joshua W. Jipp, "Hospitable Barbarians: Luke's Ethnic Reasoning in Acts 28:1–10," *JTS* 68 (2017): 23–45 (chapter 7 in this volume).

29. John Dominic Crossan, *In Parables: The Challenge of the Historical Jesus* (New York: Harper and Row, 1975), 62–63.

pation in the temple (see Lev 21:16–23; Deut 23:1). The prophet Isaiah in fact draws upon the eunuch as a representative for the kinds of outcasts who will be welcomed into God's people when God fulfills his promises (Isa 56:3–8). Eunuchs were frequently portrayed as soft, feminine, and sexually deviant as they did not conform to the masculine stereotypes of virility and strength.[30] Despite Luke's fronting of the man's identity as "eunuch" (Acts 8:27, 34, 38, 39), he activates none of the stereotypes about eunuchs. Rather, the man is humble and inquisitive as he reads Isaiah and seeks interpretive help from Philip. He welcomes Philip's interpretation, pursues baptism, and goes back home rejoicing—a model Lukan character to be sure.

Roman centurions, women, people representing other ethnic stereotypes (e.g., Pontus, Acts 18), and those with physical disabilities could be examined in detail to see that the previous three examples are not accidental but instead point to a fundamental feature of Luke-Acts: the worthlessness of stigmatic stereotypes for making sense of human existence. The recipients of divine welcome in Luke-Acts are some of society's most stigmatized (and often vulnerable) peoples: sinners, tax collectors, eunuchs, Samaritans, the poor and the hungry, the physically disabled, and barbarians. Jesus is remarkably unconcerned with a fear of the stranger, being polluted by a sinner, or conforming to societal standards and cultural norms.[31] Amos Yong has suggested that this theme indicates that those on the margins of society are included within God's people as they are, so that they can stand "as a testimony to the power of God to save all of us 'normal' folk from our discriminatory attitudes, inhospitable actions, and exclusionary social and political forms of life."[32]

Second, Luke further disrupts the notion of the other as a source of fear, pollution, and inferiority through appropriating the religious and cultural logics of non-Jewish peoples. Since Christianity does not sacralize any particular language or culture, every new culture is, thereby, destigmatized as well as relativized.[33] Lamin Sanneh has emphasized the significance of the fact that the earliest Christians did not spread the gospel message through diffusion or cultural adoption, but rather through translation, which "rests on the per-

---

30. See further Jipp, *Saved by Faith and Hospitality*, 33.
31. On Luke-Acts' subversion of popular physiognomic norms, see Mikeal C. Parsons, *Body and Character in Luke and Acts: The Subversion of Physiognomy in Early Christianity* (Grand Rapids: Baker, 2006).
32. Amos Yong, *The Bible, Disability, and the Church: A New Vision of the People of God* (Grand Rapids: Eerdmans, 2011), 69.
33. John G. Flett, *Apostolicity: The Ecumenical Question in World Christian Perspective* (Downers Grove, IL: InterVarsity Press, 2016), 276–77.

suasive nature of the idioms adopted in religious practice."[34] The contents of the Christian proclamation were "received and framed in the terms of its host culture; by feeding off the diverse cultural streams it encountered, the religion became multicultural. The local idiom became the chosen vessel."[35] When we turn to the book of Acts and its engagement with Greco-Roman religions and cultures, it presents a similar missionary dynamic that becomes a defining feature of Christian identity throughout its history. Acts makes abundant use of Greco-Roman religious discourses in order to show that the early Christian movement embodies supremely the superior elements of Greco-Roman religiosity and philosophy.[36] Acts portrays its characters and movement as working within the cultural and religious logic of a variety of aspects of Greco-Roman religiosity as a means of simultaneously criticizing and disrupting pagan beliefs, allegiances, and ways of life, *and* using said Greco-Roman cultural scripts to portray Christianity as *the* superior Greco-Roman religion. Christianity—or at least Christian discourse—emerges out of intense conflict with Greco-Roman religiosity. But, its employment of Greco-Roman religious scripts, themes, and philosophy results in deep cultural convergences between Christianity and pagan religion as the former emerges out of the latter. The Acts of the Apostles provides significant testimony to this dynamic, as it both adapts to and criticizes aspects of the culture within which it takes root.

For example, we see Luke adapting scripts, themes, and traditions from ancient Mediterranean culture as a means of communicating the gospel. In addition to the well-known example of Paul's appropriation of Stoic philosophy in his proclamation in Athens (Acts 17:16–34), I think of the following as indicating Luke's adaptation of the gospel to Greco-Roman cultural patterns and traditions: Luke's literary prefaces and their similarities to Hellenistic historiography (Luke 1:1–4; Acts 1:1–2), the portrait of Jesus as participating in four symposia (Luke 5:27–30; 7:36–50; 11:37–54; 14:1–24), the transformation of the traditions of Jesus's crucifixion into that of noble death (Luke 23; cf. Acts 4:29; 5:29), the shaping of Jesus's resurrection appearance in the literary guise of a theoxeny (Luke 24:13–35; cf. Acts 28:1–10), the use of philosophical friendship language to exalt the Jerusalem church's common life (Acts 2:41–47;

---

34. Lamin O. Sanneh, *Translating the Message: The Missionary Impact on Culture*, rev. ed. (Maryknoll, NY: Orbis, 2009), 33–34.

35. Lamin Sanneh, *Disciples of All Nations: Pillars of World Christianity*, Oxford Studies in World Christianity (Oxford: Oxford University Press, 2008), 26.

36. I have written in more detail on this in "Did Paul Translate the Gospel in Acts 17:22–31? A Critical Engagement with C. Kavin Rowe's *One True Life*," *Perspectives in Religious Studies*, PRSt 45 (2018): 361–76 (chapter 6 in this volume).

4:32–35), God's validation of the Christian movement as exemplified in the apostle's prison escapes (Acts 5:19–20; 12:1–17; 16:25–34), and the depiction of the Christian movement's power and success as validated through victorious turf wars against its competitors (8:14–25; 13:5–12; 19:11–20; 28:3–6). Throughout Acts, Luke portrays the Christian witnesses both disrupting the cultural and religious allegiances of his Greco-Roman audience and working within, rather than mocking or demonizing, their cultural and religious logics.

Reflecting on Following Our Migrant Messiah

So where does our analysis of Luke-Acts leave us as we attempt to give a faithful Christian response to the complex challenges and questions surrounding immigration? It is true that the Bible does not contain specific prescriptions for public policy, but it most certainly does provide us with a contemporary moral vision or theological imagination that can enable us to discern what faithful discipleship looks like in our world.[37] Let me offer three exhortations that move from the world of Luke-Acts to our contemporary world.

First, Luke-Acts calls us to a consistent rejection of xenophobia based upon irrational stereotypes. More than forty years ago Henri Nouwen said something that seems to me to be sadly even more true today: "Our society seems to be increasingly full of fearful, defensive, aggressive people anxiously clinging to their property and inclined to look at their surrounding world with suspicion, always expecting an enemy to suddenly appear, intrude and do harm."[38] Following Jesus our stranger-king necessitates a critical awareness and rejection of the irrational fears of our age, fears which, if left unchecked, cause us at best to turn away from our neighbors and, at worst, to participate in various forms of dehumanization, exclusion, and violence directed toward those whom we fear.[39]

The compelling force at work in anti-immigrant rhetoric is almost invariably *fear*, fear that the other will contaminate.[40] This fear often centers upon three

---

37. I set forth some thoughts on what this might look like in *Saved by Faith and Hospitality*, 142–46.

38. Henri J. M. Nouwen, *Reaching Out: The Three Movements of the Spiritual Life* (New York: Image, 1986), 49.

39. So also Hans Urs von Balthasar, *The Christian and Anxiety* (San Francisco: Ignatius, 2000).

40. Also at work is the fear of scarcity, namely, fear that immigrants and refugees will take our jobs and harm the economy. Consumer societies can distract and blind us from the

common threads: fear that the immigrant will corrupt our nation's cultural identity (related to language, religion, laws, and sense of shared history); fear that the immigrant will threaten national security (related to terrorism, violent crime, drug trafficking); and fear that the immigrant will harm the economy and national institutions (related to taxes, welfare, health care).[41] Fear that the other will pollute the purity of our nation, then, often produces all kinds of irrational ethnic stereotyping and scapegoating.[42] The stereotyping can take many forms: us vs. them, hard-working vs. lazy, civilized vs. barbaric, moral vs. the wicked, even alien vs. citizen (the coining of the term "alien" was for the purpose of labeling one as an enemy and threat to a nation).[43] The cultivation of a theological imagination from Luke-Acts will have none of this in the church. We have seen that dehumanizing stereotypes and exclusionary practices are entirely antithetical to the gospel Jesus and his disciples preach.[44]

Second, and deeply related, if Jesus is the King of Strangers, the traveling and itinerant stranger-guest, and his identity is revealed among those who hospitably welcome him on the road, then the church should expect God's presence to be found and his mission extended through "strangers," disciples "on the move," and itinerants who are disconnected from family and homeland.[45] If we take seriously Jesus's words such as, "Blessed are the poor for yours is the kingdom of God" (Luke 6:20), and if Jesus embodied God's salvation as an itinerant guest dependent upon the provisions of others, then perhaps we should expect to find God working in places and people that surprise us. If the church today imagines itself as continuing the same story and mission of Jesus, then many of our churches need to reject their obsession with the so-called

---

needs (physical and relational) of those who are lonely, hungry, and socially alienated from society. We are unable to share our resources, possessions, and live with others because we are constantly afraid that we will not "have enough" to satisfy our own desires and needs.

41. Susannah Snyder, "Fright: The Dynamics of Fear within Established Populations," in *Asylum-Seeking: Migration and Church*, Explorations in Practical, Pastoral and Empirical Theology (London: Ashgate, 2012), 85–126. See also Khalid Koser, *International Migration: A Very Short Introduction*, 2nd ed. (Oxford: Oxford University Press, 2016), 61.

42. On stereotyping and scapegoating, see Snyder, "Fright," 102–4.

43. See further Miroslav Volf, *Exclusion and Embrace: A Theological Exploration of Identity, Otherness, and Reconciliation* (Nashville: Abingdon, 1996), 57–64. On the history of the term "alien," see Heimburger, *God and the Illegal Alien*, 25–44, 65–94.

44. Personal friendships are the best way to learn about the experiences of migrants and refugees. In addition, I recommend reading two recent novels: Zadie Smith's *White Teeth* and Mohsin Hamid's *Exit West*.

45. For some reflections upon the contemporary practice of Luke's vision of itinerancy, see L. Johnson, *Prophetic Jesus, Prophetic Church*, 126–28.

normal, with strict boundaries, over the consistent witness that the church is comprised of unusual friendships, that it is a group of disciples crossing borders, transgressing boundaries and norms, to extend and receive the presence of Christ as embodied in one another.

Third, we should expect that the gospel mission can and will be facilitated through faithful disciples who speak in so-called "other tongues and languages." The Spirit of God in Acts is the Spirit of cross-cultural testimony. The Spirit enables God's people to hear God's mighty deeds not in one language only but with all the diversity and multiplicity of different languages, stories, cultural scripts, and worldviews. As Oscar Garcia-Johnson notes, "The Pentecost narrative points to the mandate and power for the church . . . to become everlastingly a flourishing intercultural community, the embodiment of the new humanity of Jesus Christ."[46] Rather than eradicating difference or forcing those different from us to assimilate, Luke-Acts testifies to a form of life where different tongues, ethnicities, and cultures are not merely tolerated but are lovingly embraced as the means whereby the church continues to hear afresh the word and work of God.[47] Those comfortably part of majority culture thereby are called not only to extend hospitality but to act as a guest willing to learn from and hear the gospel in the rituals, practices, stories, and experiences of his/her neighbor, embodying a posture and mentality whereby they are not only the hosts and givers but guests and recipients of the gospel.[48]

---

46. Oscar García-Johnson, *Spirit Outside the Gate: Decolonial Pneumatologies of the American Global South* (Downers Grove, IL: InterVarsity Press, 2019), 258.

47. See Jennings, *Acts*, 87–89.

48. See here also Amos Yong, *Hospitality and the Other: Pentecost, Christian Practices, and the Neighbor* (Maryknoll, NY: Orbis, 2008), 125, 132.

12

Jesus, the Church, and Mental Illness

Do the Scriptures say anything of relevance for the church's pursuit to care for those with mental illnesses or mental health challenges? The Scriptures do not *directly* address every question that twenty-first-century North Americans may ask, and yet the Scriptures do provide wisdom, guidance, and challenges for all questions of human existence, and this includes the problem of mental illness. It will not do for ministers of the gospel to avoid this topic by claiming that they are not medical experts or professional counselors, for while professional help (e.g., counseling, medication, hospitalization) is necessary, it is not sufficient to provide the care, love, and understanding needed by those who struggle with mental health challenges. It likely will not surprise anyone to hear that mental illness is rarely addressed in an explicit manner in most churches or sermons. There is an almost universal fear and prejudice against the mentally ill that results in them feeling unwelcome, stigmatized, and alienated from others within most settings—including many (probably *most*) churches. But if it is true that close to 3 percent of the adult population in the United States (nearly six million people) has experienced a severe and ongoing mental illness, then continuing in fear and a lack of understanding of mental illness is at best irresponsible and at worst a willful turning away from those created in the image of God.[1] The statistics elucidate the fact that, to use Amy Simpson's language, "mental illness is mainstream," but it is likely that one's own experiences, including those of their families, would suggest that everyone is surrounded by mental illness.[2]

---

1. On the statistics, see Kathryn Greene-McCreight, *Darkness Is My Only Companion: A Christian Response to Mental Illness*, 2nd ed. (Grand Rapids: Brazos, 2015), 24.

2. For more detail on the prevalence of mental illness see Amy Simpson, *Troubled Minds: Mental Illness and the Church's Mission* (Downers Grove, IL: InterVarsity Press, 2013), 33–56.

PART THREE: GOD'S ACTS FOR CHRISTIANS

The ensuing thoughts will offer biblical and theological resources for how the church ought to think and act with respect to mental illness. Specifically included is a thought experiment oriented around Luke-Acts that asks the question: What does the witness of Jesus and the early church have to say about how the church engages people who are challenged with mental health illness? What follows is not so much specific and prescriptive application but rather an examination of the witness of Jesus and the early church, and how they engaged suffering, stigma, and human vulnerability.

JESUS THE HEALER

Luke makes it plain that Jesus's short sermon in the Jewish synagogue in his hometown of Nazareth is *programmatic* for the entirety of his Gospel. Here Jesus draws upon Isaiah to proclaim that God's Spirit is upon him "to proclaim good news to the poor; he has sent me to proclaim release to the captives, sight to the blind, to bring release to the oppressed, to proclaim the year of the Lord's favor" (Luke 4:18–19). To state it simply, the object of Jesus's ministry is the vulnerable (i.e., the poor, blind, incarcerated, and oppressed), and his task is to reverse their conditions that prevent human wholeness and flourishing. If Jesus's initial sermon occupies a programmatic role in the gospel, then one should expect to find Jesus enacting this program of release and divine favor to *all people*, including the oppressed and needy. This is exactly what Jesus does in his Galilean ministry (4:31–9:50), where Luke presents a series of scenes depicting Jesus instructing and liberating human beings. This is the literary function of Luke 4:31–44, where there are a series of short vignettes that present what Jesus's ministry looks like in condensed, representative form:

- 4:33–37: Jesus provides release from demonic oppression for a man "with an unclean spirit" (4:33). The text gives a preview of the cosmic battle that takes place over humanity between the healing Messiah and Satan.
- 4:38–39: Jesus heals a woman and the fever "left her" (ἀφῆκεν αὐτήν, 4:39), thus showing that healing is one way Jesus provides *release* (cf. 4:18–19).
- 4:40–41: Luke provides a typical summary statement of Jesus's ministry: "As the sun was setting, all who had charge of persons who were sick with various illnesses brought them to Jesus. And placing his hand on each one of them, he healed them. And demons also went out from many people, shouting, 'You are the Son of God!'"

Jesus, the Church, and Mental Illness

Jesus's Galilean ministry is peppered with accounts of his healings and exorcisms: a leper (5:12–16); a paralytic (5:17–26); the slave of the centurion (7:2–10); the son of the widow in Nain (7:11–17); Jesus's response to John the Baptist's question of whether or not he is the one ("At that time Jesus healed many people of diseases, afflictions, and evil spirits, and he granted sight to many blind people. He replied to them, 'Go and report to John what you have seen and heard: the blind receive their sight, the lame walk, those with leprosy are cleansed, the deaf hear, the dead are raised, and the poor are told the good news," 7:21–22); the Gerasene demoniac (8:26–39); the daughter of Jairus (8:40–42, 49–56); the woman with the flow of blood (8:43–48); and the ministry of the twelve in the Galilean villages to heal and proclaim the gospel (9:1–6). And this is only within Jesus's Galilean ministry! The point here seems to be as emphatic as one could hope for—one of the primary ways in which *Jesus enacts his ministry of release and welcome is through healing the sick and oppressed*. A basic question to ask now is: What is the logic here? Why would release from sickness and disease be spoken of as enacting the kingdom of God?

Within Luke's Gospel, Jesus's healings reflect his *compassionate concern* (note this compassion is an enactment of his own teaching, 6:36) for holistic human flourishing and the restoration of humans to total-capacity health, well-being, and social functioning. It is important to look at "Jesus' acts of healing first and foremost from the perspective of his beneficiaries, those who were sick. Jesus was remembered as having healed people out of compassion for their needs."[3] For example, Jesus's cleansing of the leper dramatically overturns and reverses the leper's place in society (5:12–16). Of primary importance here is not the healing from actual physical ailment, but rather the implications of the leper's healing; namely, that it restores him from a place of banishment on the margins of society and from being unable to participate in the religious, communal life of Israel (Lev 13:14; 13:44–45) to now being in a place of full communion within the people of God. The result is similar with Jesus's healing of the woman with the flow of blood. Her disease was not life-threatening, but it was socially debilitating (8:43–48). Jesus's healing is a form of compassion that allows her to reenter society, religious life, and family relations. In Luke 7:11–17 Jesus restores life to the widow's son. Luke says that Jesus sees the vulnerable, marginalized widow, and "the Lord feels compassion for her"

---

3. Jan-Olav Henriksen and Karl Olav Sandnes, *Jesus as Healer: A Gospel for the Body* (Grand Rapids: Eerdmans, 2016), 70.

(7:13). His restoration of life to the dead son essentially secures her ability to have life and subsistence due to her son.

There are two healing narratives in particular in Luke that specifically exemplify how Jesus's healings are enactments of release and liberation from Satanic/demonic oppression that usher in shalom—peace, freedom, and life as intended by God. First, in the story of the Gerasene demoniac, the man is described initially as "one who had demons" (8:27) and later as "the man from whom the demons had gone" (vv. 33, 36, 38). The man's fundamental characteristic is one who is in bondage and oppression to demonic power (4:18-19). The picture is that of a totally dehumanized person, driven from society (house and city), and forced to live in the abode of the dead. He is literally "shackled in chains and bonds" (v. 29) and lives among the tombs—as one who is essentially dead (v. 27). Jesus's healing of the man results in a point-by-point overturning of the man's prior condition: he had many demons (v. 27) // demons gone from the man (v. 35); he had worn no clothes (v. 27) // he was clothed (v. 35); he did not live in a house but tombs (v. 27) // he was called to return to his own home (v. 39); demons seized him and he was out of control (v. 29) // he was in his right mind (v. 35).[4]

Second, the story of the healing of the bent woman demonstrates most obviously that Jesus's healings are enactments of *liberation* or *release* from the power of Satan (13:10-17). Thus, the story is filled with language of "binding and loosing" (v. 12: You have been set free; v. 15: each of you frees his cow/donkey; v. 16: the woman is set free from the bonds of Satan). Her affliction is due to "having an unclean spirit" (13:11). Note Jesus's pronouncement: "Ought not this daughter of Abraham, whom Satan has oppressed for eighteen years, must she not be set free from this bondage on the Sabbath"? (13:16). Her healing, then, is a form of release which signifies wholeness and freedom from diabolic and social oppression. Further note Jesus's word of inclusion to her when he refers to her as "this daughter of Abraham."

Though this point will not be greatly expanded upon, it should be noted that the healing ministry of Jesus *continues in the early church* as evinced by the book of Acts. Peter's Pentecost speech is significant here as it both provides explicit evidence that Jesus was remembered as one "attested by God among

---

4. Comparing the role of demonic invasion in the Gospel narratives with contemporary experiences of mental illness is incredibly difficult, and while relevant, it would take me too far afield from my interests here. See, however, Loren T. Stuckenbruck, "The Human Being and Demonic Invasion: Therapeutic Models in Ancient Jewish and Christian Texts," in *The Myth of Rebellious Angels: Studies in Second Temple Judaism and New Testament Texts* (Grand Rapids: Eerdmans, 2017), 161-86.

you through powerful acts, wonders, and signs which God did among you" (2:22) and indicates God's Spirit will continue to act among the church with signs and wonders (2:19; cf. 2:43).[5] Peter's healing of the lame man at the temple gate (Acts 3:1–10) and Paul's healing of the lame man in Lystra (14:8–10) are so clearly patterned after Jesus's healings (esp. Luke 5:17–26). They are both performed through prayer to Jesus *and in the name of Jesus*; the obvious conclusion is that Jesus's apostles *continue* what Jesus himself had done, but only now through the power of the risen and heavenly enthroned king (this is explicit in Acts 3:12–16).[6]

Jesus's healings, then, are a form of release and welcome that liberates humans from bondage and oppression, restores them to proper physical and social engagement, and flows from Jesus's compassion for human suffering and vulnerability. Henriksen and Sandnes state this well: "As healer, Jesus reveals a God of love and compassion, who does not turn away from the suffering of creation but instead makes possible concrete hope for redemption and fulfillment by acting in, with, and under creaturely conditions in order to reveal the kingdom.... [Jesus] engages the powers of creation in his graceful approach to humanity in order to alleviate the suffering of the sick and destitute."[7]

What does Jesus's healing ministry mean, however, for the church's call to care for those with mental illness? Heather Vacek's *Madness* examines how a variety of Protestant responses to mental illness were grounded in their Christian sense of obligation to show compassion and care for the mentally ill.[8] Despite a host of theological differences, these responses were deeply attentive to the human experience of suffering and vulnerability. The words of Dorothea Dix seem to not accidentally echo the words of Jesus: "I come to present the strong claims of suffering humanity. I come to place before the Legislature of Massachusetts the condition of the miserable, the desolate, the outcast. I come as the advocate of helpless, forgotten, insane, and idiotic men and women; of beings sunk to a condition from which the most unconcerned would start with real horror; of beings wretched in our prisons, and more wretched in our almshouses."[9] One hears in Dix's plea echoes of Jesus's care and advocacy for

---

5. The apostles are portrayed as engaging in healing in Acts 3:1–8; 5:12–16; 6:8; 8:6–7; 9:17–18; 9:32–54; 14:3, 8–10; 15:12; 16:16–18; 19:11–12; 20:7–12; 28:7–9.
6. See Henriksen and Sandnes, *Jesus as Healer*, 86–91.
7. Henriksen and Sandnes, *Jesus as Healer*, 246.
8. Heather H. Vacek, *Madness: American Protestant Responses to Mental Illness* (Waco, TX: Baylor University Press, 2015).
9. Quoted in Vacek, *Madness*, 55.

PART THREE: GOD'S ACTS FOR CHRISTIANS

the vulnerable. Dix has internalized Jesus's compassion as one who sensed the need and vulnerability of the specific people he encountered.[10]

Jesus's healing ministry functions as a reminder that Jesus cared deeply about human flourishing and stood opposed to death and that which inflicted harm and evil upon humanity. Those who seek to continue the healing ministry of Jesus, then, will "stand with those whose lives or whose flourishing are threatened and to withstand the disorders that threaten them, however we explain those disorders."[11] Amanda Porterfield has argued that the church's care for the sick continued in the early centuries of the church's existence and that this was rooted in Jesus's healing ministry. She states this well: "Care for the sick was a distinctive and remarkable characteristic of early Christian missionary outreach. Early Christians nursed the sick to emulate the healing ministry of Jesus, to express their faith in the ongoing healing power of Christ, and to distinguish Christian heroism in the face of sickness and death from pagan fear."[12] The church's indiscriminate concern for the poor was one of the major factors that led to the creation of institutions such as "poorhouses" that supported widows, the sick, and the poor, as well as hospitals, which were, "in origin and conception, a distinctively Christian institution, rooted in Christian concepts of charity and philanthropy."[13]

Hospitality and Friendship

The fundamental problem in Luke-Acts is not simply humanity's alienation from God but also *its alienation from one another*.[14] Humans were created to be friends with God as well as friends with one another. One of the surprising features of Luke's Gospel is that Jesus's analysis of those in need of "the year of the Lord's favor" and welcome includes *all people*, including but not limited to

---

10. See further Luke Timothy Johnson, *The Revelatory Body: Theology as Inductive Art* (Grand Rapids: Eerdmans, 2015), 126–29.

11. Allen Verhey, *Remembering Jesus: Christian Community, Scripture, and the Moral Life* (Grand Rapids: Eerdmans, 2002), 101.

12. Amanda Porterfield, *Healing in the History of Christianity* (Oxford: Oxford University Press, 2005), 47.

13. Gary B. Ferngren, *Medicine and Health Care in Early Christianity* (Baltimore: The Johns Hopkins University Press, 2009), 124. Very helpful here is Willard M. Swartley, *Health, Healing and the Church's Mission: Biblical Perspectives and Moral Priorities* (Downers Grove, IL: InterVarsity Press, 2012).

14. See further Joshua W. Jipp, *Saved by Faith and Hospitality* (Grand Rapids: Eerdmans, 2017), chapter 1.

those who are poor, blind, and oppressed (4:18–19). Luke portrays Jesus as a host who dispenses God's hospitality by sharing meals with strangers, sinners, outsiders, and those on the margins of society. In the ancient world, hospitality to strangers was the means whereby an enemy or outsider was converted into a friend. The "table" was reserved, then, for friends or those with whom one wanted to initiate friendship.[15] Thus, one of the primary ways in which humanity's alienation from God is overcome, within the Gospel of Luke, is through sharing meals with Jesus.

What is surprising to the religious elite about Jesus's eating practices is that his hospitality appears to be indiscriminate and offered toward all people: tax collectors (5:27–32; 19:1–10); a sinful woman (7:36–50); two women (10:38–42); the poor and hungry (9:11–17); his disciples (22:15–20); and the Pharisees (7:39; 11:37–54; 14:1–16). It is no surprise, then, that Israel's leaders consistently grumble and complain about those with whom Jesus shares meals (5:30–32; 15:1–2; 19:6–7). Their immoral lifestyle—or at least lack of serious devotion to the Torah—has disqualified them from participating in the kingdom of God. And yet Luke interprets their joyful participation in his hospitality meals as the enactment of God's recovery of his lost sheep and formerly lost children who have now been reconciled with God (throughout Luke 15).[16]

Thus, Jesus's meals create a context whereby sinners, outcasts, and those on the margins become friends with God and fellow participants in the kingdom of God. It is this reconciliation with God or friendship with God that should result in their common fellowship or union with one another as fellow friends with God and one another. This is seen, for example, when Jesus publicly declares Zacchaeus to be "a son of Abraham" (19:9) and the bent woman a "daughter of Abraham" (13:16); when the father in the parable tells his older son that "we must rejoice" at the restoration of the lost son (15:29–32), and when Jesus exalts the woman's hospitality and her recognition of her need of forgiveness, but then shames Simon the Pharisee for his lack of hospitality and attendant failure to see his need (7:44–50). Luke's sequel to his Gospel, the book of Acts, portrays the early church as a community of friends who celebrate and continue to remember Jesus's hospitality to them. The summary

---

15. Plutarch often refers to the table as having the function of "friendmaking" (e.g., *Quaest. conv.* 1 [612d–e]).

16. See Jesus's little parable of the two debtors, which also functions to interpret hospitality to and with Jesus as a sign of the reconstitution of the sinful woman's relationship with God (Luke 7:36–50). See Joshua W. Jipp, *Divine Visitations and Hospitality to Strangers in Luke-Acts: An Interpretation of the Malta Episode in Acts 28:1–10*, NovTSup 153 (Leiden: Brill, 2012), 175–82.

statements of Acts 2:42–47 and 4:32–35 show the church remembering Jesus by breaking bread with one another (2:42, 46; cf. Luke 22:19). Luke employs the language of philosophical friendship—"all things in common" (2:44; 4:32b), "one heart and soul" (4:32), and "fellowship" (2:42)—to show that the early church is a community of friends comprised of *all* people—rich and poor, Hellenist and Hebrew, man and woman, and soon Jews, and every ethnicity under heaven. The primary point here is that Luke's story presents a correspondence between divine and human hospitality or, stated differently, humanity's restoration with God results in restoration with one another. Friendship with God has as its result the creation of a community of friends. Samuel Wells states the theological dynamic well: "For Jesus, our real problem as human beings is our alienation from God and one another. That is what changes in Jesus. Jesus is the solidarity between us and God that makes those links tangible and visible and permanent and unbreakable."[17]

What is the relevance of Luke's vision of hospitality and friendship for those who are challenged by mental illness? A community of friends is precisely the gift that Christians can share with *all people* that experience deep vulnerability, stigma, and suffering. It would appear that there is a deep correspondence between the fear, exclusion, and stigma experienced by many of the characters in Luke's Gospel and mentally ill persons today. Christian community and friendship provide the possibility for vulnerable persons to experience meaningful relationships, relational wholeness, loyalty and commitment even in the midst of pain and brokenness, and fellow humans who are committed to countering the stigma and exclusion many mentally ill persons experience.[18] John Swinton has made a powerful argument that "Christian friendships based on the friendships of Jesus can be a powerful force for the reclamation of the centrality of the *person* in the process of mental health care."[19] Despite the importance of professional help offered by psychiatry and medicine, a community of friends can provide a focus upon *the person* (instead of the pathology) and thereby enable people "to explore issues of human relationships, personhood, spirituality, value, and community."[20] Just as Jesus and his friendship overturned society's evaluation of tax collectors, women, the poor, and the sick, so the church as a community of friends is able, through its friendship

---

17. Samuel Wells, *A Nazareth Manifesto: Being with God* (Malden, MA: Wiley-Blackwell, 2015), 78–79.

18. John Swinton, *Resurrecting the Person: Friendship and the Care of People with Mental Health Problems* (Nashville: Abingdon, 2000), 35–36.

19. Swinton, *Resurrecting the Person*, 37.

20. Swinton, *Resurrecting the Person*, 37.

Jesus, the Church, and Mental Illness

with the mentally ill and other vulnerable and marginalized peoples, to witness to a new, kingdom-oriented standard of evaluating one another.

One of the common refrains regarding people who struggle with mental illness is the challenge their behavior often presents to their friends and family. How should they interact with their loved one in the hospital? Why does their friend/loved one seem unpredictable and/or resist opportunities for social engagement? Could the erratic behavior of their loved one result in harm? Why does their loved one seem sad, angry, timid, etc., at all the wrong times? The challenges these questions pose to friends and family almost certainly have no real satisfying answers. Persons with mental illness are not problems to be solved but persons who require faithful, loyal, persistent, not easily offended friends who are willing to simply be *with them*.[21] Samuel Wells has argued that the most faithful form of Christian witness is what he describes as "being with" (rather than working for or working with), precisely because God's act in Christ is an act of the restoration of "being with" his people; it is an overcoming of the alienation between God and humans that is fundamentally an act of hospitality that results in friendship.[22] This is a helpful way of conceptualizing the church's engagement of those with mental illness (and those with other forms of vulnerability and suffering). Rather than treating the person as a "problem" that needs to be fixed and needs to find victory or success, the call here is for the church to simply *remain with* those who are challenged with mental illness. The call is an ordinary one of friendship, presence, fellowship, and all of the joys and struggles that characterize friendships with one another.

STIGMAS AND STEREOTYPES

One of the defining features of God's hospitality in Jesus for his people is that this welcome does not correspond to some prior existing social worth or status of the individual.[23] God's welcome is for male and female, Jew and (in Acts at least) gentile, Pharisees and sinners, rich and poor, apostles and outcasts. Luke demonstrates that God's friendship is for all people apart from their social status by frequently raising a negative cultural stereotype only to reject or subvert it. A few examples will suffice. I have written at length about how Paul's shipwreck on Malta plays on the stereotypes of the supposedly exotic

---

21. See further Wells, *Nazareth Manifesto*, 129–30.
22. Wells, *Nazareth Manifesto*, 129–30.
23. Please note that I have argued this previously in chapter 11.

islanders as uncivilized barbarians. Only here does Luke use the language "barbarian" (Acts 28:2, 4), and it seems this is almost certainly his intention to raise the stereotype of the barbarian, the non-Greek, as one who is prone to prey on shipwrecked strangers and who lacks the civilized custom of hospitality.[24] The reader is prepared, then, for an impending *inhospitality* scenario as Paul and his fellow prisoners wreck on the island. But Luke raises this stereotype only to reject it as a poor means of making sense of the Maltese, for Luke pairs "barbarian" together with φιλανθρωπία ("philanthropy"), and this is intentionally jarring for the reader. By way of summary, the Maltese execute hospitality protocols as well as any of the other characters throughout Luke-Acts. They make a fire to warm the prisoners (28:1–2); Publius, the leading man of the island, receives Paul in his home with a friendly and hospitable welcome (28:7–9); and they provide Paul with what he needs for his journey as they grant honors to him (28:9–10).

Luke does something similar, of course, with the so-called parable of the good Samaritan in Luke 10. One aspect of Jesus's genius—to use an insight from John Dominic Crossan—is seen in his forcing the lawyer and reader "to put together two impossible and contradictory words for the same person: 'Samaritan' (10:33) and 'neighbor' (10:36). . . . The story demands that the hearer respond by saying the contradictory, the impossible, the unspeakable."[25] The story packs the punch that it does precisely because the reader struggles to say, "The *Samaritan* was the neighbor to the man," and perhaps even harder, "The *Samaritan* obeyed and fulfilled the commands of the law of Moses."

A third instance of Luke's transformation of stigmas and stereotypes occurs in Luke's portrait of the first gentile convert, the Ethiopian eunuch, for he is both black and a sexual deviant by most ancient standards. The Torah forbids castrated men (those with "crushed testicles") from full participation in the temple (see Lev 21:16–23; Deut 23:1). The prophet Isaiah in fact draws upon the eunuch as a representative for the kinds of outcasts who will be welcomed into God's people when God fulfills his promises (Isa 56:3–8). Eunuchs were frequently portrayed as soft, feminine, and sexually deviant as they did not conform to the masculine stereotypes of virility and strength.[26] But despite Luke's fronting of the man's identity as a eunuch (Acts 8:27, 34, 38, 39), he acti-

---

24. See here Joshua W. Jipp, "Hospitable Barbarians: Luke's Ethnic Reasoning in Acts 28:1–10," *JTS* 68 (2017): 23–45 (chapter 7 in this volume).

25. John Dominic Crossan, *In Parables: The Challenge of the Historical Jesus* (New York: Harper and Row, 1975), 62–63.

26. See further Jipp, *Saved by Faith and Hospitality*, 33.

Jesus, the Church, and Mental Illness

vates none of the stereotypes about eunuchs. Rather, the man is silent, humble, and inquisitive as he reads Isaiah and seeks interpretive help from Philip. He welcomes Philip's interpretation and pursues baptism and goes back home rejoicing—a model Lukan character to be sure.

Roman centurions, women, and those with physical disabilities could be examined in detail to see that the previous three examples are not accidental but instead point to a fundamental feature of Luke-Acts, namely, the worthlessness of stigmatizing stereotypes for making sense of human existence. The recipients of divine welcome in Luke-Acts are some of society's most stigmatized (and often vulnerable) persons: sinners, tax collectors, eunuchs, Samaritans, the poor and the hungry, the physically disabled, and barbarians. Jesus is remarkably unconcerned with fear of the stranger, being polluted by a sinner, or conforming to good societal standards and cultural norms.[27] Amos Yong has suggested that this theme indicates that those on the margins of society are included within God's people as they are so that they can stand "as a testimony to the power of God to save all of us 'normal' folk from our discriminatory attitudes, inhospitable actions, and exclusionary social and political forms of life."[28]

In today's context one of the most stigmatized groups of people are the mentally ill. This stigma is demonstrated in a variety of ways. While some progress seems to have been made regarding the language used to describe people with physical disabilities, the same cannot be said for those who struggle with mental illness.[29] Again, John Swinton describes this dynamic clearly:

> Running alongside the biological and psychological history of people with mental health problems is a form of social experience that is fundamentally degrading, exclusionary, and frequently dehumanizing. When we look into the social experience of people with mental health problems, we discover a level of oppression, prejudice, exclusion, and injustice that is deeply concerning. Negative media images, powerful stigmatizing forces, and exclusion from basic sources of value are just some of the negative experiences

---

27. On Luke-Acts' subversion of popular physiognomic norms, see Mikeal C. Parsons, *Body and Character in Luke and Acts: The Subversion of Physiognomy in Early Christianity* (Grand Rapids: Baker, 2006).

28. Amos Yong, *The Bible, Disability, and the Church: A New Vision of the People of God* (Grand Rapids: Eerdmans, 2011), 69.

29. This point is made well by David Steele, "Crazy Talk: The Language of Mental Illness Stigma," *The Guardian*, September 6, 2012, https://www.theguardian.com/science/brain-flapping/2012/sep/06/crazy-talk-language-mental-illness-stigma.

that many people experience on a daily basis, simply because they are diagnosed as having a mental health problem.[30]

When persons in one's own local church are no longer identified as people but as a pathology (i.e., a crazy person, a loon, a schizoid, etc.), when the illness of a person becomes a source of fear or an opportunity for anxiety that one might be contaminated, then their primary identity as one who has received God's welcoming hospitality is sadly lost. One of the primary insights from those who work within disability studies is how the broader culture's perpetuation of using mental disorders as insults or for the purpose of humor directly and negatively influences engagement with persons who are actually suffering from these disorders.[31] Amy Simpson has detailed the ways in which the church often contributes, with its own unique spiritual twist, to stigmatizing the mentally ill. Some of these include the false narrative that Christians should be happy all the time, the naïve belief that mental illness is always a spiritual and never a medical matter, the desire for churches to be comprised of socially acceptable people, the worry that the mentally ill will create social disruptions, and a theological inability to engage human vulnerabilities.[32]

The subversion and rejection of stigma is dependent upon the previous point regarding hospitality and friendship. Everyone is dependent upon meaningful relationships and friendships for a sense of meaning, joy, and self-worth, but depriving those with mental illness of these friendships as a result of others' judgment and fear will inevitably lead to a deep loss of their sense of personhood.[33] Again, the call here is something that is as ordinary as it is essential and distinctly Christian, namely, the necessity for the church to engage in regular, ordinary friendships with one another and to reject stereotypes that unduly prejudice one's perceptions of the other. For persons with mental health challenges, the illnesses can too easily turn into labels that define people as sick or worse if people are not vigilant in *seeing* and *befriending* the actual person.[34] Part of the church's mission, then, is to become friends and allies who stand in solidarity with persons with mental health challenges by rejecting societal stereotypes of individuals labeled as dangerous, risky, or

---

30. Swinton, *Resurrecting the Person*, 10.
31. See here the important work of Nancy Eiesland, *The Disabled God: Toward a Liberatory Theology of Disability* (Nashville: Abingdon, 1994).
32. Simpson, *Troubled Minds*, 147–65.
33. Swinton, *Resurrecting the Person*, 95.
34. Swinton, *Resurrecting the Person*, 27.

pollutants. Of course, this stems from one's own recognition that they too are desperately in need of Christ's welcome and a recognition of their own human vulnerability.

In *Saved by Faith and Hospitality* I voiced my agreement with Heather Vacek's powerful conclusion by suggesting that the church can only continue the same mission of Jesus and the early church in Luke-Acts by rejecting its obsession with the so-called normal, with its safe and exclusive boundaries that are privileged over the witness that the church is a stigmatized community.[35] Vacek states the matter this way:

> To be a stigmatized people: to resist social norms contrary to Christian belief and practice, to eat with outcasts and tax collectors, with sinners, and with those who fail, and to remember that Christian identity is defined by baptism into the body of Christ, not by adherence (or lack of adherence) to social norms.... Being damned by association should be an expected part of Christian witness, but it is a reality difficult to embrace in a society, like modern America, where a safer, more sanitized Christian belief and practice are deemed normative.[36]

If today's churches are filled only with those whom broader society sees as safe and normal, then in what way are churches continuing the legacy of Jesus and the church in Luke-Acts? Or do churches unwittingly testify that God's welcome and friendship come only to those who are socially acceptable? Luke-Acts demands reflection upon those who are vulnerable and stigmatized in society as well as the broader cultural narratives that result in social exclusion and dehumanizing experiences for these persons. And it demands reflection upon how to provide friendship, welcome, and care for all persons within the church. One rather obvious way to do this, in addition to simply being ready and prepared for new friendships with people outside of one's social circle, is to host different kinds of support groups (or partner with other churches who already are doing this) that provide help for those with mental illnesses. Pastors and leaders (and seminary professors) might do just a little work to educate themselves on the challenges of mental illness and seek to speak, preach, and pray for one another in ways that deconstruct rather than

---

35. Jipp, *Saved by Faith and Hospitality*, 40. On the social construction of the codes and the norms of respectability as it pertains to bodies, see Iris Marion Young, *Justice and the Politics of Difference* (Princeton: Princeton University Press, 1990), 136–41.

36. Vacek, *Madness*, 168–69.

PART THREE: GOD'S ACTS FOR CHRISTIANS

reaffirm fears.[37] Further reflection could also be done upon whether today's ministries empower all people to serve and share their gifts rather than cause them to remain in a perpetual guest-like position.

God's Presence in Suffering and Weakness

The experience of suffering can quickly make one question God's presence and goodness within their life, but the Scriptures witness to the reality that God is present within one's suffering and weakness, that God often reveals himself through human vulnerability, and that God accomplishes his mission through suffering. The witness of the Scriptures with respect to human suffering is complex, and this point should *not* be taken to imply that suffering or mental illness is an inherent good or something to be sought after. But one should consider how the Scriptures often deconstruct people's notions of power, masculinity, and normalcy as privileged goods. God is often portrayed as acting and working within situations of human vulnerability. This theme is present throughout the Scriptures but most emphatically declared by Paul's surprising claims that God's power is revealed in the cross of Christ and in his bodily suffering: "I will most gladly boast all the more about my weaknesses, so that Christ's power may reside in me. So I take pleasure in weaknesses, insults, hardships, persecutions, and in difficulties, for the sake of Christ. For when I am weak, then I am strong" (2 Cor 12:9–10). But the theme is present in the Lukan writings as well. For example, in Jesus's experience of his deepest moments of suffering and vulnerability, he forgives his executioners (Luke 23:34), enacts salvation for one of the criminals on the cross (23:39–43), and entrusts himself to his Father with his last breath (23:46). Paul, as an *incarcerated prisoner* on his voyage to Rome, offers faithful proclamations of the gospel before his fellow Jews and Roman governors (Acts 22–26) and is instrumental in saving his fellow crew when they shipwreck on the way to Rome (27:1–28:10).

There are a variety of lessons here for ways in which one can learn from suffering and vulnerability, but the ways God works within suffering are particularly important. First, one's own personal experiences of suffering can enable them to sympathize with others. This is rooted in the remarkable reality that God himself has entered into human suffering through the Son of God who himself "learned obedience from the things he suffered" (Heb 5:8). Christians

---

37. According to Amy Simpson, of the pastors surveyed, only 12.5 percent said that mental illness is discussed in an open manner within their churches (*Troubled Minds*, 142).

have the call to sympathize with the pain of others and this is a participation in the divine compassion of the Messiah who had compassion on the sick and the weak.[38] Second, God's decision to work through suffering and weakness testifies that vulnerability does not detract from personhood. *Everyone* is beset by the vulnerabilities and weaknesses that characterize human existence, and these can function as reminders that everyone is needy but that they can live into their full personhood when they embrace and acknowledge their vulnerabilities and need for one another. This embrace can expose idolatrous attempts to obtain false security through "the cult of normalcy" and the rejection of one's own limitations. Thomas Reynolds says it this way: "Vulnerability is a positive feature of every human life, a life that becomes its own through dependency upon others in relationships of belonging. . . . When we engage another human being at various levels of weakness and disability we confront in ourselves something of their weakness and need."[39]

The goal here has not been to offer specific and concrete prescriptions for what the church *should do* but rather to provide some theological resources from Jesus and the early church that can help people think about the church's mandate to care for those challenged by mental illness. Remembering Jesus as healer challenges the church to continue the healing ministry of Jesus through offering compassionate care and services that lead to human flourishing. The church as a context for friendship and hospitality with one another offers the possibility of it being a place that celebrates difference and cares for one another in the midst of suffering and vulnerability. The remembrance of Jesus and the early church as those who rejected the fears of cultural stigmas and stereotypes can challenge the church to reject obsessions with normalcy and misguided notions of purity and, instead, look for means to include those that broader society has stigmatized.[40] And the realization that God is present and works within suffering can encourage people to find their joy and full personhood in the recognition of mutual dependence upon one another even in the midst of vulnerabilities.

---

38. L. Johnson, *Revelatory Body*, 126–29.

39. Thomas E. Reynolds, *Vulnerable Communion: A Theology of Disability and Hospitality* (Grand Rapids: Brazos, 2008), 117–18.

40. See here Richard Beck, *Unclean: Meditations on Purity, Hospitality, and Mortality* (Eugene, OR: Cascade, 2011).

13

Philanthropy, Hospitality, and Friendship

The subject matter of the book of Acts is the living God as revealed. This simple fact means that while Acts provides the reader with a historical explanation for the expansion of the church and its transformation into a multiethnic institution, the text also makes theological, existential, and epistemological demands upon the reader regarding the identity and activity of the living God.[1] Luke's description of the church engaged in worldwide mission, devoted to prayer, sharing possessions, challenging idolatry, and discerning divine activity in human lives and events not only tells us what happened once upon a time but also makes claims upon us about who the living God is, how God is known, and the kinds of people the church of the living God ought to be. If we are reading certain portions of Acts—e.g., Luke's summaries of the church (Acts 2:42–47; 4:32–35; 5:12–16)—then perhaps recognizing these claims will not seem to be too intractable a problem. As the church once devoted itself to prayer, apostolic teaching, fellowship, and sharing possessions so the church today must consider how to respond to the living God.

But what are we to think of Acts 27:1–28:10? This *lengthy* stretch of text narrates how Paul the prisoner was transported by ship from Caesarea to Rome, experienced shipwreck, and landed on Malta before finally arriving in Rome. The text makes for enjoyable reading: Paul surprisingly experiences the kindness of a Roman centurion; he provides prophetic insight from God that proves instrumental in saving the lives of all on board the ship when they

---

1. I have argued this point more fully in Joshua W. Jipp, "The Beginnings of a Theology of Luke-Acts: Divine Activity and Human Response," *JTI* 8 (2014): 23–44 (chapter 10 in this volume). See also C. Kavin Rowe, *World Upside Down: Reading Acts in the Graeco-Roman Age* (Oxford: Oxford University Press, 2009), 156–76.

experience shipwreck; he also provides a Eucharist-like meal, which encourages everyone on board; after the shipwreck he experiences more kindness from the barbarians on Malta; he is bit by a snake but is unharmed; and he and the Maltese share gifts with each other. This is an interesting story with some exotic encounters between Paul and strangers, undoubtedly, but does this text actually reveal something about God and the identity or character of the church to us? Does it really make a theological and existential claim upon our lives and provide meaning for how the church of God is to live today? Answering these questions requires that we explore first the literary and cultural context of Paul's sea voyage in a bit more detail and then, secondly, Paul's relationships and interactions with those who do not belong to the Christian movement.

We will see that Luke provides his readers with a final and memorable depiction of Paul's positive interaction with gentiles. The relationship between Paul and the gentiles is characterized by mutual displays of philanthropy, hospitality, and friendship. This shared hospitality between strangers continues the ministry of Jesus as described in the Gospel of Luke, provides a fitting narrative representation of Paul's final words regarding the receptivity of the gentiles to God's salvation (Acts 28:28), and calls the contemporary church to place itself in the position of guest and host with outsiders today.

The Literary and Cultural Context of Paul's Sea Voyage

Three literary and cultural observations about Paul's sea voyage will aid our interpretation of the text. Perhaps the most striking element of Luke's narration of Paul's sea voyage is its length—sixty verses in our Bibles devoted to showing how Paul was transferred from Caesarea to Rome (Acts 27:1–28:16). Travel and journeying are spoken of repeatedly throughout the book of Acts, but Luke usually avoids lengthy and technical descriptions about how the early Christian missionaries moved about from place to place.[2] Further, at this point in the narrative the reader is not expecting such a lengthy sea voyage; rather, the reader has been anticipating Paul's trial in Rome before Caesar at least since Acts 19:21 ("after I have been there [Jerusalem] it is necessary for me to see Rome"). Thus, the length of the scene and its delaying effect suggest that

---

2. On the importance of travel as a theme in Acts, see Loveday C. A. Alexander, *Acts in Its Literary Context: A Classicist Looks at the Acts of the Apostles* (New York: T&T Clark, 2007), chapters 4 and 5.

the episode bears some special importance for Luke that goes beyond *merely* providing historical information about how Paul arrived in Rome.

At this point in the narrative, when Paul the prisoner undergoes his voyage to Rome, he has had no missionary interactions with gentiles since his strengthening of the Ephesian elders in Acts 20:17–35. The apostle to the gentiles has, rather, been occupied (from Acts 21:18 until 26:32) in giving forensic speeches and defending his orthodoxy with respect to Jewish customs, beliefs, and Scriptures (a theme that will find some closure in the ending of Acts). Paul has made no gentile converts during the period of his imprisonment, and this is a marked shift in Luke's characterization of Paul. The reader knows that one of Luke's concerns is to narrate how God's salvation goes forth to the gentiles, and Paul plays the premier role in demonstrating how this takes place. Thus, in Acts 27:1–28:10 Paul reenters a gentile setting (i.e., the Mediterranean Sea) and encounters gentile characters.[3] It will not be surprising if one of Luke's agendas is to tell us something of lasting significance about Paul's relationship with the gentile peoples.

Finally, we should be aware that sea voyages, storms, shipwrecks, and subsequent encounters with exotic peoples were standard fare for Greek, Hellenistic, and Roman authors. Homer's *Odyssey*, Vergil's *Aeneid*, and numerous Greek novels employ sea voyages not only for the dramatic entertainment they provide but also as a means of providing a lasting impression of the hero's character and identity. Sea voyages and shipwrecks provide the author with an opportunity to demonstrate the hero's strength, character, and destiny and to leave a memorable portrait of the hero's identity.[4]

These three literary and contextual features of Paul's sea voyage position the reader to expect that Luke will provide significant information regarding Paul's identity and his encounter with non-Jewish peoples. When we hear Paul's final words in Acts—"God's salvation has been sent to the gentiles, they also will listen" (28:28b)—Luke may intend us to agree with Paul's declaration based, in part, on his encounters with gentiles in Acts 27:1–28:10. But when we turn to Paul's sea voyage, what do we find?

---

3. See further Daniel Marguerat, *The First Christian Historian: Writing the "Acts of the Apostles,"* trans. Ken McKinney, George J. Lauhery, and Richard Bauckham, SNTSMS 121 (Cambridge: Cambridge University Press, 2002), 217.

4. Especially helpful here is Vernon K. Robbins, "By Land and by Sea: The We-Passages and Ancient Sea-Voyages," in *Sea Voyages and Beyond: Emerging Strategies in Socio-Rhetorical Interpretation*, Emory Studies in Early Christianity 14 (Blandford Forum, UK: Deo, 2010), 47–81; Cf. Marguerat, *First Christian Historian*, 231–56.

Hospitality, Philanthropy, and Friendship Between Paul and the Gentiles

Three distinct interactions between Paul and gentiles provide a window into the lasting impression of Paul that Luke wishes to leave his readers.[5] The first named character Paul encounters when he is taken on board the ship is "Julius a Roman centurion of the Augustan Cohort" (27:1). Mention of a Roman military figure entrusted with transporting prisoners *may have* activated the stereotypes of the brave soldier and faithful citizen, but nearer at hand may have been the stereotypes of the Roman soldier as violent, brutish, and willing to use force to keep the prisoners in order—as the soldiers are, for example, more than ready to suggest the use of violence in order to prevent the prisoners from escaping when the ship wrecks (27:43; cf. Luke 23:11).[6] But Luke's characterization of the centurion is glowingly positive rather than violent. To be sure, Luke says, "Julius demonstrated philanthropy to Paul by allowing him to be cared for by his friends" (27:3). Not violent, brutish, or greedy, the military man demonstrates the prized virtue of *philanthropia*. Philanthropy—often translated as kindness, love for humanity, or generosity—was considered to be one of the premier Hellenistic virtues and was often associated with the making and maintenance of friendships through acts of mercy, kindness, hospitality, and clemency. To show philanthropy was the mark of the educated, virtuous, and civilized person such that the term was often applied to rulers who showed philanthropy through the provision of benefactions to their subjects.[7] Later the centurion shows more kindness to Paul when he saves Paul's life by disrupting the plan of the soldiers who want to kill all the prisoners when the ship wrecks on Malta (27:43). The motivation for the centurion's kindness to Paul is left unexplained, and yet this display of a military man's philanthropy toward Paul the vulnerable prisoner "unsettle[s] the authorial audience's expectations" as it casts this gentile man as favorable to Paul and as performing acts of mercy toward the vulnerable.[8]

---

5. For a detailed discussion of what follows, see Joshua W. Jipp, *Divine Visitations and Hospitality to Strangers: An Interpretation of the Malta Episode in Acts 28:1–10*, NovTSup 153 (Leiden: Brill, 2013).

6. On stereotypes of soldiers and their relevance for understanding Luke's positive depictions of the Roman centurions, see Laurie Brink, *Soldiers in Luke-Acts: Engaging, Contradicting, and Transcending the Stereotypes*, WUNT 2/362 (Tübingen: Mohr Siebeck, 2014).

7. See further, Ceslas Spicq, "La philanthropie hellénistique, vertu divine et royale (à propos de Tit 3:4)," *Studia Theologica* 12 (1958): 169–91; Mikeal C. Parsons, *Acts*, Paideia Commentaries on the New Testament (Grand Rapids: Baker Academic, 2008), 367–70.

8. Brink, *Soldiers in Luke-Acts*, 124.

But Paul not only *receives* the philanthropic kindness from Julius, Paul is also a prophetic and divine agent who secures the salvation of all of his shipmates. On three occasions, Luke portrays Paul as offering prophecies, exhortations, and encouragements that provide safety to those on board the ship. He frequently warns the leaders of the ship to refrain from immediate continuation of the journey due to the dangerous sailing conditions (27:9-11), and his prophecy comes to fruition when the typhoon threatens to destroy the ship (27:18-20). Later, after "all hope that we should be saved was taken away" (27:20), Paul receives a message from God's angel that God will see to it that Paul makes it safely to Rome and that God "will freely give to [Paul] all those sailing with [him]" (27:24b). Paul is God's prophetic instrument for the salvation of his shipmates, and as God's prophet Paul encourages everyone on board with the angel's message (27:25-26). When some of the ship's crew tries to escape due to fear that the ship would break apart against the rocks, Paul is able to advise the centurion to keep the soldiers on board: "Unless these men stay in the ship, you cannot be saved" (27:31). As Richard Pervo notes, "Paul is the cause of their deliverance and thus their savior."[9] On six occasions Luke uses forms of "to save" in order to refer to the salvation or safety of the shipmates and Paul (27:20, 31, 34, 43, 44; 28:1),[10] and given that one of Luke's primary themes is God's salvation for all people, it may be that Luke intends the reader to view God's rescue of the crew through Paul as a metaphor for the salvation of the gentiles.[11]

Paul's mediation of salvation for his shipmates is portrayed in a striking manner when Paul initiates a meal with his shipmates and takes the lead as host (27:33-38). Twice Paul exhorts everyone to "share in the nourishment" of the meal together (27:33, 34). Paul's actions whereby "he took bread, and giving thanks to God in the presence of everyone, he broke it and began to eat" (27:35) clearly mimics Jesus's sharing of meals with all people in the Gospel of Luke (e.g., Luke 9:11-17; 22:14-23; 24:28-35). Just as Jesus's meals were marked by their inclusive character, so is the meal between Paul and his shipmates characterized by the involvement of "everyone" on board the ship (see 27:33, 35, 36, and 37). Luke is clear about the purpose of this meal: "It exists for your salvation" (27:34b). The meal literally does provide salvation in that it provides the hungry crew with the needed strength to endure the impending loss of

---

9. Richard I. Pervo, *Acts*, Hermeneia: A Critical and Historical Commentary on the Bible (Minneapolis: Fortress, 2009), 662.

10. See the fine article by Susan M. Praeder, "Acts 27:1-28:16: Sea Voyages in Ancient Literature and the Theology of Luke-Acts," *CBQ* 46 (1984): 683-706.

11. On the theme of salvation in Luke-Acts, see Luke 1:47, 69, 71; 2:11, 30; 3:4-6; 6:9; 7:50; 8:12, 36, 48, 50; Acts 2:21, 40, 47; 4:9, 12; 11:14; 13:47; 14:9; 15:1, 11; 16:30, 31; 28:28.

Philanthropy, Hospitality, and Friendship

their ship, but Luke may intend his readers to view the meal as mediating divine salvation whereby the prisoners are saved by sharing in divine hospitality. The echoes of Jesus's table fellowship with sinners in the Gospel of Luke, the reference to "all 276 souls on the ship" (27:37)—which reminds the reader of earlier scenes in Acts where Luke had recounted the number of "souls" saved (2:41; 4:4)—and the repeated references to salvation throughout the sea voyage suggest that "Paul allows the Gentiles to taste God's salvation through his extension of hospitality, and thereby Luke symbolically portrays the Gentiles as being incorporated into God's people."[12]

Paul's interaction with non-Jewish peoples continues in Acts 28:1–10 where he receives another remarkable display of philanthropy and hospitality from the Maltese islanders. Paul's prophecy is fulfilled as the ship breaks apart and the crew lands on Malta (27:26; 27:44–28:1). Paul, of course, is a total stranger to the Maltese, and so this is a potentially dangerous situation. Luke refers to the Maltese as "barbarians" (28:2, 4) and thereby activates widespread cultural connotations that associated barbarians with *inhospitality* toward shipwrecked strangers. Odysseus, for example, when encountering a new land and people in his voyages often spoke the phrase, "Alas, to the land of what mortals have I now come? Are they insolent, wild, and unjust? Or are they hospitable to strangers and fear the gods in their thoughts?" (Homer, *Od.* 6.119–121).[13] Luke activates an impending *inhospitality* scenario, however, only to overturn it: "The barbarians showed us no small philanthropy" through their provision of a fire to keep the prisoners warm (28:2). Further, their kindness to the prisoners is, according to prominent Hellenistic moralists, the height of virtue since shipwrecked strangers have no means to reciprocate for hospitality received. Once again, the philanthropy of the barbarians toward the needy and vulnerable demonstrates that the Maltese belong to the same Lukan exemplars of hospitality such as Zacchaeus (Luke 19:1–10), Cornelius (Acts 10:1–11:18), and Lydia (Acts 16:11–15).[14]

After Paul's triumphal incident with the viper reveals that he is no ordinary prisoner but rather bears the powerful presence of God (28:3–6), Publius (the first man of Malta) wisely shows hospitality to Paul and his companions: "He welcomed us and for three days extended friendly hospitality to us" (28:7b).

12. Jipp, *Divine Visitations*, 256.
13. For further examples, see Jipp, *Divine Visitations*, 39–44, 257–259.
14. For a wealth of information on hospitality in Luke-Acts and the broader ancient Mediterranean world, see Andrew Arterbury, *Entertaining Angels: Early Christian Hospitality in Its Mediterranean Setting*, New Testament Monographs 8 (Sheffield: Sheffield Phoenix, 2005).

This display of hospitality and friendship to Paul elicits Paul's Jesus-like healing of Publius's father (28:8) and the healing of all the sick on the island (28:9). Luke's narration of these healings recalls Jesus's healing of Peter's mother-in-law (Luke 4:38–39) and his initial healing ministry in Capernaum (Luke 4:40–41) and suggests that Jesus's ministry is continuing to spread to the ends of the earth.

The episode concludes with the Maltese cementing their relationship with Paul: "They bestowed many honors upon us, and when we were about to sail, they put on board all the provisions that we needed" (28:10). The Maltese "barbarians" are anything but uncivilized or ignorant of the ways of hospitality toward strangers, for they reflect the attributes of ideal hosts by providing a safe conveyance for the next stage of their guest's journey. Luke may, in fact, intend for his readers to view the Maltese as eliciting a formalized guest-friendship with Paul through their hospitality. When two distinct ethnic parties engage in a mutual back-and-forth of hospitality, gifts, and friendship, it was often seen as creating a permanent, binding relationship that is on par with non-biological kinship.[15] The Maltese barbarians, then, through their *continued* enactments of hospitality appear to have initiated a binding kinship-like relationship with Paul.

Lessons for the Contemporary Church

When Paul claims that God's salvation has gone forth to the gentiles who will provide a listening and receptive audience (28:28), the examples of Julius the Roman centurion, the shared meal between Paul and his shipmates, and the hospitable Maltese barbarians provide good reason for readers to expect that the legacy and mission of Paul will continue even after his imprisonment and death. Philanthropy, shared hospitality, and friendship have been on abundant display between these gentile characters and Paul throughout his journey to Rome. The sea voyage, then, provides both a memorable glimpse of Paul's character and identity as one who was open to fresh encounters with all peoples and, surprisingly, a lasting impression of gentiles as receptive, friendly, and hospitable.

Today when we read Acts 27:1–28:10 as Christian Scripture, we are challenged to bestow (as hospitable hosts) and receive (as receptive guests) the

---

15. On the relevance of the custom of ritualized friendship (guest-friendship) for understanding the book of Acts, particularly the Peter-Cornelius episode, see Walter T. Wilson, "Urban Legends: Acts 10:1–11:18 and the Strategies of Greco-Roman Foundation Narratives," *JBL* 20 (2001): 77–99.

Philanthropy, Hospitality, and Friendship

kind of hospitality and kindness that would result in the creation of friendship and kinship relations.[16] In this text, the gifts of God—table fellowship, the salvation/safety of the shipmates, and healing—are not hoarded or held back as the exclusive property of Paul but are shared liberally and freely with those not belonging to Paul's own kinship network. They are, furthermore, shared without requiring or asking for a response.

Congregations who would continue to embody the same message and values should reflect upon where and how their gifts and resources may be put to use in service of the larger world. Paul demonstrates no hesitation in receiving kindness from a Roman military man, happily and freely shares a meal with prisoners, and shows no fear to stay in Publius's home and receive his hospitality. Thus, Luke leaves his readers with a portrait of Paul as entering into host and guest relationships with outsiders as a means of extending God's salvation to all people. Luke seems, in fact, to make a point of invoking cultural stereotypes (of Roman centurions, prisoners, and barbarians) only to overturn them—namely, to show that these are the people to whom God's salvation has and will extend and that they are not only worthy of receiving but are supremely capable of practicing and initiating friendship, hospitality, and philanthropy. As we seek to hear and be shaped by God's word in Acts 27–28, we would do well to reflect upon whether we are intentionally seeking opportunities to bestow divine hospitality and create friendship relationships with so-called outsiders. Perhaps we would do well to reflect upon whether soldiers, prisoners, and the ethnically "other" *still* represent some of the same cultural stereotypes needing to be overturned. Congregations that would take seriously the message of Acts 27–28 would, however, not *only* reflect upon how and to whom they should dispense hospitality but would also seek ways in which they might receive, learn, and experience the gifts from others who are not part of their friendship-kinship network.

---

16. Thankfully, there is now a wealth of literature devoted to recovering the Christian tradition of hospitality to strangers. The most helpful and accessible work is Christine Pohl, *Making Room: Recovering Hospitality as a Christian Tradition* (Grand Rapids: Eerdmans, 1990).

14

The Economics of Jesus in the Context of the Roman Empire and Israel's "Sacred Economy"

Jesus (in the Gospel of Luke) and his followers (in the Acts of the Apostles) represent a powerful challenge to the ancient world's economic practices, that is, its *"ordering of things, persons, and patterns of exchange."*[1] While many scholars have made valuable contributions to this topic, in this chapter I want to show how Jesus's economic practices and teachings are an extension and interpretation of Israel's "sacred economy" as seen especially in the Torah and the Prophets. In what follows, I set forth, based on Israel's Scriptures—especially the Torah and the Prophets—Israel's foundational economic teachings and then show how Jesus drew upon these teachings to offer an economic way of life that stands in contrast to the standard practices of the ancient Roman economy.

Israel's Sacred Economy

By the time of Jesus and the earliest church, the land of Israel had been occupied for centuries (except for a brief moment during the Hasmonean dynasty) by foreign empires who, despite some diversity in their methods, can be characterized as extractive regimes that exploited those living in Judea and Galilee. But while I will have occasion to look at some of the characteristics of these regimes, including their corruption, I want now to primarily examine

---

1. The phrase is from Stephen C. Barton, "Money Matters: Economic Relations and the Transformation of Value in Early Christianity," in *Engaging Economics: New Testament Scenarios and Early Christian Reception*, ed. Bruce W. Longenecker and Kelly D. Liebengood (Grand Rapids: Eerdmans, 2009), 37–59, here 39.

the Scriptures of Israel and God's sacred economy for his covenant people as set forth in the Torah.[2]

God's Promise and Pharaoh's Oppression

One of the central threads of the Torah is God's promise to give Israel a sacred land and the regulations for life in that land.[3] Beginning with Abraham and then the ensuing ancestors of Israel, the land is God's promised gift to his covenant people (Gen 12:1–4; 15:16–21; 26:2–3; 28:13–15). As the reader of the Torah awaits God's fulfillment of his promise to the patriarchs for land (something never narrated in the Pentateuch itself!),[4] the reader learns that God's promise of land is accompanied by lengthy blocks of rules and regulations for Israel's impending life in the land—a life that is to be marked by a harmonious relationship between Israel and God *and* just and peaceful relationships with their fellow humans (e.g., Exod 21–31; Lev 1–7; 11–26; Deut 4–30).

Before we look at the Torah's regulation of Israel's sacred economy, we should remind ourselves that an extremely exploitative and economically extractive ruler stands in God's way of bringing Israel into the land. We first encounter Pharaoh's extractive economic policies when during a severe famine the ruler acquires all of the land of Egypt as his sole possession (except that belonging to the priests). Due to the famine the people appeal to Pharaoh: "There is nothing left for our lord except our bodies and our land.... Buy us and our land in exchange for food. Then we with our land will become Pharaoh's slaves" (Gen 47:18–19). The narrator's note is chilling: "In this way, Joseph acquired all the land in Egypt for Pharaoh, because every Egyptian sold his field since the famine was so severe for them. *The land became Pharaoh's*" (Gen 47:20). As a result, the narrator notes that from thenceforth the Egyptians are required to give one-fifth of their produce to Pharaoh every year (Gen 47:24, 26). So it is no great surprise that later Joseph's family and their descendants find themselves under the exploitative rule of another Egyptian Pharaoh whose acquisitiveness and excessive greed leads to the enslavement of the Israelite people and their task of building "supply cities"

---

2. My use of the language "sacred economy" has been influenced by the important work of Roland Boer, *The Sacred Economy of Ancient Israel*, Library of Ancient Israel (Louisville: Westminster John Knox, 2015).

3. On the role of the land in the OT, see especially N. C. Habel, *The Land Is Mine: Six Biblical Land Ideologies*, OBT (Minneapolis: Augsburg Fortress, 1995); Walter Brueggemann, *The Land: Place as Gift, Promise and Challenge in Biblical Faith*, OBT (Philadelphia: Fortress, 1977).

4. On the lack of fulfillment of this theme in the Pentateuch as one of its driving themes, see David J. A. Clines, *The Theme of the Pentateuch*, 2nd ed. (Sheffield: Sheffield Academic, 1997).

PART THREE: GOD'S ACTS FOR CHRISTIANS

to store Pharaoh's agricultural surplus (Exod 1:8–14). Walter Brueggemann notes that the narrative depicts "a kind of restless acquisitiveness that has no restraint at all but that simply must have more, no matter what."[5] This greed and excessive desire to acquire is at the expense of human life, and the narrator emphasizes the brutality of the work imposed upon the Israelites: "So the Egyptians assigned taskmasters over the Israelites *to oppress them with forced labor*" (Exod 1:11); "But the more *they oppressed them*, the more they multiplied" (1:12a); "They worked the Israelites *ruthlessly* (1:13); they "made their *lives bitter with difficult labor . . .* and they *ruthlessly imposed* all this work on them" (1:14). God's rescue of Israel, then, stems from both his attention to the Israelites' groaning "because of their difficult labor" (stated twice in Exod 2:23–25) *and* God's remembrance of the covenant he made with Israel's ancestors—a covenant that has centered upon the promise of land. Thus, one can read the exodus story as God's judgment of an economic regime that was marked by greed, excessive desire for acquisition, and exploitation of human life and the beginning, or at least a new start, of his inauguration of a new kind of economy that resists the exploitative and extractive trappings of imperial economies.[6] Christopher Wright says it like this: "So, the paramount salvation event in the whole Old Testament scripture and history, the exodus, has economic oppression as one of its key motivational triggers, and economic freedom as one of its primary intentional objectives. Economics is written into the very fabric of Israel's redemption story."[7]

God's Land and Torah's Instruction

I want to note six characteristics of Israel's economy that indicate how it is intended to stimulate Israel toward love for God and to embody a just, peaceful, and flourishing society for all the covenant people.

1. *Since the land is God's unconditioned gift to Israel, God's people are to trust God for their daily provision and not be marked by hoarding and greedy desire.*[8] Israel's journeys in the wilderness provide an opportunity for them to learn that God is their divine host who provides for their needs (e.g., Pss 78:24–38; 105:40; Neh 9:15). He is the one who "rains down bread from heaven for you" (Exod 16:4), who gives them quail to eat (16:13) and water from the rock (17:1–

---

5. Walter Brueggemann, *Money and Possessions*, Interpretation: Resources for the Use of Scripture in the Church (Louisville: Westminster John Knox, 2016), 20.

6. Similarly, see Brueggemann, *Money and Possessions*, 20–21.

7. Christopher J. H. Wright, *Old Testament Ethics for the People of God* (Downers Grove, IL: IVP Academic, 2004), 136.

8. See further Patrick D. Miller Jr., "The Gift of God: The Deuteronomic Theology of the Land," *Int* 23 (1969): 454–65.

6). God's provision of the manna is marked by the miraculous result that those who "gathered much had no surplus and those who gathered little had no shortage" (16:16–18). Further, those who disobeyed Moses's command about storing up the food for the next day found that it became rotten and filled with worms (16:19–21). It would seem apparent that God is preparing his people for a new kind of economic system, one that operates according to divine gift and rejects the hoarding acquisitiveness of Pharaoh.

2. *The second table of the Ten Commandments is ordered against a life focused on pursuing wealth and possessions.* This is most evident in the final commandment: "Do not covet your neighbor's house. Do not covet your neighbor's wife, his male or female slave, his ox or donkey, *or anything that belongs to your neighbor*" (Exod 20:17). The regulations of the Torah embody this "love of neighbor" ethic in its prohibitions against excessive acquisitiveness. The book of Deuteronomy perhaps best exemplifies the dangers of forgetting God as the divine gift-giver and the turn toward greed and acquisition. Moses warns, for example, that Israel must be careful lest they forget God once they enter the land and experience the material goods of cisterns, vineyards, and olive groves (Deut 6:10–15). Again, "When you eat and are full, and build beautiful houses to live in, and your herds and flocks grow large, and your silver and gold multiply, and everything else you have increases, be careful that your heart doesn't become proud and you forget the Lord your God who brought you out of the land of Egypt, out of the place of slavery" (Deut 8:12–14). Once Israel forgets God as the divine gift-giver, their sense of economic self-sufficiency will invariably lead to the same greedy economic exploitation of others.

3. *Financial dealings are necessary but they must not be guided by profiteering from the poverty of a fellow neighbor.* For example, Moses states that moneylenders should not act like moneylenders when they give loans. They are not to charge interest to the poor person (Exod 22:25). Further, if they take a neighbor's clothing as collateral, the creditor must give it back to the debtor before sunset (22:26–27). One wonders whether this is simply a veiled way of telling the creditor not to take collateral from a poor person. The Israelites must realize that economic transactions *always* involve the third party—Yahweh. Hence, the creditor should be warned that if the poor person is exploited, and he cries out to God—as the Israelites did when they were oppressed by Pharaoh—then God may respond with judgment against those who oppress the poor, for "I will listen because I am compassionate" (22:27).

4. *One of the primary ways opposing the oppression of the poor is embodied is in God's demand that all Israel love and protect the vulnerable.*[9] For example,

---

9. In more detail, see Joshua W. Jipp, *Divine Visitations and Hospitality to Strangers in*

Moses declares, "You shall not wrong or oppress a resident alien, for you were aliens in the land of Egypt" (22:21). Again, "You shall not oppress an alien; you yourselves know how it feels to be an alien because you were aliens in the land of Egypt" (Exod 23:9). Israel is called upon "to love your neighbor as yourself" (Lev 19:18), but this love extends to the foreigner living among them: "When a foreigner lives with you in your land, you must not oppress him. You must regard the foreigner who lives with you as the native-born among you. You are to love him as yourself, for you were foreigners in the land of Egypt, I am Yahweh your God" (Lev 19:33–34). The contrast with Pharaoh's exploitative and extractive economy that uses and enslaves foreigners in order to secure surplus for himself could hardly be more obvious. In addition to the call to Israel to remember how they were treated by Pharaoh, Israel is also simply told that God loves the stranger: "[God] exercises justice for the fatherless and the widow, and loves the foreigner, and gives him food and clothing. You also must love the foreigner, since you were foreigners in the land of Egypt" (Deut 10:18–19). This fair treatment of the alien means that Israelites must treat them as their neighbors by giving them fair legal verdicts (1:16–17), paying fair wages for work (24:14–15), intentionally leaving behind some of the produce in their fields (Deut 24:19–22; Lev 19:9–10; 23:22), and including them within Israel's feasts and rituals (Deut 16:11–14; Lev 16:29). Similarly, Israel is commanded to give a portion of its agricultural produce (or the money received for payment) as an offering to the Lord, a percentage of which is shared with the materially and socially marginalized: orphans, widows, immigrants, and the Levites (e.g., Deut 14:22–29; 16:11).

    5. *While God is the giver of the land and he gifts the land to Israel as their inheritance, God remains the owner of the land* (cf. Josh 22:19; 2 Chr 7:20; Ps 85:1; Isa 14:2, 25; Jer 2:7; Ezek 36:5; Joel 1:6). Since Israel does not own the land—Yahweh does—they are commanded to engage in periodic debt cancellations.[10] We have seen in earlier posts the precarious nature of the landless and the way in which debt results in the cementing of a strict and virtually permanent economic hierarchy.[11] The commands to engage in debt cancellation is most famously stated in Leviticus 25 where provisions are put in place for those who have been displaced from their property to return to their land. Yahweh

---

Luke-Acts: An Interpretation of the Malta Episode in Acts 28:1–10, NovTSup 153 (Leiden: Brill, 2013), 151–56.

    10. Samuel L. Adams, *Social and Economic Life in Second Temple Judea* (Louisville: Westminster John Knox, 2014), 88–89.

    11. See also Boer, *Sacred Economy of Ancient Israel*, 162.

declares, "The land is not to be permanently sold because it is mine, and you are only foreigners and temporary residents on my land" (Lev 25:23). For this reason, there is to be a seven-year cycle where debts are cancelled (25:8–17) and a fifty-year period where land is restored to those who had fallen on difficult times (25:24–28).[12] Further, if a fellow Israelite cannot provide for himself or cannot make good on a loan, his fellow Israelite is commanded to take care of him and not to charge him any interest on a loan (25:35–37, 39–46). Why? The theological foundation is clear: "I am Yahweh your God, who brought you out of the land of Egypt to give you the land of Canaan and to be your God" (25:38). Similar commands to forgive people from their economic debts are the focus of Deuteronomy 15.[13] The first verse sets the focus: "At the end of every seven years you must cancel debts" (Deut 15:1). Moses commands Israel not to be "hardhearted or tightfisted toward your brother" but "to open your hand to him and freely loan him enough for whatever need he has" (15:8–9). Remarkably the goal of Israel's obedience to God's economy is that "there will be no poor among you" (15:4). Brueggemann forcefully summarizes Israel's economy: "Neighborliness trumps everything! . . . No permanent underclass!"[14]

6. *The Torah stipulates that when Israel enters into the land, their king must devote himself to obeying the Torah and avoid greed and acquisitiveness (Deut 17:14).* This king must not be like the rest of the kings of the nations in terms of acquisitive greed and taking. In fact, four times the text says that the king "must not take"—i.e., he must not take many horses for himself; he must not send others to Egypt to take horses; he must not take many wives; and he must not take very large amounts of silver and gold (17:16–17). Deuteronomy's law of the king is reminiscent of Samuel's rebuke of Israel for asking God for a king.[15] The verb "take" dominates the depiction of the king who will extract people, wealth, and agricultural produce for his own luxury.[16] Samuel prophesies that this king "will *take* your sons, will *take* your daughters, will *take* your best fields, vineyards, and olive orchards, will *take* one-tenth of your grain, will *take* your male and female servants as well as your young men and donkeys,

---

12. See further, Wright, *Old Testament Ethics*, 199–210.

13. See here especially Jeffries M. Hamilton, *Social Justice and Deuteronomy: The Case of Deuteronomy 15*, SBLDS 136 (Atlanta: Scholars Press, 1992).

14. Brueggemann, *Money and Possessions*, 52.

15. See further Jamie A. Grant, *The King as Exemplar: The Function of Deuteronomy's Kingship Law in the Shaping of the Book of Psalms*, Academia Biblica 17 (Atlanta: Society of Biblical Literature Press, 2004), 189–222; Gerald Eddie Gerbrandt, *Kingship according to the Deuteronomistic History*, SBLDS 87 (Atlanta: Scholars Press, 1986), 103–16.

16. Brueggemann, *Money and Possessions*, 62.

and will *take* one-tenth of your flocks" (1 Sam 8:11–18). The similarities to Pharaoh's extractive and exploitative economy are obvious. Instead, the singular command that is given Israel's monarch is that he write out, read, and obey Deuteronomy: "When he is seated on his royal throne, he is to write a copy of this instruction for himself on a scroll in the presence of the Levitical priests. It is to remain with him, and he is to read from it all the days of his life, so that he may learn to fear the Lord his God, to observe all the words of this instruction, and to do these statutes" (Deut 17:18–19). For our purposes, we can justifiably say that he is the one who is tasked with the responsibility of overseeing and implementing Israel's sacred economy. Presumably this is the same kind of royal ruler described in Psalm 72—a ruler who rules with justice, vindicates the poor, has pity on the needy, destroys those who oppress the weak, and whose rule results in prosperity and fertility. While God is depicted as the supreme shepherd who cares for his sheep and ensures their peace and prosperity, the king too is characterized as a good shepherd who provides food and protection for God's people (e.g., 1 Sam 16:11–19; 17:34; 2 Sam 7:8; Jer 23:1–5; Ezek 34).[17]

One of the major themes of the Torah is God's concern that his people implement practices that lead to the well-being and peaceful flourishing of all people within the land. God's presence in the land necessitates that his people remember that he is the divine gift giver and that he owns the land. While the land is Israel's inheritance, they must remember that they are God's guests and tenants on the land. They are dependent upon God for their agricultural provisions and the fertility of the land. Israel's society is, further, to be a place where humans are not exploited and dehumanized into a position of debt bondage through greedy moneylenders, an extractive monarch, or wealthy landowners. The goal of these laws may be summed up in the words of Deuteronomy 15:4: "There will be no poor among you." Of course, Israel's history from its entrance into the land and up until the coming of Jesus did not live up to this ideal.

Israel's Agriculture and the Prophets' Critique

In this section I want to describe both Israel's own corruption of the ideal of Torah's socioeconomic vision for life in the land and some of the challenges God's people faced as the result of living under the rule of foreign powers as providing some critical context for understanding some of the economic problems, questions, and longings experienced by the people of God up until the coming of Jesus of Nazareth.

17. Boer, *Sacred Economy of Ancient Israel*, 64–65.

The Economics of Jesus in the Context of the Roman Empire

Ancient Israel was an agrarian society, and farming, in terms of both animal husbandry and crop production, was necessary for the survival of one's household. Roland Boer describes ancient Israel as oriented toward subsistence survival, by which he means "not merely the day-to-day activities needed to ensure a minimal level of subsistence, but also carefully honed, risk-reducing, and creative forward-looking strategies that sought to ensure long-term survival."[18] Strategies for survival included the diversification of crops and animal species in order to minimize the effects of potential disease, famine, and other disasters as well as planning for some surplus in crop production in case of a low yield in harvest.[19] In other words, planned surplus was not about making a profit as much as it was an attempt to safeguard the survival of one's household in case of disaster.[20] Agricultural production also took place in extended family households and small villages where plots of land were consistently reallocated to individual units (e.g., see Gen 33:19–20; Ruth 4:3; 2 Sam 14:30–31; Jer 12:10). This too was an attempt to ensure survival by minimizing risks such as attacks from outsiders or attempts to take the land by foreigners.[21]

During the monarchy Israel's prophets testify to a situation where a few rich landowners begin to engage in a process of acquisition of the land, a situation that results in the displacement of landless tenants and the impoverishment of subsistence farmers.[22] The prophetic oracles of the eighth-century prophets Amos and Micah indicate a concern that the elites' practice of acquiring the majority of the land is destroying the lives of subsistence farmers. Walter Brueggemann argues that one of the major themes of the Prophets "is the conviction that a predatory economy that permits powerful moneyed interests to prey upon the vulnerable peasant population is unsustainable . . . because the Lord of the covenant will not tolerate such practice . . . [and] because a viable social order cannot endure such exploitative conflict and differential."[23] In the next section we will also see in more detail the ways in which royal regimes colluded with the religious leaders in order to engage in economic extraction of the majority in order to create surplus wealth for the elite. The Prophets condemn the elites for their arrogance and devotion to luxury and self-indulgence (Isa 2:12–16; Amos 6:4–7). Isaiah pronounces woes upon those

---

18. Roland Boer, *Sacred Economy of Ancient Israel*, 54.
19. Adams, *Social and Economic Life*, 84–85.
20. Boer, *Sacred Economy of Ancient Israel*, 66–67.
21. Boer, *Sacred Economy of Ancient Israel*, 71–73.
22. See Martin Hengel, *Property and Riches in the Early Church*, trans. John Bowden (Philadelphia: Fortress, 1974), 12–14.
23. Walter Brueggemann, *Money and Possessions*, 142.

"who add house to house and join field to field until there is no more room and you alone are left in the land" (Isa 5:8). The situation envisaged here is antithetical to God's demands that Israel engage in periodic but consistent debt cancellation so that the land remains in the family (see Lev 25; Deut 15) and warns Israel against exploitation of the poor (Exod 22:22–27; 23:6); instead, now the wealthy landowners give free rein to the greedy acquisition of the land of others, which thereby results in the oppression of the poor. So Micah: "They covet field and seize them, they also take houses. They deprive a man of his home, a person of his inheritance" (Mic 2:2).[24] The wealthy landowners furthermore use unjust and violent means of acquiring people's land and wealth: "For the wealthy of the city are full of violence, and its residents speak lies; the tongues in their mouths are deceitful" (Mic 6:12). They take bribes (Mic 7:3), extract material resources from the poor (Amos 5:10–12), use false balances to oppress the poor (Amos 8:4–8), and prey upon the widows and the orphans (Isa 1:23; 10:1–3).[25]

Foreigners' Control and Economic Extraction

We have noted earlier both the mixed testimony of the OT with respect to the king, namely, the hope that Israel's king would uphold justice and care for the poor by not exalting himself above his fellow Israelites (e.g., Deut 17:14–20; Ps 72), *and* the reality that even Israel's king would engage in economic extraction due to his desire to acquire an army and to support his luxurious mode of life (e.g., 1 Sam 8:11–18; 12:1–25). But the history of Jesus's ancestors was more frequently marked by the difficult experience of navigating the dominance of non-Jewish imperial rule. One of the major difficulties God's people experienced was the way in which these rulers expected their subject peoples to pay taxes and tributes. Samuel Adams describes Judah's experience of Persian rule (558–331 BCE): "To generate revenue, royal officials worked with local elites to harvest indigenous resources and collect taxes. This strategy led to hardship for many and power for the few with close ties to the royal bureaucracy."[26] In other words, the Persian overseers collaborated with a very few elite members of the local ruling class as a means of collecting taxes from

---

24. Boer, *Sacred Economy of Ancient Israel*, 118–21, argues that Micah 2 and Isaiah 5 are directed against the practice of taxing the poor in the form of labor on wealthy estates.

25. Helen Rhee, *Loving the Poor, Saving the Rich: Wealth, Poverty, and Early Christian Formation* (Grand Rapids: Baker, 2012), 28–29.

26. Adams, *Social and Economic Life*, 132.

The Economics of Jesus in the Context of the Roman Empire

the ordinary laborers and peasant farmers. One of the primary functions of debt is "to ensure economic hierarchy" and to "reinforce the hierarchy between landlord and peasant, between palatine or temple estate and laborer."[27] Thus, a consistent feature of Israel's postexilic history is the distinction between the imperial power, the local aristocracy or governing class, and the usually impoverished subsistence-level workers.

The Greek historian Herodotus notes more broadly how the Persian ruler Darius "set up twenty provincial governorships, called satrapies. The several governors were appointed and each nation was assessed for taxes; for administrative purposes neighboring nations were joined in a single unit" (*Hist.* 3.89). Herodotus then provides a detailed list of these twenty provinces and the taxes and tributes expected from each (3.90–94). Persia attempted to walk a fine line of engaging in significant economic extraction through taxes and tributes *and* moderation lest the provinces engage in rebellion.[28] We see Persia walking this fine line with Judah in its allowance and even support of the Judeans to rebuild Jerusalem and the temple. On the one hand, King Artaxerxes puts a halt to its building due to the letter he receives from the enemies of Judah who report to the king: "Let it now be known to the king that if that city is rebuilt and its walls are finished, they will not pay tribute, duty, or land tax, and the royal revenue will suffer" (Ezra 4:13). The enemies of Judah are obviously warning the Persian ruler that should they allow Judah to rebuild their city and temple, they will in turn be paid back with a rebellious province that will refuse to support the empire by paying taxes and tribute. The Persian rulers, however, later reverse this course of action and even support the rebuilding of the temple by providing imperial financing for its rebuilding and returning the sacred vessels that had been confiscated by the Babylonian ruler Nebuchadnezzar (e.g., Ezra 6–7). This so-called imperial benevolence is not what it may seem to many readers, however, for the Persians' gifts to the local Jewish governing class came with the expectations that the priestly temple aristocrats would be loyal in turn to Persia through collecting taxes and tribute for Persia.[29] Much more could be said, but here I want to look at just one text that gives us a picture of the outcome of Persia's economic policies. I quote Nehemiah 5:1–5 in full:

> There was a widespread outcry from the people and their wives against their Jewish countrymen. Some were saying, "We, our sons, and our daughters

---

27. Boer, *Sacred Economy of Ancient Israel*, 162.
28. Adams, *Social and Economic Life*, 133.
29. Brueggemann, *Money and Possessions*, 88.

are numerous. Let us get grain so that we can eat and live." Others were saying, "We are mortgaging our fields, our vineyards, and homes to get grain during the famine." Still others were saying, "We have borrowed money to pay the king's tax on our fields and vineyards. We and our children are just like our countrymen and their children, yet we are subjecting our sons and daughters to slavery. Some of our daughters are already enslaved, but we are powerless because our fields and vineyards belong to others."

The complaint here is brought against the local Jewish officials who are working for Persia and taxing their fellow kin so severely that it is leading to concerns about food supply, the loss of land, and the mortgaging of their own children and property in order to pay the king's tax. Samuel Adams summarizes the situation by noting that "a class of wealthy lenders is taking advantage of the crisis for their own benefit, and they are willing to capitalize on the vulnerability of fellow Judeans by acting as manipulative creditors in the pursuit of land and child labor."[30] Thus, Persia's extraction is creating a situation of debt bondage, which causes Israel to "cry out" just as it did in the time of the exodus for justice (Exod 2:23–25). Nehemiah demands that the wealthy nobles stop this practice of excessive extraction and claims to discontinue the wicked policies of earlier Jewish governors who had profited of their own kin through predatory economic policies (Neh 5:6–15).

While Persian rule over Judea ended with the rise of Alexander the Great, Judea's experience of imperial conquest and taxation did not, as Alexander and then his successors (the Ptolemies and the Seleucids) ruled over Judea until the Hasmonean revolt in 167 BCE. The author of 1 Maccabees describes Alexander as "gathering plunder from many nations" and collecting "a very strong army and conquering provinces, nations, and rulers, and they became his tributaries" (1 Macc 1:3, 4). After his death, his military successors caused their own great "distress over the earth" (1:8)—no doubt a reference to the Hellenistic monarchs' engagement in violent military conquest and economic exploitation of Judea.[31] The monarchs were dependent upon their armies for conquest and expansion, and this in turn required consistent economic exploitation through taxes and plunder of those they conquered. Portier-Young states the dynamic succinctly: "[Conquest] was a primary tool for economic gain, and so fueled the imperial economy."[32] As Rome began to expand its influence and

---

30. Adams, *Social and Economic Life*, 139.
31. Anathea E. Portier-Young, *Apocalypse against Empire: Theologies of Resistance in Early Judaism* (Grand Rapids: Eerdmans, 2011), 49–50.
32. Portier-Young, *Apocalypse against Empire*, 51.

The Economics of Jesus in the Context of the Roman Empire

with its defeat of the Seleucids at the Battle of Magnesia, the Seleucids were forced to pay their own tribute to Rome and in turn taxed Judea even further. The author of 2 Maccabees describes the Seleuc monarch's commission of a certain Heliodorus who is charged with the removal of wealth from the temple treasure to this end (2 Macc 3:4–39). 1 Maccabees describes a situation where the Seleucid king Antiochus IV dispatches a collector of tribute to Jerusalem who then plunders the city (1 Macc. 1:29–32), and no doubt this contributed to the Hasmonean revolt.[33]

The Hellenistic kings were the centralized economic focus of the economy and viewed themselves as directly controlling the majority of the land and property.[34] Land acquired by imperial conquest was "claimed as royal land, so that ultimately everything that was produced was somehow owed to the king and by some means went at least in part to him."[35] The king, then, leased "his" land to wealthy individuals and made provisions of land for institutions such as temples.[36] Beginning with the Ptolemies "estates and entire regions came under royal ownership as imperial authorities worked with the local aristocracy to squeeze the territories for goods and taxes."[37] The Zenon papyri (from Oxyrhynchus in Egypt) provides evidence that "a considerable amount of the land was owned directly by the king as royal lands and managed on his behalf by various people."[38] And the imperial authorities enacted their policies through local governors, priests, and temple bureaucrats who imposed their own taxes. We have seen that tax farmers or finance administrators were commissioned by the ruling authorities to collect the taxes and could potentially make a nice profit if they overcharged the taxpayers. In the time of Jesus, then, this practice resulted in a small percentage of the landed elite who controlled the majority of the land and a large percentage of landless peasants. Herod the Great's rule over Palestine continued these practices such that the land was marked by pro-Roman aristocrats localized around the temple (e.g., the Sadducees and the Sanhedrin), the few wealthy landowners, and the vast ma-

---

33. For a much more detailed description of the economic policies of the Ptolemies and Seleucids as it pertains to Judea, see Adams, *Social and Economic Life*, 145–65.

34. On the consistent policies of economic extraction by Hellenistic rulers, see John Ma, "Kings," in *A Companion to the Hellenistic World*, ed. Andrew Erskine (Malden, MA: Wiley-Blackwell, 2005), 183–86.

35. Ekkehard W. Stegemann and Wolfgang Stegemann, *The Jesus Movement: A Social History of Its First Century*, trans. O. C. Dean Jr. (Minneapolis: Fortress, 1999), 108.

36. Stegemann and Stegemann, *Jesus Movement*, 108.

37. Adams, *Social and Economic Life*, 89.

38. Sean Freyne, *The Jesus Movement and Its Expansion: Meaning and Mission* (Grand Rapids: Eerdmans, 2014), 94.

jority who lived at or below subsistence level.[39] This pattern resulted in small farmers increasingly being pushed off their land due to extreme indebtedness and the attending confiscation or appropriation of their land to the wealthy. Lack of land, oppressive demands for taxation and tribute, and increasing indebtedness resulted in incredible wealth disparities in ancient Palestine.

Roland Boer argues that "one of the first acts of those eager to see the demise of their overlords is to tear up or . . . smash the loan documents."[40] Josephus's writings are filled with freedom fighters who promise liberation from Rome and their fellow wealthy Jews who collude with Roman rule. These figures are invariably responding to the exploitative and oppressive economic policies imposed upon them from those with power and status. And one of their primary agendas seems to have been the destruction of the archives that recorded peoples' debts. For example, Josephus refers to a certain Judas the Galilean who rebuked his fellow Jews for paying tribute to Rome in the belief that only God was their lord (J.W. 2.1). Josephus also describes the Sicarii who attack those colluding with Rome and set fire to the high priest's house and Agrippa's palace; they "next carried their combustibles to the public archives, eager to destroy the money-lenders' bonds and to prevent the recovery of debts, in order to win over a host of grateful debtors and to cause a rising of the poor against the rich" (J.W. 2.427). Even though a variety of tax remissions were enacted by Herod and his successors, the Jews' refusal to pay the annual Roman tribute in 66 CE was the primary cause of the war with Rome (J.W. 2.117–118).[41] Josephus also refers to a situation in Antioch where some "scoundrels, who, under the pressure of debts, imagined that if they burnt the market-place and the public records they would be rid of all demands" (J.W. 7.61). These events indicate that "widespread indebtedness" was "a pervasive problem" in first-century Palestine.[42] The causes for the Jewish revolt against Rome have been frequently examined, but it seems right that at least one very important factor was a widespread longing for the restoration of Israel's land and the practice of Jubilee and debt cancellation.[43]

We have moved a long way from God's ideal in Torah where Israel was to share the land with one another, engage in periodic debt cancellation, and share its resources such that there would be no poor in the land (Deut 15:4). Rather,

---

39. On wealthy landowners and large estates in and near Jerusalem, see David A. Fiensy, *Christian Origins and the Ancient Economy* (Eugene, OR: Cascade, 2014), 161–63.

40. Boer, *Sacred Economy of Ancient Israel*, 197.

41. On which, see Gerd Theissen, *Sociology of Early Palestinian Christianity*, trans. John Bowden (Philadelphia: Fortress, 1978), 42–44.

42. Fiensy, *Christian Origins*, 65.

43. Fiensy, *Christian Origins*, 154.

The Economics of Jesus in the Context of the Roman Empire

the combination of imperial rule, a burdensome system of foreign taxation, tribute, and plunder, an acquisitive priestly aristocracy, and the concentration of land and wealth with a few resulted in a situation that made life and mere subsistence a constant challenge for the majority of Jews in the time of Jesus.

The Economics of Jesus

One of the most fundamental features of the Gospels' portrait of Jesus is that he proclaimed that his ministry embodied and enacted the kingdom of God: "The time is filled up, and the kingdom of God has come near. Repent and believe in the gospel" (Mark 1:15). Jesus's vision of the kingdom of God demands a thoroughgoing set of alternative economic practices that conflict with the status-quo practices.

Greed and Acquisitiveness

We have seen that God's sacred economy for Israel set forth a way of life that was to be characterized by mercy and love for one's neighbor instead of greed and exploitation. The demand to guard oneself from the desire to acquire at the expense of the good of one's neighbor is summarized in the commandment, "Do not covet your neighbor's house. Do not covet your neighbor's wife, his male or female slave, his ox or donkey, or anything that belongs to your neighbor" (Exod 20:17). And Israel's Scriptures are filled with warnings against greed precisely because it wages war against *both* one's ability to love one's neighbor *and* one's ability to worship God (e.g., Ezek 26–28).

The Gospel of Luke is filled with Jesus's criticisms against the Roman economy and its operations in ancient Palestine as something that is exploitative, extractive, hierarchical and predicated upon greed. From the beginning of Luke's Gospel, we see that Jesus's presence will mean an inauguration of *another kind of king and kingdom* and one that will challenge the current operations of Rome and Roman Palestine. Mary interprets God's miraculous act to make her virgin womb pregnant with this coming Messiah as the means whereby he will "scatter the proud . . . and topple the mighty from their thrones and exalt the lowly" (1:51b–52). Mary praises God's act as the means whereby he will give food to the hungry and will send the rich away with nothing (1:53). In accordance with Mary's prophetic anthem, Jesus is born far away from the rich and powerful who oppress and exploit such as the Caesars and governors of Rome (2:1–7). This is undoubtedly why John the Baptist's simple message of repentance is focused exclusively upon the use of possessions. Those who will be ready to embrace the coming act of God will be those who share their surplus of resources and possessions with others, turn away from exploitative and acquisitive forms of wealth generation, and who refrain from using their power to extract from the vulnerable (3:10–14).[44] This theme, namely, that those who are repentant and prepared to respond to the good news of the kingdom do so through the proper use of their possessions, while those who are unrepentant are marked by greed, runs throughout the entirety of both Luke's Gospel and his Acts of the Apostles.[45]

The text that most clearly sets forth Jesus's teaching on the dangers of greed and excessive consumption is found in Luke 12:13–34. We should remember that most people survived through subsistence agriculture, that cities were primarily places of consumption and extraction, and that wealth and power were generated from the land and those who owned and controlled the land.

In this text Jesus's teaching is interrupted by someone from the crowd who shouts out, "Teacher, tell my brother to divide the inheritance with me" (12:13). The man is likely the younger of two brothers who obviously feels that he has been swindled out of his proper share of their family inheritance. We may be reminded here of a similar situation faced by Moses who judged the people of Israel by hearing their disputes and rendering just verdicts (Exod 18). But Jesus entirely rejects the man's expectation that he will function as an arbiter of his economic dispute. Jesus's response to the man is seemingly harsh—"Who appointed me a judge or arbiter over you? (12:14b)—as he diagnoses the man's desire as consisting in greed. "Beware and watch out for every kind of greed, because one's *life* does not consist in the abundance of one's possessions" (12:15).[46] Jesus's response is stark and may strike us as unfair. After all, couldn't Jesus have at least investigated the situation to see whether the man had indeed been victimized or taken advantage of by his brother? But this was not a poor man surviving at subsistence level. And Jesus discerns that this is a man who "is seduced to want more, even at his brother's expense [and] that the man is using his energy for accumulation."[47] Rather, given the way in which wealth, status, power, and social mobility was dependent upon land, it

---

44. This theme is highlighted throughout Luke Timothy Johnson, *The Literary Function of Possessions in Luke-Acts*, SBLDS 39 (Missoula, MT: Scholars Press, 1977).

45. See here Luke Timothy Johnson, *Sharing Possessions: What Faith Demands*, 2nd ed. (Grand Rapids: Eerdmans, 2011).

46. Abraham J. Malherbe, "The Christianization of a *Topos* (Luke 12:13–34)," in *Light from the Gentiles: Hellenistic Philosophy and Early Christianity*, NovTSup 150 (Leiden: Brill, 2015), 339–51, here 348.

47. Brueggemann, *Money and Possessions*, 192.

The Economics of Jesus in the Context of the Roman Empire

is much more likely that this man wanted to enter, or advance further, in the ranks of the landed elite. And it was precisely the landed elite, among others, who were responsible for the exploitation of the poor. Behind the brother's desire for his inheritance, Jesus saw an improper and ultimately evil desire for power and the superfluous abundance of possessions.

Jesus's parable of the foolish wealthy landowner in Luke 12:16–21 is told in response to all those who, like the younger brother in verses 13–15, are tempted by greed. In this parable, there is a man whose land produces a fabulous yield; so extraordinary is the man's surplus that he has to decide how to best steward his incredible wealth. The man "reasoned to *himself*: 'What shall *I do*, since *I have* no place to gather *my crops*?' And he said, '*I will do this, I will tear down my barns* and *I will build* bigger ones and *I will gather* together there all *my* crops and *my* good things. And *I* will say to *myself*, '*Self*, you have many good things laid up for many years. Rest, eat, drink, be happy.'"[48] Jesus portrays the man as a symbol of the exploitative, extractive, consuming landowners who unjustly control the majority of the land. In an economy where most people live at a subsistence level, the man's decision to use his surplus for his own protection and security instead of sharing with the hungry demonstrates that he is painfully ignorant or simply does not care about the poor and hungry who surround him. In response to his question, "What shall I do with my surplus crops?" the divine economy that Jesus sets forth would mandate that he share his food with others. The man foolishly supposes that he can make his life secure through his accumulation of possessions, and his greed and foolish equation of his "life" with his "possessions" is on display in his excessive "I" and "my" language that wrongly supposes *he* is the owner of his possessions. Walter Brueggemann describes the man's worry as "propelled by his habitation in a culture of extraction that assumes scarcity."[49]

For Luke, those who have embraced God's alternative kingdom demonstrate it through a reorientation of their economic practices as they reject greed in order to share their surplus with others. But this is a decidedly challenging task as Luke's two volumes show that humans are tempted to trust in the accumulation of their possessions, even to the harm of their fellow neighbors, as a means of providing security and life. Thus, the Pharisees mock Jesus for the

---

48. On this parable and the broader theme of the right use of possessions in the face of death, see Matthew S. Rindge, *Jesus' Parable of the Rich Fool: Luke 12:13–34 among Ancient Conversation on Death and Possessions*, Early Christianity and Its Literature 6 (Atlanta: Society of Biblical Literature Press, 2011).

49. Brueggemann, *Money and Possessions*, 193.

stark contrast he makes between one's ability to serve God and serve money (Luke 16:13–14). Jesus here personifies money as a "master" or "lord" since greed can exert a powerful force upon people to orient their desires and aims toward it. Jesus says, "Remember Lot's wife" as an example of someone who tried to make her life secure through her possessions (17:32–33). The rich young ruler fails to enter the kingdom of God because he is unwilling to divest himself of his possessions when Jesus asks him to make a clean break with the typical economic practices of money, debt, and property (18:18–30). In Acts the villains or antagonists of the faith are frequently portrayed as greedy and making poor use of their possessions. Judas's gory end is due to his rightly receiving "the wage for his unrighteousness," namely, preferring silver to loyalty to Jesus (Acts 1:18). Ananias and Sapphira hold back the proceeds from their field instead of sharing with the community (Acts 5:1–11); Simon Magus tries to purchase the Holy Spirit (8:14–25); Demetrius's devotion to the goddess Artemis is due to his ability to profit from making silver shrines (19:23–27; cf. 16:16–18); Felix leaves Paul imprisoned hoping to receive a monetary bribe (24:24–26).

Land and Debt

The ancient Roman economy was an advanced agrarian (non-industrial) and underdeveloped economy. The landowners were dependent upon a variety of smaller sources and subgroups who cultivated and produced the crops that provided the wealth for the elite. For example, Pliny the Younger relied upon slaves to work some of his lands and rented other lands to tenants.[50] Those who mediated between the landowners and the agricultural laborers were often referred to as retainers, and they were tasked with the administration of the financial goals of the elite landowners. We are familiar with these kinds of figures from the Gospels where we see tax collectors (e.g., Luke 5:27–32; 19:1–10), managers or bailiffs (e.g., Luke 12:42–48; 16:1–8), or slaves and freedmen (e.g., Mark 12:2; Matt. 24:47–51).[51] While the tax farmers and bailiffs could make a good profit as middlemen, they did not enjoy the same status as the elite orders. Further, there was often no little discord and antagonism between the agricultural laborers or slaves and the bailiffs as the latter provided management, oversight, and discipline for the workers.[52]

---

50. Keith Bradley, *Slavery and Society at Rome*, Key Themes in Ancient History (Cambridge: Cambridge University Press, 1994), 76.
51. Fiensy, *Christian Origins*, 12–14.
52. See further, Bradley, *Slavery and Society at Rome*, 72–73.

The Economics of Jesus in the Context of the Roman Empire

Given that a small percentage of the elite controlled the land *and* in light of the fact that the majority of the population lived on the land, the landowners were easily able to exploit the economic system for their own benefit. This resulted in vast wealth disparities. The landowners generally resided in the cities, functioned as the powerful of the ruling class, and lived "off the land by controlling the peasants so as to be able to take from them a part of their product."[53] The city was responsible for the taxation system, received the profits from the rural rents, and consumed what was produced by the agricultural laborers.[54] Taxes and rents frequently forced peasant laborers into increasing forms of dependence upon those with wealth as any surplus they were able to produce was usually extracted from them.[55] The city of Rome was "a means of establishing and reinforcing political, ideological, and economic power. It was the main venue for conspicuous consumption . . . [and] became . . . the main location of elite expenditure."[56] Rome, as the primary example of the consumer city, paid for its materials and facilities through extraction from the surplus of the peasants.

The control of most of the land by the few prevented others from the kinds of entrepreneurial activities that might encourage trade, technological development, and the use of interrelated markets. Most of those who were not part of the elite orders lived at a subsistence level and sought to simultaneously provide for their family from the land and make some limited income in order to pay rents and taxes. As Garnsey and Saller have summarized, "The direct exploitation of labour by rich proprietors was a central feature of Roman imperial society. . . . Wealth was generated for members of the propertied class to a large extent by the labour of their personal dependents."[57] While some peasants owned their own land and operated their farms as family units, most agricultural workers were tenant farmers who rented the land from the elite landowners usually at very high costs.[58] Many of these tenants were legally free

---

53. John H. Kautsky, *The Politics of Aristocratic Empires* (Chapel Hill: University of North Carolina Press, 1982), 80.

54. Peter Garnsey and Richard Saller, *The Roman Empire: Economy, Society and Culture*, 2nd ed. (Berkeley: University of California Press, 2015), 83.

55. Garnsey and Saller, *Roman Empire*, 79.

56. Neville Morley, "The Early Roman Empire: Distribution," in *The Cambridge Economic History of the Greco-Roman World*, ed. Walter Scheidel, Ian Morris, and Richard P. Saller (Cambridge: Cambridge University Press, 2007), 570–91, here 578. See, however, the criticisms of this view of the "consumer city" as too one-sided by Jean Andreau, *The Economy of the Roman World*, trans. Corina Kesler (Ann Arbor: Michigan Classical Press, 2015), 20–22.

57. Garnsey and Saller, *Roman Empire*, 134.

58. They might either pay the landowners a fixed amount of money *or* a portion of the

but were not able to produce enough profit to break away from the high rents of their landlords in order to establish any level of financial independence. Others even less fortunate than the small but free peasants with some land and the tenant farmers were day laborers and slaves. Those who are familiar with the Gospels recognize that many of Jesus's parables made their point through the recognizable depictions of landowners (Luke 12:16–21; 16:19–31), tenant farmers (Mark 12:1–12), day laborers (Matt 20:1–15), and slaves (Luke 17:7–10). The use of slaves as agricultural laborers enabled the landowners to operate their farms and simultaneously withdraw from the task of competing for laborers.[59] Contemporary scholars use the language of "slave villas" to speak of certain land operations that were worked entirely by agricultural slave laborers and operated through a slave as a middle manager. Jean Andreau refers to these slave villas as "ubiquitous" throughout most of Italy.[60] This was profitable as long as the landowners had enough work to keep the slaves occupied year-round. Day laborers supplemented the work of slaves during the busy seasons of planting and especially harvest. While there are certainly exceptions, for example, the notorious wealthy freedmen and some valued slaves of socially elite masters, there was generally little difference in the economic and social value between slaves and day laborers.[61]

Jesus's attack on greed and the excessive acquisitiveness of the rich makes good sense given the situation of ancient Palestine. We have seen that God had given the land as a *gift* to his people, and thus while the land is Israel's inheritance, God was always to be understood as the owner of the land (cf. Josh 22:19; 2 Chr 7:20; Ps 85:1; Isa 14:2, 25). Since at least the time of Israel's prophets, however, the Scriptures indicate that the majority of the land was controlled by the few rich landowners and that their economic practices had led to a situation where many Israelites where displaced as tenant workers, day laborers, and peasant subsistence farmers. This situation, along with Israel's

---

harvest. The word *colonus* was often used to describe both groups of workers. See Andreau, *Economy of the Roman World*, 41.

59. Dennis P. Kehoe, "The Early Roman Empire: Production," in *The Cambridge Economic History of the Greco-Roman World*, ed. Walter Scheidel, Ian Morris, and Richard P. Saller (Cambridge: Cambridge University Press, 2007), 541–69, here 554. On the distinction between urban and household slaves, see Bradley, *Slavery and Society at Rome*, 58.

60. Andreau, *Economy of the Roman World*, 35–39.

61. On some limited possibilities for social mobility for slaves, see Dale B. Martin, *Slavery as Salvation: The Metaphor of Slavery in Pauline Christianity* (New Haven: Yale University Press, 1990). On the wealthy freedmen, see Petronius's *Satyricon* and the well-known freedmen of Claudius—Pallas, Callistus, and Narcissus.

centuries-long experience of imperial rule, meant that most small farmers and workers experienced excessive demands for taxation and tribute, which resulted in a situation of increasing indebtedness. Josephus's writings are filled with freedom fighters who are responding to the exploitative and oppressive economic policies imposed upon them from those with power and status. One of their primary goals was the destruction of the records of peoples' debt and their liberation from providing taxes and tribute. In fact, numerous parables and teachings of Jesus are oriented to the problematic experience of debt, and Jesus's teachings here seem to suppose that people know and understand well the experience or threat of debtor's prison, the suffocating enslavement of indebtedness, and the powerful desire for economic freedom (e.g. Matt 5:25–26; 6:11–12; 18:23–24; Luke 12:57–59; 16:1–9).[62]

Jesus enters into this situation with a deep commitment to provide release and freedom from those who are oppressed by economic systems and forces out of their control. In fact, scholars have for good reason seen Luke's depiction of Jesus as centering upon his inauguration of the eschatological Jubilee.[63] Jesus's first public sermon in the Gospel of Luke echoes the biblical tradition of the Jubilee: "The Spirit of the Lord is upon me, for he has anointed me to proclaim good news to the poor; he has sent me to preach *release* to the captives, sight to the blind, to bring *release* to the oppressed, to proclaim the year of the Lord's favor" (4:18–19). The twice-repeated word "release" (*aphesis*) hearkens back to Leviticus 25 where God institutes the practice of Jubilee, namely, a time of freedom and liberation when the ancestral land that had been alienated from its original owners due to debt would be returned and when indentured slaves would be released. Thus, Jesus's proclamation fits neatly with Moses's Jubilee command: "You shall proclaim freedom [i.e., release] in the land for all its inhabitants" (Lev 25:10). When Jesus quotes from Isaiah 58:6 and 61:1–2, he joins together two oracles that share the wording of release and develop the Jubilee themes of freedom and liberation for the oppressed, the hungry, and the indebted. It's worth looking at a bit of the context of Isaiah 58 in order to see how Isaiah develops the Jubilee theme: "Isn't this the fast I choose: To break the chains of wickedness, to unite the ropes of the yoke, to set the oppressed free, and to tear off every yoke? Is it not to share your bread with the hungry, to bring the poor and homeless into your house, to clothe the naked when you

---

62. On the prevalence of debt in ancient Palestine, see Douglas E. Oakman, *Jesus, Debt, and the Lord's Prayer: First-Century Debt and Jesus' Intentions* (Eugene, OR: Wipf and Stock, 2014); Fiensy, *Christian Origins*, 59–66.

63. *DJG*, s.v. "Jubilee."

see him, and not to ignore your own flesh and blood? . . . If you offer yourself to the hungry, and satisfy the afflicted one, then your light will shine in the darkness, and your night will be like noonday" (58:6–7, 10). The Gospel of Luke thereby encourages a reading of Jesus's ministry as an inauguration of the eschatological Jubilee, in that his ministry enacts God's release and liberation of his people from all that holds them captive.

The entirety of Jesus's ministry centers upon the way in which he brings release and liberation to the captives, and this takes place through his healings of the afflicted (Luke 5:12–26; 7:2–17; 13:11–17), exorcisms of the demon-possessed (4:31–44; 8:26–39), offers forgiveness of sins (5:17–26; 7:41–43), and table fellowship with outcasts (5:27–32; 7:36–50; 19:1–10). Thus, Jesus responds to John the Baptist's inquiries about whether he is the promised Messiah with a response that echoes Jesus's own declaration that he has come to enact the eschatological Jubilee: "The blind see, the lame walk, the lepers are cleansed, the mute hear, the dead are raised, and the poor hear the gospel" (7:22).

While Jesus's interpretation of the Jubilee tradition is more expansive in its focus on *all kinds of forces that oppress* humans, he also calls for God's people to turn from exploitative economic practices that lead to poverty and indebtedness. There are two ways in which Jesus enacts this Jubilee tradition through his teaching: (1) he criticizes and calls the wealthy to repentance for their exploitative oppression; and (2) he demands that his people embody mercy, as God in fact does with them, in their dealings with one another. These two points are, in fact, set forth from Jesus as one of the primary petitions his people are to pray: "Forgive us our sins even as we release/forgive everyone indebted to us" (Luke 11:4a; cf. Matt 6:12). As Nathan Eubank has stated, Jesus's prayer "does not use generic language of forgiveness but the unmistakable language of commerce. Greek speakers who encountered the prayer presumably would have heard it first as a request for debt-cancellation."[64] In other words, just as God's people experience release, liberation, and forgiveness of sins against God, so are God's people expected to engage in acts of mercy whereby one's fellow brothers and sisters are forgiven and released from their debts.[65] Or in Yoder's terms, the one who prays this prayer is called "purely and simply to erase the debts of those who owe us money; that is to say, prac-

---

64. Nathan Eubank, *Wages of Cross-Bearing and Debt of Sin: The Economy of Heaven in Matthew's Gospel*, BZNW 196 (Berlin: de Gruyter, 2013), 54.
65. See here Joel B. Green, *The Gospel of Luke*, NICNT (Grand Rapids: Eerdmans, 1997), 443–44.

tice the jubilee."[66] The one who prays this prayer is simply enacting Jesus's teaching in Luke 6:27-36 where Jesus called his people to give freely without expecting a return.

Let's look at three texts where divine judgment is promised as a warning against the wealthy who oppress and exploit the poor and where mercy is advanced as an alternative practice. In Matthew 18:23-35 Jesus tells a parable that centers upon "debt" (vv. 24, 27, 30, 32, 34) and "mercy" (vv. 26, 27, 28, 33).[67] In the parable, there was a king who had a servant who could not pay back his debt to his lord. As a result his wife, children, and all of his possessions were to be sold to pay back the debt (18:25). But in response to the servant's plea for mercy, the master "had compassion, released him, and canceled the debt" (18:27). But the servant responds to his newfound freedom by finding servants of his own who are indebted to him and demanding the payment of their debts. When they can't pay, unlike his merciful master, the man throws them into debtor's prison (18:29-30). When the master finds out, he rebukes the slave: "I forgave you all that debt because you begged me. Shouldn't you also have had mercy on your fellow servant as I had mercy on you?" (18:33). Jesus makes the point of the parable obvious. If we pray to the Father "forgives us our debts" then we too must be committed to the merciful cancellation of the debts of our fellow humans. God's merciful cancellation of our debts is meaningless and empty unless it results in our dispensing of mercy toward one another. A positive counterpart to this parable is the story of the so-called sinful woman in Luke 7:36-50, where Jesus interprets the woman's extravagant hospitality as a sign of her loving recognition of the one who has canceled her debts (Luke 7:41-42).[68]

In Luke 16:19-31 we find Jesus's scathing critique of a wealthy man who is oblivious to the situation of poverty that is right in front of his face. The rich man dines in luxury every day (16:19b), while Lazarus sits outside the rich man's gate and longs for something to eat (16:20-21). The rich man functions as a symbol of the wealthy landowners who profit off the peasants' labor and who are directly responsible for widespread poverty and displacement of many fellow Israelites.[69] At bare minimum, the rich man was obligated to show hospitality to the stranger "lying at his gate."[70] Lazarus represents the lowest

---

66. John Howard Yoder, *The Politics of Jesus* (Grand Rapids: Eerdmans, 1994), 62.

67. See here the reading offered by John R. Donahue, *The Gospel in Parable: Metaphor, Narrative, and Theology in the Synoptic Gospels* (Minneapolis: Fortress, 1988), 72-79.

68. Oakman, *Jesus, Debt, and the Lord's Prayer*, 38-39.

69. Halvor Moxnes, *The Economy of the Kingdom: Social Conflict and Economic Relations in Luke's Gospel* (Eugene, OR: Wipf & Stock, 2004), 89-90.

70. See especially Deuteronomy 14:28-29; 15:1-8.

stratum of poverty in ancient Palestine. The "absolutely poor" are those who are hungry and thirsty, have only rags for clothes, and are without lodging or hope. For the necessities of life they are dependent on the help of others, for example, through begging. The rich man is one of those, then, who is called upon by Isaiah to share his bread with the hungry, to clothe the naked "when you see him and not to ignore your own flesh and blood" (Isa 58:7b). And yet, there is no indication in the text that the rich man ever saw Lazarus.[71] When the two men die, Lazarus is carried into "Abraham's bosom," while the rich man descends to Hades (16:22b-23). While in Hades, the rich man asks if Lazarus can be sent to give a warning to his brothers, and Abraham twice tells him, "They have Moses and the prophets, let them listen to them" (16:29, 31). According to Jesus, the rich man is a Torah-breaker, for these Scriptures teach debt cancellation for the oppressed, hospitality to the poor, love of neighbor, and the extension of one's possessions to those in need.[72]

The brother of Jesus and leader of the Jerusalem church, James, carries on his brother's tradition of prophetically warning the wealthy as he criticizes the economic oppression of the poor by those with land and wealth. James squarely lays the blame for exploitation of the poor and widespread indebtedness on an uncritical participation in the normal workings of the economy. James does not exalt the virtues of the landowners, but rather sees their pursuit of luxury, wealth, and status as the greed, envy, and thirsty desire for acquisition that results in violence and oppression (Jas 4:1-2).[73] The landowners are responsible for living in luxury (5:2-3, 5), storing up wealth for their own consumption (5:3), withholding just payment from those laboring in their fields (5:4), and oppressing the righteous (5:6). We have already seen that land ownership was one of the primary ways of making wealth, that the owners (and cities) were primarily consumers, and that the peasants and agricultural laborers lived at a subsistence level. Thus, James condemns one of the primary features of the ancient economy for the way in which it enables the rich to accumulate wealth and capital at the expense of the poor. In addition, he criticizes the wealthy for using the surplus for a wasteful and luxurious lifestyle. In other words, James argues that "resources are distributed unequally in society because landowners

---

71. Bruce W. Longenecker, *Remember the Poor: Paul, Poverty, and the Greco-Roman World* (Grand Rapids: Eerdmans, 2010), 81.

72. See Wright, *Old Testament Ethics*, 146-81, 253-80.

73. On the theme of greed and envy, see Luke Timothy Johnson, "James 3:13-4:10 and the Topos περὶ φθόνου," *NovT* 25 (1983): 327-47.

exploit workers, because the rich manipulate the justice system, and because the rich squander their immoral gains on self-indulgence."[74]

Benefaction and Reciprocity

The ancient Roman economy and the creation of wealth was not driven *primarily* by market mechanisms but by the politically powerful and elite who owned the majority of arable land. In other words, the economy was not marked by an "economic rationality" that sought to maximize profits through increased entrepreneurial activity.[75] Rather, the economy was a social institution that was embedded within the broader value systems and political relations which privileged the wealthy and elite.[76] In this regard, the economy was marked by a social order that sought to preserve the prevailing social order of the day.[77] Money, however, was not the only form of capital used for exchange; one's social status also exerted a significant amount of influence upon one's ability to acquire wealth and possessions.[78]

One of the primary ways the ancient Mediterranean economy operated was through the reciprocal giving of gifts and benefits. Convention often pre-

---

74. Steve Friesen, "Injustice or God's Will? Early Christian Explanations of Poverty," in *Wealth and Poverty in Early Church and Society*, ed. Susan R. Holman (Grand Rapids: Baker Academic, 2008), 17–36, here 26. Mariam Kamell, "The Economics of Humility: The Rich and the Humble in James," in *Engaging Economics: New Testament Scenarios and Early Christian Reception*, ed. Bruce W. Longenecker and Kelly D. Liebengood (Grand Rapids: Eerdmans, 2009), 157–75, frequently makes assertions that the rich are not faulted for being rich per se, but rather, Kamell notes, James critiques "the common people who respond to him [that is, the rich man in 2:2–3] with notable groveling" (173). But this ignores what James says about the rich in 2:6–7 and 5:1–6 and underestimates the extent to which the rich, as portrayed by James, unjustly profit from the arrangement of the current economic system.

75. Kehoe, "The Early Roman Empire: Production," 549, states it this way: "For upper-class landowners, land represented a resource providing economic security rather than an investment in the modern sense. In managing their agricultural wealth, many landowners were very risk-averse, preferring strategies that maintained economic stability and their social position to ones designed to maximize wealth."

76. This system may be referred to as political capitalism in that the economy is exploited through political means to profit the elite or aristocracy. See Justin J. Meggitt, *Paul, Poverty and Survival*, Studies of the New Testament and Its World (Edinburgh: T&T Clark, 1998), 47.

77. On the notion of an embedded economy, see Karl Polanyi, *Primitive, Archaic, and Modern Economies: Essays of Karl Polanyi* (Garden City, NY: Anchor Books, 1968).

78. For what follows, see especially Garnsey and Saller, *Roman Empire*, 173–84; Richard P. Saller, *Personal Patronage under the Early Empire* (Cambridge: Cambridge University Press, 1982), 1.

scribed that one would give invitations to friends and to those from whom you hoped to receive a favor in return.[79] Social convention generally held that one would seek to do good and provide favors for friends and neighbors but to avoid and perhaps even harm one's enemies. The language that was frequently used to describe a gift or benefit is the Greek word *charis*. The return of a benefit for a prior benefit included the notion of thanksgiving or gratitude. One of the most frequently discussed of these ancient social institutions embedded within the ancient economy was patronage (*patrocinium*),[80] namely, the reciprocal exchange of favors and gifts.[81] While there were a variety of categories of patronage and a variety of important distinctions of similar social exchange (e.g., princeps/empire, landlord/tenant, patron/individuals of lower social status, etc.), usually the exchange of favors took place between "friends" of unequal status in terms of the social hierarchy.[82] The relationships were characterized by "a very strong element of inequality and difference in power."[83] In exchange for small portions of food, money, legal protection, loans, and meals the clients were expected to engage in public acts that might contribute to the social standing of their client.[84] Patrons often held banquets for their clients and often used the meal as an opportunity to distinguish their most valued clients through offering better food and superior seating arrangements. Failure to make a return on a received gift or to advertise the generosity of one's benefactor was considered an act of ingratitude and could result in enmity between the patron and the client. Given that resources were scarce—namely, honor, status, food, money, and power—patronage assumed a system of intense competition with one another for these resources.[85] The patron was consistently seeking to improve his status through constant gift giving, while the client was simultaneously indebted to the patron and caught in a suffocating web of obligations to him from which he could hardly escape.

---

79. E.g., Hesiod, *Works and Days*, 342–354: "Invite your friend, but not your enemy to dine.... Measure carefully when you must borrow from your neighbor, then, pay back the same, or more if possible, and you will have a friend in time of need.... Love your friends, visit those who visit you, and give to him who gives, but not, if he does not."

80. The actual terms *patronus* and *cliens* do not often occur in ancient Latin writings. Richard P. Saller, *Personal Patronage*, 9, argues that this is due to the "social inferiority" implied by the words.

81. See, for example, Jonathan Marshall, *Jesus, Patrons, and Benefactors: Roman Palestine and the Gospel of Luke*, WUNT 2/259 (Tübingen: Mohr Siebeck, 2009), 43–53.

82. Seneca's *On Benefits* is the most well-known ancient treatise devoted to the subject.

83. Moxnes, *Economy of the Kingdom*, 42.

84. Garnsey and Saller, *Roman Empire*, 176.

85. Rhee, *Loving the Poor, Saving the Rich*, 15.

The Economics of Jesus in the Context of the Roman Empire

Further, the giving of gifts by the patron or benefactor was often thought to result in drawing further attention to the virtue of the giver. Seneca frequently speaks of the ways in which those who give gifts from a position of superiority can humiliate and harm their recipients (*Ben.* 1.1.4–8; 2.4–5; 3.34.1).[86] This could take the form of powerful and wealthy givers delaying or hesitating in their giving of gifts, forcing the beneficiaries to feel their dependence by asking them to beg, or publicly advertising the gifts they've given (2.11, 2.13).

One significant practice related to patronage was the public acts of benefaction or euergetism, namely, the bestowal of contributions for the benefit of the city.[87] Public benefactions could take the form of building projects such as public baths, theaters, and synagogues; the provision of games and entertainment; or the provision of money, meals, and food. Benefactors were often called upon to finance grain distributions for their citizens during food shortages, but their favors were usually not granted to the lowest strata of society. In return for their love of their cities, the benefactors received public displays of gratitude and honor such as honorific inscriptions, good seats at public events, wreaths, and statues.[88] Kings and rulers were often considered to be civic benefactors *par excellence* as they used their wealth and resources as gifts for their subjects. Augustus's *Res Gestae* reads as one long list of gifts he granted to the empire, but which ultimately demonstrated his unparalleled honor and worthiness to rule. These gifts included paying for his own army to secure peace from civil war, protection from foreign threats, basic amenities of grain and oil, cash for male citizens and army veterans, and giving games and festivals (*Res Gestae* 15–18; Suetonius, *Augustus* 43).[89] Thus, the image of a generous benefactor who provided for and protected his citizens became a typical component of the script of the good king.[90]

Did favors or gifts perhaps trickle down to the impoverished and lowest stratum of society? Were the poor, the old, the ill, and the orphaned cared for through these forms of exchange? The answer to these questions is "basically no." While this may need to be qualified, most historians have argued that the

---

86. John M. G. Barclay, *Paul and the Gift* (Grand Rapids: Eerdmans, 2015), 46.

87. See Paul Veyne, *Bread and Circuses: Historical Sociology and Political Pluralism* (London: Lane, 1990).

88. Cicero says that honor (not morals or pity for the poor) is the motivation for benefaction in *Off.* 1.44.

89. See here Alison E. Cooley, *Res Gestae Divi Augusti: Text, Translation, and Commentary* (Cambridge: Cambridge University Press, 2009).

90. For more on this, see Joshua W. Jipp, *Christ Is King: Paul's Royal Ideology* (Minneapolis: Fortress, 2015), 21, 84–86.

poor only come into focus as a topic of concern with the advent of Christianity and their charitable giving endeavors.[91] Implicit throughout my description of ancient gift exchange is the fact that the exchange of gifts is a characteristic of the wealthy and elite. Numerous texts and maxims give advice about how to engage in careful discrimination and calculation *before* one gives a gift so that one will avoid the negative experience of not receiving a gracious return.[92] Thus, generosity and giving was prevalent in the ancient Greek and Roman world, but this giving took place almost exclusively among the elite. The poor did not benefit, by and large, or increase the likelihood of their survival through entering into vertical relationships of gift-exchange.[93] Benefaction was not designed, however, to benefit the poor, slaves, or non-citizens (even if the poor did sometimes receive some indirect benefit), given that the poor were unable to make returns for favors and did not occupy a social class.[94] Participating in the patronage system, in other words, presumed that you had something to offer—which the poor did not.[95]

There was, then, no systematic attempt or structural approach to alleviate poverty among the poor in Greco-Roman society.[96] While some of the absolute poor may have benefited marginally from the endeavors of benefactors, those gifts were aimed at the citizens of the city and not the destitute or the rural poor. Those who belonged to voluntary associations, for example, often used their resources to provide assistance to their members,[97] but this does not seem to have reached those in absolute poverty given that their members usually had *some* middle-range level of wealth. Voluntary associations did not recruit members from the poor to belong to their associations and thereby aid in relieving them of their poverty.[98] As Bruce Longenecker has said, "The

---

91. See, for example, Peter Brown, *Poverty and Leadership in the Later Roman Empire* (Hanover, NH: University Press of New England, 2002); Gildas Hamel, *Poverty and Charity in Roman Palestine: The First Three Centuries C.E.* (Berkeley: University of California Press, 1990).

92. A few of these texts are noted by Barclay, *Paul and the Gift*, 34.

93. See here especially Peter Garnsey and Greg Wolf, "Patronage of the Rural Poor in the Roman World," in *Patronage in Ancient Society*, ed. Andrew Wallace-Hadrill (London: Routledge, 1989), 153–70; also, Meggitt, *Paul, Poverty and Survival*, 168–70.

94. See here P. Brown, *Poverty and Leadership*, 4–5.

95. See Longenecker, *Remember the Poor*, 71–73.

96. M. I. Finley, *The Ancient Economy* (Berkeley: University of California Press, 1973), 39–40. See, however, the early rabbinic development of the *tamhui* (soup kitchen) and *quppa* (charity fund) as a means of eliminating begging and poverty. See here Gregg E. Gardner, *The Origins of Organized Charity in Rabbinic Judaism* (Cambridge: Cambridge University Press, 2015).

97. David Downs, *The Offering of the Gentiles: Paul's Collection for Jerusalem in Its Chronological, Cultural, and Cultic Contexts*, WUNT 2/248 (Tübingen: Mohr Siebeck, 2008), 102–12.

98. So Longenecker, *Remember the Poor*, 69.

vast majority of the destitute could not have pinned the slightest hope on the generosity of the associations, simply because that generosity only flowed to 'the poor' among them who had once been economically secure enough to join an association in the first place, and who were probably expected to rise up to their previous economic levels in due course."[99] Both Cicero and Seneca speak of the foolishness of wasting one's money on the poor (Seneca, *On the Brevity of Life* 23.5–24.1; Cicero, *Off.* 2.54). Anneliese Parkin notes that religious and moral institutions were not designed to meet the needs of the poor, but that "the presence of living beggars in the pagan world, which is very well attested, is mute testimony that people did give."[100] But despite some small piece of evidence demonstrating that some non-elite did give alms or do acts of mercy for the impoverished, Parkin concludes that the Greco-Roman world "had a comparatively weak religious or moral charitable ethos, seldom recorded and probably haphazardly observed."[101]

When we turn to the NT it is remarkable that both Jesus and Paul critique this economic system of exchange and directly oppose economic relationships of exchange that are marked by competition, reciprocity, and social hierarchy. Instead, both Jesus and Paul advocate economic practices of non-calculated giving (i.e., giving without respect to the recipient's social worth) of gifts and acts of mercy performed in compassionate solidarity with the hope that one will receive a return from God.

Let's turn to Jesus's Sermon on the Plain in Luke 6:17–36. Jesus's famous words come amidst a crowd of people who approach Jesus as diseased, afflicted by evil spirits, and in need of Jesus to heal them. They are those without social status or worth, the outcasts and rejects of society. They function as something of an object lesson for the disciples as Jesus then proclaims, "Blessed are the poor . . . blessed are those who hunger now . . . blessed are those who weep" (6:20–21). And, alternatively, Jesus pronounces woes on the rich and those who are satiated (6:24–25). Jesus turns the social order upside down, and then commands his disciples to "give to everyone who asks from you, and do not resist the one who takes your possessions" (6:30).[102] In other words, one does not give gifts based on social worth or merit; this is a complete rejection of the conventional wisdom that suggests one should be discriminating in the giving

---

99. Longenecker, *Remember the Poor*, 70.

100. Anneliese Parkin, "'You Do Him No Service': An Exploration of Pagan Almsgiving," in *Poverty in the Roman World*, ed. Margaret Atkins and Robin Osborne (Cambridge: Cambridge University Press, 2006), 60–82, here 61.

101. Parkin, "'You Do Him No Service,'" 75.

102. Especially helpful here is Alan Kirk, "'Love Your Enemies,' the Golden Rule, and Ancient Reciprocity (Luke 6:27–35)," *JBL* 122 (2003): 667–86.

of one's gifts and favors. Jesus's rejection of reciprocity ethics is most obvious in his commands in 6:32–35:

> If you love those who love you, what credit is that to you? For even sinners love those who love them. And if you do good deeds to those who do good things for you, what credit is that to you? Even sinners do the same thing. And if you lend from those you expect to receive a return, what credit is that to you? Even sinners lend to sinners so that they will receive back the same amount. But love your enemies and do good deeds and lend expecting nothing.

One can see in Jesus's repeated comment "even sinners..." the conventional economic practices of his day. In other words, even non-disciples give gifts and repay their debts to one another. The human economy operates with the belief that one should be calculative and discriminatory in the giving of gifts so that one can expect a good return. The task of the disciple of Jesus, however, is to give to all who ask, to love one's enemies, to give without expecting a return from one's neighbor. And this new form of giving is predicated upon the very character of God: "Then your payment will be great and you will be called children of the Most High. For he is merciful to the ungrateful and evil. Be merciful, just as your Father also is merciful" (6:35b–36). The disciple is to imitate the Father's economy, in other words, and since the Father gives gifts to everyone, even the wicked, his children are to reject reciprocity and contractual, calculating forms of exchanging goods and resources. And instead, the disciple is motivated out of a belief that when imitating God's mercy in exchanges with fellow humans, the disciple will receive "credit" or "payment" not from fellow humans but from God.

It is hard to underestimate the significance of Jesus's teaching on God as a merciful gift-giver who showers his kindness and grace upon all people apart from any corresponding social merit or worth. Thus, Jesus's parable of the so-called good Samaritan (10:25–37) interprets the meaning of Leviticus 19:18 ("love your neighbor") as encompassing love for strangers, even for those like the half-dead man who is in no situation to make a return upon the merciful gifts he receives from the Samaritan. Jesus transforms the lawyer's question from "Who is my neighbor?"—an attempt by the lawyer to place boundaries or limitations to whom he must show mercy—to "Who became a neighbor?" Jesus thus reverses the man's question about boundaries in order to indicate that there are no limitations or boundaries erected between us and our duty to show mercy.

Similarly, Jesus argues that one should not use meals as opportunities for inviting friends, family, or wealthy neighbors. Otherwise, Jesus says, "they might invite you back and you would be repaid" (Luke 14:12). Thus, one would be caught up in the web of obligations to give and receive, and to give and receive again, among one's social equals. Instead, Jesus demands that his disciples use meals as opportunities to give mercy to "the poor, maimed, lame, and blind" (14:13). These are precisely those people to whom Jesus said he had come to proclaim release, liberation, and good news in his Nazareth sermon (4:18–19) and upon whom he had pronounced blessings in his Sermon on the Plain (6:20–22). They will not have the money to pay you back, Jesus says, and in this way "you will be paid back at the resurrection of the righteous" (14:14). Again, those who show mercy to those who can't make a return payment function like the merciful Father who gives gifts to all (6:35b–36).

Finally, in Jesus's farewell testament to his disciples (Luke 22:14–38), Jesus commissions his disciples to practice meals in remembrance of Jesus, namely, in a way that imitates Jesus's sacrificial death (22:15–20). While at dinner together, a dispute takes place among the disciples as to which one of them is the greatest (22:24a). Jesus reminds them that the kings and rulers of the gentiles are obsessed with exercising their authority in such a way that they are called "benefactors" (2:25). In other words, they love to give gifts in such a way that it increases their authority and reaffirms their place in the social hierarchy. But Jesus's disciples are to remember that Jesus has been in their midst not as someone who reclined at the table but as someone who waited on tables (22:27b). And this has just been powerfully demonstrated in that he has given his own body and blood as the food and drink for their meal. Thus, meals eaten in remembrance of Jesus are opportunities for the disciples to recommit themselves to the downward mobility of Jesus, the offer of mercy and gifts to those without status and power, and as opportunities to reject the pursuit of honor.

Conclusion

Rather than summarizing what has already been a lengthy foray into the context of Jesus's economic teachings, I want to conclude by offering two ways this information might be of contemporary value to those interested in Jesus's way of life.

First, it offers possibilities for richer interpretations of the New Testament texts. Perhaps even more importantly, whether we reflect upon this or not, most of us are prone to read the NT's teachings on wealth and possessions within our contemporary free market capitalist economy. Our tendency, for example, overestimates the role of money for exchange and underestimates the extent to which exchange took place within not a free-market economy

PART THREE: GOD'S ACTS FOR CHRISTIANS

but rather a political economy that ascribed worth and the possibility for exchange upon hierarchical social orders. Thus, the theological freight in many of the biblical passages we have looked at are often underestimated as their implications go beyond "being a good steward."[103] As we have seen, when Jesus demands that his disciples give indiscriminately (Luke 6:27–36), he is calling upon his disciples to enact a new economy, namely, a new way of thinking about power, the ordering of material resources, practices of exchange, and the value of persons.[104] And this economy is predicated in virtually every respect upon *God's ordering and arrangement of power and material resources*. Stated another way, God's merciful gift in Christ for all people is the ground for new economic arrangements for the early Christians.[105] The belief that all who sit under the rule of the resurrected and enthroned Messiah are family, namely, are of "one heart and soul and mind," provides the basis for the early Christians sharing of their resources with whoever had any need (Acts 2:41–47; 4:32–35; 6:1–6). More could be said, but it is hard to underestimate the extent to which the NT's teachings on the economy results in a new family, with distinct economic practices, that correspond to God the merciful gift giver.

Second, our examination enables us to see a deep continuity between the OT/Jewish teachings and the NT. Luke's Gospel depicts Jesus's teachings as deeply rooted in texts such as Leviticus 19 and 25, Deuteronomy 15, and Isaiah 58 and 61. Jesus, in other words, is presented not so much as a radical innovator with respect to his teachings on wealth, possessions, and debt; rather, he is calling for patterns of exchange that are rooted in the scriptural teachings on Jubilee, the cancelation of debts, and love for neighbor *and* the stranger. Those who are the seed of Abraham, then, *listen* and enact the Torah and the Prophets through their economic practices (e.g., Luke 16:25–31; 19:8–9; cf. 3:7–8).

---

103. Stewardship is indeed a biblical theme, but it can often be improperly used as a monolithic lens for the Bible's teachings on wealth, possessions, and economic matters. See further Kelly S. Johnson, *The Fear of Beggars: Stewardship and Poverty in Christian Ethics* (Grand Rapids: Eerdmans, 2007).

104. See again Barton, "Money Matters," 39.

105. The economic implications are significant with respect to the argument of Barclay, *Paul and the Gift*.

Acknowledgments

A number of publishers have kindly given their permission for the republication of my previously published essays—with some revisions and changes. My thanks to all of them. The details of the original publication of each previously published essay in this collection are recorded below.

1. "The Paul of Acts: Proclaimer of the Hope of Israel or Teacher of Apostasy from Moses." *NovT* 62 (2020): 60–78. Reprinted with permission.
2. "Paul as Prophet of God's Resurrected Messiah: Prophecy and Messianism in the Lukan Depiction of Paul." Pages 217–34 in *Paul within Judaism: Perspectives on Paul and Jewish Identity*. Edited by Michael Bird, Ruben A. Bühner, Jörg Frey, and Brian Rosner. Tübingen: Mohr Siebeck, 2023. Reprinted with permission.
3. "Luke's Scriptural Suffering Messiah: A Search for Precedent, a Search for Identity." *CBQ* 72 (2010): 255–74. Reprinted with permission.
4. "Abraham in the Gospels and the Acts of the Apostles." Pages 109–25 in *Abraham in Jewish and Early Christian Literature*. Edited by Sean Adams and Zanne Domoney-Lyttle. London: T&T Clark, 2020. Reprinted with permission.
5. "'For David Did Not Ascend into Heaven...' (Acts 2:34a): Reprogramming Royal Psalms to Proclaim the Enthroned-in-Heaven King." Pages 41–59 in *Ascent into Heaven in Luke-Acts*. Edited by David K. Bryan and David W. Pao. Minneapolis: Fortress, 2016. Reprinted with permission.
6. "Did Paul Translate the Gospel in Acts 17:22–31? A Critical Engagement with C. Kavin Rowe's *One True Life*." *PRSt* 45 (2018): 361–76. Reprinted with permission.

ACKNOWLEDGMENTS

7. "Hospitable Barbarians: Luke's Ethnic Reasoning in Acts 28:1–10." *JTS* 68 (2017): 23–45. Reprinted with permission.
8. "Paul's Areopagus Speech of Acts 17:16–34 as *both* Critique *and* Propaganda." *JBL* 131 (2012): 567–88. Reprinted with permission.
9. "The Beginnings of a Theology of Luke-Acts: Divine Activity and Human Response." *JTI* 8 (2014): 23–43. Reprinted with permission.
10. "The Migrant Messiah and the Boundary Crossing Community in Luke-Acts." Pages 67–83 in *Global Migration and Christian Faith: Implications for Identity and Mission*. Edited by M. Daniel Carroll R. and Vincent E. Bacote. Eugene, OR: Cascade, 2021. Reprinted with permission.
11. "Jesus, the Church, and Mental Illness." Pages 127–48 in *For It Stands in Scripture: Essays in Honor of W. Edward Glenny*. Edited by Ardel Caneday, Anna Rask, and Greg Rosauer. St. Paul: University of Northwestern Library, 2019. Reprinted with permission.
12. "Philanthropy, Hospitality, and Friendship in Acts 27–28." Pages 65–72 in *The Book of Acts*. Christian Reflection. Waco, TX: Baylor University Press, 2014. Reprinted with permission.

Bibliography

Adams, Samuel L. *Social and Economic Life in Second Temple Judea.* Louisville: Westminster John Knox, 2014.

Alexander, Loveday. "Acts and Ancient Intellectual Biography." Pages 43–68 in Alexander, *Acts in Its Ancient Literary Context.*

———. *Acts in Its Ancient Literary Context: A Classicist Looks at the Acts of the Apostles.* LNTS 298. New York: T&T Clark, 2005 Early Christianity in Context. London: T&T Clark, 2005.

———. "'In Journeyings Often': Voyaging in the Acts of the Apostles and in Greek Romance." Pages 69–96 in Alexander, *Acts in Its Ancient Literary Context.*

Alexander, Philip S. "Jewish Law in the Time of Jesus: A Clarification of the Problem." Pages 44–58 in *Law and Religion: Essays on the Place of the Law in Israel and Early Christianity.* Edited by Barnabas Linders. Cambridge: Clark, 1988.

Allison, Dale C., Jr. *The Resurrection of Jesus: Apologetics, Polemics, History.* New York: T&T Clark, 2021.

Anderson, Kevin L. *"But God Raised Him from the Dead": The Theology of Jesus's Resurrection in Luke-Acts.* Eugene, OR: Wipf and Stock, 2006.

Andreau, Jean. *The Economy of the Roman World.* Translated by Corina Kesler. Ann Arbor: Michigan Classical Press, 2015.

Antonova, Stamenka E. "Barbarians and the Empire-Wide Spread of Christianity." Pages 69–85 in *The Spread of Christianity in the First Four Centuries: Essays in Explanation.* Edited by W. V. Harris. Columbia Studies in the Classical Tradition 27. Leiden: Brill, 2005.

Arterbury, Andrew E. *Entertaining Angels: Early Christian Hospitality in Its Mediterranean Setting.* New Testament Monographs 8. Sheffield: Sheffield Phoenix, 2005.

———. "Zacchaeus: 'A Son of Abraham'?" Pages 18–31 in *Biblical Interpretation in Early Christian Gospels.* Vol. 3, *The Gospel of Luke.* Edited by Thomas R. Hatina. LNTS 376. London: T&T Clark, 2010.

Ashton, John. *Understanding the Fourth Gospel.* 2nd ed. Oxford: Oxford University Press, 2007.

BIBLIOGRAPHY

Attridge, Harold W. *First-Century Cynicism in the Epistles of Heraclitus*. HTS. Missoula, MT: Scholars Press, 1976.

Auerbach, Erich. *Mimesis*. Princeton: Princeton University Press, 1968.

Baker, Cynthia M. "'From Every Nation Under Heaven': Jewish Ethnicities in the Greco-Roman World." Pages 79–99 in *Prejudice and Christian Beginnings: Investigating Race, Gender, and Ethnicity in Early Christianity*. Edited by Elisabeth Schüssler Fiorenza and Laura Nasrallah. Minneapolis: Fortress, 2009.

———. *Jew*. Key Words in Jewish Studies. New Brunswick: Rutgers University Press, 2017.

Balch, David L. "The Areopagus Speech: An Appeal to the Stoic Historian Posidonius against Later Stoics and the Epicureans." Pages 52–79 in *Greeks, Romans, and Christians: Essays in Honor of Abraham J. Malherbe*. Edited by David L. Balch, Everett Ferguson, and Wayne A. Meeks. Minneapolis: Fortress, 1990.

———. "ΜΕΤΑΒΟΛΗ ΠΟΛΙΤΕΩΝ—Jesus as Founder of the Church in Luke-Acts: Form and Function." Pages 139–88 in *Contextualizing Acts: Lukan Narrative and Greco-Roman Discourse*. Edited by Todd C. Penner and Caroline Vander Stichele. SBLSymS 20. Atlanta: Society of Biblical Literature Press, 2003.

Balthasar, Hans Urs von. *The Christian and Anxiety*. San Francisco: Ignatius, 2000.

Baltzer, Klaus. "The Meaning of the Temple in the Lukan Writings." *HTR* 58 (1965): 263–77.

Barclay, John M. G. *Jews in the Mediterranean Diaspora: From Alexander to Trajan (323 BCE–117 CE)*. Berkeley: University of California Press, 1996.

———. *Paul and the Gift*. Grand Rapids: Eerdmans, 2015.

Barnes, Timothy D. "An Apostle on Trial." *JTS* 20 (1969): 407–19.

Barreto, Eric D. *Ethnic Negotiations: The Function of Race and Ethnicity in Acts 16*. WUNT 2/294. Tübingen: Mohr Siebeck, 2010.

———. "A Gospel on the Move: Practice, Proclamation, and Place in Luke-Acts." *Int* 72 (2018): 175–87.

Barrett, C. K. *A Critical and Exegetical Commentary on the Acts of the Apostles: In 2 Volumes*. ICC 49. Edinburgh: T&T Clark, 1998.

———. "Paul's Speech on the Areopagus." Pages 69–77 in *New Testament Christianity for Africa and the World*. Edited by M. Glasswell and E. Fashole-Lake. London: SPCK, 1974.

Barton, Stephen C. "Money Matters: Economic Relations and the Transformation of Value in Early Christianity." Pages 37–59 in *Engaging Economics: New Testament Scenarios and Early Christian Reception*. Edited by Bruce W. Longenecker and Kelly D. Liebengood. Grand Rapids: Eerdmans, 2009.

Bates, Matthew W. *The Birth of the Trinity: Jesus, God, and Spirit in New Testament and Early Christian Interpretations of the Old Testament*. Oxford: Oxford University Press, 2015.

Beck, Brian E. *Christian Character in the Gospel of Luke*. London: Epworth, 1989.

Beck, Richard. *Unclean: Meditations on Purity, Hospitality, and Mortality*. Eugene, OR: Cascade, 2011.

Bediako, Kwame. "Africa and the Fathers: The Relevance of Early Hellenistic Christian Theology for Modern Africa." Pages 63–76 in Bediako, *Jesus and the Gospel in Africa*.

———. "How Is Jesus Christ Lord? Evangelical Christian Apologetics amid African Religious Pluralism." Pages 34–45 in Bediako, *Jesus and the Gospel in Africa*.

———. *Jesus and the Gospel in Africa: History and Experience*. Maryknoll, NY: Orbis, 2004.

———. "Jesus in African Culture: A Ghanaian Perspective." Pages 20–33 in Bediako, *Jesus and the Gospel in Africa*.

Bibliography

———. *Theology and Identity: The Impact of Culture upon Christian Thought in the Second Century and in Modern Africa*. Oxford: Regnum, 1992.
———. "Understanding African Theology in the Twentieth Century." Pages 49–62 in Bediako, *Jesus and the Gospel in Africa*.
Beers, Holly. *The Followers of Jesus as the "Servant": Luke's Model from Isaiah for the Disciples in Luke-Acts*. LNTS 535. New York: T&T Clark, 2015.
Bergh, Ronald H. van der. "Insiders or Outsiders: The Use of the Term Βάρβαρος in the Acts of the Apostles: A Problemanzeige." *Neotestamentica* 47 (2013): 69–86.
———. "The Missionary Character of Paul's Stay on Malta (Acts 28: 1–10) according to the Early Church." *Journal of Early Christian History* 3 (2013): 83–97.
Bird, Michael F. *Jesus among the Gods: Early Christology in the Greco-Roman World*. Waco, TX: Baylor University Press, 2022.
Blum, Edward J., and Paul Harvey. *The Color of Christ: The Son of God and the Saga of Race in America*. Chapel Hill: University of North Carolina Press, 2012.
Bock, Darrell L. *Proclamation from Prophecy and Pattern: Lucan Old Testament Christology*. JSNTSup 12. Sheffield: JSOT Press, 1987.
———. *A Theology of Luke and Acts: God's Promised Program, Realized for All Nations*. Biblical Theology of the New Testament Series. Grand Rapids: Zondervan, 2012.
Boer, Roland. *The Sacred Economy of Ancient Israel*. Library of Ancient Israel. Louisville: Westminster John Knox, 2015.
Boers, Hendrikus. *What Is New Testament Theology? The Rise of Criticism and the Problem of a Theology of the New Testament*. Philadelphia: Fortress, 1979.
Borgen, Peder. *Philo of Alexandria, an Exegete for His Time*. NovTSup 86. Leiden: Brill, 1997.
Bovon, François. *Luke: The Theologian*. 2nd rev. ed. Waco, TX: Baylor University Press, 2006.
Bradley, Keith. *Slavery and Society at Rome*. Key Themes in Ancient History. Cambridge: Cambridge University Press, 1994.
Braulik, Georg P. "Psalter and Messiah: Towards a Christological Understanding of the Psalms in the Old Testament and the Church Fathers." Pages 15–40 in *Psalms and Liturgy*. Edited by Dirk J. Human and Cas J. A. Vos. JSOTSup 410. London: T&T Clark, 2004.
Brawley, Robert L. "Abrahamic Covenant Traditions and the Characterization of God in Luke-Acts." Pages 109–32 in *The Unity of Luke-Acts*. Edited by J. Verheyden. BETL 142. Leuven: Leuven University Press, 1999.
———. *Luke-Acts and the Jews: Conflict, Apology, and Conciliation*. SBLMS 33. Atlanta: Scholars Press, 1987.
———. *Text to Text Pours Forth Speech: Voices of Scripture in Luke-Acts*. ISBL. Bloomington: Indiana University Press, 1995.
Brink, Laurie. *Soldiers in Luke-Acts: Engaging, Contradicting, and Transcending the Stereotypes*. WUNT 2/362. Tübingen: Mohr Siebeck, 2014.
Brown, Peter. *Poverty and Leadership in the Later Roman Empire*. Hanover, NH: University Press of New England, 2002.
Brown, Raymond E. *The Death of the Messiah: From Gethsemane to the Grave; A Commentary on the Passion Narratives in the Four Gospels*. AYBRL. New York: Doubleday, 1994.
Bruce, F. F. *Commentary on the Book of Acts*. NICNT. Grand Rapids: Eerdmans, 1970.
Brueggemann, Walter. *The Land: Place as Gift, Promise, and Challenge in Biblical Faith*. OBT. Philadelphia: Fortress, 1977.

BIBLIOGRAPHY

———. *Money and Possessions*. Interpretation. Louisville: Westminster John Knox, 2016.
Buell, Denise Kimber. "Early Christian Universalism and Modern Forms of Racism." Pages 109–24 in *The Origins of Racism in the West*. Edited by Miriam Eliav-Feldon, Benjamin Isaac, and Joseph Ziegler. Cambridge: Cambridge University Press, 2009.
———. *Why This New Race: Ethnic Reasoning in Early Christianity*. New York: Columbia University Press, 2005.
Burnett, Anne Pippin. "Pentheus and Dionysus: Host and Guest." *CP* 65 (1970): 15–29.
Burrus, Virginia. "The Gospel of Luke and the Acts of the Apostles." Pages 133–55 in *A Postcolonial Commentary on the New Testament Writings*. Edited by F. F. Segovia and R. S. Sugirtharajah. Bible and Postcolonialism 13. London: T&T Clark, 2007.
Butticaz, Simon David. *L'identité de l'église dans les Actes des apôtres: De la restauration d'Israël à la conquête universelle*. BZNW 174. Berlin: de Gruyter, 2011.
Byron, Gay L. *Symbolic Blackness and Ethnic Difference in Early Christian Literature*. London: Routledge, 2002.
Cadbury, Henry J. *The Book of Acts in History*. London: Black, 1955.
———. "Lexical Notes on Luke-Acts: III. Luke's Interest in Lodging." *JBL* 45, (1926): 305–22.
———. "The Speeches in Acts." Pages 402–27 in *The Beginnings of Christianity: Part 1, The Acts of the Apostles*. Edited by F. J. Foakes Jackson and Kirsopp Lake. Vol. 5, *Additional Notes to the Commentary*. Edited by Kirsopp Lake and Henry J. Cadbury. London: Macmillan, 1933.
Cameron, Averil. *Christianity and the Rhetoric of Empire: The Development of Christian Discourse*. Berkeley: University of California Press, 1991.
Carroll, John T. "Luke's Crucifixion Scene." Pages 108–24 in *Reimaging the Death of the Lukan Jesus*. Edited by Dennis D. Sylva. Athenäums Monografien, Theologie 73. Frankfurt am Main: Anton Hain, 1990.
Carter, J. Kameron. *Race: A Theological Account*. Oxford: Oxford University Press, 2008.
Cartledge, Paul. *The Greeks: A Portrait of Self and Others*. 2nd edition. Oxford: Oxford University Press, 1997.
Chrysostom, John. "Homilies in the Acts of the Apostles." In vol. 11 of *The Nicene and Post-Nicene Fathers of the Christian Church*. Translated by Henry Browne. Oxford: Oxford University Press, 1851.
Clark, Elizabeth A. *History, Theory, Text: Historians and the Linguistic Turn*. Cambridge: Harvard University Press, 2004.
Clines, David J. A. *The Theme of the Pentateuch*. 2nd ed. Sheffield: Sheffield Academic, 1997.
Cochran, Elizabeth Agnew. "Bricolage and the Purity of Traditions: Engaging the Stoics for Contemporary Christian Ethics." *JRE* 40 (2012): 720–29.
Cohen, Shaye J. D. *The Beginnings of Jewishness: Boundaries, Varieties, Uncertainties*. Berkeley: University of California Press, 1999.
Conzelmann, Hans. "The Address of Paul on the Areopagus." Pages 217–30 in *Studies in Luke-Acts: Essays Presented in Honor of Paul Schubert*. Edited by Leander E. Keck and J. Louis Martyn. Mifflintown, PA: Sigler, 1966.
———. *The Theology of St. Luke*. Philadelphia: Fortress, 1982.
Cooke, G. "The Israelite King as Son of God." *ZAW* 73 (1961): 202–25.
Cooley, Alison E. *Res Gestae Divi Augusti: Text, Translation, and Commentary*. Cambridge: Cambridge University Press, 2009.
Cosgrove, Charles H. "The Divine Δεῖ in Luke-Acts: Investigations into the Lukan Understanding of God's Providence." *NovT* 26 (1984): 168–90.

Bibliography

Crossan, John Dominic. *In Parables: The Challenge of the Historical Jesus*. New York: Harper and Row, 1975.
Croy, Clayton. "Hellenistic Philosophies and the Preaching of the Resurrection (Acts 17:18, 32)." *NovT* 39 (1997): 21–39.
Crump, David Michael. *Jesus the Intercessor: Prayer and Christology in Luke-Acts*. WUNT 2/49. Tübingen: Mohr Siebeck, 1992.
Cunningham, Scott. *"Through Many Tribulations": The Theology of Persecution in Luke-Acts*. JSNTSup 142. Sheffield: Sheffield Academic, 1997.
Dahl, Nils A. "The Story of Abraham in Luke-Acts." Pages 139–58 in *Studies in Luke-Acts*. Edited by Leander E. Keck and J. Louis Martyn. Mifflintown, PA: Sigler, 1966.
Dawsey, James M. *The Lukan Voice: Confusion and Irony in the Gospel of Luke*. Macon, GA: Mercer University Press, 1986.
Dibelius, Martin. "Paul on the Aeropagus." Pages 26–77 in *Studies in the Acts of the Apostles*.
———. "The Speeches in Acts and Ancient Historiography." Pages 138–85 in *Studies in the Acts of the Apostles*.
———. *Studies in the Acts of the Apostles*. Translated by Mary Ling. London: SCM, 1951.
Dillon, Richard J. "Previewing Luke's Project from His Prologue (Luke 1:1–4)." *CBQ* 43 (1981): 205–27.
Doble, Peter. "Luke 24.26, 44—Songs of God's Servant: David and His Psalms in Luke-Acts." *JSNT* 28 (2006): 267–83.
———. *The Paradox of Salvation: Luke's Theology of the Cross*. SNTSMS 87. Cambridge: Cambridge University Press, 1996.
———. "The Psalms in Luke-Acts." Pages 83–119 in *The Psalms in the New Testament*. Edited by Steve Moyise and Maarten J. J. Menken. NTSI. New York: T&T Clark, 2004.
Dodd, C. H. *According to the Scriptures: The Sub-Structure of New Testament Theology*. London: Collins, 1952.
Donahue, John R. *The Gospel in Parable: Metaphor, Narrative, and Theology in the Synoptic Gospels*. Minneapolis: Fortress, 1988.
———. "A Neglected Factor in the Theology of Mark." *JBL* 101 (1982): 563–94.
Downs, David J. *The Offering of the Gentiles: Paul's Collection for Jerusalem in Its Chronological, Cultural, and Cultic Contexts*. WUNT 2/248. Tübingen: Mohr Siebeck, 2008.
Duling, Dennis C. "The Promises to David and Their Entrance into Christianity—Nailing down a Likely Hypothesis." *NTS* 20 (October 1973): 55–77.
Dupertuis, Ruben R. "Bold Speech, Opposition, and Philosophical Imagery in the Acts of the Apostles." Pages 153–68 in *Engaging Early Christian History: Reading Acts in the Second Century*. Edited by Ruben R. Dupertuis and Todd Penner. Durham: Acumen, 2013.
Dupont, Jacques. "'Assis à la droite de Dieu': L'interprétation du Ps. 110, 1 dans le Nouveau Testament." Pages 94–148 in *Resurrexit: Actes du Symposium International sur la Résurrection de Jésus (Rome 1970)*. Edited by Edouard Dhanis. Vatican City: Libreria Editrice Vaticana, 1974.
———. *Études sur les Actes des apôtres*. LD 45. Paris: Cerf, 1967.
———. "'Filius meus es tu'. L'interpretation de Ps 2,7 dans le Nouveau Testament." *RSR* 35 (1948): 522–43.
———. "La Destinée de Judas Prophétisée par David (Actes 1,16–20)." *CBQ* 23 (1961): 41–51.
———. "Les discours de Pierre dans les Actes et le Chapitre XXIV de l'évangile de Luc." Pages

329–74 in *L'Évangile de Luc: Problèmes littéraires et théologiques; Mémorial Lucien Cerfaux*. Edited by F. Neirynck. BETL 32. Gembloux: Duculot, 1973.

———. *L'utilisation apologétique de l'Ancien Testament dan les discours des Actes*. ALBO 40. Paris: Publications Universitaires, 1953.

Eaton, John H. *Kingship and the Psalms*. SBT 2/32. London: SCM, 1976.

Edwards, Mark. "Quoting Aratus: Acts 17,28." ZNW 83 (1992): 266–69.

Eiesland, Nancy. *The Disabled God: Toward a Liberatory Theology of Disability*. Nashville: Abingdon, 1994.

Escobar, Samuel. *In Search of Christ in Latin America: From Colonial Image to Liberating Savior*. Downers Grove, IL: InterVarsity Press, 2019.

Eskola, Timo. *Messiah and the Throne: Jewish Merkabah Mysticism and Early Christian Exaltation Discourse*. WUNT 2/142. Tübingen: Mohr Siebeck, 2001.

Eubank, Nathan. *Wages of Cross-Bearing and Debt of Sin: The Economy of Heaven in Matthew's Gospel*. BZNW 196. Berlin: de Gruyter, 2013.

Eyl, Jennifer. "Divination and Miracles." Pages 215–34 in *T&T Clark Handbook to the Historical Paul*. Edited by Ryan S. Schellenberg and Heidi Wendt. London: T&T Clark, 2022.

Ferngren, Gary B. *Medicine and Health Care in Early Christianity*. Baltimore: Johns Hopkins University Press, 2009.

Fiensy, David A. *Christian Origins and the Ancient Economy*. Eugene, OR: Cascade, 2014.

Finley, M. I. *The World of Odysseus*. London: Chatto and Windus, 1977.

———. *The Ancient Economy*. Berkeley: University of California Press, 1973.

Fitzmyer, Joseph A. *The Acts of the Apostles*. AYBC. New Haven: Doubleday, 1998.

———. "David, 'Being Therefore a Prophet . . .' (Acts 2:30)." CBQ 34 (1972): 332–39.

———. *The Gospel According to Luke X–XXIV: A New Translation with Introduction and Commentary*. AB 28A. Garden City, NY: Doubleday, 1985.

Flett, John G. *Apostolicity: The Ecumenical Question in World Christian Perspective*. Downers Grove, IL: InterVarsity Press, 2016.

Frankenberg, Ruth. *White Women, Race Matters: The Social Construction of Whiteness*. Minneapolis: University of Minnesota Press, 1993.

Fredriksen, Paula. "How Jewish Is God? Divine Ethnicity in Paul's Theology." JBL 137 (2018): 193–212.

———. *Paul: The Pagans' Apostle*. New Haven: Yale University Press, 2017.

Frei, Hans W. *The Eclipse of Biblical Narrative: A Study in Eighteenth and Nineteenth Century Hermeneutics*. New Haven: Yale University Press, 1974.

———. *The Identity of Jesus Christ*. Philadelphia: Fortress, 1975.

Freyne, Sean. *The Jesus Movement and Its Expansion: Meaning and Mission*. Grand Rapids: Eerdmans, 2014.

Friesen, Steve. "Injustice or God's Will? Early Christian Explanations of Poverty." Pages 17–36 in *Wealth and Poverty in Early Church and Society*. Edited by Susan R. Holman. Grand Rapids: Baker Academic, 2008.

Gager, John G. *Who Made Early Christianity? The Jewish Lives of the Apostle Paul*. New York: Columbia University Press, 2015.

García-Johnson, Oscar. *Spirit Outside the Gate: Decolonial Pneumatologies of the American Global South*. Downers Grove, IL: InterVarsity Press, 2019.

Gardner, Gregg E. *The Origins of Organized Charity in Rabbinic Judaism*. Cambridge: Cambridge University Press, 2015.

Garland, Robert. *Introducing New Gods: The Politics of Athenian Religion*. London: Duckworth, 1992.
Garnsey, Peter, and Richard Saller. *The Roman Empire: Economy, Society and Culture*. 2nd ed. Berkeley: University of California Press, 2015.
Garnsey, Peter, and Greg Wolf. "Patronage of the Rural Poor in the Roman World." Pages 153–70 in *Patronage in Ancient Society*. Edited by Andrew Wallace-Hadrill. London: Routledge, 1989.
Garrett, Susan R. *The Demise of the Devil: Magic and the Demonic in Luke's Writings*. Minneapolis: Fortress, 1989.
Gärtner, Bertil. *The Areopagus Speech and Natural Revelation*. Translated by Carolyn Hannay King. ASNU 21. Uppsala: Gleerup, 1955.
Gaston, Lloyd. *No Stone on Another: Studies in the Significance of the Fall of Jerusalem in the Synoptic Gospels*. NovTSup 23. Leiden: Brill, 1970.
Gaventa, Beverly Roberts. *From Darkness to Light: Aspects of Conversion in the New Testament*. OBT. Philadelphia: Fortress, 1986.
———. "Toward a Theology of Acts: Reading and Rereading." *Int* 42 (1988): 146–57.
Geary, Patrick J. *The Myth of Nations: The Medieval Origins of Europe*. Princeton: Princeton University Press, 2002.
Gebhard, Elizabeth R. "The Gods in Transit: Narratives of Cult Transfer." Pages 451–76 in *Antiquity and Humanity: Essays on Ancient Religion and Philosophy Presented to Hans Dieter Betz on His 70th Birthday*. Edited by Adela Yarbro Collins and Margaret M. Mitchell. Tübingen: Mohr Siebeck, 2001.
Gerbrandt, Gerald Eddie. *Kingship According to the Deuteronomistic History*. SBLDS 87. Atlanta: Scholars Press, 1986.
Gilbert, Gary. "The List of Nations in Acts 2: Roman Propaganda and the Lukan Response." *JBL* 121 (2002): 497–529.
Gill, David W. J. "Achaia." Pages 433–54 in *The Book of Acts in Its First Century Setting*. Vol. 2, *The Book of Acts in Its Graeco-Roman Setting*. Edited by David W. J. Gill and Conrad Gempf. Grand Rapids: Eerdmans, 1994.
Given, Mark. "Not Either/or But Both/and in Paul's Areopagus Speech." *BibInt* 3 (1995): 356–72.
Goodman, Martin. "The Persecution of Paul by Diaspora Jews." Pages 379–87 in *The Beginnings of Christianity: A Collection of Articles*. Edited by Jack Pastor and Menachem Mor. Jerusalem: Yad BenZvi, 2005.
Grant, Jamie A. *The King as Exemplar: The Function of Deuteronomy's Kingship Law in the Shaping of the Book of Psalms*. Academia Biblica 17. Atlanta: Society of Biblical Literature Press, 2004.
Gray, Patrick. "Athenian Curiosity (Acts 17:21)." *NovT* 47 (2005): 109–16.
———. "Implied Audiences in the Areopagus Narrative." *TynB* 55 (2004): 205–18.
———. *Paul as a Problem in History and Culture: The Apostle and His Critics through the Centuries*. Grand Rapids: Baker Academic, 2016.
Green, Joel B. Afterword to *Reading Luke: Interpretation, Reflection, Formation*. Edited by Craig Bartholomew, Joel B. Green, and Anthony C. Thiselton. Grand Rapids: Zondervan, 2005.
———. "The Death of Jesus, God's Servant." Pages 1–28 in *Reimaging the Death of the Lukan Jesus*. Edited by Dennis D. Sylva. Athenäums Monografien Theologie. Frankfurt am Main: Hain, 1990.

BIBLIOGRAPHY

———. *The Gospel of Luke.* NICNT. Grand Rapids: Eerdmans, 1997.
———. "Jesus and a Daughter of Abraham (Luke 13:10–17): Test Case for a Lucan Perspective on Jesus' Miracles." *CBQ* 51 (1989): 643–54.
———. "The Problem of a Beginning: Israel's Scriptures in Luke 1–2." *BBR* 4 (1994): 61–86.
———. "Scripture and Theology: Failed Experiments, Fresh Perspectives." *Int* 56 (2002): 5–20.
———. *The Theology of the Gospel of Luke.* Cambridge: Cambridge University Press, 1995.
Greene-McCreight, Kathryn. *Darkness Is My Only Companion: A Christian Response to Mental Illness.* 2nd ed. Grand Rapids: Brazos, 2015.
Griffith, Terry. "'The Jews Who Had Believed in Him' (John 8:31) and the Motif of Apostasy in the Gospel of John." Pages 183–92 in *The Gospel of John and Christian Theology.* Edited by Richard Bauckham and Carl Mosser. Grand Rapids: Eerdmans, 2008.
———. *Keep Yourselves from Idols: A New Look at 1 John.* JSNTSup 233. London: Sheffield Academic, 2002.
Gruen, Erich S. *Heritage and Hellenism: The Reinvention of Jewish Tradition.* Berkeley: University of California Press, 1998.
———. *Rethinking the Other in Antiquity.* Princeton: Princeton University Press, 2011.
Haacker, Klaus. "Das Bekenntnis des Paulus zur Hoffnung Israels nach der Apostelgeschichte des Lukas." *NTS* 31 (1985): 437–51.
Habel, Norman C. *The Land Is Mine: Six Biblical Land Ideologies.* OBT. Minneapolis: Augsburg Fortress, 1995.
Haenchen, Ernst. *The Acts of the Apostles: A Commentary.* Philadelphia: Westminster, 1971.
Hahn, Scott W. *The Kingdom of God as Liturgical Empire: A Theological Commentary on 1–2 Chronicles.* Grand Rapids: Baker, 2012.
———. *Kinship by Covenant: A Canonical Approach to the Fulfillment of God's Saving Promises.* AYBRL. New Haven: Yale University Press, 2009.
Hall, Edith. *Inventing the Barbarian: Greek Self-Definition through Tragedy.* Oxford: Clarendon, 1989.
Hall, Jonathan M. *Hellenicity: Between Ethnicity and Culture.* Chicago: University of Chicago Press, 2002.
Hall, Robert. *Revealed Histories: Techniques for Ancient Jewish and Christian Historiography.* JSPSup 6. Sheffield: Sheffield Academic, 1991.
Hamel, Gildas H. *Poverty and Charity in Roman Palestine: The First Three Centuries C.E.* Berkeley: University of California Press, 1990.
Hamilton, Jeffries M. *Social Justice and Deuteronomy: The Case of Deuteronomy 15.* SBLDS 136. Atlanta: Scholars Press, 1992.
Hamilton, Mark W. *The Body Royal: The Social Poetics of Kingship in Ancient Israel.* Biblical Interpretation Series 78. Leiden: Brill, 2005.
———. *Jesus, King of Strangers: What the Bible Really Says about Immigration.* Grand Rapids: Eerdmans, 2019.
Hamm, Dennis. "Luke 19:8 Once Again: Does Zacchaeus Defend or Resolve?" *JBL* 107 (1988): 431–37.
———. "Sight to the Blind: Vision as Metaphor in Luke." *Bib* 67 (1986): 457–77.
Harris, Sarah. *The Davidic Shepherd King in the Lukan Narrative.* LNTS 558. London: T&T Clark, 2016.
Harrisville, Roy A., and Walter Sundberg. *The Bible in Modern Culture: Baruch Spinoza to Brevard Childs.* 2nd ed. Grand Rapids: Eerdmans, 2002.

Bibliography

Hart, Trevor A. *Faith Thinking: The Dynamics of Christian Theology*. Downers Grove, IL: InterVarsity Press, 1995.

Hartog, François. *The Mirror of Herodotus: The Representation of the Other in the Writing of History*. Translated by Janet Lloyd. Berkeley: University of California Press, 1988.

Hay, David M. *Glory at the Right Hand: Psalm 110 in Early Christianity*. SBLMS 18. Nashville: Abingdon, 1973.

Hayes, Christine. *What's Divine about Divine Law? Early Perspectives*. Princeton: Princeton University Press, 2015.

Hays, Richard B. "Christ Prays the Psalms: Paul's Use of an Early Christian Exegetical Convention." Pages 122–36 in *The Future of Christology: Essays in Honor of Leander E. Keck*. Edited by Wayne A. Meeks and Abraham J. Malherbe. Minneapolis: Fortress, 1993.

———. *Echoes of Scripture in the Gospels*. Waco, TX: Baylor University Press, 2016.

———. *Echoes of Scripture in the Letters of Paul*. New Haven: Yale University Press, 1989.

———. "Reading Scripture in Light of the Resurrection." Pages 216–38 in *The Art of Reading Scripture*. Edited by Ellen F. Davis and Richard B. Hays. Grand Rapids: Eerdmans, 2003.

Heimburger, Robert W. *God and the Illegal Alien: United States Immigration Law and a Theology of Politics*. Cambridge: Cambridge University Press, 2018.

Hemer, Colin J. *The Book of Acts in the Setting of Hellenistic History*. WUNT 49. Tübingen: Mohr Siebeck, 1989.

Hengel, Martin. *Property and Riches in the Early Church: Aspects of a Social History of Early Christianity*. Translated by John Bowden. Philadelphia: Fortress, 1974.

Henriksen, Jan-Olav, and Karl Olav Sandnes. *Jesus as Healer: A Gospel for the Body*. Grand Rapids: Eerdmans, 2016.

Herman, Gabriel. *Ritualised Friendship and the Greek City*. Cambridge: Cambridge University Press, 1987.

Heschel, Susannah. *The Aryan Jesus: Christian Theologians and the Bible in Nazi Germany*. Princeton: Princeton University Press, 2008.

Holmås, Geir Otto. "'My House Shall Be a House of Prayer': Regarding the Temple as a Place of Prayer in Acts within the Context of Luke's Apologetical Objective." *JSNT* 27 (2005): 393–416.

Hommel, H. "Platonisches Bei Lukas: Zu Acta 17.28a." *ZNW* 48 (1957): 193–200.

Hood, Jason B. *The Messiah, His Brothers, and the Nations: Matthew 1.1–17*. LNTS 441. New York: T&T Clark, 2011.

Hooker, Morna D. *Jesus and the Servant: The Influence of the Servant Concept of Deutero-Isaiah in the New Testament*. London: Nisbet, 1959.

Horst, Pieter W. van der. "The Altar of the 'Unknown God' in Athens (Acts 17:23) and the 'Cult of the Unknown Gods' in the Hellenistic and Roman Periods." *ANRW* 2.18.2 (1990): 1426–56.

Hoskyns, Edwyn Clement. *The Fourth Gospel*. London: Faber and Faber, 1947.

Hubbard, Benjamin. "The Role of Commissioning Accounts in Acts." Pages 187–98 in *Perspectives on Luke-Acts*. Edited by Charles H. Talbert. Edinburgh: T&T Clark, 1978.

Huizenga, L. A. *The New Isaac: Tradition and Intertextuality in the Gospel of Matthew*. NovTSup 131. Leiden: Brill, 2009.

Hume, Douglas A. *The Early Christian Community: A Narrative Analysis of Acts 2:41–47 and 4:32–35*. WUNT 2/298. Tübingen: Mohr Siebeck, 2011.

Hunt, Steven A. "And the Word Became Flesh—Again? Jesus and Abraham in John 8:31–59."

BIBLIOGRAPHY

Pages 81–109 in *Perspectives on Our Father Abraham: Essays in Honor of Marvin R. Wilson*. Grand Rapids: Eerdmans, 2012.

Hurtado, Larry W. *Destroyer of the Gods: Early Christian Distinctiveness in the Roman World*. Waco, TX: Baylor University Press, 2016.

———. *Why on Earth Did Anyone Become a Christian in the First Three Centuries?* Milwaukee: Marquette University Press, 2016.

Hutchinson, John, and Anthony D. Smith, eds. *Ethnicity*. Oxford: Oxford University Press, 1996.

Hvalvik, Reidar. "Paul as a Jewish Believer—according to the Book of Acts." Pages 121–51 in *Jewish Believers in Jesus: The Early Centuries*. Edited by Oskar Skarsaune and Reidar Hvalvik. Grand Rapids: Baker Academic, 2017.

Jennings, Willie James. *Acts*. Belief. Louisville: Westminster John Knox, 2017.

———. *The Christian Imagination: Theology and the Origins of Race*. New Haven: Yale University Press, 2010.

Jenson, Robert W. "Toward a Christian Theology of Israel." *Pro Ecclesia* 9 (2000): 43–56.

Jervell, Jacob. *Die Apostelgeschichte*. Kritisch-exegetischer Kommentar über das Neue Testament (Meyer-Kommentar). Göttingen: Vandenhoeck & Ruprecht, 1998.

———. *Luke and the People of God: A New Look at Luke-Acts*. Minneapolis: Augsburg, 1972.

———. *The Theology of the Acts of the Apostles*. Cambridge: Cambridge University Press, 1996.

Jeska, Joachim. *Die Geschichte Israels in der Sicht des Lukas: Apg 7,2b-53 und 13,17-25 im Kontext antik-jüdischer Summarien der Geschichte Israels*. FRLANT 195. Göttingen: Vandenhoeck & Ruprecht, 2001.

Jipp, Joshua W. "The Acts of the Apostles." Pages 350–67 in *The State of New Testament Studies: A Survey of Recent Research*. Edited by Scot McKnight and Nijay K. Gupta. Grand Rapids: Baker Academic, 2019.

———. "The Beginnings of a Theology of Luke-Acts: Divine Activity and Human Response." *JTI* 8 (2014): 23–44.

———. *Christ Is King: Paul's Royal Ideology*. Minneapolis: Fortress, 2015.

———. *Divine Visitations and Hospitality to Strangers in Luke-Acts: An Interpretation of the Malta Episode in Acts 28:1-10*. NovTSup 153. Leiden: Brill, 2013.

———. "Does Paul Translate the Gospel in Acts 17:22–31? A Critical Engagement with C. Kavin Rowe's One True Life." *PRSt* 45 (2018): 361–76.

———. "Hospitable Barbarians: Luke's Ethnic Reasoning in Acts 28:1–10." *JTS* 68 (2017): 23–45.

———. "Luke's Scriptural Suffering Messiah: A Search for Precedent, a Search for Identity." *CBQ* 72 (2010): 255–74.

———. "The Paul of Acts: Proclaimer of the Hope of Israel or Teacher of Apostasy from Moses." *NovT* 62 (2020): 60–78.

———. "Paul's Areopagus Speech of Acts 17:16–34 as *Both* Critique *and* Propaganda." *JBL* 131 (2012): 567–88.

———. *Reading Acts*. Eugene, OR: Cascade, 2018.

———. *Saved by Faith and Hospitality*. Grand Rapids: Eerdmans, 2017.

Johnson, Aubrey. *Sacral Kingship in Ancient Israel*. Cardiff: University of Wales Press, 1967.

Johnson, Kelly. *The Fear of Beggars: Stewardship and Poverty in Christian Ethics*. Grand Rapids: Eerdmans, 2007.

Johnson, Luke Timothy. *The Acts of the Apostles*. SP 5. Collegeville, MN: Liturgical Press, 1992.

Bibliography

———. *Among the Gentiles: Greco-Roman Religion and Christianity*. AYBRL. New Haven: Yale University Press, 2009.

———. "Fragments of an Untidy Conversation: Theology and the Literary Diversity of the New Testament." Pages 276–89 in *Biblical Theology: Problems and Perspectives, In Honor of J. Christiaan Beker*. Edited by Steven J. Kraftchick, Charles D. Myers, and Ben C. Ollenburger. Nashville: Abingdon, 1995.

———. "Imagining the World Scripture Imagines." *Modern Theology* 14 (1998): 165–80.

———. "James 3:13–4:10 and the *Topos* περὶ φθόνου." *NovT* 25 (1983): 327–47.

———. *The Literary Function of Possessions in Luke-Acts*. SBLDS 39. Missoula, MT: Scholars Press, 1977.

———. *Prophetic Jesus, Prophetic Church: The Challenge of Luke-Acts to Contemporary Christians*. Grand Rapids: Eerdmans, 2011.

———. *The Revelatory Body: Theology as Inductive Art*. Grand Rapids: Eerdmans, 2015.

———. *Scripture and Discernment: Decision Making in the Church*. Nashville: Abingdon, 1983.

———. *Septuagintal Midrash in the Speeches of Acts*. The Père Marquette Lecture in Theology, 2002. Milwaukee: Marquette University Press, 2002.

———. *Sharing Possessions: What Faith Demands*. 2nd ed. Grand Rapids: Eerdmans, 2011.

Johnson Hodge, Caroline. "The Question of Identity: Gentiles as Gentiles—but Also Not—in Pauline Communities." Pages 153–73 in *Paul within Judaism: Restoring the First-Century Context to the Apostle*. Edited by Mark D. Nanos and Magnus Zetterholm. Minneapolis: Fortress, 2015.

Juel, Donald. *Messianic Exegesis: Christological Interpretation of the Old Testament in Early Christianity*. Philadelphia: Fortress, 1988.

———. "Social Dimensions of Exegesis: The Use of Psalm 16 in Acts 2." *CBQ* 43 (1981): 543–56.

Kamell, Mariam. "The Economics of Humility: The Rich and the Humble in James." Pages 157–75 in *Engaging Economics: New Testament Scenarios and Early Christian Reception*. Edited by Bruce W. Longenecker and Kelly D. Liebengood. Grand Rapids: Eerdmans, 2009.

Kautsky, John H. *The Politics of Aristocratic Empires*. Chapel Hill: University of North Carolina Press, 1982.

Keener, Craig S. *Acts: An Exegetical Commentary*. 4 vols. Grand Rapids: Baker Academic, 2012–2015.

Kehoe, Dennis P. "The Early Roman Empire: Production." Pages 541–69 in *The Cambridge Economic History of the Greco-Roman World*. Edited by Walter Scheidel, Ian Morris, and Richard P. Saller. Cambridge: Cambridge University Press, 2007.

Kelley, Shawn. *Racializing Jesus: Race, Ideology and the Formation of Modern Biblical Scholarship*. London: Routledge, 2002.

Kennedy, Rebecca F., C. Sydnor Roy, and Max L. Goldman, trans. *Race and Ethnicity in the Classical World: An Anthology of Primary Sources in Translation*. Indianapolis: Hackett, 2013.

Kilgallen, John J. "Your Servant Jesus Whom You Anointed (Acts 4,27)." *RB* 105 (1998): 185–201.

Kinman, Brent. "Parousia, Jesus' 'A-Triumphal' Entry, and the Fate of Jerusalem (Luke 19:28–44)." *JBL* 118 (1999): 279–94.

BIBLIOGRAPHY

Kinzer, Mark S. *Jerusalem Crucified, Jerusalem Risen: The Resurrected Messiah, the Jewish People, and the Land of Promise*. Eugene, OR: Cascade, 2018.

Kirk, Alan. "'Love Your Enemies,' the Golden Rule, and Ancient Reciprocity (Luke 6:27–35)." *JBL* 122 (2003): 667–86.

Klassen, William. *Judas: Betrayer or Friend of Jesus?* Minneapolis: Fortress, 1996.

Klauck, Hans-Josef. *Magic and Paganism in Early Christianity: The World of the Acts of the Apostles*. Edinburgh: T&T Clark, 2000.

Klawans, Jonathan. *Josephus and the Theologies of Ancient Judaism*. Oxford: Oxford University Press, 2012.

Kleinknecht, Karl Theodor. *Der leidende Gerechtfertigte: Die alttestamentlich-jüdische Tradition vom "leidenden Gerechten" und ihre Rezeption bei Paulus*. WUNT 13. Tübingen: Mohr Siebeck, 1988.

Konradt, Matthias. *Israel, Church, and the Gentiles in the Gospel of Matthew*. Translated by Kathleen Ess. Baylor-Mohr Siebeck Studies in Early Christianity. Waco, TX: Baylor University Press, 2014.

Konstan, David. *Friendship in the Classical World*. Cambridge: Cambridge University Press, 1997.

Koser, Khalid. *International Migration: A Very Short Introduction*. 2nd ed. Oxford: Oxford University Press, 2016.

Lake, Kirsopp. "Your Own Poets." Pages 246–51 in *The Beginnings of Christianity: Part 1, The Acts of the Apostles*. Edited by F. J. Foakes Jackson and Kirsopp Lake. Vol. 5, *Additional Notes to the Commentary*. Edited by Kirsopp Lake and Henry J. Cadbury. London: Macmillan, 1933.

Langton, Daniel R. *The Apostle Paul in the Jewish Imagination: A Study in Modern Jewish-Christian Relations*. Cambridge: Cambridge University Press, 2010.

Lash, Nicholas. *Theology on the Way to Emmaus*. London: SCM, 1986.

LeDonne, Anthony. *The Historiographical Jesus: Memory, Typology, and the Son of David*. Waco, TX: Baylor University Press, 2009.

Levenson, Jon D. *Abraham Between Torah and Gospel*. The Père Marquette Lecture in Theology 2011. Milwaukee: Marquette University Press, 2011.

———. *Resurrection and the Restoration of Israel: The Ultimate Victory of the God of Life*. New Haven: Yale University Press, 2006.

Lieu, Judith M. "The Christian Race." Pages 239–68 in Lieu, *Christian Identity in the Jewish and Graeco-Roman World*. Oxford: Oxford University Press, 2004.

Litwa, M. David. *IESUS DEUS: The Early Christian Depiction of Jesus as a Mediterranean God*. Minneapolis: Fortress, 2014.

Long, Anthony A. *Epictetus: A Stoic and Socratic Guide to Life*. Oxford: Clarendon, 2002.

———. "Hellenistic Ethics and Philosophical Power." Pages 138–56 in *Hellenistic History and Culture*. Edited by Peter Green. Hellenistic Culture and Society 9. Berkeley: University of California Press, 1993.

———. "Philo on Stoic Physics." Pages 121–40 in *Philo of Alexandria and Post-Aristotelian Philosophy*. Edited by Francesca Alesse. Studies in Philo of Alexandria 5. Leiden: Brill, 2008.

Longenecker, Bruce W. *Remember the Poor: Paul, Poverty, and the Greco-Roman World*. Grand Rapids: Eerdmans, 2010.

Lövestam, Evald. *Son and Saviour: A Study of Acts 13, 32–37; With an Appendix, "Son of God" in the Synoptic Gospels*. Translated by Michael Petry. Lund: Gleerup, 1961.

Bibliography

Lucass, Shirley. *The Concept of the Messiah in the Scriptures of Judaism and Christianity.* LSTS 78. New York: T&T Clark, 2011.
Lundin, Roger, Clarence Walhout, and Anthony C. Thiselton. *The Promise of Hermeneutics.* Grand Rapids: Eerdmans, 1999.
Luz, Ulrich. *Matthew 1–7: A Commentary.* Translated by Wilhelm C. Linss. Minneapolis: Augsburg Fortress, 1985.
Lynch, Matthew. *Monotheism and Institutions in the Book of Chronicles: Temple, Priesthood, and Kingship in Post-Exilic Perspective.* FAT 2/64. Tübingen: Mohr Siebeck, 2014.
Ma, John. "Kings." Pages 183–86 in *A Companion to the Hellenistic World.* Edited by Andrew Erskine. Malden, MA: Wiley-Blackwell, 2005.
MacIntyre, Alasdair. *Three Rival Versions of Moral Enquiry: Encyclopaedia, Genealogy, and Tradition.* Notre Dame: University of Notre Dame Press, 1990.
Mack, Michael. *German Idealism and the Jew: The Inner Anti-Semitism of Philosophy and German Jewish Responses.* Chicago: University of Chicago Press, 2003.
MacMullen, Ramsay. *Christianizing the Roman Empire: A.D. 100–400.* New Haven: Yale University Press, 1984.
———. *Paganism in the Roman Empire.* New Haven: Yale University Press, 1981.
Malherbe, Abraham J. "The Christianization of a Topos (Luke 12:13–34)." In *Light from the Gentiles: Hellenistic Philosophy and Early Christianity*, 339–51. Supplements to Novum Testamentum 150. Leiden: Brill, 2015.
———. "'Not in a Corner': Early Christian Apologetic in Acts 26:26." Pages 209–29 in *Light from the Gentiles: Hellenistic Philosophy and Early Christianity: Collected Essays, 1959–2012.* NovTSup 150. Leiden: Brill, 2014.
———. "Pseudo-Heraclitus, Epistle 4: The Divinization of the Wise Man." *Jahrbuch Für Antike Und Christentum* 21 (1978): 42–64.
Mamdani, Mahmood. *Citizen and Subject: Contemporary Africa and the Legacy of Late Colonialism.* Princeton: Princeton University Press, 1996.
Marcus, Joel. "Crucifixion as Parodic Exaltation." *JBL* 125 (2006): 73–87.
———. *Mark 8–16.* AYBC 27A. New Haven: Yale University Press, 2009.
———. *The Way of the Lord: Christological Exegesis of the Old Testament in the Gospel of Mark.* Louisville: Westminster John Knox, 1992.
Marguerat, Daniel. *Les Actes des Apôtres (1–12).* CNT. Geneva: Labor et Fides, 2007.
———. *The First Christian Historian: Writing the "Acts of the Apostles."* Translated by Ken McKinney, Gregory J. Laughery, and Richard Bauckham. SNTSMS 121. Cambridge: Cambridge University Press, 2002.
———. "Paul and the Torah in the Acts of the Apostles." Pages 98–117 in *Torah in the New Testament: Papers Delivered at the Manchester-Lausanne Seminar of June 2008.* Edited by Peter Oakes and Michael Tait. LNTS 401. London: T&T Clark, 2009.
Marshall, I. Howard. *The Acts of the Apostles.* Sheffield: Sheffield Academic, 1992.
———. *The Gospel of Luke: A Commentary on the Greek Text.* NIGTC. Grand Rapids: Eerdmans, 1978.
Marshall, I. Howard, and David Peterson, eds. *Witness to the Gospel: The Theology of Acts.* Grand Rapids: Eerdmans, 1998.
Marshall, Jonathan. *Jesus, Patrons, and Benefactors: Roman Palestine and the Gospel of Luke.* WUNT 2/259. Tübingen: Mohr Siebeck, 2009.
Martens, John W. "The Meaning and Function of the Law in Philo and Josephus." Pages

27–40 in *Torah Ethics and Early Christian Identity*. Edited by Susan J. Wendel and David M. Miller. Grand Rapids: Eerdmans, 2016.

Martin, Clarice J. "A Chamberlain's Journey and the Challenge of Interpretation for Liberation." *Semeia* 47 (1989): 105–35.

Martin, Dale B. *Inventing Superstition: From the Hippocratics to the Christians*. Cambridge: Harvard University Press, 2004.

———. "Paul and the Judaism/Hellenism Dichotomy: Toward a Social History of the Question." Pages 29–61 in *Paul Beyond the Judaism-Hellenism Divide*. Edited by Troels Engberg-Pedersen. Louisville: Westminster John Knox, 2001.

———. *Slavery as Salvation: The Metaphor of Slavery in Pauline Christianity*. New Haven: Yale University Press, 1990.

Matera, Frank J. *Passion Narratives and Gospel Theologies: Interpreting the Synoptics through Their Passion Stories*. Theological Inquiries. New York: Paulist, 1986.

Matson, David Lertis. *Household Conversion Narratives in Acts: Pattern and Interpretation*. JSNTSup 123. Sheffield: Sheffield Academic, 1996.

Matthews, Shelly. *Perfect Martyr: The Stoning of Stephen and the Construction of Christian Identity*. Oxford: Oxford University Press, 2010.

Mbiti, John S. *New Testament Eschatology in an African Background: A Study of the Encounter between New Testament Theology and African Traditional Concepts*. Oxford: Oxford University Press, 1971.

McWhirter, Jocelyn. *Rejected Prophets: Jesus and His Witnesses in Luke-Acts*. Minneapolis: Fortress, 2013.

Meeks, Wayne A. "Judaism, Hellenism, and the Birth of Christianity." Pages 17–28 in *Paul Beyond the Judaism/Hellenism Divide*. Edited by Troels Engberg-Pedersen. Louisville: Westminster John Knox, 2001.

Meggitt, Justin J. *Paul, Poverty and Survival*. Studies of the New Testament and Its World. Edinburgh: T&T Clark, 1998.

Meier, John P. "The Historical Jesus and the Historical Law: Some Problems within the Problem." *CBQ* 65 (2003): 52–79.

Ménard, Jacques E. "*Pais Theou* as a Messianic Title in the Book of Acts." *CBQ* 19 (1957): 83–92.

Mettinger, Tryggve N. D. *King and Messiah: The Civil and Sacral Legitimation of the Israelite Kings*. CBOT 8. Lund: Gleerup, 1976.

Miller, David M. "Reading Law as Prophecy: Torah Ethics in Acts." Pages 75–91 in *Torah Ethics and Early Christian Identity*. Edited by Susan J. Wendel and David M. Miller. Grand Rapids: Eerdmans, 2016.

Miller, Patrick D., Jr. "The Gift of God: The Deuteronomic Theology of the Land." *Int* 23 (1969): 451–65.

Minear, Paul S. *To Heal and to Reveal: The Prophetic Vocation According to Luke*. New York: Seabury, 1976.

Mitchell, Alan C. "The Social Function of Friendship in Acts 2:44–47 and 4:32–37." *JBL* 111 (1992): 255–72.

Mitchell, David C. *The Message of the Psalter: An Eschatological Programme in the Book of Psalms*. JSOTSup 252. Sheffield: Sheffield Academic, 1997.

Miura, Yuzuru. *David in Luke-Acts: His Portrayal in the Light of Early Judaism*. WUNT 2/232. Tübingen: Mohr Siebeck, 2007.

Moessner, David P. "'The Christ Must Suffer': New Light on the Jesus—Peter, Stephen,

Paul Parallels in Luke-Acts." Pages 238–71 in Moessner, *Luke the Historian of Israel's Legacy.*

———. *Lord of the Banquet: The Literary and Theological Significance of the Lukan Travel Narrative.* Minneapolis: Fortress, 1989.

———. *Luke the Historian of Israel's Legacy, Theologian of Israel's "Christ": A New Reading of the "Gospel of Acts" of Luke.* BZNW 182. Berlin: de Gruyter, 2016.

———. "Paul in Acts: Preacher of Eschatological Repentance to Israel." *NTS* 34 (1988): 96–104.

———. "Paul in Acts: Preacher of Eschatological Repentance to Israel." Pages 292–301 in Moessner, *Luke the Historian of Israel's Legacy.*

———. "Reading Luke's Gospel as Ancient Hellenistic Narrative: Luke's Narrative Plan of Israel's Suffering Messiah as God's Saving 'Plan' for the World." Pages 125–54 in *Reading Luke: Interpretation, Reflection, Formation.* Edited by Craig G. Bartholomew, Joel B. Green, and Anthony C. Thiselton. Grand Rapids: Zondervan, 2005.

———. "Two Lords 'at the Right Hand'? The Psalms and an Intertextual Reading of Peter's Pentecost Speech (Acts 2:14–36)." Pages 215–32 in *Literary Studies in Luke-Acts: Essays in Honor of Joseph B. Tyson.* Edited by Richard P. Thompson and Thomas E. Phillips. Macon, GA: Mercer University Press, 1998.

Moessner, David P., Daniel Marguerat, Mikeal C. Parsons, and Michael Wolter, eds. *Paul and the Heritage of Israel: Paul's Claim upon Israel's Legacy in Luke and Acts in the Light of the Pauline Letters.* Vol. 2 of *Luke the Interpreter of Israel.* LNTS 452. London: T&T Clark, 2012.

Momigliano, Arnaldo. *Alien Wisdom: The Limits of Hellenization.* Cambridge: Cambridge University Press, 1975.

Morley, Neville. "The Early Roman Empire: Distribution." Pages 570–91 in *The Cambridge Economic History of the Greco-Roman World.* Edited by Walter Scheidel, Ian Morris, and Richard P. Saller. Cambridge: Cambridge University Press, 2007.

Mowery, Robert L. "Lord, God, and Father: Theological Language in Luke-Acts." *SBLSP* (1995): 82–101.

Mowinckel, Sigmund. *He That Cometh: The Messiah Concept in the Old Testament and Later Judaism.* Translated by G. W. Anderson. Grand Rapids: Eerdmans, 2005.

Moxnes, Halvor. *The Economy of the Kingdom: Social Conflict and Economic Relations in Luke's Gospel.* Eugene, OR: Wipf & Stock, 2004.

Moxnes, Halvor, Ward Blanton, and James G. Crossley. *Jesus Beyond Nationalism: Constructing the Historical Jesus in a Period of Cultural Complexity.* London: Routledge, 2014.

Nasrallah, Laura Salah. *Christian Responses to Roman Art and Architecture: The Second-Century Church amid the Spaces of Empire.* Cambridge: Cambridge University Press, 2010.

Nauck, Wolfgang. "Die Tradition und Komposition der Areopagrede: Eine Motivgeschichtliche Untersuchung." *ZTK* 53 (1956): 11–52.

Neagoe, Alexandru. *The Trial of the Gospel: An Apologetic Reading of Luke's Trial Narratives.* SNTSMS 116. Cambridge: Cambridge University Press, 2002.

Neuer, Werner, and Adolf Schlatter. "Adolf Schlatter on Atheistic Methods in Theology." Translated by David R. Bauer. Pages 211–25 in *Adolf Schlatter: A Biography of Germany's Premier Biblical Theologian.* Translated Robert W. Yarbrough. Grand Rapids: Baker, 1996.

Newbigin, Lesslie. *The Gospel in a Pluralist Society*. Grand Rapids: Eerdmans, 1989.
Nouwen, Henri J. M. *Reaching Out: The Three Movements of the Spiritual Life*. New York: Image, 1986.
Novakovic, Lidija. *Raised from the Dead According to Scripture: The Role of Israel's Scripture in the Early Christian Interpretations of Jesus' Resurrection*. T&T Clark Jewish and Christian Texts Series 12. London: T&T Clark, 2012.
Oakman, Douglas E. *Jesus, Debt, and the Lord's Prayer: First-Century Debt and Jesus' Intentions*. Eugene, OR: Wipf and Stock, 2014.
Oliver, Isaac W. "The 'Historical Paul' and the Paul of Acts." Pages 51–80 in *Paul the Jew: Rereading the Apostle as a Figure of Second Temple Judaism*. Edited by Gabriele Boccaccini and Carlos A. Segovia. Minneapolis: Fortress, 2016.
———. *Luke's Jewish Eschatology: The National Restoration of Israel in Luke-Acts*. Cambridge: Cambridge University Press, 2021.
———. *Torah Praxis after 70 CE: Reading Matthew and Luke-Acts as Jewish Texts*. WUNT 2/355. Tübingen: Mohr Siebeck, 2013.
Omi, Michael, and Howard Winant. "Racial Formation." Pages 405–15 in *The New Social Theory Reader*. 2nd ed. Edited by Steven Seidman and Jeffrey C. Alexander. London: Routledge, 2008.
O'Neill, J. C. *The Theology of Acts in Its Historical Setting*. London: SCM, 1961.
O'Toole, Robert F. "Acts 2:30 and the Davidic Covenant of Pentecost." *JBL* 102 (1983): 245–58.
———. *Acts 26: The Christological Climax of Paul's Defense (Ac 22:1–26:32)*. AB 78. Rome: Pontifical Biblical Institute, 1978.
———. "Christ's Resurrection in Acts 13,13–52." *Bib* 60 (1979): 361–72.
Padilla, René. "Mensaje biblico y revolucion." *Certez* 10 (1970): 197.
Pao, David W. *Acts and the Isaianic New Exodus*. WUNT 2/130. Tubingen: Mohr Siebeck, 2000.
———. "Disagreement among the Jews in Acts 28." Pages 109–18 in *Early Christian Voices: In Texts, Traditions, and Symbols; Essays in Honor of François Bovon*. Edited by David H. Warren, Ann Graham Brock, and David W. Pao. BibInt 66. Leiden: Brill, 2003.
Parker, Robert. *Polytheism and Society at Athens*. Oxford: Oxford University Press, 2005.
Parkin, Anneliese. "'You Do Him No Service': An Exploration of Pagan Almsgiving." Pages 60–82 in *Poverty in the Roman World*. Edited by Margaret Atkins and Robin Osborne. Cambridge: Cambridge University Press, 2006.
Parsons, Mikeal C. *Acts*. Paideia Commentaries on the New Testament. Grand Rapids: Baker Academic, 2008.
———. *Body and Character in Luke and Acts: The Subversion of Physiognomy in Early Christianity*. Grand Rapids: Baker, 2006.
Penner, Todd C. "Civilizing Discourse: Acts, Declamation, and the Rhetoric of the *Polis*." Pages 65–104 in *Contextualizing Acts: Lukan Narrative and Greco-Roman Discourse*. Edited by Todd C. Penner and Caroline Vander Stichele. SBLSymS 20. Atlanta: Society of Biblical Literature Press, 2003.
———. *In Praise of Christian Origins: Stephen and the Hellenists in Lukan Apologetic Historiography*. New York: T&T Clark, 2004.
Pervo, Richard I. *Acts*. Hermeneia: A Critical and Historical Commentary on the Bible. Minneapolis: Fortress, 2009.

Bibliography

Pfremmer De Long, Kindalee. *Surprised by God: Praise Responses in the Narrative of Luke-Acts.* BZNW 166. Berlin: de Gruyter, 2009.

Piotrowski, Nicholas G. *Matthew's New David at the End of Exile: A Socio-Rhetorical Study of Scriptural Quotations.* NovTSup 170. Leiden: Brill, 2016.

Placher, William C. *The Domestication of Transcendence: How Modern Thinking about God Went Wrong.* Louisville: Westminster John Knox, 1996.

Plümacher, Eckhard. *Lukas als hellenistischer Schriftsteller: Studien zur Apostelgeschichte.* SUNT 9. Göttingen: Vandenhoeck & Ruprecht, 1972.

Pohl, Christine. *Making Room: Recovering Hospitality as a Christian Tradition.* Grand Rapids: Eerdmans, 1990.

Polanyi, Karl. *Primitive, Archaic, and Modern Economies: Essays of Karl Polanyi.* Garden City, NY: Anchor Books, 1968.

Porterfield, Amanda. *Healing in the History of Christianity.* Oxford: Oxford University Press, 2005.

Portier-Young, Anathea E. *Apocalypse against Empire: Theologies of Resistance in Early Judaism.* Grand Rapids: Eerdmans, 2011.

Praeder, Susan M. "Acts 27:1–28:16: Sea Voyages in Ancient Literature and the Theology of Luke-Acts." *CBQ* 46 (1984): 683–706.

Radl, Walter. *Paulus und Jesus im lukanischen Doppelwerk: Untersuchungen zu Parallelmotiven im Lukasevangelium und in der Apostelgeschichte.* Bern: Lang, 1975.

Rahlfs, Alfred, and Robert Hanhart, eds. *Septuaginta.* Stuttgart: Deutsche Bibelgesellschaft, 1935.

Räisänen, Heikki. *Beyond New Testament Theology: A Story and a Programme.* 2nd ed. London: SCM, 2000.

Reicke, Bo. "Die Mahlzeit mit Paulus auf den Wellen des Mittelmeers Acts 27,33–38." *TZ* 4 (1948): 401–10.

Reinhartz, Adele. "John 8:31–59 from a Jewish Perspective." Pages 787–97 in vol. 2 of *Remembering for the Future: The Holocaust in an Age of Genocide.* Edited by John K. Roth, Elisabeth Maxwell, Margot Levy, and Wendy Whitworth. London: Palgrave, 2001.

Rese, Martin. *Alttestamentliche Motive in der Christologie des Lukas.* SZNW 1. Gütersloh: Mohn, 1969.

Reynolds, Thomas E. *Vulnerable Communion: A Theology of Disability and Hospitality.* Grand Rapids: Brazos, 2008.

Rhee, Helen. *Loving the Poor, Saving the Rich: Wealth, Poverty, and Early Christian Formation.* Grand Rapids: Baker, 2012.

Ricoeur, Paul. "Philosophical Hermeneutics and Theological Hermeneutics." *SR* 5 (1975): 14–33.

———. *Time and Narrative,* Vol. 1. Translated by Kathleen McLaughlin and David Pellauer. Chicago: University of Chicago Press, 1984.

Rindge, Matthew S. *Jesus' Parable of the Rich Fool: Luke 12:13–34 among Ancient Conversations on Death and Possessions.* Early Christianity and Its Literature 6. Atlanta: Society of Biblical Literature Press, 2011.

Rives, J. B. "Christian Expansion and Christian Ideology." Pages 15–42 in *The Spread of Christianity in the First Four Centuries: Essays in Explanation.* Edited by William V. Harris. Leiden: Brill, 2005.

Robbins, Vernon K. "By Land and by Sea: The We-Passages and Ancient Sea Voyages." Pages

47–81 in *Sea Voyages and Beyond: Emerging Strategies in Socio-Rhetorical Interpretation*. Emory Studies in Early Christianity 14. Blandford Forum, UK: Deo, 2010.

Roberts, J. J. M. "The Old Testament's Contribution to Messianic Expectations." Pages 39–51 in *The Messiah: Developments in Earliest Judaism and Christianity*. Edited by James H. Charlesworth. Minneapolis: Fortress, 1992.

Root, Michael. "The Narrative Structure of Soteriology." Pages 263–78 in *Why Narrative? Readings in Narrative Theology*. Edited by Stanley Hauerwas and L. Gregory Jones. Eugene, OR: Wipf & Stock, 1997.

Rowe, C. Kavin. *Early Narrative Christology: The Lord in the Gospel of Luke*. BZNW 139. Berlin: de Gruyter, 2006.

———. "The Grammar of Life: The Areopagus Speech and Pagan Tradition." *NTS* 57 (2011): 31–50.

———. *One True Life: The Stoics and Early Christians as Rival Traditions*. New Haven: Yale University Press, 2016.

———. *World Upside Down: Reading Acts in the Graeco-Roman Age*. Oxford: Oxford University Press, 2009.

Runesson, Anders. *Divine Wrath and Salvation in Matthew: The Narrative World of the First Gospel*. Minneapolis: Fortress, 2016.

Ruppert, Lothar. *Jesus als der leidende Gerechte? Der Weg Jesu um Lichte eines alt- und zwischentestamentlichen motivs*. SBS 59. Stuttgart: Katholisches Bibelwerk, 1972.

Said, Edward W. *Orientalism*. New York: Vintage Books, 1979.

Saller, Richard P. *Personal Patronage under the Early Empire*. Cambridge: Cambridge University Press, 1982.

Salmeier, Michael A. *Restoring the Kingdom: The Role of God as the "Ordainer of Times and Seasons" in the Acts of the Apostles*. Princeton Theological Monograph Series 165. Eugene, OR: Pickwick, 2011.

Sanders, Jack T. *The Jews in Luke-Acts*. London: SCM, 1987.

Sanders, James A. "A Hermeneutic Fabric: Psalm 118 in Luke's Entrance Narrative." Pages 140–53 in *Luke and Scripture: The Function of Sacred Tradition in Luke-Acts*. Edited by Craig A. Evans and James A. Sanders. Minneapolis: Fortress, 1993.

Sandnes, Karl Olav. "Paul and Socrates: The Aim of Paul' s Areopagus Speech." *JSNT* 50 (1993): 13–26.

Sandys-Wunsch, John, and Laurence Eldredge. "J. P. Gabler and the Distinction between Biblical and Dogmatic Theology: Translation, Commentary, and Discussion of His Originality." *SJT* 33 (1980): 133–58.

Sanneh, Lamin O. *Disciples of All Nations: Pillars of World Christianity*. Oxford Studies in World Christianity. Oxford: Oxford University Press, 2008.

———. *Translating the Message: The Missionary Impact on Culture*. Rev. ed. Maryknoll, NY: Orbis, 2009.

Satlow, Michael L. *Creating Judaism: History, Tradition, Practice*. New York: Columbia University Press, 2006.

Schaper, Joachim. "Die Septuaginta-Psalter als Dokument jüdischer Eschatologie." Pages 38–61 in *Die Septuaginta zwischen Judentum und Christentum*. Edited by Martin Hengel and Anna Maria Schwemer. WUNT 2/72. Tübingen: Mohr Siebeck, 1994.

———. *Eschatology in the Greek Psalter*. WUNT 2/76. Tübingen: Mohr Siebeck, 1995.

Schlatter, Adolf. "The Theology of the New Testament and Dogmatics." Pages 117–66 in *The*

Nature of New Testament Theology: The Contribution of William Wrede and Adolf Schlatter. Edited and translated by Robert Morgan. London: SCM, 1973.

Schnabel, Eckhard J. "Contextualising Paul in Athens: The Proclamation of the Gospel Before Pagan Audiences in the Graeco-Roman World." *R&T* 12 (2005): 172–90.

Schneider, Gerhard. *Die Apostelgeschichte*. 2 vols. HTKNT 5. Freiburg: Herder, 1982.

———. *Die Apostelgeschichte: Teil 2*. Freiburg: Herder, 1982.

Scholes, Robert, and Robert Kellogg. *The Nature of Narrative*. New York: Oxford University Press, 1966.

Schröter, Jens. "Salvation for the Gentiles and Israel: On the Relationship between Christology and People of God in Luke." Pages 227–46 in *From Jesus to the New Testament: Early Christian Theology and the Origin of the New Testament Canon*. Translated by Wayne Coppins. Baylor-Mohr Siebeck Studies in Early Christianity. Waco, TX: Baylor University Press, 2013.

Schubert, Paul. "The Place of the Areopagus Speech in the Composition of Acts." Pages 235–61 in *Essays in Divinity*. Vol. 6, *Transitions in Biblical Scholarship*. Edited by J. Coert Rylaarsdam. Chicago: University of Chicago Press, 1968.

Schwartz, Seth. *Imperialism and Jewish Society: 200 B.C.E. to 640 C.E.* Princeton: Princeton University Press, 2001.

Scott, James C. *Domination and the Arts of Resistance: Hidden Transcripts*. New Haven: Yale University Press, 1990.

Shauf, Scott. *Theology as History, History as Theology: Paul in Ephesus in Acts 19*. BZNW 133. Berlin: de Gruyter, 2005.

Siker, Jeffrey S. *Disinheriting the Jews: Abraham in Early Christian Controversy*. Louisville: Westminster John Knox, 1991.

Simpson, Amy. *Troubled Minds: Mental Illness and the Church's Mission*. Downers Grove, IL: InterVarsity Press, 2013.

Skinner, Christopher W. *Reading John*. Cascade Companions. Eugene, OR: Cascade, 2015.

Skinner, Matthew L. *Intrusive God, Disruptive Gospel: Encountering the Divine in the Book of Acts*. Grand Rapids: Brazos, 2015.

Sleeman, Matthew. *Geography and the Ascension Narrative in Acts*. SNTSMS 146. Cambridge: Cambridge University Press, 2009.

Smit, Peter-Ben. *Fellowship and Food in the Kingdom: Eschatological Meals and Scenes of Utopian Abundance in the New Testament*. WUNT 2/234. Tübingen: Mohr Siebeck, 2008.

Smith, Dennis E. "Table Fellowship as a Literary Motif in the Gospel of Luke." *JBL* 106 (1987): 613–38.

Smith, Jonathan Z. *Drudgery Divine: On the Comparison of Early Christianities and the Religions of Late Antiquity*. Chicago: University of Chicago Press, 1990.

Snyder, Susanna. "Fright: The Dynamics of Fear within Established Populations." Pages 85–126 in *Asylum-Seeking, Migration and Church*. Explorations in Practical, Pastoral and Empirical Theology. London: Ashgate, 2012.

Soards, Marion L. *The Speeches in Acts: Their Content, Context, and Concerns*. Louisville: Westminster John Knox, 1994.

Somov, Alexey, and Vitaly Voinov. "'Abraham's Bosom' (Luke 16:22–23) as a Key Metaphor in the Overall Composition of the Parable of the Rich Man and Lazarus." *CBQ* 79 (2017): 615–33.

Soulen, R. Kendall. *Distinguishing the Voices.* Vol. 1 of *The Divine Name(s) and the Holy Trinity.* Louisville: Westminster John Knox, 2011.

———. *The God of Israel and Christian Theology.* Minneapolis: Fortress, 1996.

Spicq, Ceslas. "La philanthropie hellénistique, vertu divine et royale (à propos de Tit 3:4)." *Studia Theologica* 12 (1958): 169–91.

Squires, John T. *The Plan of God in Luke-Acts.* SNTSMS 76. Cambridge: Cambridge University Press, 1993.

Steele, David. "Crazy Talk: The Language of Mental Illness Stigma." *The Guardian*, September 6, 2012. https://www.theguardian.com/science/brain-flapping/2012/sep/06/crazy-talk-language-mental-illness-stigma.

Stegemann, Ekkehard W., and Wolfgang Stegemann. *The Jesus Movement: A Social History of Its First Century.* Translated by O. C. Dean Jr. Minneapolis: Fortress, 1999.

Stenschke, Christoph W. *Luke's Portrait of Gentiles Prior to Their Coming to Faith.* WUNT 2/108. Tübingen: Mohr Siebeck, 1999.

Sterling, Gregory E. *Historiography and Self-Definition: Josephos, Luke-Acts, and Apologetic Historiography.* NovTSup 64. Leiden: Brill, 1992.

———. "The Interpreter of Moses: Philo of Alexandria and the Biblical Text." Pages 415–35 in *A Companion to Biblical Interpretation in Early Judaism*, edited by Matthias Henze. Grand Rapids: Eerdmans, 2012.

———. "'The Jewish Philosophy': Reading Moses via Hellenistic Philosophy according to Philo." Pages 129–54 in *Reading Philo: A Handbook to Philo of Alexandria.* Edited by Torrey Seland. Grand Rapids: Eerdmans, 2014.

———. "*Mors Philosophi*: The Death of Jesus in Luke." *HTR* 94 (2001): 383–402.

———. "'Opening the Scriptures': The Legitimation of the Jewish Diaspora and the Early Christian Mission." Pages 199–217 in *Jesus and the Heritage of Israel: Luke's Narrative Claim upon Israel's Legacy.* Edited by David P. Moessner. Harrisburg, PA: Trinity Press International, 1999.

Strauss, Mark L. *The Davidic Messiah in Luke-Acts: The Promise and Its Fulfilment in Lukan Christology.* JSNTSup 100. Sheffield: Sheffield Academic, 1995.

Strelan, Rick. "Recognizing the Gods (Acts 14.8–10)." *NTS* 46 (2000): 488–503.

Striker, Gisela. "*Ataraxia*: Happiness as Tranquility." Pages 183–95 in *Essays on Hellenistic Epistemology and Ethics.* Cambridge: Cambridge University Press, 1996.

Stuckenbruck, Loren T. "The Human Being and Demonic Invasion: Therapeutic Models in Ancient Jewish and Christian Texts." Pages 161–86 in *The Myth of Rebellious Angels: Studies in Second Temple Judaism and New Testament Texts.* Grand Rapids: Eerdmans, 2017.

Stuhlmacher, Peter. "Adolf Schlatter's Interpretation of Scripture." *NTS* 24 (1978): 433–46.

———. *Historical Criticism and Theological Interpretation of Scripture: Toward a Hermeneutics of Consent.* Translated by Roy A. Harrisville. Philadelphia: Fortress, 1977.

Subramanian, J. Samuel. *The Synoptic Gospels and the Psalms as Prophecy.* LNTS 351. New York: T&T Clark, 2007.

Swartley, Willard M. *Health, Healing and the Church's Mission: Biblical Perspectives and Moral Priorities.* Downers Grove, IL: InterVarsity Press, 2012.

Swetnam, James. "The Meaning of Πεπιστευκότας in John 8,31." *Bib* 61 (1980): 106–9.

Swinton, John. *Resurrecting the Person: Friendship and the Care of People with Mental Health Problems.* Nashville: Abingdon, 2000.

Bibliography

Tannehill, Robert C. "Israel in Luke-Acts: A Tragic Story." *JBL* 104 (1985): 69–85.
———. *The Narrative Unity of Luke-Acts: A Literary Interpretation*. Vol. 2, *The Acts of the Apostles*. Minneapolis: Fortress, 1990.
Taylor, Vincent. *The Passion Narrative of St Luke: A Critical and Historical Investigation*. Edited by Owen E. Evans. SNTSMS 19. Cambridge: Cambridge University Press, 1972.
Theissen, Gerd. *Sociology of Early Palestinian Christianity*. Translated by John Bowden. Philadelphia: Fortress, 1978.
Thiessen, Matthew. *Contesting Conversion: Genealogy, Circumcision, and Identity in Ancient Judaism and Christianity*. Oxford: Oxford University Press, 2011.
Thompson, Alan J. *The Acts of the Risen Lord Jesus: Luke's Account of God's Unfolding Plan*. NSBT 27. Downers Grove, IL: Intervarsity Press, 2011.
———. *One Lord, One People: The Unity of the Church in Acts in Its Literary Setting*. LNTS 359. London: T&T Clark, 2008.
Tiede, David L. *Prophecy and History in Luke-Acts*. Philadelphia: Fortress, 1980.
Torrance, Thomas F. *Space, Time and Resurrection*. Grand Rapids: Eerdmans, 1976.
Tutu, Desmond. "Whiter African Theology?" Pages 364–69 in *Christianity in Independent Africa*. Edited by E. Fashole-Luke et al. London: Collings, 1978.
Tyson, Joseph B. *Luke, Judaism, and the Scholars: Critical Approaches to Luke-Acts*. Columbia: University of South Carolina Press, 1999.
Vacek, Heather H. *Madness: American Protestant Responses to Mental Illness*. Waco, TX: Baylor University Press, 2015.
Vanhoozer, Kevin J. *Biblical Narrative in the Philosophy of Paul Ricoeur: A Study in Hermeneutics and Theology*. Cambridge: Cambridge University Press, 1990.
Verhey, Allen. *Remembering Jesus: Christian Community, Scripture, and the Moral Life*. Grand Rapids: Eerdmans, 2002.
Veyne, Paul. *Bread and Circuses: Historical Sociology and Political Pluralism*. London: Lane, 1990.
Vielhauer, Philipp. "On the 'Paulinism' of Acts." Pages 33–50 in *Studies in Luke-Acts*. Edited by Leander E. Keck and J. Louis Martyn. Philadelphia: Fortress, 1968.
Volf, Miroslav. *Exclusion and Embrace: A Theological Exploration of Identity, Otherness, and Reconciliation*. Nashville: Abingdon, 1996.
Wagner, J. Ross. "Psalm 118 in Luke-Acts: Tracing a Narrative Thread." Pages 154–78 in *Early Christian Interpretation of the Scriptures of Israel: Investigations and Proposals*. Edited by Craig A. Evans and James A. Sanders. JSNTSup 148, SSEJC 5. Sheffield: Sheffield Academic, 1997.
Walls, Andrew F. "Kwame Bediako and Christian Scholarship in Africa." *International Bulletin of Missionary Research* 32 (2008): 188–93.
———. *The Missionary Movement in Christian History: Studies in the Transmission of Faith*. Maryknoll, NY: Orbis, 1996.
———. "The Rise of Global Theologies." Pages 19–34 in *Global Theology in Evangelical Perspective: Exploring the Contextual Nature of Theology and Mission*. Edited by Jeffrey P. Greenman and Gene L. Green. Downers Grove, IL: InterVarsity Press, 2012.
Walton, Steve. "'The Heavens Opened': Cosmological and Theological Transformation in Luke and Acts." Pages 60–73 in *Cosmology and New Testament Theology*. Edited by Jonathan T. Pennington and Sean M. McDonough. LNTS. London: T&T Clark, 2008.

Ward, Roy Bowen. "The Works of Abraham: James 2:14–26." *HTR* 61 (1968): 283–90.
Weaver, John B. *Plots of Epiphany: Prison-Escape in Acts of the Apostles*. BZNW 131. Berlin: de Gruyter, 2004.
Wells, Samuel. *A Nazareth Manifesto: Being with God*. Malden, MA: Wiley-Blackwell, 2015.
Wendel, Susan. *Scriptural Interpretation and Community Self-Definition in Luke-Acts and the Writings of Justin Martyr*. NovTSup 139. Leiden: Brill, 2011.
Wendt, Heidi. *At the Temple Gates: The Religion of Freelance Experts in the Roman Empire*. New York: Oxford University Press, 2016.
Weren, W. J. C. "Psalm 2 in Luke-Acts: An Intertextual Study." Pages 192–96 in *Intertextuality in Biblical Writings: Essays in Honour of Bas Van Iersel*. Edited by Sipke Draisma. Kampen: Kok, 1989.
White, Hayden. "Narrativity in the Representation of Reality." Pages 1–25 in *The Content of the Form: Narrative Discourse and Historical Representation*. Baltimore: Johns Hopkins University Press, 1987.
Wilckens, Ulrich. *Die Missionsreden der Apostelgeschichte: Form und traditionsgeschichtliche Untersuchung*. WMANT 5. Neukirchen-Vluyn: Neukirchener Verlag, 1961.
———. "Kerygma und Evangelium bei Lukas (Beobachtungen zu Acta 10,34–43)." *ZNW* 49 (1958): 223–37.
Williams, Catrin H. "Patriarchs and Prophets Remembered: Framing Israel's Past in the Gospel of John." Pages 187–212 in *Abiding Words: The Use of Scripture in the Gospel of John*. Edited by Alicia D. Myers and Bruce G. Schuchard. Atlanta: SBL Press, 2015.
Williamson, H. G. M. "'The Sure Mercies of David': Subjective or Objective Genitive?" *JSS* 23 (1978): 31–49.
Wills, Lawrence M. "The Depiction of the Jews in Acts." *JBL* 110 (1991): 631–54.
Wilson, Brittany E. *Unmanly Men: Refigurations of Masculinity in Luke-Acts*. Oxford: Oxford University Press, 2015.
Wilson, Gerald H. *The Editing of the Hebrew Psalter*. SBLDS 76. Chico, CA: Scholars Press, 1985.
———. "The Use of Royal Psalms at the 'Seams' of the Hebrew Psalter." *JSOT* 11/35 (1986): 85–94.
Wilson, Stephen G. *Leaving the Fold: Apostates and Defectors in Antiquity*. Minneapolis: Fortress, 2004.
———. *Luke and the Law*. SNTSMS. Cambridge: Cambridge University Press, 1983.
Wilson, Walter T. "Urban Legends: Acts 10:1–11:18 and the Strategies of Greco-Roman Foundation Narratives." *JBL* 120 (2001): 77–99.
Winter, Bruce. "On Introducing Gods to Athens: An Alternative Reading of Acts 17:18–20." *TynB* 47 (1996): 71–90.
Wolterstorff, Nicholas. "Living within a Text." Pages 202–13 in *Faith and Narrative*. Edited by Keith E. Yandell. Oxford: Oxford University Press, 2001.
Wright, Christopher J. H. *Old Testament Ethics for the People of God*. Downers Grove, IL: IVP Academic, 2004.
Wrogemann, Henning. *Intercultural Hermeneutics*. Translated by Karl E. Böhmer. Vol. 1 of *Intercultural Theology*. Downers Grove, IL: InterVarsity Press, 2016.
Wycherley, R. E. "St. Paul at Athens." *JTS* 19 (1968): 619–21.
Yarbrough, Robert W. "Modern Reception of Schlatter's New Testament Theology."

Bibliography

Pages 2:417–31 in *The Theology of the Apostles: The Development of New Testament Theology*. Translated by Andreas Köstenberger. Grand Rapids: Baker, 1999.

———. *The Salvation Historical Fallacy? Reassessing the History of New Testament Theology*. Dorset, UK: Deo, 2004.

Yoder, John Howard. *The Politics of Jesus*. Grand Rapids: Eerdmans, 1994.

Yong, Amos. *The Bible, Disability, and the Church: A New Vision of the People of God*. Grand Rapids: Eerdmans, 2011.

———. *Hospitality and the Other: Pentecost, Christian Practices, and the Neighbor*. Maryknoll, NY: Orbis, 2008.

Young, Iris Marion. *Justice and the Politics of Difference*. Princeton: Princeton University Press, 1990.

Zwiep, Arie W. *The Ascension of the Messiah in Lukan Christology*. NovTSup 87. Leiden: Brill, 1997.

———. "*Assumptus Est in Caelum*: Rapture and Heavenly Exaltation in Early Judaism and Luke-Acts." Chap. 2 in Zwiep, *Christ, the Spirit and the Community of God: Essays on the Acts of the Apostles*. WUNT 2/293. Tübingen: Mohr Siebeck, 2010.

———. *Judas and the Choice of Matthias: A Study on Context and Concern of Acts 1:15–26*. WUNT 187. Tübingen: Mohr Siebeck, 2004.

Index of Authors

Adams, Samuel L., 252, 255–59
Alexander, Jeffrey C., 127
Alexander, Loveday, 9, 14, 138–39, 146, 148, 241
Alexander, Philip S., 10
Allison, Dale C., Jr., 34
Anderson, Kevin L., 85, 89, 92, 99
Andreau, Jean, 265–66
Antonova, Stamenka E., 130
Arterbury, Andrew E., 72, 138, 245
Ashton, John, 81
Attridge, Harold W., 118, 159
Auerbach, Erich, 195

Baker, Cynthia M., 11, 124
Balch, David L., 103, 165, 179
Balthasar, Hans Urs von, 222
Baltzer, Klaus, 28
Barclay, John M. G., 16, 112, 273–74, 278
Barnes, Timothy D., 151
Barreto, Eric D., 128, 134, 142, 211, 214, 218
Barrett, C. K., 93, 96, 140, 155, 161, 168
Barton, Stephen C., 248, 278
Bates, Matthew W., 90–91
Bauckham, Richard, 38, 180, 201
Bauer, David R., 189
Beck, Brian E., 198
Beck, Richard, 239
Bediako, Kwame, 109–12, 121
Beers, Holly, 36

Bergh, Ronald H. van der, 130–31
Bird, Michael F., 170
Blanton, Ward, 125
Blum, Edward J., 125
Bock, Darrell L., 54, 93, 187–88
Boer, Roland, 249, 252, 254–57, 260
Boers, Hendrikus, 189, 191
Borgon, Peter, 113
Bovon, François, 45, 49
Bradley, Keith, 264, 266
Braulik, Georg P., 46
Brawley, Robert, 5, 62, 74, 76–77
Brink, Laurie, 132, 243
Brown, Peter, 274
Brown, Raymond E., 44, 50
Bruce, F. F., 93
Brueggemann, Walter, 249–50, 253, 255, 257, 262–63
Buell, Denise Kimber, 125, 128, 133–34, 218
Burnett, Anne Pippin, 150, 175
Burrus, Virginia, 144
Butticaz, Simon David, 5, 97
Byron, Gay L., 133

Cadbury, Henry J., 129, 131, 144, 212
Cameron, Averil, 141, 171–72
Carroll, John T., 49
Carter, J. Kameron, 125
Cartledge, Paul A., 130
Clark, Elizabeth A., 193

305

INDEX OF AUTHORS

Clines, David J. A., 249
Cochran, Elizabeth Agnew, 108
Cohen, Shaye J. D., 6, 17, 124
Conzelmann, Hans, 48, 151, 154
Cooke, G., 86
Cooley, Alison E., 273
Cosgrove, Charles H., 56
Crossan, John Dominic, 132, 219, 234
Crossley, James G., 125
Croy, N. Clayton, 168
Crump, David Michael, 199
Cunningham, Scott, 50

Dahl, Nils A., 69–71, 76, 78
Dawsey, James M., 52
De Long, Kindalee Pfremmer, 197
Dibelius, Martin, 104, 144, 147, 154–55, 159, 161
Dillon, Richard J., 192
Doble, Peter, 44, 51–52, 55, 62–64
Dodd, C. H., 64
Donahue, John R., 198, 269
Dostoevsky, Fyodor, 194
Downs, David, 274
Duling, Dennis C., 90
Dupertuis, Ruben R., 181
Dupont, Jacques, 56, 58, 63, 90, 100

Eaton, John H., 54, 86
Edwards, Mark J., 163
Eisland, Nancy, 236
Eldredge, Laurence, 190
Escobar, Samuel, 212
Eskola, Timo, 90, 92, 98–99
Eubank, Nathan, 268
Eyl, Jennifer, 172

Ferngren, Gary B., 230
Fiensy, David A., 260, 264, 267
Finley, M. I., 274
Fitzmyer, Joseph A., 44, 90, 96
Flett, John G., 108–9, 112
Frankenberg, Ruth, 128
Fredriksen, Paula, 5, 16, 18, 24
Frei, Hans W., 195, 202, 210
Freyne, Sean, 259
Friesen, Steve, 271

Gabler, J. P., 190–91
Gager, John G., 3, 17
Garcia-Johnson, Oscar, 224
Gardner, Gregg E., 274
Garland, Robert, 150
Garnsey, Peter, 265, 271–72, 274
Garrett, Susan R., 174
Gärtner, Bertil, 104, 144, 161, 164
Gaston, Lloyd, 43
Gaventa, Beverly Roberts, 192, 204, 217
Geary, Patrick J., 129, 151
Gebhard, Elizabeth R., 150
Gerbrandt, Gerald Eddie, 253
Gilbert, Gary, 146, 183
Gill, David W., 147
Given, Mark D., 117, 155, 167
Goldman, Max L., 133
Goodman, Martin, 18
Grant, Jamie A., 253
Gray, Patrick, 3, 153, 155, 160
Green, Joel B., 43, 48, 53–55, 70–71, 187, 191–92, 196, 200, 268
Green-McCreight, Kathryn, 225
Griffith, Terry, 78–79
Gruen, Erich S., 115, 129

Haacker, Klaus, 15, 33, 135
Habel, N. C., 249
Haenchen, Ernst, 10, 94, 154, 167
Hahn, Scott W., 86, 88, 97
Hall, Edith, 130
Hall, Jonathan M., 124
Hall, Robert, 12, 31
Hamel, Gildas, 274
Hamid, Mohsin, 223
Hamilton, Jeffries M., 253
Hamilton, Mark W., 86, 213
Hamm, Dennis, 40
Harris, Sarah, 26
Harrisville, Roy A., 189
Hart, Trevor, 196
Hartog, François, 129
Harvey, Paul, 125
Hay, David M., 58
Hayes, Christine, 114
Hays, Richard B., 44, 46, 62, 66–67

Index of Authors

Heimburger, Robert W., 210, 223
Hemer, Colin J., 129, 140
Hengel, Martin, 255
Henriksen, Jan-Olav, 227, 229
Herman, Gabriel, 136-38
Heschel, Susannah, 125, 128
Hodge, Caroline Johnson, 133
Holliday, Carl R., 144
Holmås, Geir Otto, 20
Hommel, H., 163
Hood, Jason B., 68
Hooker, Morna D., 45
Horst, Pieter W. van der, 156-57
Hoskyns, Edwyn Clement, 79
Hubbard, Benjamin, 34
Huizenga, L. A., 82
Hume, Douglas A., 178
Hunt, Steven A., 80-81
Hurtado, Larry W., 169-71
Hutchinson, John, 126
Hvalvik, Reidar, 5, 127, 135

Jennings, Willie James, 21, 123-26, 139, 215-16, 224
Jenson, Robert W., 21, 124
Jervell, Jacob, 5-7, 15, 23, 27, 57, 75, 94-95, 135, 140, 149, 155, 165, 187
Jeska, Joachim, 12
Jipp, Joshua W., 9, 11, 23, 28, 30, 35, 37, 72-73, 80, 98, 116-17, 120, 122, 129-30, 135-36, 141-42, 170-71, 180, 182, 209-10, 213, 215, 219-22, 230-31, 234, 237, 240, 243, 245, 251, 273
Johnson, Aubrey R., 86
Johnson, Kelly S., 278
Johnson, Luke Timothy, 25, 32, 38, 40, 55, 57, 64, 85, 91, 95-96, 99-100, 120, 140-42, 170, 173, 191, 195, 201, 206, 210, 212, 217, 223, 230, 239, 262, 270
Juel, Donald, 44, 90

Kamell, Mariam, 271
Kautsky, John H., 265
Keener, Craig S., 7-8, 34, 76, 84
Kehoe, Dennis P., 266, 271
Kelley, Shawn, 125-27
Kellogg, Robert, 194

Kennedy, Rebecca F., 132-33
Kilgallen, J. J., 63
Kinman, Brent, 29
Kinzer, Mark S., 27
Kirk, Alan, 275
Klassen, William, 58
Klauck, Hans-Josef, 119, 151, 157, 159, 163-64
Klawans, Jonathan, 19
Kleinknecht, Karl Theodor, 47
Konradt, Matthias, 67
Konstan, David, 177
Koser, Khalid, 223

Lake, Kirsopp, 163
Langton, Daniel R., 3
Lash, Nicholas, 190, 195
Laughery, Gregory J., 180, 201
LeDonne, Anthony, 65
Levenson, Jon D., 66, 69, 80
Lieu, Judith M., 134
Litwa, M. David, 115, 170
Long, Anthony A., 113, 118, 148, 156
Longenecker, Bruce W., 270, 274-75
Lövestam, Evald, 93, 96
Lucass, Shirley, 87
Lundin, Roger, 193
Luz, Ulrich, 68
Lynch, Matthew, 87

Ma, John, 259
MacIntyre, Alasdair, 191
Mack, Michael, 125
MacMullen, Ramsay, 173
Malherbe, Abraham J., 118, 120, 160, 182, 262
Mamdani, Mahmood, 123
Marcus, Joel, 48-49, 69
Marguerat, Daniel, 10, 17, 19, 38-39, 58, 136, 180, 201, 205, 242
Marshall, I. Howard, 44, 140, 187
Marshall, Jonathan, 272
Martens, John W., 114
Martin, Clarice J., 133
Martin, Dale B., 117, 127, 154, 266
Martin, Hubert H., Jr., 151
Martyn, J. Louis, 69
Matera, Frank J., 44

INDEX OF AUTHORS

Matson, David Lertis, 9
Matthews, Shelly, 4, 19, 21
Mbiti, John S., 109
McKinney, Ken, 180, 201
McWhirter, Jocelyn, 19, 34
Meeks, Wayne A., 127
Meggitt, Justin J., 271, 274
Meier, John P., 10
Ménard, Jacques E., 63
Mettinger, Tryggve N. D., 86
Miller, David M., 6, 19
Miller, Patrick D., Jr., 250
Minear, Paul S., 19, 34
Mitchell, Alan C., 177
Mitchell, David C., 46, 53
Miura, Yuzuru, 45
Moessner, David P., 5, 16, 19, 28, 38, 58, 77, 90, 183, 192, 211
Momigliano, Arnoldo, 129
Morgan, Robert, 188
Morley, Neville, 265
Mowery, Robert L., 202
Moxnes, Halvor, 125, 269, 272

Nasrallah, Laura Salah, 124, 128, 146, 165, 183
Nauck, Wolfgang, 121, 163
Neagoe, Alexandru, 14
Neuer, Werner, 189
Newbigin, Lesslie, 107
Nouwen, Henri J. M., 222
Novakovic, Lidija, 91-92

Oakman, Douglas E., 267, 269
Oliver, Isaac W., 6-7, 26-27, 29, 32-33, 41
Omi, Michael, 127
O'Neill, J. C., 10
O'Toole, Robert F., 14, 58, 91-94, 136

Padilla, René, 212
Pao, David W., 35-36, 39-40, 45, 57, 93, 97, 133, 144, 158, 216
Parker, Robert, 152
Parkin, Anneliese, 275
Parsons, Mikeal, 71, 220, 235, 243
Penner, Todd C., 146, 172, 179, 182

Pervo, Richard I., 135, 141, 149, 151, 153-54, 157-58, 162-63, 167, 244
Piotrowski, Nicholas G., 65
Placher, William C., 195
Plümacher, Eckhard, 148
Pohl, Christine, 247
Polanyi, Karl, 271
Porterfield, Amanda, 230
Portier-Young, Anathea E., 258
Praeder, Susan M., 244

Radl, Walter, 37, 135
Reicke, Bo, 135
Reinhartz, Adele, 78
Rese, Martin, 93
Reynolds, Thomas E., 239
Rhee, Helen, 256, 272
Ricoeur, Paul, 193-94, 207
Ringe, Matthew S., 263
Rives, J. B., 170, 172
Robbins, Vernon K., 242
Roberts, J. J. M., 86
Root, Michael, 195-96
Rowe, C. Kavin, 58, 89, 103-8, 119-21, 139, 144-47, 151, 154, 158, 169, 182, 190, 210, 240
Roy, C. Sydnor, 133
Runesson, Anders, 66, 69
Ruppert, Lothar, 47

Saller, Richard P., 265, 271-72
Salmeier, Michael A., 196
Sanders, Jack T., 10
Sanders, James A., 60
Sandnes, Karl Olav, 148, 227, 229
Sandys-Wunsch, John, 190
Sanneh, Lamin O., 108-9, 139, 220-21
Satlow, Michael L., 11-12
Schaper, Joachim, 47
Schlatter, Adolf, 188-91
Schnabel, Eckhard J., 103
Schneider, Gerhard, 94, 147, 154
Scholes, Robert, 194
Schröter, Jens, 11, 17, 24
Schubert, Paul, 167
Schwartz, Seth, 4

Index of Authors

Scott, James C., 145
Seidman, Steven, 127
Shauf, Scott, 191, 201
Siker, Jeffrey S., 68, 71–72, 76
Simpson, Amy, 225, 236, 238
Skinner, Christopher W., 78, 217
Sleeman, Matthew, 20, 34, 84, 86, 91, 98–99, 158
Smit, Peter-Ben, 73
Smith, Anthony D., 126
Smith, Dennis E., 121
Smith, Jonathan Z., 126
Smith, Zadie, 223
Snyder, Susannah, 223
Soards, Marion L., 55
Somov, Alexey, 74
Soulen, R. Kendall, 21–22, 124–25
Spicq, Ceslas, 243
Squires, John T., 56, 202
Steele, David, 235
Stegemann, Ekkehard W., 159
Stegemann, Wolfgang, 159
Stenschke, Christoph J., 140
Sterling, Gregory E., 77, 112–13, 115, 121, 145, 183
Strauss, Mark L., 26, 43–44, 89–90, 92–95
Strelan, Rick, 183
Striker, Gisela, 155
Stuckenbruck, Loren T., 228
Stuhlmacher, Peter, 188, 191
Subramanian, J. Samuel, 51–52
Sundberg, Walter, 189
Swartley, Willard M., 230
Swinton, John, 232, 234, 236

Tannehill, Robert C., 40, 56, 59, 94, 135
Taylor, Vincent, 53
Thiessen, Matthew, 6–7, 134, 160
Thiselton, Anthony C., 193
Thompson, Alan J., 84, 97, 100, 178
Tiede, David L., 5, 45
Torrance, Thomas F., 85

Tutu, Desmond, 110
Tyson, Joseph B., 5

Vacek, Heather H., 229, 237
Vanhoozer, Kevin J., 193–94
Verhey, Allen, 230
Veyne, Paul, 273
Vieljauer, Philipp, 135
Voinov, Vitaly, 74
Volf, Miroslav, 223

Wagner, J. Ross, 60, 99
Walhout, Clarence, 193
Walls, Andrew F., 108–9, 112, 139
Walton, Steve, 85, 100
Ward, Roy Bowen, 80
Weaver, John B., 122, 176, 212
Wells, Samuel, 232–33
Wendel, Susan, 22, 39, 75, 77–78
Wendt, Heidi, 173
Weren, W. J. C., 62
White, Hayden, 193
Wilckens, Ulrich, 55, 138
Williams, Catrin H., 80–81
Williamson, H. G. M., 95
Wills, Lawrence M., 10
Wilson, Brittany E., 216
Wilson, Gerald H., 46
Wilson, Stephen G., 8, 18
Wilson, Walter T., 138–39, 179, 246
Winant, Howard, 127
Windisch, Hans, 130
Winter, Bruce, 149, 152
Wolf, Greg, 274
Wolterstorff, Nicholas, 196
Wright, Christopher J. H., 250, 253, 270
Wrogemann, Henning, 111, 121
Wycherley, R. E., 147

Yarbrough, Robert W., 188–89
Yoder, John Howard, 268–69
Yong, Amos, 110, 220, 224, 235

Ziegler, Joseph, 133
Zwiep, Arie W., 57, 84, 91–93

Index of Subjects

Abraham, 6–7, 13, 65–66, 76–78, 81–83, 215
almsgiving, 24, 275
ascension, 84–86, 92n31, 97

barbarians, 128–33, 140–41, 219, 234, 245–47
benefaction, 243, 271–77

circumcision, 6–7, 18
covenants: Abrahamic, 65–72, 75–76, 86; Davidic, 86–87, 95–96

Davidic psalms, 12–14, 45–47, 49–54, 56–58, 63–64, 86–91, 95–97
divine visitation, 28–29, 40, 81, 131, 140, 198–99, 211–13

election, 4–5, 12–13, 20–22, 31, 42, 66, 75–76, 82, 123–24, 126–28, 134
Epicureanism, 103, 117, 155–56, 168
ethnicity, 5, 11n28, 24, 124–25, 128–29, 132–39, 142–43, 179, 205–6, 218
exploitation, 72, 248–51, 255–58, 264–71

friendship, 122, 128, 133–39, 141–42, 177–79, 214–16, 218–19, 230–39, 243, 247

god-fighters, 175–76

healing, 40–41, 71, 74, 99–100, 137, 141, 172–74, 198–99, 226–30, 239, 246–47
hospitality, 9, 72–74, 80–82, 128–32, 135–43, 177, 179–80, 211–13, 219–20, 231–36, 241, 243, 245–47

idolatry, 77–78, 145, 147–49, 153–55, 158, 160, 164–66, 168
Isaianic servant, 34–36, 44–45, 53–55, 64

John the Baptist, 27, 66, 71

kingdom: Davidic, 29, 32–33, 86–90; of God, 67, 85, 92, 97, 100, 197, 231, 261

law of Moses, 10, 18–19, 23, 43, 113–15, 234, 251

magic, 173–74
mental health, 226, 229, 232–40
Messiah: Davidic, 11, 17, 25–29, 32, 45–46, 53, 64–65, 88–92; royal reign of, 11, 30, 84–86, 92, 97–100; suffering, 43–45, 48–49, 53–55, 59, 64
missiology, 107–12

Paul: calling and commission of, 34–36; and messianic controversy, 7–10, 16–22; as prophet, 37–42, 244; on Torah observance, 3–7, 16, 135
philosophy, 103–6, 111–16, 119–21, 144–46, 149, 153–54, 171–72, 180–83, 221
prayer, 61, 98, 268–69
psalms. *See* Davidic psalms

Index of Subjects

resurrection, 11, 13–16, 21, 24–25, 29–33, 42, 45, 58, 69, 74–75, 84–85, 89–90, 93–96, 167–68, 202–3

reversal, 60, 72–73, 128, 156, 245, 276

salvation, 26–27, 30, 35–36, 40–41, 66–68, 71–73, 133–34, 141, 214, 218, 244–47

servant. *See* Isaianic servant

Socrates, 147–49

Spirit, 18, 20–21, 56, 97–98, 204–6, 217–18, 224

Stoicism, 103–7, 114–20, 155–56, 159, 162–64

suffering, 229, 238–39

superstition, 117–19, 153–57, 168

temple, 20, 28, 159–60, 257, 259

visions, 20, 40, 98, 204, 207–8, 217

Index of Scripture

Old Testament

Genesis

1	160
1:26	165
1:26–27	165
2:6 LXX	161
2:7	165
4:14 LXX	161
6:7 LXX	161
7:4 LXX	161
7:23 LXX	161
10 LXX	215
11 LXX	215
11:30	70
12–21	70
12:1–4	68, 249
12:2–7	70
13:14–17	70
15	81
15:1–6	68
15:13–14	77
15:14	77
15:16–21	249
17:1	70
17:1–5	68
17:22	70
18	80
18:4	72
18:11–13	70
22	82
26:2–3	249
27:21–22 LXX	162
28:13–15	249
32:8	161
33:19–20	255
47:18–19	249
47:20	249
47:24	249
47:26	249
49:29–32 LXX	77

Exodus

1:8–14	250
1:11	250
1:12	250
1:13	250
1:14	250
2:23–25	250, 258
3:6	69
3:12	77
16:4	250
16:13	250
16:16–18	251
16:19–21	251
17:1–6	250–51
18	262
20:11	158
20:17	251, 262
21–31	249
22:21	252
22:22–27	256
22:25	251
22:26–27	251
22:27	251
23:6	256
23:9	252

Leviticus

1–7	249
11–26	249
13:14	227
13:44–45	227
16:29	252
19	278
19:9–10	252
19:15–19	138, 204
19:16–18	74
19:18	252
19:33–34	74, 252
21:16–23	216, 220, 234
23:22	252
25	252, 256, 267, 278
25:8–17	253
25:10	267
25:23	215, 253
25:24–28	253

312

Index of Scripture

25:35–37	253
25:38	253
25:39–46	253
26:1	158
26:30	158

Deuteronomy

1:16–17	252
4–30	249
6:10–15	251
8:12–14	251
10:17	208
10:17–19	138, 204
10:18–19	252
14:22–29	252
14:28–29	73, 269
15	253, 256, 278
15:1	253
15:1–8	73, 269
15:4	253–54
15:7–11	74
15:8–9	253
15:14	260
16:11	252
16:11–14	252
17:14	253
17:14–20	256
17:16–17	253
17:18–19	254
23:1	216, 220, 234
24:14–15	252
24:19–22	252
26:1–11	215
28:29 LXX	162

Joshua

22:19	252, 266
22:22 LXX	8

Judges

16:26 LXX	162

Ruth

4:3	255

1 Samuel

1–2	26, 70
2:1–10	26
8:11–18	254, 256
12:1–25	256
16:11–19	254
16:13	86, 97
17:34	254

2 Samuel

7	87, 94
7:8	254
7:10–14	96
7:12	32, 87, 90
7:12–14	12, 63, 76, 86, 88, 94, 96
14:30–31	255
22:6	89
22:51	13, 32

2 Kings

2	84
2:7–12	84

1 Chronicles

12:38	178
17:4–14	13, 32
17:11	87
17:12	88
17:14	88
17:17–18	87
17:20–21	87
29:15	215
29:21–24	178

2 Chronicles

7:20	252, 266
29:19 LXX	8

Ezra

4:13	257
6–7	257

Nehemiah

5:1–5	257–58

5:6–14	258
9:6–36	12, 31
9:15	150

Job

5:14 LXX	162

Psalms

1	53
1–2	52
1:5–6	52
2	32, 46, 53–54, 58–59, 61–64, 86, 94–95, 98
2:1–2	32, 49, 62, 94, 98
2:1–3	62, 95
2:2	63, 86
2:2–3	86
2:4–9	62
2:6–7	63, 95
2:6–8	87
2:6–9	86
2:7	11, 13, 93–95
2:8–9	87
2:9	47
2:10–12	62
2:11	52
2:12 Heb.	52
5	256
6:9 LXX	72
7:4	47
15 LXX	90–92, 97
15:8–11 LXX	95
15:9–10 LXX	90
15:10 LXX	32, 93, 95
15:11 LXX	91
16	44, 58, 91
16:8–11	89, 95
16:9–10	90
16:10	13–14, 32, 93, 95–96
17 LXX	97
17:5 LXX	89
17:49–50 LXX	89
17:51 LXX	89
18:4	89
18:12 LXX	54

313

INDEX OF SCRIPTURE

18:48–49	89	88 LXX	100	118	59–62, 64
18:50	86, 89	88:4 LXX	50, 54	118:5–9	59
20:6	86	88:20 LXX	50	118:8–9	60
21:8 LXX	49	88:20–21 LXX	49, 54	118:14–15	60
21:9 LXX	50	89	47, 49, 54, 88	118:14–17	60
21:19 LXX	49	89:3	54, 86	118:15–29	60
22	47, 49–51, 64	89:4 Heb.	54	118:22	59–60
22:7	49	89:19	88	118:26	28
22:8	50–51	89:19–20	49, 54	131 LXX	97
22:9–10	50	89:20	86	131:10 LXX	54
22:14–18	47, 86	89:20–21	99	131:11 LXX	90
22:18	49	89:20–21 Heb.	54	132	44, 46, 58
30:6 LXX	51, 53	89:20–38	13, 32	132:11	86, 89–90
30:15 LXX	51	89:23	87	132:11 LXX	90
30:19 LXX	52–53	89:24	88	132:11–12	11
31	49, 52–53, 64	89:26–28	86	132:17	86
31:5	51, 53	89:27–38	11	134:17 LXX	162
31:10–14	51	89:29	88	144:11–14	87
31:14	51	89:38	86	145:3 LXX	62
31:18	52	89:38–42	88	145:5–6 LXX	61
37:12 LXX	51	105:40	250	146	59, 61–62, 64
38	49, 64	108:8 LXX	55, 57	146:3	62
38:5–8	47, 86	108:28 LXX	54, 57	146:5	158
38:11	51	109	57, 64, 91	146:5–6	61
39:13	215	109 LXX	92, 97		
68:18 LXX	54	109:1 LXX	58, 90–92, 97, 99	**Isaiah**	
68:22 LXX	50	109:3	47	1:23	256
68:26 LXX	55, 57	109:8	55, 57, 100	2:12–16	255
69	47, 49, 51, 58, 64	109:27	58	2:18	158
69:1–2	57	109:28–31	57	4:15–16	68
69:1–4	57	109:31	57–58	5:8	256
69:16–20	47, 86	110	44, 48, 58, 62, 98	6	40
69:17	57	110 LXX	91	6:1–13	34
69:19–29	57	110:1	11, 89–90, 97	6:9	38
69:21	50	110:1–2	58, 87	6:9–10	17, 38–41
69:24	47	110:2	87	9:1–2	68
69:25	55, 57	110:5–6	58	10:1–3	256
69:26	100	113:15 LXX	162	10:11	158
69:30–36	57	114:4	89	11:1–2	86, 97
72	254, 256	117 LXX	100	11:10–13	178
72:5–7	87	117:8–9 LXX	60	12:15–21	68
72:8	87	117:10 LXX	100	14:2	252, 266
72:15–16	87	117:11 LXX	100	14:25	252, 266
77:70 LXX	54	117:12 LXX	100	19:1	158
78:24–38	250	117:14–15 LXX	60	21:9	158
85:1	252, 266	117:22 LXX	59, 99		

Index of Scripture

25:5–7	68	61	278	**Amos**	
25:6–8	68	61:1	41, 74	5:10–12	256
28:16–20	68	61:1–2	267	6:4–7	256
31:7	158	61:1–3	86, 97	8:4–8	256
32:15	97	66:1–2a	158	9:11	208
37:19	164			9:11–13	15
40–66	35	**Jeremiah**			
40:3–5	40	1:1–19	34	**Micah**	
40:5	41	1:7–8	34	2	256
40:15	138	1:8	36	2:2	256
40:18–20	164	2:7	252	5:2	26
41:7	164	2:19 LXX	8	6:12	256
41:10	36	6:15 LXX	29	7:3	256
42	158	7:8–15	28		
42:1	54, 158	10:19	164	**Zechariah**	
42:5	158	12:10	255	9–14	46
42:5 LXX	157	12:27	28		
42:6	26, 68, 158	16:19	164	**NEW TESTAMENT**	
42:6–7	34	22:5	28		
42:8	158	23:1–5	254	**Matthew**	
43:1–5	36	23:5–6	96	1:1	65, 68
43:10–12	35			1:2–6	66
43:11	158	**Ezekiel**		1:6–11	66
44:1–4	97	9–11	28	1:12–16	66
44:8	35	26–28	261	1:16–17	66
45:20	166	34	254	2:1–12	68
46:6	158	34:5–23	178	2:5–6	65
46:7	164	34:22–31	96	3:2	66
49:1–6	138	36:5	252	3:7	66
49:5–6	35	36:26–27	97	3:9	66
49:6	15, 26, 41	37:14	97	4:17	66
49:6 LXX	36	37:15–28	178	4:25	68
49:10 LXX	162	37:24–28	96	5:25–26	267
52:13	53, 99			6:11–12	267
53	44–45, 54–55	**Daniel**		6:12	268
55:3	13–14, 32, 93, 95	2:21	161	7:13–23	67
55:6 LXX	162	5:4	158	7:21–29	68
56:3–8	220, 234	5:23	158	7:28–29	68
58	267, 278	7:13–14	68	8:1	68
58:6	74, 267	8	161	8:5–13	67–68, 72
58:6–7	268			8:10	67–68
58:7	270	**Joel**		8:11	68
58:10	268	1:6	252	8:11–12	67
60:1–6	68	3:1–5	97	8:12	68
60:1–11	26			13:14–15	40

315

INDEX OF SCRIPTURE

13:36–43	68	1:5–25	210	2:46	151
13:38	68	1:5–2:52	25	3:1–6	71
16:27	67	1:6	52	3:4–6	13, 40–41, 214, 244
18:23–24	267	1:7	70	3:6	40
18:23–35	269	1:11	70	3:7	174
18:24	269	1:15	70	3:7–8	278
18:25	269	1:17	52, 71	3:7–9	40
18:26	269	1:18	70	3:8	71, 73–74
18:27	269	1:26–30	110	3:9	71
18:28	269	1:27	47	3:10–14	71, 262
18:29–30	269	1:31–35	26, 30, 62	3:22	62, 197
18:30	269	1:32	47, 70	3:34	70
18:32	269	1:32–33	11, 26, 89	4:16	31
18:33	269	1:45	198	4:18	40
18:34	269	1:46–55	26, 198	4:18–19	41, 74, 213, 226, 228, 231, 267
20:1–5	266	1:47	244		
21:9–15	65	1:51–52	261	4:18–29	71
21:33–45	67	1:51–53	71	4:24–28	40
21:43	67	1:53	261	4:27	228
21:45	67	1:54	54	4:29	228
22:23–33	69	1:54–55	70	4:30	151
24:47–51	264	1:55	70	4:31–44	226, 268
25	213	1:64	198	4:31–9:50	226
		1:68	110	4:33	226
Mark		1:68–74	89	4:33–37	226
1:15	261	1:68–79	198	4:35	228
2:12	198	1:69	47, 54, 94, 244	4:38–39	226, 246
4:12	40	1:71	244	4:40–41	226, 246
10:52	198	1:72–73	70	5:12–16	227
12:1–2	266	1:73	70	5:12–26	268
12:2	264	1:76	71	5:17–26	99, 227, 229, 268
12:18–27	69	1:78	110	5:25	198
12:23	69	2:1–7	212, 261	5:27–30	121, 221
12:24	69	2:4	47	5:27–32	72, 205, 213, 230, 264, 268
12:26–27	69	2:8–20	210		
15:24	49	2:10	214	5:30–32	231
15:31	49	2:11	28, 30, 47, 244	5:32	52
15:39	52	2:20	198	5:35	202
15:40	51	2:26	30	6:9	244
		2:28	198	6:17–36	275
Luke		2:30	40, 198, 244	6:20	213, 223
1–2	27, 70	2:30–32	13, 15, 75	6:20–21	275
1:1	192, 196	2:31	133	6:20–22	277
1:1–4	121, 183, 221	2:32	40, 214	6:23	39
1:4	192	2:34–35	71	6:24–25	275
		2:43	54	6:27–36	269, 278

Index of Scripture

6:30	275	9:53	212	13:17	199
6:32–35	276	9:57	212	13:22	212
6:35–36	276–77	9:58	212	13:23	72
6:36	227	10	234	13:23–30	72
7:2–10	132, 227	10:1–13	9	13:25	72
7:2–17	268	10:1–16	198	13:26	72
7:11–17	227	10:11	38–39	13:26–29	74
7:13	228	10:17–20	141	13:27	72–74
7:16	198	10:18–19	174	13:29	72
7:18–23	198	10:19	174	13:30	73
7:21–22	227	10:21	199	13:31–35	28
7:21–23	40	10:21–24	212	13:33	202, 212
7:22	268	10:22	199	13:33–34	28, 39
7:36–39	73	10:23	199	13:35	28, 199
7:36–50	121, 131, 205, 212–13, 221, 231, 268–69	10:23–24	40, 200	14:1	73
		10:25–37	276	14:1–6	212
		10:26–29	74	14:1–16	231
7:39	231	10:33	234	14:1–24	121, 221
7:41–42	269	10:36	234	14:11	73
7:41–43	268	10:38	212	14:12	276–77
7:44–50	231	10:38–42	131, 213, 231	14:13	214
7:50	244	11:4	268	14:14	52, 277
8:10	40	11:11–12	174	14:16–24	73
8:12	244	11:37–44	73, 212	14:18–19	277
8:26–39	227, 268	11:37–54	74, 121, 221, 231	14:25	212
8:27	228	11:47–48	28	15	231
8:33	228	11:48	39	15:1–2	73, 231
8:36	228, 244	11:50–51	28	15:1–32	73
8:38	228	12:13	262	15:7	52
8:39	192	12:13–15	263	15:10	73
8:40–42	227	12:13–34	262	15:16	73
8:43–48	227	12:14	262	15:28–29	73
8:48	244	12:15	262	15:29–32	231
8:49–56	227	12:16–21	263, 266	16:1–8	264
8:50	244	12:42–48	264	16:1–9	267
9:1–6	227	12:57	52	16:13–14	264
9:10	192	12:57–59	267	16:19	73, 269
9:11–17	231, 244	13:6–9	73	16:19–31	73, 266, 269
9:11–18	213	13:10	71	16:20	73
9:22	98, 201–2	13:10–17	228	16:20–21	269
9:31	202	13:11	71, 228	16:21	73
9:35	62, 197	13:11–17	268	16:22	73
9:44	202	13:12	228	16:22–23	69, 73, 270
9:45	200	13:13	198	16:23	73
9:51–56	28	13:15	228	16:25–31	278
9:51–62	212	13:16	71, 228, 231	16:29	74, 270

317

INDEX OF SCRIPTURE

16:31	74, 270	20:17	59–60, 202	23:46–47	132
17:7–10	266	20:19	59	23:47	51–54, 200
17:18	199	20:20	52	23:48	200
17:25	202	20:27–38	69	23:49	51, 200
17:32–33	264	20:41–44	48, 58	23:50	52
18:9	52	20:42	45–46	23:51	202
18:18–30	264	21:27	98	24	43
18:31	202, 212	22–23	202	24:6	202
18:32	202	22:2	202	24:7	37
18:33	202	22:3	175, 202	24:8–12	203
18:34	56, 212	22:14–23	244	24:12	200
18:35–37	212	22:14–38	277	24:13–35	122, 221
18:35–43	40	22:15–20	231, 277	24:16	200
18:38	48	22:19	232	24:19–21	29
18:41	199	22:24	277	24:20	37
18:41–43	212	22:24–30	17, 179	24:24–27	203
18:43	198–99	22:25	277	24:25–27	19
19:1	212	22:27	151, 277	24:26	43, 56, 60, 202
19:1–3	72	22:31	202	24:26–27	37, 56
19:1–10	72, 131, 213, 231,	22:37	45, 54, 56, 202	24:28–35	203, 244
	245, 264, 268	22:39–46	54	24:31	200
19:3	72	22:42	202	24:34	200
19:5	72	22:48	202	24:35	200
19:6–7	231	22:53	174, 202	24:36	151
19:8–9	278	23	121, 183, 221	24:36–43	203
19:9	72, 231	23–24	54	24:44	56–57, 202
19:10	72	23:4	37, 52	24:44–46	43
19:11	212	23:7–8	200	24:44–47	60
19:11–27	48	23:11	243	24:44–49	19, 203, 207–8,
19:28	212	23:12	64, 95		214
19:28–40	28	23:14–15	37, 52	24:45	45
19:28–44	48	23:14–16	37	24:47	36, 133, 205, 208
19:31	28	23:15	37	24:47–48	214
19:33	28	23:22	37	24:48–49	203
19:37	199	23:25	202	24:49	97
19:38	28	23:33–46	47	24:52–53	200
19:39	29, 199	23:34	49, 238		
19:41–44	21, 29, 42, 213	23:34–46	49	**John**	
19:42	199	23:35	49–51, 54, 200	1:11–12	80
19:44	29, 199	23:36	50	1:12	80
19:45–48	58	23:37	48	2:23–25	79
19:47	199	23:38	48	3:11	80
20:1	59	23:39	48	3:32–33	80
20:1–19	59	23:39–43	238	5:43	80
20:2	59	23:41	52	6:21	80
20:16	59	23:46	51, 53, 238		

318

Index of Scripture

6:60–61	79	1:8	35, 85–86, 89, 97–98, 133	2:22–36	13, 58, 89, 91
6:60–71	79			2:23	203
6:61	79	1:9–11	34, 84, 86, 89, 92, 96	2:23–24	167
6:66	79	1:10–11	92	2:24	89, 94, 203
6:70	79	1:15	151	2:24–25	203
7:1–8:30	79	1:15–17	25	2:25	25–26, 56–57, 92
8:30	79	1:15–26	55, 100, 179	2:25–28	89
8:31	78, 81	1:16	27, 55–57	2:25–29	95
8:31–59	78–79	1:16–17	25, 27	2:28–32	25
8:33	78–79	1:18	175, 264	2:29	57, 90, 96, 180
8:34–36	81	1:18–19	57	2:29–32	96
8:37	81	1:20	45, 57–58	2:29–36	97
8:39	80–81	1:21	56	2:30	89
8:43	81	1:22	207	2:30–32	26, 41
8:44	78–79	1:27	26	2:30–36	11, 34
8:45	81	1:33	27	2:31	90, 95–96
8:45–46	79	1:41–56	25	2:31–33	89
8:46	81	1:54	27	2:32	27, 94, 203, 207
8:48	79	1:54–55	26	2:32–36	48, 92
8:56	81	1:67	25	2:33	92, 178, 214
8:58	81	1:68	26	2:33–35	203
8:59	81	1:68–79	77	2:34	57, 91–92
11:45–46	78	1:69–70	26	2:34–35	27, 89, 91
13:2	79	1:72–75	77	2:35	91
13:20	80	1:73–74	26	2:36	92
13:27	79	1:76	25, 27	2:36–38	25
17:8	80	1:76–79	27	2:37–41	167–68
		1:78	26	2:38	25–26
Acts		1:78–79	26	2:40	244
1	60	2	11, 58	2:41	99, 245
1–4	55	2:1–13	20, 92, 110, 206–7, 214	2:41–47	122, 221, 278
1–5	17			2:42	177, 232
1–7	20	2:2	95	2:42–47	39, 100, 137, 178–79, 232, 240
1:1–2	121, 183, 221	2:4	26, 214		
1:1–8	203, 207	2:5–11	123, 146, 183, 208	2:43	229
1:3	97	2:8	214	2:44	177, 232
1:3–4	85	2:11	26, 215	2:44–45	177
1:4	97	2:12–13	39, 168	2:46	177, 232
1:4–5	214	2:14–16	92	2:47	244
1:4–8	97, 208	2:14–36	97	3	53, 76
1:5	97	2:16–21	97, 208	3–4	100
1:6	35, 85, 97	2:17–36	206	3–5	98
1:6–11	92, 98–99	2:19	229	3:1–8	229
1:7–8	97	2:21	244	3:1–10	74, 98, 100, 229
		2:22	151, 229	3:1–4:4	59
		2:22–32	206	3:4–6	27

319

INDEX OF SCRIPTURE

3:6	27, 41, 69, 99–100	4:18	41	6:2			178
3:11–26	74, 167, 206	4:19	52, 180	6:7			181
3:12	99	4:21	181	6:8			229
3:12–16	229	4:23–28	98	6:8–8:1			4
3:13	53–54, 74–76, 99	4:23–31	20, 98	6:11–14			4
3:13–14	54	4:24	59, 61–62	7			12, 31
3:13–15	206	4:24–30	95	7:1–5			215
3:14	52	4:25	54, 56–57, 63, 95	7:2			76, 215
3:15	75, 203, 207	4:25–26	54, 59, 62–63, 94	7:2–8			74, 78
3:16	100	4:25–27	32, 94	7:2–53			76
3:17–18	75	4:25–28	203	7:3			76
3:18	30, 203	4:25–31	63	7:4			76
3:18–26	19	4:27	54, 63, 95	7:5			76
3:19	100	4:28	203	7:6			78
3:19–20	75, 99	4:29	121, 180–81, 221	7:6–7			77
3:19–21	34, 99	4:29–30	64, 98	7:7			77
3:20–21	30, 99–100	4:30	63, 95, 98, 100, 180	7:9			215
3:21	56, 75, 99	4:31	98	7:9–10			215
3:22	93–94	4:32	177, 232	7:9–16			78
3:22–26	17, 77	4:32–35	39, 74, 100, 122,	7:11–12			215
3:25	74–75		177, 180, 232, 240,	7:12			13
3:25–26	76		278	7:14–53			19
3:26	75, 93	4:35	222	7:15–16			77
4	59–60, 62	4:38–39	137	7:16–17			74
4–5	182	4:40–41	137	7:17			77
4:1	59	5:1–11	100, 175, 264	7:18–36			78
4:1–2	60	5:4	175	7:19			215
4:1–4	19	5:5	175	7:19–29			215
4:1–6	20	5:9	175	7:22–23			215
4:1–31	58	5:11	175	7:27			27
4:2	206	5:12–16	100, 229, 240	7:30–33			215
4:4	99, 245	5:17	7, 21, 42	7:32			69, 74
4:5	60	5:17–21	20	7:37			93–94
4:5–6	59	5:17–26	176	7:39–43			77
4:6	60	5:19–20	122, 222	7:44–45			100
4:7	59, 100, 151	5:20	176	7:45			57
4:8	59–60	5:27–32	167	7:49–50			158
4:9	244	5:29	121, 181, 221	7:51–53			39
4:9–10	99	5:30	203, 206	7:52			52
4:10	99–100, 203	5:30–31	99	7:53			19
4:10–11	100, 203	5:30–32	206	7:53–54			167
4:11	59–60, 62	5:31	58, 206	7:54–60			42, 91, 98
4:11–12	60	5:32	207	7:54–8:3			19
4:12	60–61, 100, 244	5:33	181	7:55–56			98, 158
4:13	180–81	6	126	7:55–60			206
4:17	100	6:1–6	137, 278	7:58			207

Index of Scripture

7:59	98	9:19–25	30	10:47	204, 218		
8	55, 181, 215	9:19–29	7	10:48	138		
8:1	216	9:22	8	11:1–18	179		
8:1–4	98, 216	9:23	8	11:14	244		
8:1–25	39	9:26–30	30, 208	11:15	138		
8:3	176	9:27	192	11:15–17	205		
8:4–5	216	9:31	216	11:15–18	18, 39		
8:5	216	9:32–54	229	11:17	205		
8:5–8	174	9:36	7	11:18	205, 208		
8:6–7	229	10	219	12:1–17	122, 222		
8:8	174	10:1–6	132	12:1–25	176		
8:9	174	10:1–48	131, 179, 181	12:3–5	176		
8:9–13	174	10:1–11:18	20, 206–7, 245	12:17	192		
8:10	174	10:2	7	12:20–23	100, 142, 182		
8:13	174	10:3	208	13	9, 12, 76		
8:14	216	10:3–6	204	13:1	36, 218		
8:14–17	20, 206	10:8–9	137	13:2	36		
8:14–25	122, 222, 264	10:9	204, 208	13:3–37	206		
8:15	216	10:15	204	13:4	7		
8:18–23	175	10:17	204, 217	13:4–5	174		
8:25	216	10:19	204, 217	13:5	12, 37		
8:26	216	10:20	204	13:5–12	122, 222		
8:26–40	45, 181, 206–7, 217	10:22	52, 204	13:6	174		
		10:23	204, 217	13:11	174		
8:27	132, 216, 220, 234	10:23–27	138	13:13–41	11, 21, 31, 58		
8:32–33	206	10:23–48	134	13:14	37–38		
8:34	132, 216, 220, 234	10:25–26	140	13:15	31, 38, 168		
8:36	216	10:28	204, 217	13:16	12, 31		
8:38	132, 216, 220, 234	10:31	7	13:16–23	75		
8:39	132, 216, 220, 234	10:33	132, 219	13:16–41	75, 93		
9	34	10:34	138, 204, 217	13:16–14:28	36		
9:1	34, 176	10:34–35	133	13:17	12		
9:1–9	34	10:35	138, 180	13:19	12		
9:1–19	40, 206–7	10:36	132, 138, 142, 208, 218–19	13:20	12		
9:3	34			13:21–22	12, 31		
9:3–7	208	10:36–43	138	13:22	32, 57, 94		
9:4	176	10:38	208	13:23	12–13, 32, 76, 90, 93		
9:5	34	10:39	207	13:23–37	75		
9:10	34	10:40	203	13:26	7, 12, 31–32, 74, 76		
9:11	34	10:41	207	13:27	7, 38		
9:13	34	10:42	167	13:27–29	95		
9:15	31, 34–35, 37, 176	10:42–43	208	13:30	13, 32, 93, 203		
9:15–16	38, 208	10:43–44	167	13:30–37	76		
9:17–18	208, 229	10:43–48	138	13:30–39	206		
9:17–19	36	10:44–46	204–6, 208, 217	13:31	207		
9:19	8	10:44–48	138	13:32	13		

321

INDEX OF SCRIPTURE

13:32–33	93	14:15–17	161	17:16	147, 153, 155, 166
13:32–36	98	14:17	161	17:16–21	104, 147, 153, 166
13:32–37	13, 89, 93	14:19	9, 21, 42	17:16–34	144–45, 168, 181, 218, 221
13:33	13, 32, 45, 93–94, 203	14:22	206		
		15:1	18, 244	17:17	117, 148
13:33–37	32, 94	15:1–5	18	17:17–20	148, 150, 152
13:34	32, 57, 93, 95–96, 203	15:1–29	179	17:18	103, 119, 148–49, 163, 167, 181
		15:5	7, 18		
13:34–35	14, 95	15:7–11	18	17:18–19	153, 166
13:34–39	20	15:10	19	17:18–20	148
13:35	32, 95–96	15:11	205, 244	17:19	150–52
13:36	32, 57, 96	15:12	229	17:20	148–49, 152
13:37	32, 96, 203	15:14–18	205	17:20–23	154
13:38	12, 31	15:15	208	17:21	117, 153, 155, 166
13:38–39	18, 99, 206	15:16	57	17:22	104, 117, 119, 151, 166
13:38–41	14	15:16–17	15	17:22–23	163
13:39	19	15:39	146	17:22–31	103–4, 116, 153
13:40–41	32	16–18	143	17:23	104, 119–20, 156–57, 165
13:41	168	16:1–5	6		
13:42–43	7	16:6–10	20	17:23–29	167
13:42–45	39	16:7	179	17:24	103, 119, 145, 157–58, 165–66
13:42–47	38	16:7–10	36		
13:42–52	24	16:11–15	9, 131, 134, 218, 245	17:24–25	100, 103, 157–59
13:43	8–9			17:25	119, 157–58, 165–66
13:44	38	16:12–13	7	17:26	103, 105, 160–61, 165
13:44–45	8	16:13	37	17:26–27	160–61, 166
13:45	21, 42	16:15	180	17:26–29	166
13:46	21, 36, 38, 42	16:16–18	175, 229, 264	17:27	119, 161, 163
13:46–47	8	16:19	151	17:27–28	164
13:46–48	13	16:20–23	18	17:27–29	166
13:47	15, 36, 40–41, 244	16:25–34	122, 176, 222	17:28	103, 118–19, 163–65
13:47–52	17	16:30	244	17:28–29	103, 119, 163, 165
13:48	39	16:31	244	17:29	164–66, 180
13:49	39	16:40	180	17:30	119, 157, 165–66
13:49–51	8	17	104–7, 112, 116, 121	17:30–31	165, 167
13:50	136	17:1	37	17:31	105, 120, 145, 158–59, 166–67, 203, 206
13:51	38	17:1–9	9, 180		
14:1	7, 37	17:1–11	7	17:31–32	31
14:1–7	21, 42	17:2–3	31	17:32	120, 167–68
14:2–5	9	17:3	56	17:32–34	39, 167
14:3	229	17:4	9, 136	17:33	151
14:4–7	24	17:5	21, 42	17:34	151, 168
14:8–10	229	17:5–8	17	17:54–60	21
14:8–18	140, 142	17:5–9	9, 21, 42	18	220
14:8–20	147	17:6	9	18:1–6	38
14:9	244	17:13	9	18:1–8	9

Index of Scripture

18:1–11	180	21:30	151	24:26	182
18:2–4	37	21:33	151	24:27	37
18:4	7, 39	21:37–40	132	25:2	136
18:5	31	22	5, 34	25:3	6
18:5–6	9, 17	22–26	127, 181, 238	25:5–6	24
18:6	21, 39, 42	22–28	5, 21, 23, 33, 135	25:10–11	23
18:8	9	22:1–3	5, 33, 135	25:25	182
18:9–10	36, 38	22:1–21	20	26	34
18:12–13	17	22:2	5, 24	26:4–5	5, 24, 135
18:12–17	182	22:3	5, 6, 24	26:5	7
18:13–15	8	22:3–6	136	26:6–7	6, 37, 135
18:17	151	22:9–11	136	26:6–8	15, 33, 206
18:19	7	22:10–21	38	26:7	33
19	9	22:12	7	26:15–16	35
19:8	7, 9, 37	22:13	136	26:15–18	20, 38, 136
19:8–40	142	22:14	34, 52	26:15–23	208
19:11–12	229	22:14–16	35	26:16	34
19:11–17	174	22:15	207	26:16–17	182
19:11–20	122, 167, 222	22:16	36	26:17	34
19:13	167	22:17	6–7, 20	26:17–18	34
19:18–19	174	22:17–21	208	26:18	20, 40–41
19:21	241	22:21	15	26:18–19	15
19:23–27	264	22:21–22	17	26:19–23	33
19:23–41	167	22:22	23	26:22	7, 14, 182
19:28–41	182	22:29	37	26:22–23	6, 19, 135, 206
20:7–12	229	23:1	5, 135	26:23	15, 30, 33, 41
20:16	6	23:3	7, 23	26:26	181–82, 207
20:17–35	242	23:5	5, 135	26:27	33
20:18–35	181	23:5–6	24	26:29	37, 182
20:20–21	181	23:6	37	26:31	37
20:26–27	181	23:11	37, 136	26:31–32	182
20:28	206	23:12–22	6	26:32	242
20:33	181	23:26–35	37	27	146
20:34–35	181	23:29	8, 182	27–28	247
21–27	135	24:5	7	27:1	243
21:7–17	131	24:10–13	23	27:1–44	180
21:15–29	127	24:11–14	6	27:1–28:10	238, 240, 242, 246
21:18	242	24:11–17	20		
21:20–21	3, 7, 23	24:14	7, 14	27:1–28:16	241
21:20–26	5, 135	24:14–15	6, 19, 33, 135	27:3	131–32, 140, 180, 243
21:20–27	127	24:15	14, 37	27:9	6
21:21–26	7	24:17	24, 52	27:9–11	244
21:23–27	6	24:17–24	7	27:9–12	180
21:26	7	24:24–26	264	27:13–20	180
21:27–28	4, 16	24:25	182	27:18–20	244
21:28	23	24:25–27	42	27:20	244

323

INDEX OF SCRIPTURE

27:20–26	136	28:7–10	136–37, 174, 180	9:4	21
27:23	37	28:8	137, 246	11:1	21
27:24	244	28:9	137, 246		
27:24–26	37, 180	28:9–10	219, 234	**1 Corinthians**	
27:25–26	244	28:10	137, 140, 246	14:11	129
27:26	245	28:11	139		
27:30	244	28:12–15	131	**2 Corinthians**	
27:31	244	28:16	38	12:9–10	238
27:33	244	28:17	7, 23, 136		
27:33–38	139, 180, 244	28:17–19	33	**Galatians**	
27:34	244	28:17–20	33	3:16	66
27:35	244	28:17–31	37		
27:36	244	28:19	7, 27	**Hebrews**	
27:37	244–45	28:20	6, 15, 19, 33, 37, 135	1:5	90, 94
27:43	243–44	28:22	7, 27	5:5	94
27:44	244	28:23	7, 15, 19, 37	5:8	238
27:44–28:1	245	28:23–28	9, 38		
28	38, 128, 139	28:24	39	**James**	
28:1	244	28:24–25	39	2:2–3	271
28:1–2	136, 180, 219, 234	28:25	39	2:6–7	271
28:1–10	122–23, 128, 134, 141, 179, 218, 221, 245	28:25–27	17	2:20–26	80, 82
		28:25–28	21, 41–42	4:1–2	270
28:2	129, 131, 137, 140, 219, 234, 245	28:26	38, 40	5:1–6	271
		28:27	41	5:2–3	270
28:3–6	122, 137, 222, 245	28:28	13, 141, 241–42, 246	5:3	270
28:4	124, 219, 234, 245			5:4	270
28:4–6	135	**Romans**		5:5	270
28:5	174	1:2–4	94	5:6	270
28:6	140	1:16–17	8		
28:7	129, 136–37, 139–40, 180, 245	3:1–2	21	**1 Peter**	
		7:7	21	1:18	18
28:7–9	219, 229, 234	7:12	21		

Index of Other Ancient Sources

Deuterocanonical Books

Tobit
7:17 — 158

Judith
8:18 — 158

Wisdom of Solomon
7:18 — 161
9:1 — 158
9:9 — 158
13:6–9 — 164
13:8–19 — 166
14:1–31 — 166
14:8 — 158
15:11 — 166
15:16–17 — 164

Bel and the Dragon
5 — 164

1 Maccabees
1:3 — 258
1:4 — 258
1:8 — 258
1:29–32 — 259
1:41–43 — 8
1:51–52 — 8
2:15 — 8
2:19–28 — 8
2:49–70 — 8

2 Maccabees
3:4–39 — 259
14:35 — 159

3 Maccabees
2:9 — 159

4 Maccabees
4:26 — 8

Old Testament Pseudepigrapha

1 Enoch
2:1 — 161
90:6–12 — 12, 31

4 Ezra
3:14 — 81

Jubilees
12:5 — 164
20:7–8 — 164

Psalms of Solomon
17 — 46
17:21–32 — 46, 94
17:22 — 86
17:23–24 — 47
17:24 — 47
18 — 46
18:5–8 — 86

Testament of Abraham — 81

Dead Sea Scrolls

Florilegium (4QFlor) — 94a

Ancient Jewish Writers

Philo

On the Change of Names
223 — 113

On the Confusion of Tongues
141 — 113

On the Creation of the World
3 — 114

325

INDEX OF OTHER ANCIENT SOURCES

On the Embassy to Gaius
156   113
245   113

On the Life of Joseph
254   8

On the Life of Moses
1.1–3   113
1.31   8
2.48   114
2.52   114
2.216   113

On the Special Laws
2.163–167   113

On the Virtues
65   113

That Every Good Person Is Free
57   113

Josephus

Against Apion
2.262   150
2.265   150
2.266–268   150

Jewish War
2.1   260
2.117–118   260
2.427   260
7.47–53   8
7.61   260

GRECO-ROMAN LITERATURE

Aeschylus

Agamemnon
60–62   130
362–363   130
395–402   130
525–527   130
701–704   130
745–749   130

Eumenides
470–489   152

Apuleius

Metamorphoses
5.6.3   153
6.20.5   153
11   153

Aratus

Phaenomena
5   119, 163

Aristobulus
frag. 4b   163

Aristotle

Nicomachean Ethics
1166a31–32   177
1169a18–22   177
1169b18–23   177

Politica
5.11   154

Augustus

Res Gestae
15–18   273

Cicero

De legibus
22–29   161

De natura deorum
1.20.55   155
1.85   156
1.117   157
2.65.162   155
2.74   151
154   114

De officiis
1.19   153
1.44   273

2.54   275
3.28   161, 179

De republica
3.22   114

Epistulae ad Atticum
1.5   151
1.6   151

In Verrem
2.4.25   131, 179

Pro Flacco
62   148

Demosthenes

Orations
18.127   149

Dio Chrysostom

"The Hunter"   179
6.51–54   131

Orations
12   165
12.27–30   162
12.60–62   162
13   178
38   178
39   178
40   161, 178
41   178
54.3   148
78.45   181

Diogenes Laertius

Lives of Eminent Philosophers
1.110   156
2.20   148
2.21   148
2.45   148
2.91–92   157
2.101   152
2.116   152
2.122   148

Index of Other Ancient Sources

7.33	117, 156
7.168–169	152
10.120	156
10.135	155

Dionysus of Halicarnassus

Antiquitates romanae

2.2.2	178
2.11.2	178

Epictetus

Diatribai

1.12.26	118
1.14.6	163
1.14.14	118
1.30	181
2.5.13	118
2.8	118, 156
2.8.10–117	118
4.7.6–7	118

Euripides

Bacchae

45–46	175
256–259	150

Helen

155	130
789	131

Trojan Women

865–866	130

Herodotus

Histories

2.57	129
3.89	257
3.90–94	257
4.103	131
5.3	180

Hesiod

Works and Days

342–354	272

Homer

Odyssey

	180, 195, 242
4.30–37	179
6.119–121	130, 245
7.159–166	179
9.172–176	130
9.252–370	130
9.416	162
13.200–202	130

Julian

Orations

5.159	150

Lucian

True Story

1.28–29	132
2.46	132

Lucretius

On the Nature of the Universe

5.1194–1203	155

Ovid

Metamorphoses

1.163–252	179
1.197–198	130
8.617–724	179

Tristia

5.10.37	129

Pausanias

Description of Greece

1.1.4	156
5.14.8	156
24.3	154

Petronius

Satyricon 266

114	132

Plato

Apology

1.17C	148
17.30B	148
24B	148
29D	181

Euthyphro

1C	148
2B	148

Phaedo

99b	162

Timaeus

37c6–7	163

Plutarch

De Alexandri magni fortuna aut virtute

323	178

De curiositate

513D–518B	153

De Herodoti malignitate

857a	129

Demetrius

902	149

De superstitione

164EF	157
165C	156
171F	153

Quaestionum convivialum libri IX

1 [612d–e]	231

Stoicos absurdiora poetis dicere

1034B	156, 165

Table-Talk

612 D–E	177

INDEX OF OTHER ANCIENT SOURCES

Pseudo-Aristotle

Xenophanes
977a — 172

Pseudo-Heraclitus

Epistle 4
4 — 118

Seneca

De beneficiis
1.1.4–8 — 272
1.5.4 — 273
2.4–5 — 132
2.11 — 273
2.13 — 273
3.9.3 — 273
3.34.1 — 132
3.35.4 — 273
4.9.1 — 132
4.11.1–3 — 118
  — 132

Epistulae morales
41.1 — 118
41.1–2 — 162
88.36–38 — 153

94.47–50 — 159
95.35 — 117
95.47 — 117

On the Brevity of Life
23.5–24.1 — 275

Stoicorum Veterum Fragmenta
1:537 — 117, 156

Suetonius

Augustus
43 — 273

Thucydides

History of the Peloponnesian War
3.38.5 — 152

Virgil

Aeneid
1.538–539 — 180, 242
  — 131
1.538–543 — 179

Xenophon

Apology
10–11 — 148

Cyropaedia
3.3.58 — 154

Memorabilia
1.1.1 — 148–49
1.1.10 — 8

Early Christian Literature

John Chrysostom

Homilies in the Acts of the Apostles
1–55 — 131

Justin Martyr

1 Apology
5.4 — 148

2 Apology
10.5 — 148

328